TQM
for Training

Other Books in the McGraw-Hill TQM Series

TQM
for Training

Elaine Biech

Compliments of
Oculus Consulting Group
Transform Your Organization's Vision into Reality
A Professional Services Organization

McGraw-Hill, Inc.

New York   San Francisco   Washington, D.C.   Auckland   Bogotá
Caracas   Lisbon   London   Madrid   Mexico City   Milan
Montreal   New Delhi   San Juan   Singapore
Sydney   Tokyo   Toronto

Library of Congress Cataloging-in-Publication Data

Biech, Elaine.
    TQM for training / Elaine Biech.
        p.   cm.
    Includes bibliographical references and index.
    ISBN 0-07-005210-7
    1. Total quality management.   2. Employees—Training of.
I. Title.
HD62.15.B54   1994
658.3'124—dc20   94-18842
                                                      CIP

ISBN 0-07-005210-7

The sponsoring editor for this book was James H. Bessent, Jr., the editing supervisor was Fred Dahl, and the production supervisor was Donald F. Schmidt. It was set in Baskerville by Inkwell Publishing Services. Printed and bound by R. R. Donnelley & Sons Company.

This book is printed on recycled, acid-free paper containing a minimum of 50 percent recycled de-inked fiber.

Dedicated to
Shane and Thad,
true examples of quality

Contents

Preface and Acknowledgments

✳ Thousands of books have been written about quality. What sets this one apart? Two things. First, it has been written specifically for the HRD and training professional. Second, it goes well beyond theory to provide practical put-to-use-today ideas. These ideas can be found next to the ✳.

The words in this book were not created in a vacuum. Therefore, the reader will notice the use of "we" throughout this book, even though a singular author is listed. That "we" represents the coauthors that helped create this book. To the many people who were an intricate part of authoring this book: "Thanks!"

Thanks to Dan Greene and Garland Skinner, my personal quality gurus who shaped my quality thinking and my words.

Thanks to the women behind the scene who more often are in front leading: Beth Drake, Sonya Zimmerman, Robin Lucas, D.C. Campbell, and Carol Gardner.

Thanks to friends and colleagues who provided ideas, insight, encouragement, advice, mentoring, and inspiration: Tom Birrenkott, L.A. Burke, Richard Chang, Vicki Chvala, Michael Danahy, John

Hurley, Linda Kane, Shirley Krsinich, Pam Schmidt, and Michele Wyman.

Thanks to all the *ebb associates* customers who have challenged me to think more creatively:

General Casualty, Hershey Chocolate Company, Land O'Lakes, Lands' End, Langley Research Center—NASA, Naval Aviation Depot—Norfolk, Naval Supply Center—Hawaii, Newport News Shipbuilding, Pre-Mix Industries, Supervisory of Shipbuilding—Newport News, Valley Bancorporation.

Thanks to Jim Bessent, editor for McGraw-Hill, who pushed to have this book reach the quality level it has.

And all of you deserve much more than the simple thank-you that appears here, though that is the limitation of the ink on this page. Thanks for helping me write this book.

ebb

TQM
for Training

1

TQM Is a Philosophy

Why Should HRD and Training Professionals Be Committed?

What Is TQM?

TQM, TQL, CQI, CPI, QIP, EIP, CIP ... whatever you call it, chances are very good that you will someday be asked for your involvement. And, if you are a Human Resource Development (HRD) professional, you will probably be expected to help with others' involvement.

This book will use TQM as a matter of consistency, though most of the listed acronyms embody similar characteristics. Our definition clarifies the concept of quality improvement more than any letters ever could. Don't be distracted by the title; learn from the text. How do we define TQM (or your favorite alphabet combo)?

Quality improvement (or TQM) is a customer-focused, quality-centered, fact-based, team-driven, senior-management-led process to achieve an organization's strategic imperative through continuous process improvement.

In its most eminent portrayal, TQM is a philosophy; in its most ethereal, it's a concept; in its most practical, it's a way of life; and in the bottom-line world of business, it's a business strategy to achieve the competitive advantage.

TQM is not a program that has a start and end time like so many programs that you have designed, delivered, and implemented. It is not something else to do and it is not practiced to achieve normal goals. It cannot be achieved by individuals. It is not easy (Dr. W. Edwards Deming liked to say, "No instant pudding."). And it certainly is not "business as usual."

Several key components must exist for TQM to flourish:

- It has a customer focus: internal and external.
- Emphasis is on continuous process improvement in a systems approach.
- It is data-based.
- Teamwork is essential.
- Employees must be involved.
- A vision must be developed, communicated, and applied.
- Senior management must be involved and lead the effort.
- Managers must coach and guide the organization through changes.
- Training is imperative at all levels.

This book will explore these components in general and as they relate to your HRD Department and the training profession. (*Note:* You will find both the acronym "HRD" and the word "training" used throughout the text depending on the sentence structure and the content. We view training and development as a key part of the HRD department, but also include organization development, career de-

> "If it's just common sense, why aren't we doing it?"

velopment, human resource planning, performance management systems, and so on.)

We are often told that this is just common sense. And our response is, "If it's just common sense, why aren't we doing it?" The answers are many:

- *It's difficult to change old habits.* Everyone has a comfortable way to complete the tasks required to get the job done, and everyone experiences a slight amount of discomfort if asked to change. Think about some simple changes you've been asked to make in the past. Perhaps you needed to change the way you drove to work due to construction. Or, remember how difficult it seemed to read your telephone bill's new format? These are little things compared to what TQM asks you to do: Change the way you plan, interact, and work to get the job done. TQM requires you to change the way you do business.

- *Opposite behaviors have been rewarded in the past.* If you've had a successful career, it is not likely that it has been because you've constantly changed processes to improve them, but rather that you were able to stabilize processes and get them running smoothly. You've probably also been good at solving problems and putting out fires yourself, rather than coaching a team or an empowered work force to do it. In addition, you've probably been very goal-driven and have never given up a chance to reach that goal so that others could be successful for the good of the larger system. TQM requires you to reward and expect to be rewarded for different behaviors.

- *It requires thinking differently.* The two previous items suggest that a new thinking process is needed—a systems thinking approach. You will need to think about what is good for the whole, not its parts; what is good for the entire company, not just the training department. TQM asks you to adopt a systems thinking approach.

- *We are impatient and short-term orientated.* American companies have been accused of "microwave management," looking for the quick fix and implementing "flavor-of-the-month" programs. Management wants something that will work—*now*. You can see by now that TQM is none of these. It takes time to change individuals and company cultures. This means that the goals must be oriented toward more than the next quarterly report. It means that annual strategic plans are a minimum and that three-year, five-year and longer plans should become the norm. TQM requires you to be patient and take a long-term focus.

- *Fear may prevent change.* What might people be afraid of? They may be afraid of change, of failure, of questions, of management, of the system, of success. Any of these could immobilize employees and prevent them from doing what is "just common sense." TQM requires that you take risks, do things differently, and face the fears that may prevent success.

- *It requires new skills and knowledge.* Actually, this is good news for training departments. It translates into work for you. That means, however, that HRD will need to get up to speed first, to recognize and deliver the new skills and knowledge that is necessary to implement a TQM effort. TQM requires that you acquire new skills and knowledge.

- *It requires wisdom.* To be successful, you will need to go beyond new skills and knowledge to achieving wisdom. Wisdom is the result of learning new skills and applying them to the situation. Your task as an HRD professional will be to identify how to put people into situations that allow wisdom to develop. As an individual you will need to achieve your own wisdom—that "aha!" that clarifies how it all fits together and why. TQM requires you to develop wisdom.

- *It's hard work!* No one said it was easy—just effective. There will be days when you may wonder why your company ever started this effort. But the payoff is great. TQM requires hard work.

As you might imagine, the dichotomy between "this is just common sense" and why we're not "doing it" creates numerous issues that lead to failure or less than total success in many organizations.

Why TQM?

Companies initiate a quality improvement effort to:

- Increase customer satisfaction ("delight" your customer is heard often).

- Increase customer retention.
- Reduce customer complaints.
- Attract new customers.
- Increase organizational effectiveness.
- Reduce costs due to less waste and rework.
- Improve profitability.
- Achieve a greater market share.
- Maintain a competitive advantage.

But why should HRD implement a TQM effort? There are three key reasons: (1) increase internal customer satisfaction, (2) improve department effectiveness, and (3) help the company maintain a competitive advantage.

Increase Internal Customer Satisfaction. TQM provides a broader view of the customer to include anyone who is next in line for your product or service. Everyone produces something, therefore, everyone has a customer. *Internal customers* are those company employees who are supported or served by other company employees. The HRD Department's internal customers are those other departments to whom you provide training services or materials, individuals to whom you provide career development services, including any participants in your training sessions, as well as their managers. Your internal customers require and deserve HRD's best. A quality improvement effort can help you design products and services that help them meet their changing needs. And it can prepare them for the future to better meet their customers' needs.

At times the HRD Department may even think of its own employees as customers. TQM can increase their satisfaction as well, leading to improving the HRD Department's effectiveness.

Improve the HRD Department's Effectiveness. TQM encourages a department to more clearly define its key priorities and to communicate them more effectively. As a result, employees are working on the right things at the right time. This is the opportunity to change behaviors that gives employees pride in what they are doing.

TQM further encourages increased employee involvement. Improving processes is a job for those who are performing the work. TQM provides both the tools and the environment in which to make changes that result in improved efficiency and customer satisfaction.

> *"TQM creates an opportunity for employees to improve processes which make a meaningful contribution to the organization."*

Teamwork, communication, and management-employee relations all improve. Employees find more opportunities to contribute in a meaningful way to the organization and, as a result, their job satisfaction increases. The more their satisfaction increases, the more meaningful the contributions they make. Peter Senge suggests that employees are born with this innate desire to contribute meaningfully, but that our organizational systems have taken that away. Dr. W. Edwards Deming called them willing workers. And Abraham Maslow gave us a model to understand that people choose behaviors that are intrinsically rewarding.

TQM creates an opportunity for employees to improve processes which make a meaningful contribution to the organization. Employees are rewarded by this and therefore choose the behavior that is rewarding. TQM continues to create the opportunity for them to do so. Increased employee satisfaction leads to more meaningful contributions which lead to an even greater level of employee satisfaction. This can be one continuous upward spiral, resulting in higher morale and lower turnover. Focus your TQM implementation on changing behaviors and providing a supportive culture. The attitude change will occur as a result.

Assist Your Organization to Maintain a Competitive Advantage. Ultimately, TQM helps a company achieve success, improve profitability, enjoy a competitive advantage, and be the supplier of choice. Lofty statements, but they translate directly to the training department as job security and pride to be a part of a successful, well-respected company. Training is one of the departments that makes up the whole of the company and plays a key role to achieve that success.

TQM provides a common language from department to department. It also introduces the idea of internal customers. Companies of the past have often thought of other departments as competition, or even enemies, rather than customers. When things go wrong, TQM encourages people to look at the process rather than finger pointing to place blame. Each of these prevents problems and leads to overall organizational effectiveness. Although it is difficult to trace the exact contribution to the bottom line, we know there is a strong correlation between satisfying cultures and successful companies.

How Do You Implement a TQM Effort? Learn, Live, and Lead the Philosophy

You may understand the "what" and the "why" of TQM, but the more difficult question is, "How" do you implement a TQM effort?

A quality improvement implementation must have a two pronged approach. It must introduce the concept of continuous improvement and the tools that support it. But it must also focus on changing the culture to ready itself for accepting and implementing the changes created by continuous improvement. If this sounds like a great deal of work, you're right. Let's follow the *Learn, Live, Lead Model* throughout this book.

Step one is learn. Most organizations are ignorant of the philosophy, lifestyle, beliefs, and paradigms that comprise a TQM culture. We first must gain knowledge through training and studying.

Step two is live. "Walk the talk" is the phrase most often heard. We must live it, experience it, truly understand it. This is how we acquire wisdom.

Step three is lead. To achieve a TQM culture requires both knowledge and wisdom. Then and only then will the leadership be able to lead the paradigm shift that must occur.

Learn, live, lead. Learn—gain knowledge. Live—acquire wisdom. Lead—shift the paradigm. This is the philosophy necessary to implement TQM in your organization as well as your HRD Department. Keep this model in mind as you go through this book as a part of your learning.

You can find numerous suggestions for how to learn, live, and lead your quality improvement effort in the appendices. We will cover implementation in your HRD Department more completely in Chap. 7.

What Can You Expect?

- *It will be more difficult than you expected.* No matter how many books you read or how many gurus you talk to, you will not be able to plan for everything that may occur. TQM requires cross-functional teamwork, which is different from the way most organizations work today. Different translates to difficult in most organizations. Changing the culture of an organization and your department will be difficult.

> *"It will be more difficult than you expected."*

- *Resistance will occur from some individuals at all levels.* There will always be that 10 percent that resist everything. However, in this case there will most likely be a larger percentage. Since the change is so all-encompassing, it will affect everyone throughout the organization and at all levels.

- *There will be complaints and frustration.* Since there is no recipe for TQM, answers will not always be readily available. This will cause frustration.

- *It will take more time and effort than originally anticipated.* Since your organization has most likely never initiated an effort such as TQM, it will be difficult to anticipate the time and resources that will be required to reach success.

- *Outside distractions will occur and will have an adverse impact on the implementation effort.* The home office gets involved in a new initiative that takes necessary attention from TQM, a specific division meets with unexpected competition, an out-of-state plant experiences a strike, the market plummets—each may provide distractions and excuses to slow the implementation effort.

- *It will be difficult at times to measure the implementation process.* What do you measure? The number of training days or the effectiveness of the training? The number of times the president makes a "TQM appearance" or the level of satisfaction employees achieved from the appearance? The ability of employees to recite the company's guiding principles or their ability to put them into practice? The answer is all of these. Even if you decide what to measure, you'll then face how to measure. And once you do measure, it's likely that you may find the results disheartening. The truth is that sometimes it may seem as if you are going backward: More employees complain about safety issues, everyone, it seems, wants to have a say in decisions, and expectations are higher for everyone. In reality, what has happened is that TQM has provided an opportunity for employees to be heard. What may appear as going backward, may indeed be giant leaps forward!

- *The implementation strategy will require adjusting to lessons learned.* Just because you spent four months developing the perfect TQM implementation plan, it does not mean that you will follow through on it. In the spirit of true continuous improvement, you should plan on evaluating your progress against what you expected. Then evaluate the lessons learned to make adjustments. Expect to learn much about your company culture and use this knowledge as your backdrop for implementing within the training department. Make changes as they are needed throughout the implementation plan.

Initially, employees will feel as if they are doing twice as much. And to some extent, they will be working two systems at once. They will try to maintain the current way of doing things as well as serve on teams, act as facilitators, track their processes, and gather data. You'll hear about all the extra work required by TQM, "in addition to my *real* work!" Expect to hear this until a critical mass has formed and TQM becomes the *way* to work.

Figure 1.1 is an often used illustration of how the TQM transition occurs. As an organization moves through the implementation

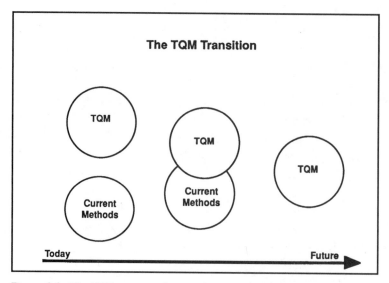

Figure 1.1. The TQM transition illustrates how an organization moves through the implementation of TQM.

phases, the TQM method gradually takes over. Time varies from organization to organization and from department to department. It depends on two things: how close the two were together initially, and how much support and reinforcement exists for the change to occur.

You'll face resistance, both active and passive. "If I hold my breath long enough, this too shall pass." Know that it's natural. It needs to be managed, but put the majority of your energy into helping those people who support the change and anticipate success.

Why Should HRD Be Committed?

TQM is the strategy to achieve a successful future for HRD and your organization. It is the opportunity that HRD has been awaiting. As a training professional, you have always known the value that your department could add in its various roles: the value of the training role, the value as a change agent, the value of your organizational development (OD) role.

You're probably thinking about the time that your organization introduced a new appraisal system and neglected to get HRD involved early to provide training for managers in the new system. Or the time a new management development design was researched and HRD was the last to know. Or even the last downsizing, sure it was small, but your department's OD skills could have prevented some of the issues that arose.

TQM offers a significant opportunity to HRD Departments in many organizations. With a focus on a systems and teamwork approach, chances of your department being left out of the loop decreases. With a focus on training, the important role that your department plays in the organization is elevated to new heights. And with the focus on internal customers, your department may finally be able to pursue the support role to line that you have been advocating.

TQM opens the door to rich opportunities to have a positive influence over the major changes the philosophy will bring to your company.

HRD's role is changing. HRD's importance is finally being recognized. HRD must be committed. It's the opportunity you've been awaiting.

2

TQM Is Customer-Focused

Who Is the Customer in the Training Process?

TQM is a customer-focused management strategy and a direct path to achieve the organization's goals and its strategic imperative. Understanding and anticipating your customers' needs and expectations is a vital ingredient to success. Delighting the customer—both internal as well as external—is a basic principle of TQM and powers the motivation for TQM.

Focus on the Customer

Internal customers, as explained in Chap. 1, are those who are next in line for your product. Training's internal customers are the employees in your organization who receive products and services from the training department, regardless of what these products or services are.

A customer focus means that you manage through the customers' eyes. The customers' needs drive quality improvement. As a supplier, for example, you:

- Work with customers to gain a mutual understanding of their wants, needs, and requirements.

- Ask them about your performance and what you could do differently or better.

- Listen to what they say and take action to improve their experience (the event called quality).

- Reflect their feedback into your processes and into your suppliers' processes to improve the event for everyone.

- Measure yourself through your customers' eyes and welcome their measurement of you.

- Suggest ways they could be better customers and ways they could help you better meet their needs. Being a "better customer," for example, could mean that they tell you about their problems immediately so that they can be corrected quickly.

- Make it a point to know their business so well that you not only anticipate their needs, but can meet them before they recognize them.

- Consider if your responsibility to give them the competitive advantage.

It's interesting that the importance of the customer wasn't evident to companies in the United States until recently. Now the Malcolm Baldrige National Quality Award criteria allocate 30 percent of their points to customer satisfaction.

In the past, training departments may not have been as responsive to their customers' needs as the customers would have liked. Each department (including training) was viewed as being the most knowledgeable in its areas of expertise and was expected to take the lead to make decisions about what was best for the other departments. These other departments were not seen as customers.

Therefore, a training department would create a program listing based on its knowledge of the most popular training programs, send it to other departments, and wait for them to sign up. If classes weren't filled, manager's arms might be twisted or quotas distributed to get classroom participants. The thought was that there must be something wrong with the other departments; they don't know what's good for them.

TQM has brought the customer terminology to organizations. Training departments now recognize that they exist to serve the other departments and that these other departments and the company as a whole must have input into the entire process. This may even include designing the needs assessment to ensure that the correct questions are asked based on the company's direction.

Who Is HRD's Customer?

HRD has many customers. Most of them are probably internal though you may have a few external customers depending on the process. In most cases the customer-supplier relationship will shift back and forth depending on the stage the process is in. For example,

> "Always think of your customers as suppliers first. Work closely with them so that they can supply you with the information you need and, in turn, you can supply them with the products and services that meet their needs and expectations."

when training is developing a program at the request of another department, that department's management may provide information about what should be taught (i.e., objectives and sample materials). At that point training is the customer and the other department is the supplier. Once the session is designed and training delivers it, the employees and managers of the other department are the customers. Always think of your customers as suppliers first. Work closely with them so that they can supply you with the infor-

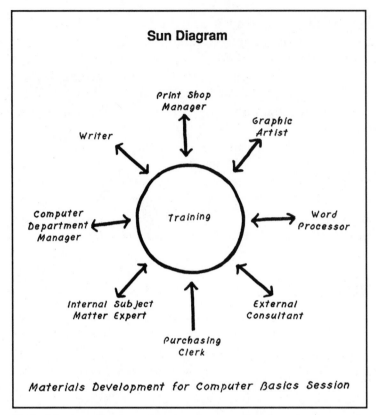

Figure 2.1. A sun diagram can focus the customer-supplier relationship discussion for a particular task.

mation you need and, in turn, you can supply them with the products and services that meet their needs and expectations.

✳ You may wish to use a sun diagram such as the one shown in Fig. 2.1 to show these customer-supplier relationships. To develop a sun diagram for a particular process, draw a circle in the center of a flipchart pad. Place the name of your department (or group) in the center. At the bottom of the page identify the process you are considering. Around the outside, list all the people you come in contact with throughout the process. Draw arrows from the supplier to the customer. As you discuss the relationships, you will find most of the arrows pointing in both directions. Conduct this activity as a group. You will find the discussion at least as beneficial as the diagram.

Some examples of the HRD Department's customers during specific processes could include the following:

Materials Development Process:

Internal Customers	External Customers
■ Print shop	■ Consultant designers
■ Graphic arts	■ Artists
■ Word processing	■ Printing companies

Facilities Arrangement Process:

Internal Customers	External Customers
■ Facilities staff	■ Hotel staff
■ Travel department	■ Caterers
■ Cafeteria	

Training Delivery Process:

Internal Customers	External Customers
■ Training session participants	■ Guest instructors
■ Participants' managers	

Notice that you might not think of many of these as your customers. In reality they are, though they are your suppliers as well. The internal customer-supplier relationship is much more difficult and complex to define than the external customer-supplier relationship. However, for the HRD Department, it is probably the most common relationship and an important way to emphasize how to begin to look at processes and improving them.

What Does Your Customer Need?

Once you have identified your customers, you will need to know what their needs, expectations, and requirements are.

■ Do you know what your customers want?

■ Do you know what your customers need?

- Do you know what your customers think?
- Do you know what your customers feel?
- Do you know your customers' level of satisfaction?
- Do you know what suggestions they have?

How do you find out the answers to these questions? Probably, the first idea that pops into your head is to send them a survey. But there is an easier, faster, more practical approach. You can listen to them! You will be amazed at what you will learn if you just give your customers a forum for discussing what's on their mind.

It sounds too easy, but it's not. Improving your customer satisfaction requires a good deal more than improving the product or service you provide. Take for example the department that had you develop a time management course for them last month. You spent a lot of time preparing materials that were typo-free. You convinced the manager of the department that you really needed a full day to teach all the aspects of time management. And in addition, you went out of your way to get the training room with the great view on the third floor.

Your course evaluations weren't as good as you thought they might be. They said things like, "not applicable to what I do," and "too long; could have been taught in four hours," and "room too cold."

How did you respond? "Time management is time management! Can't they make the transition from the general to the specific?" "Too long? They just wanted to get back to their desks." "Too cold? Can't please everyone!"

What happened? You did a great job providing the products and services that you believed your customer wanted and needed. You provided added value to your basic fare. However, you didn't heed some early messages your customer was sending you and you didn't meet some of their expectations.

You have a more sophisticated customer today than even two years ago. In fact, *you* are a more sophisticated customer today. Think of any service situation: banking, shopping, eating in a restaurant. Chances are very good that your expectations are higher today than they were just two years ago.

I have a higher expectation level of car rental agencies than I did just two months ago. You know the routine: late for the flight, locate rental car parking, unload luggage, remember to check the mileage, don't forget the papers in the glove box, struggle with the luggage, find the desk, wait in line, computer down, credit card's rejected, must complete paperwork manually, blood pressure rising.

Two months ago the routine started the same but ended very differently. Late for the flight, locate rental car parking, unload luggage, attendant hands me a receipt! One of the car rental agencies in a large city had equipped its employees with hand-held computers. The attendant checked the mileage and gas gauge, and completed my paperwork while I unloaded my luggage. Surprised? Yes! Met my expectations? Exceeded them! Next time? I will have a higher expectation level for this company and especially for its competitors.

With everyone in the world who is not "trying harder," the chances of customers bumping up against better and better service is very good. Better service means higher expectations next time.

Your internal customers will have consistently higher expectations. What do internal customers want?

- Increased customization
- Increased quality
- Decreased turnaround time
- Improved timeliness
- Lower cost

How does this translate to the training department? In the time management course example, the customer expected the training to be customized and to use examples, role plays, data, and scenarios related to that department. The customer probably expected to see high-quality materials, typo-free on paper that you couldn't see through. The customer also expected to see some form of technology used to enhance learning (e.g., video, or an overhead projector). With regard to turnaround time, the customer probably expected the course to be designed and developed within a very minimal amount of time. We sometimes get requests for "next week." The customer also expected timeliness. If you promised the customer delivery in a month, you are expected to live up to that commitment. And finally, everyone in your company is looking for cost savings.

For the training department this translates to offering more learning at a lower per participant cost.

✳ During the next two weeks track your discussions with your internal customers. What common themes emerge? How can you translate what your customers are saying into needs that you can

> *"You will want your measurements to go beyond a mere head count and tell you what the heads think and feel."*

meet? Do your discussions reveal any needs your customers might have in the future?

✳ Have people in your department call three customers each week: one happy, one unhappy, and one indifferent. The purpose is to learn what each one needs.

✳ Evaluate the last three programs or services HRD offered. How many came from customers' ideas? What comparisons can you make between those that were offered as a result of customers' requests and those that were not?

What to Measure

Advice about what to measure? In Chap. 5 we will explore fact-based decision making and measuring the right things, but let's think about that with regard to your customer.

You want your measurements to go beyond a mere head count and tell you what the heads think and feel. You will want to measure satisfaction level. How satisfied are customers with your present performance today? But you will also want to go beyond that.

You will want to gather data about how you can support your customers in the near future. So you will want to ask questions about what they believe they might need soon. This doesn't necessarily prevent any last minute requests that they might have, but at least your department might anticipate them. This means you can more easily meet their needs on request (i.e., What do they believe they will need tomorrow?). But you will want to go beyond even that.

You will want to gather data about future trends so that you can keep your own department appraised about what might be on the horizon. This means staying on top of training needs in general, technology of the future as well as the direction your company is heading. For example, were you ready for diversity training? ADA training? Can you explain reengineering to your Vice President of Information Systems? Can you discuss with ease the latest development in your company's industry? Can you list the training needs that will most likely be necessary to move your company into the twenty-first century?

Each of these are examples of what is necessary to stay in touch with and anticipate your customers' needs.

How Do You Learn About Your Customers' Needs?

What do you need to do?

- *Ask more questions.* Spend time with your customers on a regular basis getting to know them and their problems. What will they need in the next 12 months? Next two years? If you provide training services to them, what skills will be needed to fulfill the organization's expectations?

- *Learn to listen better.* Once you ask the questions, listen to their answers, but don't take them at face value. Probe for more. Remember all those "tips for active listening" that you taught in a listening course? Now is the time to use them: make eye contact, show interest, listen for both the content and the intent, attend to the body language, use paraphrase, and demonstrate understanding. Often a skilled listener can help customers more clearly define their own situation. And as a result, you learn more about your customers' needs.

- *Think in terms of exceeding your customer's expectations.* You and your department should focus on how you can go the extra mile. Your customer may ask for something, but how can you provide more, better, sooner? A word of caution here: Be sure that the extra is something that is truly useful to your customer. Don't spend valuable time providing something that really doesn't matter to your customer.

- *Develop ways to measure your customers' satisfaction level.* You certainly will continue to have training session participants complete the typical "smile sheets," but don't forget about other methods and other customers. Have you built in a way to follow up with training session participants to learn how much of what was presented in the classroom was implemented on the job? Do you follow up with the participants' managers to identify their satisfaction level with the course? Chapter 3 provides a list of specific questions you can ask customers.

- *Welcome your customers' measurement of you.* Be pleased that your customers take the time to provide input to you that will help your department better meet their needs. No one enjoys receiving complaints from customers and the tendency is to cover them up or to justify why it can't be changed. A customer complaint, however, identifies a process problem and an opportunity for improvement. Therefore, a positive attitude toward the customer input and a willingness to improve the process must be encouraged by all employees. Meeting customers' needs means that you remain in business.

- *Develop ways to stay in touch with your customers' anticipated needs.* In addition to informal discussions with your customers, you should conduct a more formal needs assessment on an annual basis. Tie the needs assessment to your organization's strategic plan and be certain that you are asking the kind of questions that will elicit useful responses. Don't provide a list of training topics and ask department managers to choose their top five. Ask open-ended questions, and then be sure to follow-up if you need more information.

- *Accept the customer's perceptions as real data.* It will be time wasted if you ask for input and then do not use it. Don't brush off negative feedback with "but they don't understand ...." Their perceptions are reality to them. Accept them and use the data to make improvements.

- *Invite customers to be on your team.* When planning for future products or services or when improving present processes, ask a customer to be a member of the team. They can provide a perspective that no one in your department can.

✽ One way to stay in touch with your customers is to help keep them informed. You should be reading industry-specific journals to stay informed about what is going on in your organization. When you read an article that you believe is pertinent to another department, send a copy to your contact in that department. This does three things: First, it builds rapport with your customers. Second, it provides an opportunity to open discussion which will help you understand your customer better. And, third, it's a way to show that you are exceeding your customers' expectations.

✽ Discuss customer expectations and customer satisfaction at your next staff meeting. It is important to understand everyone's perspective. Do you hear comments such as

- "Customers expect the impossible!"
- "They always want it yesterday!"
- "If they knew how much I had to do, they'd appreciate me more!"
- "Customers don't understand our department problems!"
- "They should try to solve their problems before they call us!"

Comments such as these indicate a lack of understanding of true customer satisfaction. The department needs to realize that without customer demands and customer problems, the department would not be in business. This discussion could lead to a "Customer Bill of Rights" or a "Valuing Customers" statement.

Your challenge in this should be to know your customers' next needs before they do! That's an impressive customer focus.

"Your challenge in this should be to know your customers' next needs before they do!"

3

TQM Is Quality-Centered

How Do You Determine the Quality of HRD's Products and Services?

What Is Quality?

Quality is the measure of satisfaction that occurs between a customer and supplier that only they can define. In other words, quality is what the customer says it is.

But if quality improvement is meant to be fact-based, shouldn't there be some way to measure customer satisfaction?

> "Quality is the measure of satisfaction that occurs between a customer and supplier that only they can define."

You will probably want to jump right in and ask your customer questions. Before you do that, think in terms of what your customers want, how you must measure it, and how you will find out. Internal customer satisfaction surveys can be an excellent tool. However, you must plan ahead to ensure that the data you gather will be valuable.

What Does Your Customer Want and How Do You Find Out? Beyond the Smile Sheet

Your customer wants high-quality services and products. How do they define "quality?" You will need to have specific measures. What will you measure? Turn-around time, accuracy, cost, length of time, size, and quantity are all easily quantifiable. But you will also want to measure your department's responsiveness, availability, thoroughness, and follow-through. How do you come across to others? These aren't as easy to quantify, but are still critical for measuring your customers' satisfaction.

✳ For example, if you wanted to learn other departments' levels of satisfaction with some of the courses you are now offering, you might consider asking the following questions:

- What percentage of time does training deliver courses in the time you requested?
- How many times each year should training offer course A?
- When is the best time to offer specific courses?
- How would you rate the accuracy of the materials produced by training?
- How would you rate the quality of the materials produced by training?
- How relevant is the content in course A to your department?
- How satisfied are you with training's responsiveness to your requests?
- How satisfied are you with the availability of training's staff?
- What kind of follow-up do you expect from training?
- What courses would you like us to offer that we don't offer presently?

- What other ways could we provide knowledge to your department?
- How could we be more helpful to you?

You should be constantly looking for ways you can improve the quality of the products and services HRD provides customers. To do this you need to be constantly looking for ways you can improve the quality and quantity of feedback you gather from your customers. In addition, you should determine how everyone in the department can get involved. They, too, need to be informed so that everyone is serving the customer.

How can you get information? Although questionnaires and surveys are excellent ways to gather data, you could try some of these more creative ways to get feedback from your customers.

- *Spend a day with your customers.* This allows you to get to know them and their specific needs. Nothing beats being there, in the other person's place to learn how you can help make it easier.

- *Conduct a focus group.* A focus group is a practical technique to get feedback about your current and potential products and services. Although focus groups have typically been used in marketing, they are a unique technique that more and more trainers are using to acquire immediate, in-depth feedback. The focus group can evaluate a program that has just been conducted, training materials that are about to be used, or the training department's performance for the past year. More information about conducting a focus group can be found in the appendices.

- *Visit several managers and ask just two questions.* Those two questions are: "What *bugs* you most about our department? Is there anything you can say that *brags* about our department?" Share the results with the rest of the department. You may wish to use a force-field analysis to strengthen the "brags" and to eliminate the "bugs."

- *Have everyone on staff call two managers.* Call managers in other departments to learn what they need from HRD. Bring the group together to combine the lists and to determine how your customers define quality.

- *Follow up with participants.* Call participants from recent sessions. How are they using the information? Although this is very specific, it is a good practice especially for new programs.

- *Follow up with recent participants' managers.* Use this follow-up to learn whether they see any change in behavior or skills of the participants. This helps everyone understand that the department's customers go beyond the participants in a program.

- *Invite your internal customers to a round table discussion.* Again use this opportunity to learn about services they would like to see improved. A round table discussion is less structured and more informal than a focus group. Depending on your customers and your relationship with them, it may be more effective than the formality of a focus group.

- *Reward people for learning about and acting on customers' needs.* Announce the action at the next staff meeting, send a note to the individual's supervisor (if different from you), or post the idea where everyone can read about it. If you want to encourage this behavior, you will need to reward it.

- *Post all results where everyone can see them.* Whether the results are good or bad, or from a survey or individual interviews, the results should be available for everyone to see. This will help everyone in the department understand the customers' quality expectations.

And, of course there is still valuable data in the participant session evaluations—smile sheets. You may want to go back and glean more information, looking for trends. Have you compiled the data? Do you compare the same sessions from month to month? Do you compare the same questions from session to session? All of this is data that may give you a clue about how to improve the quality of the services and products you provide to your customers.

Consider these notes before you initiate other data gathering activities.

- *Test your questions or survey before you begin actual data gathering.* Are the questions clear? Are you getting the data you need? Conduct your interview or survey with a sample group to ensure that you are asking the right questions.

- *Ask open-ended questions as well as those that will give you numeric data.* Objective data is a necessity, but subjective data often adds the explanation for the numbers. Although it may be more difficult to analyze, subjective data often gives you the human side of the information and answers the "why's."

- *Sometimes customers are more honest with outsiders than with their supplier.* If you have a less than positive relationship with your customers, you should consider hiring someone outside your organization, or perhaps outside your department to conduct the data gathering.

- *Don't be surprised if your customers respond with, "It's about time someone asked me!"* If you've never asked your customers what they want, they may not know how to respond to you. You might hear all kinds of things—including nothing. Don't give up. Give the process time. Give your customers time to figure out this new training department technique!

- *Keep your feedback system simple.* The easier the system, the more your customers will use it. Questionnaires that take more than 20 minutes to complete will not get the attention you want them to have. Interviews that take more than 30 minutes will not be seen as helpful to your customers. Know what you want; then ask it in the most succinct way you can. Remember you will want to go back for follow-up data.

- *Involve as many people in your department as you can.* You will achieve two things with more involvement. First, you will obtain more ideas both in the initial design as well as improvement ideas. Second, you will achieve more buy-in right from the start.

- *Get back to the people who provided you with data.* Thank them and share results. It is human nature to be curious about the findings of any research, especially if you have contributed. As quickly as you can, compile the data and provide it to your customers—perhaps in a condensed form. Include your planned

> "Don't be surprised if your customers respond with,
> 'It's about time someone asked me!'"

actions if you know them. And finally, be certain to thank them for taking valuable time to provide input to your process. Each of these represents another positive opportunity to interact with your customers.

How do you define your customers' measure of quality? Find out what you're giving them. Find out what they want. Then identify the gaps. This will provide you with opportunities for improvement.

Remember, at this point you are not solving problems. In fact, you aren't even learning. You are simply asking questions about "how," "what," "why," and "when." You are gathering data. The learning will occur when you analyze the data. The solutions will occur when you assign an individual or a team to determine the root cause and recommend improvements. Ask questions. Every question about services, products, and processes could potentially lead to improvements in quality for HRD and your customer.

In addition, remember that your goal is total customer satisfaction (i.e., knowing your customers' needs before they do). All of this data should be examined for what they tell you they need now, but you should also be thinking about their future needs. As you examine the data, you might ask yourself the following questions.

- What are the future trends in our business?

- What are the future trends in human resource needs?

- What is the next step that follows what this customer is requesting?

- How does this customer tie into the organization's strategic plan?

- How do you translate the customer's request to your options? For example, "A four-day session is too long, can it be cut down to two?" could translate to eight half-day sessions; to two full-day sessions, one week apart with a project between the sessions; to a computer-based training with support from a trainer.

- Based on the data, what do I believe this customer needs next?

Knowing what your customers need before they do is quite a challenge. Besides examining the data from your customer, what else can you do? You need to stay in touch with senior management and the direction of the organization. You also need to stay on top of what's happening in your company's industry by reading journals and attending industry-related seminars or joining the industry's association. It's also important to read books by futurists to get a generalist's view of the future. And don't forget to network with others in the training field about what they are doing, both within your oganization's industry and outside.

HRD's Chain Reaction

Dr. W. Edwards Deming is the American credited with introducing quality to the Japanese in the 1950s. His Quality Chain Reaction provides a logical rationale for implementing a quality improvement effort. It says that if an organization improves quality, costs will decrease due to fewer errors and more efficient use of materials and time. This causes an improvement in productivity and leads to capturing the market due to higher quality and lower prices. Therefore, a company will stay in business and provide more jobs. This is the chain of events that occurs to define quality as well as to produce the result.

Perhaps we can explain HRD's quality improvement efforts as a modification of Deming's Chain Reaction in Fig. 3.1. Deming says that if an organization begins with quality, its costs will decrease

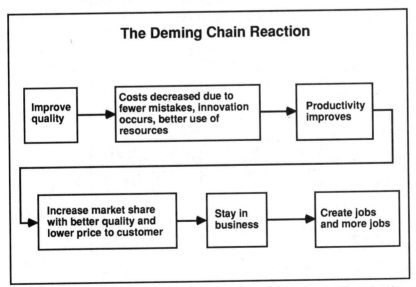

Figure 3.1. Deming's Chain Reaction provides the rationale for why an organization should start with quality.

because there will be less rework and errors. Perhaps you can remember a time when you were in charge of a project that was fraught with problems. Did you pay additional overtime to make the deadline? Did you pay a premium price to the printer to complete the job in less than the normal time? Did short timelines force people to hurry and make more errors? Did short tempers cost the department a decrease in morale? Each of these is a cost that could be eliminated or at least decreased.

According to Deming, this cost reduction leads to improved productivity, increased market share, and lower prices. All of this translates into staying in business and providing more jobs.

Figure 3.2 illustrates the rationale for implementing a TQM effort in your HRD department. It also displays the chain of events that occurs to determine the benefits of improving the quality of HRD's products and services.

If your training department improves the quality of its services and products (as defined by the customer), the increased effectiveness and efficiency should result in more relevant and appropriate materials and learning opportunities for the employees of your organization. Learning occurs both within the training department as well as outside the department. Inside the department, employees are learning more about their customers as well as how to do their jobs better. Outside HRD you are creatively meeting other depart-

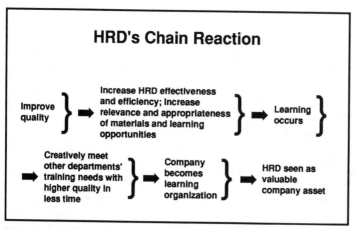

Figure 3.2. HRD's Chain Reaction is a modification of Dr. Deming's Quality Chain Reaction that provides a rationale for implementing a TQM effort.

ments' training needs with higher-quality products and services in less time. The result is that the company potentially becomes a learning organization. HRD is seen as a valuable company asset, contributing to the bottom line.

How will you know when you have achieved quality? You won't. There is always room for improvement. If you don't improve things, someone else will. You will know that you are approaching a quality department when you have total customer satisfaction. And that can be defined as knowing what your customers need before they do.

> *"If you don't improve things, someone else will."*

4

TQM Is Process-Oriented

What Processes Will HRD Improve?

Everything you do is a process. From the time you get up in the morning until you go to bed at night (getting up and going to bed are each processes, too), you are managing processes. And each of those processes is most often a part of another process. Many processes fit together to create a system. Becoming process-oriented and thinking in terms of systems is a new and exciting way to think about how to get your job done.

What are the benefits of systems thinking and being process-oriented?

- Provides a clearer sense of the system you work in.

- Helps you focus holistically on problems and more easily identify root causes.

- Prevents problems from occurring.

Initially you will see the relationship of everything that goes into completing your job. This will lead you to understand how everything in your department, and then the organization, fits together and how each part affects the other parts and the whole. This will give you a new sense of the system that you are working within. "What does diversity training have to do with our strategic plan anyway?"

Being process-oriented helps you focus holistically on problems and more easily identify root causes of problems. Knowing that every time something goes wrong, there are at least five inputs to the process that must be examined gives you the advantage to find and eliminate the true cause of the problem. How many times have you "fixed" the same problem? Examining the entire process also prevents you from "fixing the blame" on someone. The easiest response when anything goes wrong is to figure out whose fault it is. If you think about the entire process, you will realize that there are at least four other inputs to the process to consider and that any one of them could be the root cause. "You mean the form we use to order copies is confusing and it wasn't Sue's forgetfulness after all?"

Being process-oriented eventually prevents problems from occurring. Focusing on the process means that you will put the customer's needs first. It means that you will get customer involvement early in any process. That will prevent errors, reduce rework, and decrease frustration. "So we should ask production for input to the program objectives?"

In the long run, a process-orientation and a systems-thinking approach will improve communication between you and other individuals, between HRD and other departments, and between training staff and their customers. Everyone will be looking at the process to figure out what went wrong and how to prevent it from happening again. Everyone will begin to ask "what's the process?" rather than going off and just completing the task. "So if I had just explained the process up front, you would have been able to reserve the training room in time?"

What Is a Process?

A *process* is a series of steps that when combined produce a result. Every process has inputs that come from a supplier and outputs that go to your customer.

> *"A process is a series of steps that when combined produce a result."*

As you can see in Figure 4.1, the process starts with an identified (or perceived) customer need. Your supplier provides you with services and products. You use this input in your process. You have five components that you manipulate to add value to the process: people, materials, methods, machines, and environment. You produce an output in the form of services and products that goes to your customer. An astute process manager will measure the customer's satisfaction level and feed that into the process the next time. Every process has its own boundaries, its starting (input) and ending (output) points. Be sure that you have these clearly defined before you begin to examine a specific process.

What You Will Find When You Examine Processes

You will find at least four things when you examine processes.

- Variation
- Nonvalue added steps
- Quality costs
- Opportunities for improvement

Variation.   You will find variation in every process. Variation is the result of the unique combination of the five components of a process: people, materials, methods, machines, and environment. Excessive variation leads to waste of valuable resources. The key to process improvement is to locate the root cause of the variation and then

> *"Variation is the result of the unique combination of the five components of a process: people, materials, methods, machines, and environment."*

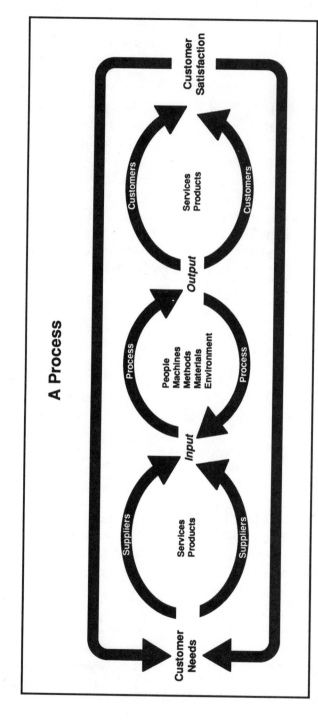

Figure 4.1. A process is a series of steps that when combined produce a result (output) in the form of a service or product for a customer.

either remove or decrease it, if it is not adding value to your process. Or, if the variation is adding value above what you ever expected, make it a permanent part of the process.

Two kinds of variation exist: normal and abnormal. *Normal variation* is always present and can never be completely eliminated. Sometimes it is called *common cause variation* because it is the result of the five components of a process (people, materials, methods, machines, and environment) working together naturally. Each component contributes to the total variation. Normal variation is also called *chronic,* since it has either been a part of the process for some time or recurs frequently. Normal variation is predictable within limits.

Examples of normal variation inherent in the process may include:

- Inconsistent material (e.g., your supplier sends you binders and you find 5 percent have defective rings).

- Limitations of machines (e.g., your copier jams if too many copies are made in too short a time).

- Inconsistent methods (e.g., everyone in the department has a different level of "completion" before handing off new designs to word processing).

Abnormal variation is not always present, and, unlike normal variation, can be eliminated in most cases. Sometimes it is called *special cause variation* because it is the result of a unique event. This causes variation beyond what is inherent in the system. Abnormal variation is also called *sporadic* because you don't know when it will occur. Abnormal variation is unpredictable.

Examples of abnormal variation not normally a part of the process may include:

- Unavailable materials (e.g., the order for binders was misplaced).

- A broken machine (e.g., your copier finally breaks down and can't be repaired until the next day).

- A blizzard (e.g., your department loses development time in an already tight schedule).

Understanding the two kinds of variation is important because it tells you what action is required to improve the process. If you have normal variation you need to examine the entire process, all five components. If abnormal variation has been introduced to your process you must try to isolate the unique event. If the variation is bad, it can be eliminated; if the variation is good, it can be made a part of the ongoing process.

For example, you have tracked course registration errors over the past two years and have calculated upper and lower control limits so you know what is normal. One month the number of errors shoots much higher than the expected limit. You would know that something unique occurred to create this abnormal variation. Since you do not want this to occur next month, you would seek out the cause and correct it. On further investigation, you discover that the automated registration phone system is not rewinding the tapes consistently, and you have it repaired immediately.

On the other hand, several months later the error rate is much lower than the control limit. This is good, so you would want to determine what happened and try to recreate it. Can you determine what occurred? This is abnormal variation, too—good abnormal variation. So you have a good chance to find something if you look for it. Upon investigation you find that you had hired temporary help two weeks that month while the department secretary was on vacation. The temp inadvertently sent old registration forms with the course announcements. It's time to check those old forms to identify the difference.

Nonvalue Added Steps.   You will find nonvalue added work in every process. Nonvalue added work is a step in your process (or a complete process in some cases) that does not contribute to meeting your customers' expectations. Nonvalue added work exists in the form of duplication of work, getting unnecessary approvals, waiting for instructions, attending unnecessary meetings, reworking others' outputs, writing reports that are not read, collecting unused data, and looking for errors. Sometimes nonvalue added steps have been a part of the process for so long that we fail to see them as such.

For example, a particular journal that your HR library subscribes to was difficult to locate on the shelf. Several years ago someone came up with a great idea to put a label on the spine each month when it arrived and before it was placed in the library. About three months ago, after receiving customer feedback, the association started to print the name, volume, and date on the spine. The person who placed the labels on the spine joined the department last year. No one ever told her why she was placing the labels on the spine, so she just continued to do it, even though she was covering up the very information her label represented.

And how about that report that your predecessor requested from department heads. Do you really use it? Or do you ask for other information? Over time, nonvalue added work creeps into your processes in the form of duplication, errors, rework, outdated procedures, and double inspection.

There are two keys to finding nonvalue added work. First, recognize that you will not likely be able to determine your own nonvalue added work. If we could, we would have eliminated it long ago. Second, encourage everyone to ask "why?" about everything that they do. A flow chart (discussed in Chap. 5) is a useful tool to help discover nonvalue added work.

✳ This activity requires that you have a good working relationship with the people who report to you. Choose several individuals and let them know that you are looking for nonvalue added work that can be eliminated. Ask the question, "What nonvalue added work do I create for you?" Then listen and take notes. Do not deny what you hear. Think about it and determine what you can change. It is almost impossible to identify the nonvalue added work that you create. If you knew what it was, chances are you would stop doing it! That's why you will need to ask others for input.

> *"Over time nonvalue added work creeps into your processes in the form of duplication, errors, rework, outdated procedures, and double inspection."*

Quality Costs.   You will find quality costs in every process. You will find costs to control the process such as proofing new copy (appraisal costs), or training new employees or developing a room arrangement checklist (both are prevention costs). You will also find costs of failure to control the process such as publishing an inaccurate course description or delivering training that does not meet the customer's needs. Discovering these quality costs should be seen as positive. They represent opportunities for HRD to improve its processes and to become a world-class training department. They represent opportunities for improvement. (If you wish to study quality costs and their control in depth, read *Total Quality Control* by Armand V. Feigenbaum.)

Opportunities for Improvement.   You will find opportunities for improvement in every process. To locate those opportunities you must examine your processes. Breaking down your HRD processes and examining all the components should become second nature to you.

For example, if you believe that designing new training programs has always seemed to take too long, produced too much frustration, and was frequently behind schedule, the program design process is probably a good candidate as an opportunity for improvement. Yet, what you have probably done in the past is put up with the frustration, made excuses for the lateness, and found someone to blame for the entire mess.

In the past, most of us have not been very good at examining our processes when something went wrong. What does examining your process mean? How do you break down a process? How do you improve processes? Continuous process improvement is the bottom line of TQM.

Continuous Process Improvement

Continuous process improvement is an organized system that uses a predetermined methodology for examining processes. The methodology chooses a process, looks at the way the process works today, gathers baseline data, analyzes the data to determine the root cause for less than perfection, looks for possible solutions, tests those solutions, implements the process improvement, standardizes the improvement, and monitors it for the future.

Many of you will recognize the description as the PDCA (Plan-Do-Check-Act) cycle, displayed in Fig. 4.2. This road map for continuous process improvement was initially developed by Walter Shewhart.

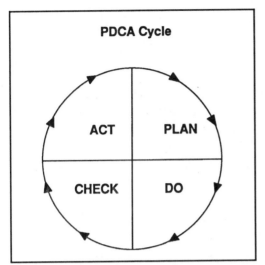

Figure 4.2. The PDCA Cycle, initially developed by Walter Shewhart, provides a methodology for process improvement.

Most recently is has been called the Deming Cycle because Deming used the wisdom of the PDCA cycle to help people understand the concept of continuous process improvement.

Plan. As the name suggests, this is the planning step. You plan which process you will improve, examine the data to determine possible improvements, determine how you will measure the improvement, establish a target, and decide who will be involved in the improvement effort.

Do. In the do step the process improvement is implemented—often as a trial run. Data is collected before, during, and after the improvement.

Check. In this step the preimprovement data is compared to the postimprovement data. This analysis provides information about whether the root cause of the unwanted variation has been corrected. Prior to Deming's death he began to call this step "study," referring to the need to study the data.

Act. The act step uses the analysis from the check step to determine the next action. If the root cause was found and corrected, the improvement would be standardized to "hold the gain" and the cycle would start again with another process. If the root cause was not corrected, if the original target was not reached, or if there is room for further improvement, the cycle would begin again.

The continuous nature of the cycle provides a clear understanding for why it is the basis for continuous process improvement. Remember that continuous process improvement can be at two levels: small, incremental improvements (i.e., the Japanese way); or large, breakthrough improvements (i.e., the American way. *Breakthrough,* as defined by J.M. Juran, generally refers to the organized creation of beneficial change, generally to an unprecedented level of performance.

Japan is known for making very small improvements in thousands of places in a singular process. For example, adding a check list to the outside of a registration packet could be considered an incremental improvement. It is not uncommon for a Japanese worker to submit hundreds of improvement ideas each year.

Americans, on the other hand, are much more interested in looking for the one big improvement that creates a breakthrough in the system. For example, putting the entire registration process on a computer could be considered a breakthrough improvement. Both small, incremental improvements and large, breakthrough improvements may make processes shorter, easier, more accurate, or faster. Both put money on the bottom line. Both are important; both are necessary. And both can be successful.

Continuous process improvement—the phrase says it all. Examine your processes. Improve them. Continuously.

How to Choose Processes

The HRD Department has literally thousands of processes that it depends on to get its work out the door. This simply means that there will be no shortage of processes from which to choose when you decide to initiate a process improvement effort.

✳ A great team activity is to have all department employees list all of their processes and then get together to share them as a department. It is a fantastic learning experience for everyone.

Some of those processes may include:

Training course design	Audio visual design
External trainer selection	Course evaluation
Course description composition	Deliver training
Evaluate training requests	Certify trainers
Maintain AV equipment	Purchase supplies
Develop training schedules	Maintain library
Analyze performance problems	Classroom set up
Administer apprentice program	Promote courses
Keep out skills on the cutting edge	Update materials

As you begin to narrow this list you should ask yourself these questions:

- Has the organization provided you with any guidelines you need to consider?
- Which processes will make a difference to your customers?
- Which processes have caused reoccurring problems?
- Which processes incur a high level of nonvalue added effort?
- Which processes have the highest level of complaints?

If this is one of your department's first improvement projects, avoid the most difficult process. Choose one that is easily correctable. This will provide reinforcement to other teams that see the progress. Also choose a process that takes place within a positive environment, an area where management supports TQM.

Which Processes Will HRD Improve?

When determining which processes to improve, think about your customer first. Which processes will your customer benefit from the most? You might consider choosing the process that receives the most customer complaints or the process that prevents your customers from completing their jobs. Or it might be the process that is so complex that no one, least of all your customers, understands it.

Next, think in terms of your organization. Which processes will help the organization reach its strategic imperative? Examine the strategic plan to determine which processes link the closest to the organization's long-term goals. You might consider choosing the process that provides training of a specific skill required to fulfill the goal. If the strategic plan requires the training department to work closely with another department, you might choose a process that is owned by both departments.

Next, think in terms of your department. Which processes do you have the most control over? It's always easiest to improve processes which you own completely, that is the beginning and the end of the process and everything between is solely under your control. You have the authority and the ability to change them. And remember, you can rally a great deal of support for improving a process that makes everyone's job easier. So consider choosing the process that receives the most complaints from the training staff. They will welcome improving a process that will save them time, reduce their frustration, or eliminate problems.

You should also consider resources in the form of hours and dollars. There are two ways of looking at this. First, how much time and money might you expect will be required to improve a particular process? Don't start to improve a process that you can't complete for lack of either. Second, how much time and money is the present process costing you unchanged? Often the recognition of this fact alone will create enough urgency to start a successful process improvement effort.

And last, think in terms of the process itself. Which process is stable enough from which to obtain and analyze *baseline data* (initial data collected that provides you with a solid foundation from which to measure improvement)? At least initially, don't choose a process that you cannot measure or one that is so wildly out of control that it will be difficult to make changes. Save those processes until later when your department has some experience with improving processes.

✳ A criteria matrix, such as the example in Fig. 4.3, will help you select the process that is the best candidate. List the criteria (e.g., customer benefit, company benefit, department control, resource requirement, and stability) across the top. List the potential processes down the side. Then use a numeric voting system to select:

Criteria Matrix

Potential Processes	Customer Benefit	Company Benefit	Department Control	Reasonable Resource Requirement	Process Stability	Total
Logistical Support of Training	2	0	0	1	1	4
Hiring New Trainers	2	2	2	3	0	9
Training Registration	3	1	3	1	0	8
Training Course Design	3	2	3	2	0	10
Upgrading Technology Systems	3	3	3	1	3	13

3 = Meets criteria completely
2 = Meets criteria to some extent
1 = Meets criteria very little
0 = Does not meet criteria

Figure 4.3. A criteria matrix is an excellent tool to use to make decisions. It combines objective ratings with your own subjective values.

3 = meets criteria completely; 2 = meets criteria to some extent; 1 = meets criteria very little; 0 = does not meet criteria. Add the totals of each line to find which one or two to select. This can be

done individually or as a team. In the example in Fig. 4.3 you would select "upgrading technology systems."

For additional discussion about more generic process identification and selection see the appendices.

Once you've chosen your processes you're ready to begin gathering data.

What Does This Mean to a Manager?
Process Management versus Results
and Inspection Management

The most fundamental change that must occur during this decade is that we must begin to manage processes. However, our obsession with the bottom line and final results prevents this from happening. We set things up, let them run, and hope for the best. When we get good results we are relieved but rarely study why. When the results are less than what we wanted, we quickly place the blame on someone. Why is that universal? Probably because people are the most flexible component of the process. They can adjust to the situation. You can kick your computer all day long and it will not adjust its

> "The most fundamental change that must occur during this decade is that we must begin to manage processes."

process to meet your needs. So we blame somebody. Call it human error. And, just to ensure that it doesn't happen again, let's add another inspection step.

Process management asks us to think in terms of the entire system. What are the inputs that go into the process that lead to the results? When something goes wrong, we realize that there are five components of the process, not just people.

If you're a manager moving into process management, consider these guidelines:

- Make continuous process improvement a way of life.

- Integrate the philosophy into everyday activity as quickly as you can.

- Measure the savings of each improvement.

- Review improvements regularly to ensure you are "holding the gains."

- When things go wrong, be sure to ask about the process, not the person.

- Train everyone to ensure that the department gets the full benefit of everyone's experience, expertise, skills, and knowledge.

- Involve everyone.

- Provide many opportunities so that everyone shares the sense of satisfaction.

The bottom line is that process management will make your job as an HRD manager easier if you allow it to do so. If your employees understand that you really need their help, if you have provided training so that they understand what they are to do, and if you provide reinforcement at the end, you may be surprised by the results. It will free you from being a controlling manager, to becoming a planning manager; from looking back at what happened, to looking ahead toward the future.

✳ Completing one of the numerous short forms of the Malcolm Baldrige National Quality Award can be an excellent activity for your department. It can help everyone see a big picture of how your department stands against the Baldrige criteria. This may also provide some ideas for selecting processes. At the very least it is an excellent discussion starter for your department about the topic of quality improvement.

5
TQM Is
Fact-Based

Where Is HRD's Data?

Fact-Based Decision Making

Measurement and analysis are a vital part of a quality culture and continuous process improvement. Anything within the entire process can be measured. The measurement might include the inputs to the process from the supplier, the transformation or value added that occurs within the organization, or the results of the contact with the customer.

Before you jump in and begin measuring everything in the HRD Department, think carefully about why you want measures. Data collection is important. In fact, one of the seven categories in the Malcolm Baldrige National Quality Award asks about data collection. However, a company is not awarded points on collecting lots of data, but rather on the appropriateness of the data collection. Before you begin collecting data in your department, be sure it is tied to the department's goals and that your department's goals are tied to the organization's goals and strategic imperative. You will read more about this in Chap. 7.

A baseline will establish beginning points, measure progress toward targets, and identify effectiveness of improvement efforts. Process performance and process capability to meet customer expectations are essential data and can only be determined by listening to the process through process performance data and listening to the customer through various feedback mechanisms.

Measurement and analysis of the customer-supplier interface—both internal and external—is a must. Appropriate measures that can effectively describe the quality characteristics of the process, the interface, and the product or service must be mutually established. Key measures might include quantity, efficiency, timeliness, or effectiveness of products and services. In Chap. 3 we discussed your customers' expectations of quality and measures for those expectations. You may need to translate those measures to your own process measures to make them meaningful to you. Your department may also want to track trends of major processes over time. It will provide information that could prevent a problem from getting out of hand or highlight areas for improvement.

This data is used to measure progress and to plan for the future. To be most effective the data needs to be accurate, consistent, up-to-date, and available to those who need it. The diagnostic tools will help you measure and analyze the process.

Diagnostic Tools You Will Use to Evaluate Processes

As you discuss quality improvement with people, you will hear much about the tools of quality. The tools are imperative to assist you with making fact-based decisions.

> "Be wary of people who believe that 'the tools' are all there is to TQM."

However, be wary of people who believe that "the tools" are all there is to TQM. You can readily see by this book that there is much more and the tools are just one factor of the whole.

You will also hear about the seven tools, and yet if you count them here, you will find eight:

1. Flow chart

2. Tally sheet

3. Pareto chart

4. Cause and effect diagram

5. Scatter diagram

6. Histogram

7. Run chart

8. Control chart

Depending on whom you read, Deming, Juran, Joiner's *Team Handbook*, or Goal QPC's *Memory Jogger*, you will find a different one left out each time. It might be the flow chart or the tally sheet or the scatter diagram. In addition, you will find them called different names. Don't get wrapped up in this because it doesn't matter. Just learn to use the tools and use them often. They will be valuable to you whether you are a member of a process improvement team or whether you are gathering data on your own processes. This chapter provides a brief description and how you might use each in an HRD Department. For more information and detail you should read one of the resources listed at the end of the tools description.

Flow chart.   Figure 5.1 depicts a *flow chart*—a visual representation of the process steps, using standard symbols connected by arrows that show the flow of the process. To construct a flow chart, identify major activities, decisions, inputs, and outputs that are a part of the process. Then use the standard symbols to show the activity and arrows to show the flow.

Like everything else in the diagnostic tools, there is no one set of standard symbols. Most often an oval or a circle represents the beginning and ending of a process, a rectangle represents a process

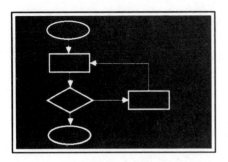

Flow Chart

Figure 5.1. The flow chart is probably the most useful of all the diagnostic tools.

step and a diamond represents a decision step (yes/no; go/no go; approved/not approved; passes/doesn't pass inspection). You will most likely encounter other symbols that will be introduced by people from various backgrounds such as electronics, engineering, or computer programming. Some of these other symbols may include a D-shape to represent a delay, a tiny circle with a letter in its center used to connect flow charts from one page to another, an upside-down triangle for storage, an arrow for transportation, or a curve-bottomed box to represent documentation.

For ease of communication, your organization should agree on its own standard set of symbols so that flow charts are easily understood from one department to the next. Our recommendation is to keep it as simple to use as possible.

Before you begin to construct a flow chart, remember to define the boundaries clearly. Where does the process start—specifically. At the time the receptionist answers the phone or when the registration form is handed off to a trainer? Also be certain you are charting only one process. It's very easy to begin to chart the physical process and get bogged down in the paperwork process. Agree up front about whether you are following the physical process or the documentation.

A flow chart will probably be the first diagnostic tool you use when improving a process. It may be the most important tool you use since it provides the best overall picture of what is occurring in the process. Use the appropriate level of detail within the chart to serve your purpose. Try to phrase all questions from a decision diamond as a "yes" or "no" question. Be sure to get input from the people who work in the process.

A flow chart may also be called a flow process chart or a process flow diagram.

Uses for the flow chart:

- Illustrates work/process flow.

- Illustrates document and paperwork flow.

- Isolates duplication of effort.

- Identifies unnecessary tasks.

- Isolates problem areas.

- Points out misunderstandings.

- Identifies process bottlenecks.

- Illustrates changes to the process.

- Trains employees in improved methods.

How might you use a flow chart in the training department? You will probably find it very beneficial to flow chart many of the processes that relate directly to the delivery of services to the rest of the organization. Examples include the training session design process, making room arrangements, material printing process, hiring consultants, the training registration process, the team building process from assessment through evaluation, the training assessment process, the process of making changes to training materials, or the course catalog production process.

✳ If you would like to have fun introducing the flow chart to your department, hold a lunch-time meeting. Bring in all the ingredients and utensils for making a sandwich. Have teams flow chart the process of making a sandwich. Then have teams switch flow charts and make the sandwich following another team's flow chart. The flow charts will likely leave out some obvious steps. The discussion over eating the successfully made sandwiches can focus around: What problems did you encounter as you tried to construct the flow chart? What problems occurred as you tried to follow another team's flow chart to make the sandwich? How

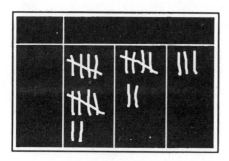

Tally Sheet

Figure 5.2. A tally sheet is the most basic, yet important, of the diagnostic tools.

might flow charts be useful to us in our department? What processes might we want to flow chart in the training department? What lessons might we take away from this experience as we begin to construct other flow charts?

Tally Sheet. Figure 5.2 shows a *tally sheet* which is the primary tool used to record and arrange raw data in a systematic manner. You have probably used a tally sheet often. To create a tally sheet, first determine the data to be recorded and design the form so it is clear and easy to use. Tally sheets vary in type and complexity. You will probably want to test the sheet before a project begins.

To ensure success, be certain that everyone agrees on what is being observed. It might be useful to keep separate sheets for different days, operators, or other components to discover patterns. You will want to strive for random observations and fight against biased data collection. Make sure there is time allowed for collecting data.

A tally sheet may also be called a check sheet, data sheet, or checklist.

Uses for the tally sheet:

- Provides data on frequency of events.
- Helps translate opinions into facts.
- Acts as the initial attempt to measure process characteristics.
- Pinpoints the location of defects and causes.

■ Establishes the original source for other charting techniques.

How might you use a tally sheet in the HRD Department? You could use it to collect an infinite amount of data (be sure you always have a reason to collect data) including, why people cancel, types of questions asked about a training course, types of follow-up phone calls, number and type of special requests by participants or even which refreshments are not eaten.

Pareto Chart.   A Pareto chart is displayed in Fig. 5.3. Developed by Vilfredo Pareto, a nineteenth-century Italian economist, to describe the distribution of wealth, a *Pareto chart* reveals the 80-20 rule. Dr. J.M. Juran identified a wider application to reveal which few (vital) causes have the greatest effect. A Pareto chart is a bar chart that displays the relative importance or frequency of collected data. To develop a Pareto chart, you will use data from the tally sheets or other forms of data collection, list the categories from left to right on the horizontal axis in order of decreasing frequency, cost or rate, and then add a cumulative percent line.

The key objective of the Pareto chart is to distinguish the "vital few" from among the "useful many." (*Note:* Juran introduced the Pareto principle as distinguishing the vital few from the "trivial" many, though most recently uses the "useful" many to suggest that all errors are worthy of eventual correction.) The Pareto chart needs to be read using your practical experience and knowledge since the most frequent occurrence may not always be the most important.

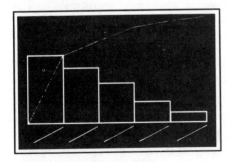

Pareto Chart

Figure 5.3. The Pareto chart is the classic of TQM diagnostic tools.

For example, you may be looking at frequency of errors when cost per error might be more important. An example of this might be that after constructing your Pareto chart for the kinds of errors discovered after a training program had been designed and printed reveals that typing errors occur with the most frequency. However, if you use the same data and construct a Pareto chart examining the cost of these errors you find something different. The second Pareto chart shows that although "artist renderings" are only fourth in frequency, it is first in cost, since the cost of each error was much higher. You now will need to decide which error to attack first: typing errors which occurred most frequently, or artist errors which are the most costly.

A Pareto chart may also be called a Pareto analysis, a Pareto diagram, or the 80-20 rule.

Uses for the Pareto Chart:

- Isolates the factors that offer the greatest payback.

- Measures the impact of changes—used before and after analysis.

- Provides direction to team, "Where do we go from here?"

- Establishes hierarchy of the data.

How might you use a Pareto chart in the HRD Department? A Pareto chart would provide you with the "vital few" error types on tests, follow up questions asked, types of unsolicited training requests, problems identified as the reasons for team building, cancellations by department, types of training design delays, errors made on transparencies, reasons materials are late from suppliers, or the kind of phone calls received by the HRD Department.

Cause and Effect Diagram. Figure 5.4 displays the fishbone-like sketch of a cause and effect diagram. Developed by Kaoru Ishikawa, a *cause and effect diagram* is a visual display of the relationship between causes and a specific problem, condition, or symptom. It helps to identify the possible causes for variation. To develop a cause and effect diagram, first determine the effect (the problem, condition, or symptom) being examined. List that on the right side. Then draw a fishbone-like diagram. The traditional approach is to establish the major cause categories and list them at the primary "bones." Next begin to brainstorm causes within each of these categories.

✻ A second method for this construction is to brainstorm all the possible causes on a blank piece of paper. Next identify the major categories and place the items in the correct category on a predrawn cause and effect diagram. Finally, go back to the brainstorming mode and fill in the "bones" that have a minimum number of causes. Also look at the entire diagram to see if any of the connections might generate other ideas.

As you select the effect, remember to stay within the scope of the process and before you get started, ensure that you have group consensus and full understanding of the problem. Keep the diagram simple; be concise. The objective is to find the root cause so that you can eliminate it.

Don't be satisfied with superficial causes, go for the one deep in the system. Ask: Why? Why? Why? Strive for the breakthrough! What is the one key cause that might be eluding you? What is the one cause that might be preventing you from unprecedented performance?

✻ Sometimes it is useful to work on a cause and effect diagram in two stages. Bring your group together to construct the initial diagram. When energy seems low or the group seems to run out of ideas, end the session. Assign everyone the task to continue to think about the causes and let them know when you will get

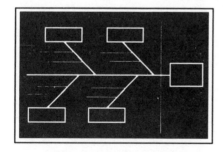

Cause and Effect Diagram

Figure 5.4. The cause and effect diagram is useful to find the root cause.

together to complete the cause and effect diagram. Often times, going away to "sleep on it" generates some of the true root causes and gets to the breakthough thinking you are trying to create.

The cause and effect diagram may also be called a fishbone diagram, an enumeration diagram, or an Ishikawa diagram.

Uses for the cause and effect diagram:

- Breaks down complicated issues.
- Separates symptoms from causes.
- Gives the team a blueprint from which to ask questions.
- Assists the team to identify the potential primary causes.
- Reduces subjective "finger pointing" tendency while identifying causes.

How might you use a cause and effect diagram in the HRD Department? You could use it to discover the reasons for unproductive meetings, reasons for class "no shows," reasons department managers cancel classes, reasons training is not perceived as effective, reasons materials are returned to suppliers, reasons rooms are not available, or the reasons training materials are lost.

Scatter Diagram.   A *scatter diagram*, Fig. 5.5, is a visual presentation of the strength of the relationship between two variables. Collect paired samples of data on two process variables and plot the data on an x and y axis. The pattern will tell you whether there is a relationship between the two variables and the strength of that relationship.

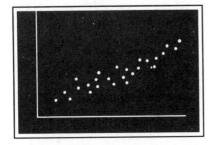

Scatter Diagram

Figure 5.5. The scatter diagram shows the strength
of the relationship between two variables.

Remember that single measurements provide the best analysis; stay away from averages. The scatter diagram only displays the relationship of variables, not proof of cause and effect. The closer the points lie in a pattern, the stronger the relationship.

The scatter diagram may also be called an XY graph.

Uses for the scatter diagram:

- Provides a means of testing whether two variables are related.

- Measures the impact of changing one element of a process on another.

How might you use a scatter diagram in the HRD Department? You might examine the relationship between training billing errors and day of the month, number of registration errors and number of classes taught, number of design errors and hours of overtime or the number of course "no shows" and the levels in the organization. Each of these might show a relationship between the two variables.

Histogram. A *histogram* (Fig. 5.6) is a bar chart that displays the distribution and variation of data in a process. It provides a snapshot of what the process is doing at a particular time. After obtaining the frequency of data on a tally sheet, you will determine the appropriate number of classes, the class width, and class boundaries. This allows you to insert the data into the appropriate classes and display it in a bar chart format. A histogram construction worksheet can be found in the appendices.

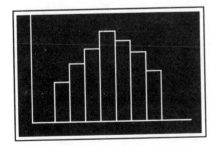

Histogram

Figure 5.6. A histogram displays the distribution and variation of data.

Remember that the pattern of the data is greatly affected by the number of classes you choose to use. The data displayed in a histogram represents the output of the process only. Although the normal curve histogram is most prevalent, don't expect it in every situation. A histogram with twin peaks usually means that more than one source is influencing the data. The histogram is a snapshot of the process—it doesn't show trends over time.

Uses for the histogram:

- Depicts the variation of the data to establish the capability of the process.

- Compares process capability in relation to specifications or valid customer requirements.

- Measures the impact of change when used in before-and-after analysis.

How might you use a histogram in the HRD Department? A histogram could give you a snapshot of how many minutes late classes start, how many people spoke in class and how often, how many errors there are in new class materials, how many people are using the new career development resources, or the number of errors made in follow-up tests.

Run Chart. A *run chart* (Fig. 5.7) is a line graph used to display data as it occurs over time. To develop a run chart, determine the characteristic to be measured and plot its values as they occur. Connect the data points to ease interpretation.

Knowledge of the process is critical to interpretation: a downward trend is not always an improvement. Keep data in sequential order as you collect it. Label carefully; don't rely on your memory. Ensure that the time period is appropriate to show trends over time.

The run chart may also be called a line graph.

Uses for the run chart:

- Shows events over time.
- Identifies trends.
- Indicates a change in the process.
- Provides a before-and-after analysis.

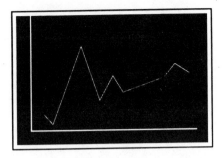

Run Chart

Figure 5.7. A run chart is probably the most familiar to you and displays data over time.

How might you use a run chart in the HRD Department? It could show the trends over time of many things including course "no shows," the number of minutes a class starts late, number of hours of overtime worked, evaluations of various classes, number of minutes to set up classrooms, number of special requests, number of unsolicited training requests throughout the year for a specific session or all sessions, or the number of ergonomic requests throughout the year.

Control Chart. Figure 5.8 displays a control chart. A *control chart* identifies the type of variation in a process by adding statistically calculated upper and lower control limits to a run chart. To develop a control chart, data is collected from a process. The upper and lower control limits are calculated by taking the collected data from the process and plugging them into statistical formulas. Do not change the process while collecting the data.

When working with control charts, get help from someone who is knowledgeable about them. There are various control charts and each has its own special consideration for data collection and calculation. You will also want to ensure that you are using the right type of control chart. However, don't leave interpretation of control charts entirely up to the experts. Interpretation is not pure statistics. Knowledge of the process and common sense are equally important.

Probably the biggest point of confusion is that upper and lower control limits are statistically calculated and are *not* specification

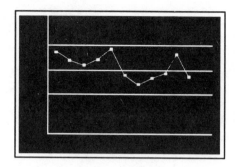

Control Chart

Figure 5.8. A control chart is used to identify the type of
variation.

limits. Control charts represent the process talking to you; specifications represent the customer talking to you. What does this mean?
To construct the control chart you gathered data on the process—
what the process was producing. So, it makes sense that reading the
control chart will tell you what the process is doing. The upper and
lower control limits are based on the process over time—*not the
specifications.* Being in control means the process is stable and
predictable, that events occur within the upper and lower control
limits (created by the process itself) and do not produce any abnormal patterns.

Since the specifications come from the customer and provide you
with the requirements as identified by the customer, you can see that
they have nothing to do with whether the process is in control or not.
Technically this means that it is possible that the process is "in
control" and producing junk! Again, recognize that if you have
trouble understanding the concept of *control*, it is the most difficult
and most misunderstood concept in TQM. It is definitely a labeling
issue, and what most people's definition of "in control" means to
them personally.

Uses for a control chart:

- Determines whether the variation in a process is normal or abnormal.

- Provides management with information to determine what type of
  action to take.

- Allows comparison of the output of a process in control to customer requirements/specifications.

- Measures the impact of changes—used in before-and-after analysis.

How might you use a control chart in the HRD Department? You could use control charts to track time of producing materials for a class that's taught often, number of errors in newly designed materials, number of classes taught each month, number of days of training provided weekly, cost to design new training, travel costs, or travel arrangement errors.

For a more detailed discussion of the diagnostic tools, see either ASTD's INFO-LINE issue 9109, *Diagnostic Tools for Total Quality* or Goal QPC's *Memory Jogger.*

Other Tools. There are many other tools that can assist you. A few such as brainstorming, force field analysis, Gantt charts, and Nominal Group Technique you will have used as an HRD professional. Others such as the pairwise ranking, storyboarding, multivoting or matrices, although not "the seven tools" and not readily connected to quality improvement, are useful. Still others are very quality improvement specific such as quality function deployment, benchmarking, the affinity diagram, and the rest of the seven management and planning tools. Although you don't need them to get started, you will eventually wish to learn more about them. See the appendices for further descriptions.

All of the tools are useful. Remember two things: (1) The tools are not everything and (2) don't get sidetracked by the names. Learn and use as many as you can, as often as you can.

Where Is HRD's Data?

Data is everywhere. The previous examples should give you some ideas. If not, stand in the middle of your office area and look at

> *"You are surrounded by data."*

what people are doing. Data could be gathered on every process that you see.

You are surrounded by data. The tools will help you collect and analyze data, but you need to initiate the process by asking questions. One of the most important questions for you to ask is, "Why are we collecting this data?" If the response doesn't fall into one of the following categories, you will probably want to dig deeper.

- To determine ways to improve services or products for our customer.

- To improve a process related to the organization's strategic imperative.

- To improve a process that meets our department's goals.

- To add value or remove nonvalue added steps to a process.

- To make a fact-based decision.

Data should be collected for a good reason. Remember, more is not always better.

6

TQM Is
Team-Driven

When Should HRD
Use a Team Approach?

A recent survey asked executives in Human Resources (HR) to rank what they valued most in employees. The survey, conducted by the outplacement firm Challenger, Gray and Christmas, listed "team player" (40%) almost twice as often as the second highest, "dependable" (22%) out of seven candidates. This may be an indication of the importance that HR places on teamwork.

What Do You Mean Teamwork?

TQM, teamwork. Teamwork, TQM. You can hardly mention one without the other. But what does that mean? Teamwork in a TQM environment must be focused on your customer (Chap. 2) and grounded in continuous process improvement (Chap. 4). Actually teamwork has a dual meaning in a TQM environment. The teamwork that you probably think of initially is the process improvement teams that attack a process and improve it for the customer. These teams are very important, but there is another meaning for teamwork that is absolutely crucial to the success of your effort. It is teamwork in the macro sense. That is the teamwork that occurs in any of the following examples.

- Collaboration in place of competition between two departments.
- Cooperation between union and management.
- Joint effort between the organization and its suppliers.
- Interaction to learn the customers' needs.
- Coordination of the vision at the executive level.
- Pooling of resources between two departments to achieve what they could not alone.
- Mutual agreement between management and employees.
- Combined action between line and staff.
- Participation in decision making by everyone.
- Coordinated action within a cross-functional team to improve processes.
- Synergy throughout the organization.

> *"TQM teamwork. Teamwork TQM.*
> *You can hardly mention one without the other."*

This teamwork is a result of a shared vision, a dedication to the customer, and a clear understanding of how the organization's systems and processes work together and a shared commitment to improve.

This is the teamwork that must occur daily, naturally, and with pleasure if it is to drive your TQM effort.

This will only occur if teams are made up of empowered employees.

Explaining Employee Empowerment

The *Learn, Live, and Lead Model* can be expanded to include *Listen* and *Let* at the beginning and the end of the series: Listen, Learn, Live, Lead, and Let. Extending your initial leadership responsibilities with Listen and Let expands the boundaries of responsibility for TQM to employees. Notice that the boundary is expanded at both the front end and the back end of the model.

The word *listen* means that you will truly hear what employees are telling you—both the content and the intent of the message.

The word *let* means to give permission, to allow, to authorize, to empower. Let the people go within defined boundaries. Individuals and teams need to be given the authority, responsibility, and accountability to create, innovate, experiment, suggest, implement, monitor, and adjust. Empowering employees means to stop stopping them!

Empowerment is one of those elusive words that is hard to get your hands around. Let's try. Empowerment is not something you do to people. It is a set of conditions that must be created that allows people to reach their maximum potential and frees them to act in the most beneficial way for the customer, their department, and the company.

Three things must occur for employees to feel empowered. You must:

> *"Empowering employees means to stop stopping them!"*

- Educate

- Enable

- Encourage

To be successful, teams in the HRD Department must be made up of empowered people. The leadership of the department must create the atmosphere for empowerment to flourish.

This area is probably one of the most difficult to conquer since the hierarchical chain of command and the rigid pyramids of power are so firmly entrenched in most organizations. Further, all employees from the top to the bottom are totally programmed for success in that framework. Consequently, the existing paradigms deter and often prevent leaders and employees alike from even intellectually buying in or knowing how to empower either individuals or teams. Leaders believe it is their responsibility to *tell* people what and how. While employees believe it is their lot in life to be *told*.

HRD leaders and managers will need to force themselves to break old paradigms and create new ones.

Truly the force multiplier of your TQM effort will be employee empowerment and teamwork. Read more about empowerment in Chap. 8.

Teamwork

Allowing teams to work on processes or issues is not new. The problem that most often manifests itself, however, is that leaders, bosses, and supervisors can't restrain themselves from:

- Giving teams the answers up front.
- Telling them where to look for the answer.
- Concluding the answer before the facts are presented.
- Expecting the team to confirm their suspicions.
- Implementing the changes and expecting teams to support them.
- Always finding fault and having teams go back to the drawing board.
- Putting their twist on recommendations, (Good idea, but let's ...).
- Withholding facts.

To be successful, teams need to have all the facts at their disposal, their charter clearly defined, and their authority, responsibility, and resources mutually understood. Information needs to be readily available for the team to use as data. In addition, teams need access to the right people.

Teams need to have a clearly defined charter. A charter sets the expectation for the team. It describes the process the team will work to improve, identifies customer needs, and delineates other information that the team may need to more clearly understand its charge: who's affected, who will be involved, and what the data presently suggests. The key players are also identified and may include the team leader, team members, the facilitator, the champion, the process owner, and/or the manager responsible for the team. The charter most often is a written document signed and dated by management. A sample charter format will be explained in Chap. 7.

Teams need to have their authority, responsibility, and resources mutually understood. Everyone on the team, as well as those who work in the process that is to be improved and those who work with the team members, needs to have each of these clarified. Everyone involved must understand the authority the team has to request data, interview individuals, conduct research, and to plan, schedule, attend, and provide follow-up to meetings. Everyone, especially the team, must understand the specifics around responsibility that may include the following questions: In what format will the final recommendation be provided? What is the completion deadline? What milestones should be reported? To whom and when? Everyone must also understand what resources are available to the team (i.e., How much time will team members be given to work on the process? Does the team have a budget? How does the team request additional resources if necessary?).

Teams also need to break paradigms that tend to hobble them.

"Teams need to break paradigms that tend to hobble them."

People are so used to trying to give bosses what they think they want that they let that drive them. They attempt to fit the answers with supporting facts and will fail to allow the process to speak for itself. Sacred cows, tradition, hidden agendas, and empires taint objectivity. Teams in these situations are destined to fail.

After a team has a clear understanding of its boundaries and has all the facts, leaders must demonstrate a willingness to *let* it happen and take a risk. If the team has been properly chartered, has followed the process improvement methodology, and has based its decisions on data, chances are that any proposed improvement it suggests will be at least as good and probably more on target than any individual (who is detached from most processes) could suggest.

Further, even if the recommendation is not as good as what the boss would do, the payoffs are greater. The team's idea will get better buy in, greater ownership, and more likelihood of implementation and success. The team will take responsibility for problems with implementations and will be more likely to see further improvement opportunities.

The long-term payoffs are immense because the team knows that they were *listened* to and will believe that they will be listened to again.

Both HRD employees and managers believe wholeheartedly that improvements are necessary and possible. Every HRD Department believes that it could identify substantial improvements. Yet the concerns are that:

- The people *fear* that management will reject their recommendations.

- Managers *fear* that the people will make recommendations they can't implement or will have to reject.

This same fear is a barrier to empowerment.

This fear is real and is based on lack of trust between management and the people. This lack of trust has been built on many experiences over a significant period of time. If teamwork and empowerment are to occur, trust must be established.

The first step must come from management. People must believe that management really wants to improve the process, that management will support recommendations, even if risky, and that management trusts them. Management must demonstrate a willingness to put the organization's well-being in their hands.

> *"When teams face up to their awesome responsibility unbelievable things happen."*

When teams face up to their awesome responsibility unbelievable things happen. Teamwork in this sense is foreign to most employees and managers, therefore, they need to be taught. They need to be taught to work together as partners in process improvement. *Listen, Learn, Live, Lead, Let.*

❋ If you believe that there is a need to build trust and decrease fear in your HRD Department, you might consider having everyone in the department read *Driving Fear Out of the Workplace* by Kathleen D. Ryan and Daniel R. Oestrich. Follow this with a department discussion. You may wish to use a discussion leader if you believe that more could be accomplished.

Initiating HRD's Teamwork

Your Department.　Your present culture will establish the ease with which the HRD Department is able to move to a team-driven culture. What has occurred in the past, what people have gotten rewarded for, how they will continue to get rewarded, and how their work has been defined will all affect your department's ability to be more team oriented. The ideas in Chap. 7 will help you get started.

You may also need to think in terms of bringing in someone from the outside to assist you with a Team Building Intervention.

Outside Your Department.　You need to think about building teams in several ways. Of course the most important team you can build is the one with your internal customers, those departments to whom you deliver training services, materials, or other educational counseling.

You need to think about building teams with those that you typically think of as your internal suppliers, such as the cafeteria, facilities staff, and graphic arts. You will also think of your external suppliers such as hotels, guest instructors, and printing companies. Make yourself their favorite customer and see the change in service. You will already have laid the ground work for process improvement.

The HRD Department may be asked to be members of other department's teams. HRD frequently gets called in to be an internal consultant because its expertise in training, education, and OD skills is valued. Or because part of the solution might be additional training.

✳ You may also begin some preliminary steps to create a team culture with some very simple things.

- Pair people up for tasks they usually do alone—good cross-training potential.
- If you aren't doing so now, begin to schedule regular staff meetings.
- If you already have regular staff meetings, consider having shorter ones more often—there's usually a better exchange of information.
- Consider rotating the leadership role for those meetings among your staff.
- Plan a Jump-Over-the-Hump-Day meeting every Wednesday at 11:45 to briefly update everyone about what's happening in the organization.
- Encourage a job swap between your department and another to enhance understanding and teamwork.
- Complete an information audit. Where does everyone in the department get their information to make decisions?
- Identify six ways you can change that will decrease fear. Share these with your boss.
- Identify six ways you can build trust. Share these with your staff.
- If you have already implemented action teams in your HRD Department, visit a meeting. Self-evaluate your behavior and communication.

No, every decision isn't made by teams. You do not need to reach consensus on everything. However, a solid team foundation will improve everyone's decision-making ability because there will be improved communication which provides better input.

The motto of one of our clients is "Happy people, making happy products for happy customers." When you walk into their plant you see it, you feel it. You just know they have the sort of teamwork that works.

7

TQM Is a Transformation

How Do We Get There from Here?

Okay! You're ready to begin. How do you get started?
  This chapter makes several assumptions:

- The entire organization is initiating a TQM effort.

- The HRD Department will design its effort based on the organization's vision, strategic imperative, and strategic plan.

- This is something that HRD wants to do.

  This chapter focuses on getting the TQM effort started in your training department. Chapter 9 will focus on getting the TQM effort started in the entire organization and your role in that task. One of the first steps you should consider is to conduct a survey.

Conducting the Department Survey

At some point you may decide to gather some data about the readiness of your department to implement a TQM effort. You may create your own survey using the one in the appendices as a model. You will need to determine what needs to be measured in your department. The survey in the appendices measures nine areas of quality implementation readiness which include: recognition, management skills/leadership, commitment to change, organizational alignment, communication, teamwork, quality improvement readiness, job satisfaction, and creativity/innovation. What do each of these areas measure?

Survey Categories.　The *recognition area* measures the effectiveness of the reward and recognition systems that are in place in the department. You need to give attention to this area before getting involved in a TQM effort. You will be asking people to change their behaviors and that requires reinforcement to make the change. You will need to know what people think about the systems that are in place so that you will know how to reinforce the change. This will also be valuable data for making changes in the recognition system itself.

The *management skills/leadership* area measures many things from the ability of a manager to create a vision and lead a change effort to the day-to-day skills of coaching and using employees' input to make decisions. It examines the skills a manager models and successfully performs to implement a TQM effort. If you are going to have a leadership role in this effort, it provides employees' perceptions about your ability to lead the change.

The *commitment to change* area measures the willingness of the department to implement change, improve processes and the way you do business today. It will give you an idea of the employees' perceptions about the willingness of the department to do what needs to be done to implement TQM.

The *organizational alignment* area measures how well everything fits together: the vision, the strategic plan, and the objectives. It also measures whether employees understand and support the department's direction. TQM requires that everyone is on board and contributing to one focused goal. This information will tell you how far off from that requirement the department is now.

The *communication* area measures exactly what you might imagine: How well we listen, exchange information, and provide feedback. When you measure the communication in your department, think not only in terms of upward communication and downward communication, but also horizontal communication. TQM requires that everyone communicates in all directions.

> *"TQM will be most successful in a department that has both a need and a desire to implement TQM."*

The *teamwork* area measures how well the department works together on setting goals and objectives and getting the work done. To some extent it should also measure the amount of responsibility people take for successes or failures and for making improvements when necessary. Pushing decision making and responsibility down to the lowest level is important if TQM is to succeed.

The *quality improvement readiness* area measures whether employees believe there is a need for TQM. It might examine the internal need to the department as well as the external need to other departments as customers or suppliers. TQM will be most successful in a department that has both a need and a desire to implement TQM.

The *job satisfaction* area measures the satisfiers that individuals get from doing their job. You should measure those that are most important to your training department. This area is not necessarily something for which you establish objectives and goals to try to increase the rating. However, it is probably the most important area to observe for an increase in its score. Increased job satisfaction is a result of a satisfactorily implemented TQM effort.

The *creativity/innovation* area measures the acceptance and encouragement for employees to take risks and create and present new ideas. It should also look at the results of developing those new ideas. TQM is a new way to do business; innovation is a key.

You can consider these categories or others. Does your department need to have a baseline on these satisfaction areas? All of them? What others should be measured? What questions will give you the information you need? You should also determine the best format for the survey. This survey takes two measurements on a five-point scale:

what exists now and what the employee believes should exist. You may choose to add other open-ended questions, a different scale, or a completely different format.

Getting Involvement.   Once again this is a good way to get involvement from others in your department. Your training department has needs assessment expertise within it. Take advantage of it by asking employees to assist with developing the survey.

To get the most honest, accurate data you will need to allow for both anonymity as well as near 100-percent return of the survey. In addition, employees should be given time to complete the survey. The best method to achieve all of this is to bring everyone together at one time, allow time (45 minutes for our survey) for them to complete the survey, and have them place the completed surveys in a box or envelope. For additional anonymity ask someone outside the department to administer the survey—this person can disseminate and collect the surveys. You may even ask this same person to compile the data. Do what is necessary to get good data.

Survey Timing.   Ideally this survey should be administered at the point in time when everyone in your department knows about the transition, but the actual implementation and training have not yet occurred. This timing will provide you with the best baseline data because employees will have knowledge of the change, but the work toward that change hasn't actually started.

This survey gives you baseline data. Accept the results. Figure out what you need to improve. Then put the survey away and forget it—for a while anyway. You should wait at least 18 to 24 months after implementation has begun to repeat your survey. If you can wait longer that's even better. Give the culture time to shift. If you conduct the survey earlier (say, at 12 months) its very possible that you will see the scores go down. Why? Employees will have higher expectations. They may not have known how great things could be! Therefore, it's usually better to wait the 18 to 24 months to conduct the follow-up survey.

One last word about timing: Get the survey results back to employees *immediately* after the survey is completed. Don't sit and ponder the results for weeks, trying to come up with answers, as you may have in the past. An immediate turnaround will have more impact and shows that you care. Besides, if TQM is *not* business as usual, this will demonstrate that fact.

These thoughts about surveys can easily be transferred to others you might conduct. Remember, do what is necessary to get good data. You will want sound baseline data from which you can measure progress.

Now let's examine the planning and implementation that can get you started.

Creating Your Training Department's Implementation Plan

Your training department will function most effectively if everyone's efforts are focused on a singular vision and directed toward a common goal. However, that goal must not be set in a vacuum. The training department will not be totally successful if it tries to improve its performance independently. Your department's plan must be based on the company's plan—a systems approach. In addition, the training department must pay particular attention to its interaction points with other departments. These are the "connectors" in the process flow chart. It is at these hand-off points that the ball gets dropped most often.

Many words are tossed around when people discuss planning: vision, mission, strategic plan, values, guiding principles, compelling reason, purpose, philosophy, beliefs, aspiration statements. As a department, you will want to use the same words that your company uses for consistency. To keep this design simple, four terms will be used which are defined as follows:

- *Compelling reason.* The compelling reason is the power behind a TQM implementation. It is simply a statement of *why* you are implementing TQM. The discussion that surrounds establishing a compelling reason begins initial dialogue among management and forces them to examine the company and the surrounding environment in a more critical light than ever before.

- *Vision.* The vision is the overarching purpose of the organization. It is *what* the organization wants to be. It provides a framework to make decisions that guide the processes that produce the products and services for customers. Most people see the vision as something to strive for but for all practical purposes will usually remain just out of reach.

- *Strategic imperative.* This is the goal—the attainable goal—that provides a measurable target for the organization. It also describes *why* you're in business.

- *Strategic plan.* The strategic plan is *how* an organization intends to reach its strategic imperative. It is the means that it will use to achieve its goal.

Each of these definitions can be brought down to the department level. How could you approach each as an HRD Department?

What's Your Department's Compelling Reason? The HRD Department's senior management must first clarify why the department will be initiating a TQM effort. What is the compelling reason? Survival? Improve quality? Competition? Internal customer demand? Told to do it? Company-led initiative? This information is valuable in understanding why a department would want to go through all the work of implementing a TQM effort.

It is especially imperative to know how passionate the leadership is about TQM, since much of the responsibility lies with them and can't be delegated out. The management team must reach a consensus on the compelling reason for implementing a quality improvement effort. The result of this first step in the planning process should be a singular statement that clarifies the compelling reason. This provides a clear message to the rest of the department and visually displays teamwork by the management team.

Envisioning Your Future. Only if you have an image of the future will you be able to create it. The vision and values should "come out of the bowels" of your department says Stephen Covey, author of *The 7 Habits of Highly Effective People.* Employees who have a vision guiding their daily work can make better decisions resulting in less

> *"Only if you have a vision of the future will you be able to create it."*

needed control. The vision supports the "Let" in the *Listen, Learn, Live, Lead,* and *Let Model.*

How do you develop a vision for your department? First, examine your organization's vision. If it meets your department's needs, there may be no reason to go beyond adopting it. If your department decides to develop your own vision, you need to remember a few guidelines.

- A vision should be a stretch. It is not an objective that you expect to accomplish. A vision should be written as something that everyone strives toward, but that is just out of reach. It should anticipate the future. If you come close to reaching your vision, you should adjust it to greater heights or new directions.

- It should be written in the present tense, as if you are already living the vision, even though you know that it is written as a timeless statement that you may never reach.

- It should encourage as much involvement as possible.

- It should be short; aim for a maximum of two sentences.

- It should encompass everyone in the department as well as customers, suppliers, and other stakeholders.

- It should be fun and energizing ... and even inspirational, if possible.

✳ Here's a simplified way to create a vision. If your department is small (22 or fewer) bring all of the employees of the HRD Department together. If you have a large department, the process may involve only management initially. Educate everyone about what a vision statement means and what it encompasses. You may choose to provide prereading. One of Stephen Covey's books would be good background. It may also be helpful to "seed" participants' thinking by presenting several examples from other organizations.

Next, have individuals write words and phrases on pages that are taped to a wall. Out of that, have each person begin to craft a vision statement. Read each aloud and post the statements. As a group, narrow it down as much as you can. Ensure that everyone is participating in the discussion. Get it as close to final copy as you can.

You will probably need a couple of volunteers to finalize the wordsmithing. They will bring it back to the group for finalization. If you have a large department, you would take the vision statement out to everyone else for their input. Use the contributions and make adjustments before working it into its final form. You may also choose a subcommittee to determine how you will keep the vision in front of the department. Where will it be printed? Who should know about it? How will you use it?

(*Note:* Throughout the process, do not attach names—either verbally or visually—to any of the words, phrases, or final copy. Once the vision is finalized and agreed on, it can be signed by everyone in the department.)

✳ Want to be more creative in your vision development? Consider these suggestions for describing your future vision.

Letter to an industry publication editor	Letter to a friend
Dialog between two employees	Radio/TV newscast
Press release from the year 2000	Write a short story
Memo from the company president	Write a poem
Poster for a future corporate event	Metaphor
Industry-specific award	Choreograph a dance
Present a brief skit	Draw a picture
Write and sing a song	Develop a jingle
Flow chart a process	Enact a conversation
Write a radio commercial	Create new job titles
Prepare the CEO's "To Do List for a week in the year 2000"	
Develop a new organizational structure	

✳ Want to be really creative? We know one plant manager who wanted everyone to understand the importance of creating the division's message. He wanted his people to imagine what people would be saying about the success of the division long after he was gone. To make his point, he made a video of his funeral, including him in a casket, with flowers and all the trappings of a real funeral. As people wrote eulogies they addressed the division's vision.

✻ Another HRD Department we know had an artist attend all of their visioning sessions. In the end he created a picture of their vision. Shouldn't a vision be visual?

One last word of caution, remember that everyone's view may not be included. What is important to an individual, may not be important to the organization. A true collabortive effort is required.

Remember, a vision leaps over obstacles, puts aside present problems, and describes the preferred dreams of the future. Though it may seem an arduous task, *creating* the vision is actually the easiest step. You now need to ensure that it is clearly communicated, that you are building commitment to the vision, and that what people do is aligned to the vision.

Clarify Your Strategic Imperative. Your department's strategic imperative comes directly from the organization's strategic plan. What specifically do you need to do to support the company? This might be considered the department's mission.

> "TQM becomes the way things are done, rather than something else to do."

Strategic Planning to Focus Your Energy. Strategic planning aligns the work to the vision. This is critical to the success of TQM in that it focuses the energies, resources, and the effort toward the achievement of the overall aim of the organization—the strategic imperative. It creates a road map to the future and a framework for day-to-day operation. TQM and strategic planning have an interesting relationship. Strategic planning can facilitate the orderly, systematic implementation of TQM while at the same time TQM becomes the glue that holds it all together. In this sense, TQM becomes the way things are done rather than something else to do.

In addition, the aspects of a TQM culture enhance the process of strategic planning. That is, the customer-focused, quality-centered, process-oriented, fact-based, team-driven, senior-management-led components of TQM actually reinforce the ability of an organization, department, or group to develop a worthwhile strategic plan. As strategic planning continues within a TQM culture, it enables the culture to improve. The strategic plan enhances the TQM culture that enhances the next strategic plan. Each enhances the other in a very natural, cyclical way.

In the real world of limited resources, the coordination of your HRD Department's strategic plan to the organization's strategic business plan provides you with a focus toward efficiency. Your department will maximize its application of resources in areas which will yield the greatest return and ultimately support the organization's goal.

The development of a strategic plan should be a senior-management led initiative with maximum involvement, participation, input, and feedback from all levels of the department. To ensure that you get participation from everyone, you need to ask for input before it is developed, during its development, and after its completion. You can assign individuals from a cross section of your department—all areas and all levels—to participate on a team to develop the plan.

✴ There are numerous ways to get input into your strategic plan. Any of your favorites will work. The most creative method we've seen is to open with a statement: "The organization has decided to close the HRD Department, unless we can prove to the company in the next two days how we will support the strategic imperative and how we will contribute to continuous improvement and the bottom line over the next three years." Ensure that people realize that this is a joke. After the laugh is over, employees should recognize that this is a serious activity and you should get some serious, committed input.

The strategic plan should be a living entity rather than a shelved document. It should guide the department as it meets the changing environment. Consequently, it must be monitored and mid-course improvements applied as the strategic goals or the means to achieve them shift. As your department gains knowledge and develops wisdom, you may wish to refine your strategic plan so that it better reflects the potential within a TQM environment.

The key to all this planning is that the HRD Department must remain focused on the organizational mission and/or vision. Synergy will be created and energy conserved when everyone is heading in the same direction. The following company example is one that is in the process of refinement. However, it shows how the corporate mission statement for implementing a continuous improvement effort led to the HRD Department vision.

- *Corporate mission statement.* Continuous improvement will create an environment that recognizes the value of all employees and encourages everyone to be involved in improving processes that will enable us to exceed customer expectations.

- *HRD Department mission statement.* Our mission is to work together as a team to anticipate and address work force issues to create a supportive environment where all employees have an opportunity to achieve their potential.

- *HRD Department vision.* Bringing out the best in all of us, by going beyond customer expectations.

For more information about developing a strategic plan, read ASTD's INFO-LINE issue 9206, *Strategic Planning for Human Resource Development.*

The Implementation Framework

Once your planning is in place, HRD will have a direction.

Remember, for TQM to work most effectively, it must start at the top. Because of that, we are working with the assumption that the entire organization is initiating a TQM effort. Therefore, you will, of course, follow the same model, use the same process improvement methodology, establish the same structure, use the same terminology, and whatever else your company has established to ensure consistency.

No matter what is planned for your company, several key elements exist in the majority of all TQM implementation plans. Generic names are used to describe these elements.

- Steering committees
- Action teams

- Training and support

- Communication

- Reward and recognition

How do you translate these to your HRD Department?

Steering Committee. Most organizations implement a temporary, artificial TQM structure of ESC's (Executive Steering Committees), QMB's (Quality Management Boards), LIT's (Lead Implementation Teams), or Lead Teams designed to get the effort started. The steering committee defines, manages, and provides resources for the TQM process. They are responsible for both implementing cultural change and directing the process improvement effort.

Ideally the work of these teams will someday become a more natural part of the organization's routine. As Fig. 1.1 in Chap. 1 illustrates, the way you do business today and the TQM effort become the one way everything is accomplished. In the meantime, the HRD Department will need to determine its team's roles, responsibilities, and membership.

The training department's steering committee is usually made up of the senior manager and that person's direct reports. Some organizations choose to have the senior manager plus a diagonal cut

> "The amount of time invested is often the first sign of commitment to the rest of the department."

through the organization. And, of course, if your company has a specific model you will follow that. Either can work and there are advantages and drawbacks to each. You will also want to determine when and how often the steering committee should meet. A typical team might begin to meet for four hours every other week to begin to make other implementation plans. An organization that wants to move quickly might meet more often. The amount of time invested is often the first sign of commitment to the rest of the department. (Remember, however, quantity will not automatically get you quality.)

The steering committee will begin by looking at the department's strategic plan and determining how to implement process improvement in the department. In addition, the committee will be evolving from a group of individuals to a team. This can take place either formally and faster, or naturally and slower. Though most steering committees allow the team to form naturally and slower, there is much to be said for the team that invests in a formal team-building intervention.

First, of course, is that they become a team faster. But even more important than that, they are able to achieve more sooner. In addition, the rest of the organization sees them acting like a team—which is what they are telling the rest of the organization to do. So they are actually "walking the talk."

What do we mean by a team-building intervention? Simply that the steering committee leaves the workplace for a couple of days and contracts with someone who has expertise in building teams to take them through a series of exercises to enhance communication, build trust, and improve the various interpersonal relationships. Generally, the session is intense with some quick gains. Of course this does not mean that the steering committee will not need further team development after the session. Team development is a more ongoing, continuous improvement. Generally, a team will leave the team-building session with an action plan that will address this continuous team development. Dennis Kinlaw, in his book, *Developing Superior Work Teams*, provides a more in-depth discussion about the difference between team building and team development.

Action Teams.   Chapter 6 highlights the importance of teams in a TQM effort. How do you get those teams started in your department? You need to identify processes for the teams to improve. You could do that in several ways. One way is to identify your customers and the processes that are most important to them. You could also look at the company's strategic imperative and the processes that your department needs to improve to support that direction. (Refer to Chap. 4 or the appendices for a more detailed description of identifying and selecting processes.)

Identifying processes can start in many ways. The steering committee can suggest processes that need improving based on the strategic plan and the assessment. Or you can design a nominating system in which anyone can nominate a potential process. In any case, once you have a number of processes identified, specific processes will need to be selected and assigned to a team for improvement.

Choosing processes can be done by the steering committee or subgroups within your department. Once you've chosen the process, choose teams based on who works within the process. You may also place a customer of the process on the team. Think in terms of who needs to buy into the potential changes and who has information that the team needs. The best members on the team are those that work within the process.

You should also consider having a manager on the team. This is an opportunity for management and employees to work together. Some companies keep management off the teams because they are afraid that they will dominate the team action. This isn't fair to the team or management. Both have something to learn, both can benefit from the experience, and both add a necessary dimension. Your training program that supports the TQM effort should discuss this issue so that it's out in the open. In addition, if your teams have facilitators, it is their responsibility to ensure balanced participation on the team.

The Action Team Charter.   The team is given a charter that describes the improvement: the process, its boundaries, the customer expectations, preliminary data, and anything else that might be pertinent. This charter is typically a single written page (see Fig. 7.1 for an example).

What would you expect to put in each of these sections of the team charter? Let's go through each.

The *title* indicates the name of the process. It is most useful for tracking and for clarity when employees begin to discuss various processes. Examples for the training department might be the "graphic arts request process" or "training referral process" or "program evaluation process."

Initiated by identifies who initiated the charter. Depending on the implementation plan in your organization, it could be many different people. Often, the individual who initiated the charter is a member, or even the leader of the team. Why? Not due to default, but generally the initiator has a natural stake in the process. The initiator may be the process owner, an affected customer of the process, or a worker within the process.

The *description of the process* is probably the most important section of the charter. It describes the process from start to finish,

---

Team Charter

TITLE:

INITIATED BY:

DESCRIPTION:

STATEMENT OF CUSTOMER NEEDS:

PRELIMINARY DATA ANALYSIS:

DEPARTMENTS AND WORK AREAS AFFECTED:

CANDIDATES FOR TEAM:

FACILITATOR'S NAME:

CHAMPION'S NAME:

HRD DEPT. SIGNATURE: _____   **DATE:** _____

Figure 7.1. The team charter provides the team with the direction for the process improvement.

identifying the boundaries (the specific beginning and end) of the process, who is involved in the process, what is occurring now, what should be occurring, the time if important, and any recent changes that have occurred within the process.

The *statement of customer needs* keeps the team focused where it should be—on the customer. What does the customer—whether internal or external—need from this process. Try to be as specific as possible. "Needs fewer errors," or "requires faster turnaround time" is adequate if that's all you have. However, generally a discussion with the customer will generate more specifics such as, "needs 99-percent accuracy" or "requires document returned within two working days."

The *preliminary data analysis* identifies the facts we already know about the process. This information will come from the records you already have. It might be as simple as "Nine customer complaints in October" or as complex as the attachment of control charts that show the process out of control.

To complete the section for *departments and work areas affected* requires some homework. The individual completing the charter needs to know enough about the process to know who the customer, supplier, and other stakeholders are that may need to change what they do if the process is changed. Support departments such as information systems, purchasing, accounting, and even your own department, training, should be considered.

Candidates for the team are those people who have been selected to be on the team. Usually these individuals have been invited and their respective supervisors notified before the charter is written. The word "candidates" usually refers more to the fact that others might be added rather than that some of those listed might be deleted.

The *facilitator's name* and the *champion's name* give these two individuals specific responsibilities. The facilitator is not an official member of the team, but has the responsibility to attend all team meetings to ensure that the best team dynamics are used and that the team has the skills it needs to move through the improvement process. The champion, most often a manager, is also not an official member of the team and does not attend all team meetings. The champion's responsibility is to ensure that the team has everything it needs from anywhere in the organization. A manager is usually the champion since the role requires the authority to open doors anywhere in the organization.

The *HRD Department signature* and *date* make the entire document official. This means that the team is officially sanctioned, has the authority, responsibility, and resources (see Chap. 6) to improve the identified process.

Recognize that this charter is only an example. You should develop your own based on the information that you believe your department and organization will need. As you do that, think about the tracking system you will want for the process improvements and who you expect to complete the charter. Also, remember to keep it simple.

The team then works together using the improvement methodology (a variation of the PDCA) chosen by the organization, keeping management and the rest of the department informed along the way.

If you are a part of a large corporation, it is likely that teams will begin in departments as functional teams. As the implementation progresses, cross-functional teams will appear between departments.

Team Training Suggestions. TQM requires training for everyone, starting at the top. If you are a manager, don't embarrass yourself by trying to get out of training because you "already know this stuff." When you attend the training sessions, you will find that there will be as much value in the team building aspect and hearing the discussion as in the information that will be taught. Besides, not attending will be interpreted as a lack of commitment. A word of advice to all managers: Nothing should interfere with your ability to attend the TQM training sessions—not illness, not fires that only you can put out, not phone calls, not even meetings with the company president. That means attending the entire session, the entire time. Rumors will already be flying about your lack of commitment to the effort. Squelch them with action.

The training design (see Chap. 10 for ideas) usually depends on the organization's implementation plan, but it will probably include some form of awareness training for everyone, team training for action teams, and sometimes management training for managers to prepare them to support the effort.

As an HRD professional, you know how important just-in-time training is for true skill transfer to occur. The model that seems to work best is one in which everyone receives awareness training quickly. This becomes a part of the communication effort and gives all employees a flavor for what's happening. Teams should be given training as soon as the process they will be improving is selected. The training can be designed so that the teams are completing some of the initial steps of their processes and are actually working on building their teams in the session. Training for managers should give them the skills to coach and mentor teams as well as others in the department.

Plan to Ensure Support for the Team.   Support for the team effort needs to come from at least two places: facilitators and management coaching.

Most TQM teams derive their support from facilitators. Facilitators are not members of the team, but they attend all team meetings to facilitate the team (e.g., ensuring the team stays focused, attending to team dynamics, providing just-in-time training as required). They are most effective if they know little about the process that is being improved. In fact, most organizations suggest that the facilitators for a team come from a different department. This ensures that they will maintain objectivity and keep their focus on the teamwork rather than get involved in the process. Facilitators work closely with the team leader to ensure that they are consistent and working for the success of the team.

TQM teams should also receive support and coaching from management. However, some guidance and a word of caution is necessary here. Management support can easily be perceived as meddling, taking over, or "the way it's always been." If you are a manager, you will want to support the team and at the same time be wary of the perceptions that might occur.

✳ A manager could sit down with a team at one of its first meetings and open a candid discussion around the difference between coaching and meddling. They could all agree about the best way to handle the situation if the team does feel that management is taking over. It could be as simple as opening the discussion at a regularly scheduled team meeting. If this is a big change for the manager or the department, it might be more formal—such as producing a document that identifies how the team perceives the problem or an agreement to have the facilitator moderate a discussion among all parties. The truth is that just having the manager open the discussion sends a positive signal that it is okay to bring up the concern. So typically it will never reach the more formal mediation techniques.

As management plans to support and coach teams, there is a fine line between support and meddling, between coaching and interfering. What should a manager do?

- Provide data when necessary, but don't add subjective qualifiers.

- Open doors to other managers when necessary, but don't meddle by doing so before being asked by the team.

- Support the team members' on-the-job workload, but don't simply load up someone else which could lead to discontent and jealousy.

- Stay informed and interested in the progress, but don't appear to be hovering.

- Provide help and assistance when needed, but don't appear to be interfering.

- Encourage the team, but don't appear to be pushing them.

- Provide ideas when asked, but don't provide your solutions.

- Have faith, but don't appear to be ignoring them.

- Ensure recognition, but be sure it's appropriate for the team and its level of effort.

- Implement the solutions; do not wait.

> "As management plans to support and coach teams, there is a fine line between support and meddling, between coaching and interfering."

Yes, it is difficult. It is especially difficult to walk the fine line between some of these suggestions. But then, no one said it would be easy, especially when everyone will have a different perception. The best advice is to keep the lines of communication open.

If you are a manager in the HRD Department, you need to think in terms of how you can assist your department. But who helps you? Many organizations provide one-on-one coaching for all managers and departments. This helps managers know what to do in an environment that may be changing daily. Frequently, employees grasp the concepts and move forward faster than their managers. Managers have been busy maintaining their responsibilities of the past and haven't had the same opportunity to practice the new skills the way their employees have. Coaching ensures that managers are given the same opportunities for growth that employees have been given.

✻ One of the best ways for leaders to continue to hone their skills is to pair up with a buddy. Two individuals can serve as mentors to each other to work through the difficult situations, to find answers to questions, and to continue to learn together. This works most effectively if the pair meets both regularly and spontaneously. For example, they may set aside every other Tuesday for lunch to discuss a book they have both agreed to read. They should feel very comfortable calling the other on the spur of the moment for advice about a situation that may have occurred during the week.

Resource Support for the Teams.   Resources come in the form of money and time. How will you budget training for your department? In addition, the most important resource that teams will need is time: time to meet, time to gather data, time to implement ideas. How your department handles the time issue will be a measure of commitment. Teams that go off to three days of training and come back to stacks of work on their desks will not feel very supported.

✻ In some organizations the manager is required to fill in for the employee who is attending TQM classes. This prevents the work from piling up while the employee is learning the skills that are so important to the company's future.

Hopefully the organization has thought about providing facilitators, coaching, and resources to your department. You need to determine how to tap into it.

Communication. Too many efforts have failed for the lack of a good communication network. In fact, it is probably the number one reason why some efforts are successful and others are not. It will be crucial to create communication links that keep people informed and involved.

Certainly, it is top management's responsibility to communicate the initial TQM vision to the organization. Often this public announcement (in the form of a speech) is the first communication that most employees receive. Generally the next communication will be the awareness training which will provide more "how-to" communication. A video tape should also be made for those employees who are in branches or who join the organization at a later date. You can keep the communication flowing with newsletters, announcements, or memos. Our preference is that you plan to build the communication about TQM into the vehicles you now have available. That is, rather than start a new TQM newsletter, ensure that there is a column in the regular company newsletter or your department newsletter to communicate TQM progress. Build the TQM message into other existing communication methods including memos, agendas, annual reports, earnings statements, bulletin boards, and any others at your disposal.

But the most important communication will come from the less formal communication network: staff meetings, operations briefings, and one-on-one discussions. If your weekly staff meetings do not address the TQM effort, you are sending a strong communication message. If you do not show interest in your department action teams, you are sending a strong communication message. And both of these messages are negative. Again, attend to building TQM progress messages into routine meetings and conversations.

✳ One organization sent video tapes and a letter to each employees' home, encouraging them to discuss the TQM effort with their families. Did this make an impact on the employees? Absolutely! The message was "we're serious about this."

The communication plan for your department does not need to be elaborate. It *does* need to be two-way and readily accessible to everyone. Ask questions. Give information. You need to keep this in front of you constantly. What's the purpose? You'll want to identify resources needed, identify continued training needed, stay on top of the concerns and issues, examine the level of commitment, stay in touch with involvement and most important, revisit the vision to determine whether you're on target.

Reward and Recognition.   How will you communicate your satisfaction with individual and team efforts as well as their results? In fact, most organizations don't change the overall system until they are well into the implementation effort. This is appropriate. The organization needs to determine what implications TQM will have on the organization and where the most needed changes exist in the reward and recognition system. Without this data premature changes would be meddling with the system.

This does not mean, however, that your department cannot supplement the organization's reward and recognition system until that time occurs.

You will want to adopt some plan that rewards those who conform to the new set of values and priorities that are established. This could be anything from a pat on the back and a thank you to recognition for teams and celebrating their success. What will be seen as rewards to employees of the training department?

✳ Don't take on this task yourself. Establish a team or use some other mechanism for asking employees in your department to develop ways to recognize and celebrate your department's successes. It's important to get others involved because you will have more buy in. You will probably also have more ideas, as well as ideas that are meaningful to the people in your department. And, don't forget, it's easier!

Questions to Ask Others

Earlier we spent time with a TQM readiness survey for your department. It provided you with an implementation baseline: Where are you today? Answering this question now is important so that after you implement TQM you can measure the department again to learn where the department improved and where the department still needs additional improvement.

Just because you asked lots of questions then, doesn't mean you should stop. Remember, communication is a major reason for the success or failure of TQM efforts. At this time you will want to ask questions that will help you learn what to do within your implementation efforts. (Remember learn, live, and lead?) The following questions will provide insight from several different views. Ask the questions. Listen to the responses. Learn from the insight.

> *"Communication is a major reason for the success or failure of TQM efforts."*

Ask Your Customers

- During the last _____ _____ (e.g., six months) describe the times we exceeded your expectations.

- During the last _____ _____ (e.g., six months) describe the times we did not meet your expectations.

- In your opinion, what services or products do we most need to improve?

- List all the ways we could help to improve your performance.

- What are your most critical needs that we can fulfill?

- What would we need to do for you to brag about us?

- What do we do or provide that is in excess of your needs?

Ask Your Employees

- What do you personally expect out of the quality improvement effort?

- How do you explain our quality improvement effort to others?

- How can we encourage the involvement of everyone?

- How do you want to be involved?

- What would you like to see us do?

- What do our customers say about us?

- What do our suppliers say about us?

- How well are the processes working in your area? How do you know?

- Who are your internal customers? What do they expect of you?

- Can you and your colleagues produce quality work every time? Why or why not?

- What skills do you need to help you on the job?

Ask Other Departments or Organizations That Have Invested in Quality

- What was the most valuable step you took to initiate your quality effort?

- How do you ensure that you are visibly supporting the effort?

- What are you trying to achieve by implementing a quality improvement effort?

- How much time did you invest the first year? Doing what?

- What were the major obstacles that you faced when implementing your quality improvement effort?

- What is the vision for your department and the organization?

- What is the most difficult for you in this effort?

- What commitment is necessary for this type of effort to succeed?

- What is the most valuable piece of advice you can give me?

✳ As you begin your implementation process it would be wise to involve the entire training department. Naturally, you will need to stay within the guidelines established by your organization. You can open that communication by bringing everyone together to create a list of the implementation methods that will work best within the department. Provide everyone with a sheet that looks similar to the one in Fig. 7.2. After a brief introduction about the purpose of the activity, ask them to complete the page, identifying several critical TQM implementation "methods to avoid" and those to include in the training department's implementation plan. If you have a small department (less than 22 people) open the discussion to the entire group and list methods to avoid as they come up on flipchart paper. Do the same with the "methods to

Implementation Methods for the Training Department

Avoid These	Include These

Figure 7.2. Use the implementation methods worksheet to get involvement in your department.

include." If you have a large department, you may conduct several of these sessions or choose a cross section of people to generate input.

This activity can accomplish several things. First, it can clear up any misperceptions people may have. Second, it gives you an opportunity to explain what has been decided at the executive level. Third, it offers everyone an opportunity to contribute to the process, which can lead to buy-in. Fourth, it brings attention to any potential problems with the implementation plan.

What can you expect to hear? On the first side you may hear: avoid ...

"too much paperwork."

"bureaucracy."

"force feeding information."

"getting us excited and then not letting us do something."

"leaving out middle managers."

"gurus and gospel.

"assuming everyone is at the same level."

On the second side you may hear: include ...

"lots of involvement."

"letting people know that failure is okay."

"realistic timelines."

"top-management commitment and participation."

"a process model."

"success stories and examples."

"making it a part of the way we do everything."

"plenty of training."

"allowing changes along the way."

Enjoy the activity. It can be a great starting point.

8

TQM Is Lead from the Top

What Does That Mean?

"Institute leadership." These two words have been canonized in Deming's Fourteen Points.

Deming believed strongly that leadership commitment and support are imperative to successfully improve quality. To succeed, TQM must be the chosen business strategy by senior management. There are several reasons for this.

- Senior management leads the organization in goal setting, resource planning, future focusing, and deciding how to stay in business. TQM is a business strategy. Who else can lead it?

- Senior management has established and implemented the systems, policies, and procedures that need to be changed to be more customer-focused and systems oriented. Who better to fix them?

- Senior management controls the resources. And resources are needed to implement TQM. Who else will commit the resources for TQM?

- Senior management is the model for the rest of the organization. Most employees emulate their bosses. Who should be modeling the behaviors?

Senior-Management Leadership and Commitment

Lack of senior-management commitment and support is reported most often as the reason most TQM efforts fail. Although this is probably somewhat true in many instances, let's be careful about heaping all the blame on senior management. Each person in the organization has at least some control over some processes. Each of you shares in the responsibility to make this business strategy work. Don't blame your bosses for why you can't do your part to achieve success.

Senior management must be leaders. Leaders must be committed. Commitment implies risk and trust. Commitment means providing training, tools, resources, authority, responsibility, freedom, and encouragement. And it means doing things "their" way or "our way" rather than always "my" way. Commitment means asking, listening, and acting instead of deciding, telling, and directing.

Leaders must appreciate the potent power of people working collectively and that the people are the force multiplier that will account for unprecedented levels of performance. Their creative energy must be unshackled, and leadership is the key. Your vision and plan covered in Chap. 7 will have little effect without the 100-percent support of everyone in the department.

You're a Leader, Where Do You Start?

Begin by understanding the compelling reason for change. Why does your organization need to change? Why does the HRD Department need to change? Then recognize that TQM is not only a proven way, but the chosen way—the chosen business strategy to make the necessary changes to achieve your strategic imperative.

Next, focus on what needs to be changed. Leaders need to focus on at least three elements:

- Providing a unified focus
- Implementing process improvement
- Changing the culture

Providing a Unified Focus.   The unified focus is the vision and strategic plan that was discussed in Chap. 7. A unified focus is the glue that holds the implementation together and the fuel that energizes everyone to make changes. Without a unified focus, commitment, synergy, and a sense of urgency will not become a reality.

Implementing Process Improvement.   Implementing process improvement is the heart of TQM change and is the change that will keep the company in business. This was discussed in Chap. 4. Work processes must change to improve products and services to customers. Without process improvements you will not delight your customers.

Changing the Culture.   The cultural change has been discussed throughout this book. But the leadership must begin the cultural change within themselves. They must begin to identify how they are leading the organization and what must change to support the vision they see. The leaders of the organization must accept the responsibility for the cultural change. Processes are wrapped in the culture. It is not possible to change one without the other. Without a cultural change, process improvement efforts do not last and become artificial flag waving exercises.

Change Will Occur in Phases.   All of these changes occur in three distinct phases. The first is in the initial *planning phase* when the emphasis is on organizing and developing the strategy to gain knowledge and experience, to begin to identify processes, and to

> *"Processes are wrapped in the culture.*
> *It is not possible to change one without the other."*

begin to understand the organization's culture. The organization is
investigating what TQM is and how others have implemented it. It is
a time of excitement and newness. Everyone has a checklist of things
to begin. Awareness training is established, though the training is
conducted in a sterile environment. In addition, the organization
makes a first attempt at establishing formal action teams. You can
recognize the planning phase by the hustle and bustle of making
plans, the excitement of designing a new future, and the sense of
early optimism.

The second phase is the *transition phase*. It occurs when sufficient knowledge and wisdom have occurred so that those within
the organization can define and execute a unified focus that makes
sense, understand what process improvement means, and begin to
view the cultural changes initiated by senior management. This
phase doesn't begin until most employees have had awareness
training. The way of doing business is starting to change substantially and employees talk in terms of processes, customers, and
suppliers. Ownership for constant improvement is spreading
throughout the organization. That's the positive side of the transition phase.

Interestingly, this phase is also typified by chaos, confusion, and
frustration. Why? Upper management is pushed from the bottom by
employees who have bought into the plan and who want things to
move faster. When this doesn't occur, the "willing workers" are
frustrated and confused. The managers caught in the middle find it
difficult to cope with the situation. Actually these are signs of success!
The fact that employees feel empowered enough to disagree openly
certainly means that the culture is changing. The fact that you as a
leader didn't know that there was any dissent before, doesn't mean
it didn't exist. This can be a scary time for leaders who may be asking
themselves, "Why did we ever start this?"

> "The fact that you as a leader didn't know that there
> was dissent before, doesn't mean it didn't exist."

What do you do as a leader to help your organization through the
transition phase? Actually, nothing more than we have already
suggested. Don't give up and continue to focus on these elements:

- Provide a unified focus by constantly communicating a clear vision at all levels.

- Implement process improvement by modeling what you expect others to do.

- Change the culture by continuing to provide strong, visible leadership and commitment.

Keep the faith! If you have a good implementation plan in place the organization will continue to flourish and move forward. Training department leaders, of course, have responsibility for the implementation plan. Chapter 10 provides guidelines for ensuring that your implementation plan will successfully move you through the transition phase. Just remember, the transition phase is the most exciting yet frustrating, most challenging yet rewarding change phase of all.

The third phase, the *vision phase*, occurs when everyone lives the vision, improves processes, and feels a part of the new culture. Continual improvement is no longer a new dimension, in fact, it is a given. Employees cross department lines for improved communication. The obsession to exceed both internal and external customer needs is apparent at all levels and this is occurring easily because decision making has been pushed down to the lowest level. Change is a way of life and Peter Senge would say that there is a "passion for learning." Certainly this sounds like the organization has "made it," but with the constant change and improvements that are necessary, no organization ever really "makes it." As a leader, you can expect your department and organization to experience these phases.

Do the phases sound familiar? It's learn, live, and lead again, but this time from an organizational viewpoint.

Don't Make These Phase Mistakes.   As a leader you must be aware of the phases your organization will go through so that you recognize that it is quite natural. If you don't recognize the phases, you run the risk of making some critical errors, such as taking your eye off the ball in the planning phase when everyone seems to be enthusiastic about the TQM implementation. Or you might become upset and frustrated during the transition phase and try to issue more edicts and more demands to "do it or else!" when what this phase really demands is compassion, not commands; leadership, not management. Or you might also give up during the transition phase, asking, "Why did we ever start this mess?" And the mistake you could potentially make in the vision phase is that you might not know when a hands-off approach is better. You might stay too intimately involved and actually be preventing progress.

As your organization moves through these change phases you will need to focus on creating an empowered work force, so let's explore what that means.

Empowerment

Much has been written about empowerment and what it means. It has been described as removing barriers, encouraging employee commitment and risk taking, reinforcing creativity and innovation, enabling people to implement solutions, increasing responsibility, believing and trusting people, and having freedom from fear, and even the "opposite of enslavement."

Empowerment is a term used in the *Malcolm Baldrige National Quality Award* to clarify the role that an organization's human resource plans play in providing quality services and products to customers. Empowerment is defined as employees' authority to act.

Empowerment can become complicated quickly. It can begin to sound like a religion or a cult. Therefore, because it has become so difficult to describe, some people have banned the word from their vocabulary and insist that it is meaningless. However, we know of at least one CEO who accepted the word again, once he understood a clear definition of empowerment, what an empowered leader needed to do and the results empowerment could achieve.

Empowerment is not something you do to people. Empowerment is a set of conditions that must be created that allows people to reach their maximum potential and frees them to act in the most beneficial way for the customer, their department, and the company.

We believe there are three key elements that a leader must complete for empowerment to occur: educate, enable, and encourage.

Educating. Educating starts with understanding who your people are—their style—and what they will need. The many facets of educating include mentoring, coaching, counseling, and teaching. The empowering leader will delegate the challenging tasks to develop others and then let go of the authority for those tasks. It also means using the basics of listening and communicating. The empowering leader will provide a vision or at least clear goals and direction. The empowering leader measures competence (willingness and ability) before delegating tasks and is adept at providing support without taking over.

Educating must also include the timely and adequate flow of information required to do the job. The empowering leader shares organizational information regularly and will also share information that lets people know how they're doing on a regular basis.

Enabling. Enabling starts with providing the appropriate resources to get the job done. It also means identifying and removing roadblocks, driving fear out of the workplace, giving employees influence over their environment, and sharing accountability while delegating authority and responsibility.

The organization's climate also has a great influence on whether the individual is enabled to do the job. The empowering organization has a strong vision and values that support leadership. Policies and procedures support the vision and rules exist only if absolutely necessary.

Encouraging. Encouraging starts with expecting the best from people. No one comes to work planning to mess up. The empowering leader trusts humans and encourages initiative, ideas, and risk taking. Empowering leaders have good feedback skills and encourage learning from every situation. The empowering leader recognizes the importance of maintaining and building self-esteem so that people can accept the power. It also means that the empowering leader knows how to show appreciation and how to individualize reinforcement for each person.

The work itself must also provide encouragement. It must be meaningful so that the employee knows that it is important to the success of the organization. The job must provide challenge and variety to encourage enthusiasm. The empowered leader will provide new experiences, job rotation, special assignments, and new settings for employees. They try to tailor the job to match the employee's style and abilities. Empowered leaders will also encourage the individual to make direct contact with customers and suppliers. A job that provides intrinsic reinforcement and is motivating, creates an empowered environment.

✳ Want to know if your people think you're an empowering leader? Create a 12-question form that identifies what you need to do to empower your people, four questions for each of the areas: educate, enable, and encourage. Provide this to your people and ask them to respond on a five-point scale anonymously regarding your skill/behavior level. What kind of questions? Figure 8.1 provides you with an example. However, remember that this exercise will be most beneficial if you create questions that will be most pertinent to you and your situation.

✳ Need other suggestions for creating a climate that supports empowerment? Try these.

- Identify three responsibilities you could delegate to someone else.
- Ask people in your department to identify tasks they'd like to try.
- Hold scheduled meetings to discuss improvement ideas.
- List 10 ways you could recognize and reward people.
- Plan 15-minute meetings with all your people within 30 days to let them know how they're doing.
- Interview someone you know who is doing a great job of developing people and implement some of that person's suggestions.
- Ask people if they're getting the support they need from you.
- Ask all employees in your department what they see themselves doing in 10 years. Then begin to think about how you could give those people the experiences they need.

Walk the Talk

As leaders of the HRD Department you have a responsibility to model the role that emulates what the organization and the department are trying to accomplish. Creating an empowered workplace is just one

Empowerment Skills

I'm interested in improving my leadership skills. **Please rate me on a 1-5 scale based on your interaction with me.**

Educate

	Minimum Degree				High Degree

To what degree:
1. do I provide you with all the information you need to do your job?
    1 2 3 4 5
2. are you being prepared to be successful in the future?   1 2 3 4 5
3. are you satisfied with the opportunities available to learn new skills and abilities?   1 2 3 4 5
4. do I model behaviors that empower you?   1 2 3 4 5

Enable

To what degree:
5. do you feel comfortable disagreeing with me?   1 2 3 4 5
6. are barriers eliminated so you can do your job?   1 2 3 4 5
7. do you feel comfortable experimenting and taking risks?   1 2 3 4 5
8. do you feel a part of our future vision?   1 2 3 4 5

Encourage

To what degree:
9. do you feel adequately appreciated for your contributions?   1 2 3 4 5
10. are you positively challenged in your job?   1 2 3 4 5
11. are you recognized, rewarded, reinforced and celebrated for your accomplishments?   1 2 3 4 5
12. are you satisfied with the amount and type of feedback you receive from me?   1 2 3 4 5

Comments:

Figure 8.1. This questionnaire is an example of one you could develop to learn about your skills as an empowering leader.

of your responsibilities. You will also want to measure up to the following checklist:

- Establish a constancy of purpose so that every decision made and every action taken in your organization leads it one step closer to achieving the defined culture.
- Be as involved in process improvement as you expect everyone in your department to be.
- Integrate a quality improvement focus into everything you do.
- Insist that your direct reports integrate a quality improvement focus into everything they do.
- Establish an aggressive customer focus.
- Begin to see yourself as a supplier to meet a variety of internal customer needs.
- Change policies, procedures, and systems to support the desired culture.
- Insist on establishing data-based measures for each key process in your department.
- Pave the way with resources.
- Encourage risk taking and creative thinking.
- Break down barriers.
- Be a coach.
- Open doors for customer-employee interactions.
- Get out into the department and share your vision with all employees.
- Ask questions of employees and then listen to their responses.
- Listen to employees concerns, issues, and suggestions; follow up immediately when possible.
- Teach the quality concepts to employees—in the classroom and out of it.
- Continue to learn and talk about your learning with others.

- Insist on a system that rewards quality-focused behavior and accomplishments.

More specific ideas are listed in the appendices under the learn, live, lead theme. Or copy and use Fig. 8.2 as a quick reminder.

Leaders must recognize and accept their role to learn, live, and lead the transformation. They need to set the example—to exemplify the new principles in their own actions and reactions. Leaders must reward the behaviors that support the new culture rather than the old. (Beware of reverting back at crunch time.)

Lead from the Top: What Does That Mean?

According to Deming, all leaders need to acquire a system of profound knowledge to successfully run a business. He defined four areas of profound knowledge:

- An understanding and appreciation for systems.
- Knowledge of statistics and the theory of variation.
- Some theory of knowledge.
- Knowledge of psychology.

A *system* of profound knowledge indicates the interdependent nature of the four areas. According to Deming, an organization cannot achieve its maximum potential without its leaders and managers having profound knowledge and the discretion to apply it as they work together. We all have new roles to play and new skills to develop.

> *"Leaders must recognize and accept their role to learn, live, and lead the transformation. They need to set the example—to exemplify the new principles in their own actions and reactions."*

Figure 8.2. This executive to do list is a reminder for what needs to be completed by the leadership.

Deming offered his 14 points for management and his system of profound knowledge as a means of transforming the present management style to a new dimension of leadership—one that maximizes and integrates the positive attributes of the traditional style with new and broader perspectives and skills in a quality-focused environment. This means that most of us have new roles to play and new skills to develop. Few of us can profess to have profound knowledge. You can read more about profound knowledge in *The Deming Dimension* by Henry R. Neave.

❋ If you have already implemented TQM in your training department, you will want to answer the following questions. The answers will give you some insight about how you're doing. Although it may not be what you wanted to hear, recognize that *you* answered the questions and only *you* can change the answers to them.

Learn
- What is the most recent book you have read about quality? When?
- How much of your personal and organizational time are you investing in learning about quality?
- Which quality journal did you last read? How long ago?
- How many quality journals do you read on a regular basis?
- When was the last time you discussed a quality article with someone? Who?
- What did you last learn from an employee about quality improvement?
- How much time have you spent interviewing leaders in other organizations about quality concepts?
- What skills are you personally trying to improve?
- When was the last time you went to a colleague to ask for help?

Live
- On which of your processes are you presently taking data?
- Which personal process did you last improve? How?
- How did you last support and reward a team effort?
- Do you use a quality improvement philosophy as a framework for effective management? How?
- Which diagnostic tool did you last use? How?

- How much of your time is spent focusing on your customers?
- How do you coach others?
- How do you visibly promote and live a strong commitment to the vision, values, and continuous improvement?
- How do you interact with individuals at all levels to create awareness, develop skills, and reinforce success?
- How many process improvements have you implemented in your area in the last month?
- When was the last time you exceeded a customer's expectations? How do you know?
- How many times did employees feel comfortable enough to disagree with you yesterday?

Lead
- How many teams are improving processes in your area?
- How many cross-functional teams are in your organization?
- How do you reward teamwork?
- When was the last time you talked to an external customer? About what?
- When was the last time your employees made a decision that you disagreed with, but encouraged them to implement anyway?
- How do you encourage risk, innovation, change, and improvement?
- Do you hold line managers as accountable for service and quality improvement as financial results?
- Have you committed the necessary financial and human resources for a full implementation effort?
- How have you integrated improvement efforts with current strategic and financial planning?
- What was the last resource you gave up to assist a colleague in another area?
- What is your plan for total employee involvement?

Since you've read chapters that focused on unified focus and on process improvement, let's focus on the cultural change that must occur within senior management. If you're at the *learn* level, there are several books that can get you started.

- *Not Bosses But Leaders* by John Adair
- *The Empowered Manager* by Peter Block
- *The 7 Habits of Highly Effective People* or *Principle Centered Leadership* by Stephen R. Covey
- *Leadership Is an Art* or *Leadership Jazz* by Max DePree

9

HRD's Role in Implementing TQM in the Rest of the Company

Part 1—Strategy

Hopefully, HRD will be involved in the company's TQM implementation plan. First, congratulations! All companies do not believe that their HRD Departments are prepared to handle a task this significant. (More about this in Chap. 11.) Next, roll up your sleeves; there is much work ahead of you. However, heed this warning: *HRD cannot implement TQM without line involvement.*

If a well-meaning company leader has delegated the entire implementation effort to the HRD Department, it leads to several problems:

- It sends a signal of low priority.

- It says that line management is too busy to lead the effort.

- It prevents integration with the day-to-day work of the organization.

- It will eventually be thought of as a program and will end like every other program.

> *"If you want the effort to succeed get someone from
> line management to lead the effort and complement
> that individual with your skills."*

If you want the effort to succeed get someone from line management to lead the effort and complement that individual with your skills.

A Corporate Implementation Strategy

This chapter will just scratch the surface of implementing a quality improvement effort. It will provide a big picture guide to get you started. There are many books and seminars that can provide more in-depth assistance for your implementation design and start-up efforts. Several are listed in the appendices.

Chances are HRD will be a member of a company-wide steering committee. This is a great opportunity for HRD to dust off the Organizational Development (OD) skills that your company may have neglected for some time.

The following guidelines will put you in the correct frame of mind before you begin to help with the task of planning your company's TQM design.

Think Customer.   The design and the approach must be customer driven. Who are the customers: internal as well as external? Employees should be one of your answers.

Customization Is Critical.   Reference everything you know about your organization. Then design an approach based on where you are, where you want to go, and which approach will get you there best. Yes, each of the Quality gurus have strengths, and organizations can benefit by using the concepts. Yet, when an organization establishes a quality improvement process, it should fit the philosophy into its process, rather than try to fit its process into one of the philosophies. Therefore, do not take a canned approach and expect it to work. Instead, establish an integrated approach that is consistent with your culture and values. The approach must be customized to meet your needs.

Flexibility Will Be Important. Every organization that has implemented TQM admits that they made changes and improvements along the way. Recognize that continuous improvement also applies to implementing TQM. Expect change and plan for mid-course improvements to ensure that these changes occur smoothly.

People Are the Key to Success. A formal quality improvement effort will have little chance of succeeding unless effective interactive people skills are in place at all organizational levels. Employees should not feel that you are "doing TQM to them." Provide the tools, skills, and resources to implement TQM as the vision dictates, but use the organization's employees to ensure that the effort is seen as theirs.

Your approach should build trust, improve communication, and answer the question, "What's in it for me?" The people must implement TQM; they will make it work. They must all *Learn, Live,* and *Lead.*

Remember, the plan must be customized. Someone else's plan will

> "Remember, the plan must be customized. Someone else's plan will fail."

fail. At the minimum, the following six elements must be addressed in your organization's implementation plan:

- Senior management leadership and support
- Strategic planning
- Focus on the customer
- Employee training and recognition
- Employee empowerment and teamwork
- Systems approach that encompasses measurement

Each of these has been or will be discussed in this book.

Figure 9.1 provides a master implementation plan as a big-picture approach. Sequentially the plan moves from top to bottom and left to right. This is a general statement, however, and you should customize to meet your organization's needs. It is possible that you may spend three to nine months in the plan column, depending on

Master Implementation Plan

	PLAN	PROCEED	PERPETUATE
Steering Committee	Define membership Form/train Clarify role	Work as a team Demonstrate commitment	Long range planning Maintain momentum
Strategy	Create the vision Name the effort	Focus on integration Provide symbols to facilitate the shift	Develop long term focus
Structure	Form design team Determine infrastructure Develop implementation plan	Implement the plan Early middle management involvement	Absorb structure into daily management system
Logistics	Resource planning Determine who coordinates Define budgetary requirements	Deploy the plan and monitor Anticipate time requirements	Integrate into daily activity
Communication	Communicate plans and vision to everyone Develop communication plan	Communicate successes Communicate progress and lessons learned Utilize new media	Encourage cross functional communication
Education and Training	Develop JIT training plan Custom design materials	Awareness for all Team skills for teams Management coaching skills CI tools	Assess and continue to meet growing needs Create learning environment Cross functional skill base
Teamwork	Identify team roles Determine team selection criteria Develop methodology	Pilot team projects Select facilitators	Encourage spontaneity Cross functional teamwork Involve customers and suppliers on teams
Customer Focus	Identify customers Introduce internal customer concept	Survey their satisfaction Customer needs driven into workplace	Lead our customers and suppliers into the future Exceed customer expectations
Measure Progress	Determine key performance indicators	Track, evaluate and adjust plan COQ design	Benchmark against others Survey the customers
Reward and Recognition	Determine team and individual recognition	Celebrate success Reward teams Implement results quickly	Link performance to goals Adapt appraisal and compensation systems
Cultural Responsiveness	Identify cultural obstacles	Drive out fear Focus on processes Introduce new language	Encourage constant improvement Ensure policies and procedures support desired culture
Management Responsibility	Learn as much as possible	Live as a model	Lead for continuous improvement

© 1992 ebb associates used with permission

Figure 9.1. The master implementation plan illustrates how much must be done and a general sequence to follow.

where your organization is in its development and how many resources will be dedicated to the effort. It may be two years before you reach the third column, perpetuate.

Implementation Must Start at the Top

It's imperative that the implementation start at the top and extend to everyone in the organization. Therefore, selecting a steering committee is the first step. This team should be made up of the senior executives in the organization. Most often it is the company president and the immediate vice presidents who will set the tone for the entire effort. This team must establish a strategy that answers these questions: what are we doing, why are we doing it, and what is our vision? The team may at the same time also determine a mission statement and create a strategic plan. As an HRD professional, you may lead this strategy planning effort or you may be asked to recommend someone who will. You may also be a member of the team. Chapter 7 will get you started on this task.

Generally, the steering committee's responsibilities fall into several areas: establish a focus, provide resources, create/support a culture that's conducive to TQM, drive out fear, ensure total awareness, and create a feedback loop with the rest of the organization.

A word of advice: Don't skimp on the planning. "Go slow to go fast." A well thought-out plan will prevent problems and issues from arising at a later date.

Move the Effort Through the Organization

You will need to decide how to move the implementation through the organization. You may choose to implement on a department by department basis or to move down through the organization across all departments on a level by level basis. Each has its advantages.

Department by department advantages include:

- Everyone in a department is talking the same language.
- You have the opportunity to choose positive pockets of support that want to get involved within the organization.

- You have more control over success and these successes can serve as role models and examples for other departments.

- When training is conducted you will have an opportunity to conduct real team building with intact groups.

- The training session usually strengthens the department due to a clearer understanding of each other.

  Level by level advantages include:

- Everyone at the same level is talking the same language.

- You have the opportunity to allow time for the concepts to take hold before moving to the next level.

- You demonstrate the importance of top-down implementation.

- When training, people from other divisions, departments, and areas get to know each others' problems and concerns better. It is possible that you could have two departments represented that have had an adversarial relationship in the past and this is the first time they've had a chance to discuss the "process" rather than placing blame. You need to take advantage of the situation and surface the issues.

- Training is an opportunity to strengthen the relationships throughout the organization.

Choose the method that seems most logical for your organization. Understanding your organization will be beneficial to making this decision. (See Chap. 10 for questions you might ask yourself.)

Tracking Mechanisms

Our suggestion is to keep tracking mechanisms simple. Your TQM effort should not deplete another forest.

Many organizations get by with just three documents: a team charter, a process improvement record, and a good meeting agenda and note system.

A team charter, as discussed and illustrated in Chap. 7, is important to get the team started. It identifies specifically what the team will do by providing a description of the process including its boundaries,

Process Improvement Record

Process _____   Starting Date _____

Team Leader_____   Department _____

Phase	Accomplished, Notes, Data, and Comments	Date Completed
I. Select and Target		
II. Identify and Plan		
III. Collect and Analyze		
IV. Change and Test		
V. Evaluate and Adjust		
VI. Implement and Monitor		
	Attach all documentation	

Figure 9.2. The process improvement record is a living record that tracks the teams' progress.

what the customer expects, a preliminary data analysis, the departments or areas affected, and who will work with the team.

A process improvement record, like the one in Fig. 9.2, documents the team's progress in a macro way following the steps of the particular methodology (6-step, 7-step, or another derivation of the PDCA cycle) your organization has chosen. It is usually completed at the end of each process improvement step. The process improvement record is a living document that tracks the team's progress. It includes narrative comments to describe the actions and decisions the team has taken throughout the improvement process. Process improvement records are often valuable to other teams that might be looking at a similar process.

The agenda and meeting note (minutes) system documents the team's progress on a meeting by meeting basis. It also provides insight for other teams that may be improving a similar process, but it is most valuable to the team itself. At times the team will need to go back to review what happened on what date, or what a specific decision was, or to review some data. A good agenda and meeting note system will assist with the answers.

✳ Each team should keep a file for the process it is improving. Generally it is easiest to organize according to the process improvement methodology your organization is using. A team can use a three-ring binder with divider sheets numbering each step of the improvement methodology. Meeting agendas, notes, data collection sheets, and an updated process improvement record can be placed chronologically behind each divider.

> *"... keep tracking mechanisms simple.*
> *Your TQM effort should not deplete another forest."*

Generally, a recorder is responsible for keeping the documentation updated, although the entire team will assist. The final records are kept on file for anyone in the organization to examine. If you have a TQM coordinator or a process improvement manager, that individual usually receives the final documentation.

Celebration Plan

It's not likely that you will immediately turn your organization's reward and recognition system upside down. However, you do need to have a plan in place to recognize teams and individuals for their efforts, results, and participation and to celebrate their successes. There are two reasons: First, people do or will continue to do what gets rewarded, and second, everyone should know about the successes that are occurring in the organization. It tells them what is getting recognized, helps them identify appropriate new behavior, and encourages them to strive for success.

> *"... people do or will continue to do what gets rewarded."*

Recognition can take many forms. You will need to develop your own ideas or take some from this list:

- Certificates, plaques
- Pins
- Monetary awards
- Letters from the president (not form letters)
- Time off
- Articles in the company newsletter or local newspaper
- Celebrations, such as Quality Improvement Day or Team Recognition Day
- The simple, but powerful, "thank you"

As you put your plans together, be sure that you have employees at all levels on the team helping with the design. Also, build in a peer review system. Awards and recognition should not just be handed down by management.

❋ One training department in a government agency developed a "Recognition Cookbook." It was used by the entire organization to supplement a system that could not be easily changed. The idea behind it was to provide employees with recipes for providing recognition. These recipes included tips, cautions, suggestions, and a variety of specific ideas that range from positive statements to more formal on-the-spot cash awards (with the criteria).

A recognition store accompanied the cookbook to provide thank-you cards, balloons, and other recognition items such as coffee mugs, clip holders, T-shirts, pens, and caps. One of the unique items in the store was a recognition insert card, like the one pictured in Fig. 9.3. You could easily personalize it for your department. It can become a very personal and special way to thank people.

One last thought. We generally discourage competition, that is, recognizing the "team of the year" or the "employee of the year." There is little specific value in such a plan, and it may create problems among teams and individuals competing for the glory. Teams may withhold information from other teams that, if shared, could multiply the effect of the process improvement. Individuals may spend

---

To _____   **Date**_____

From _____

Thank you for _____

I would like to recognize you by doing something special for you.

❑ Bring coffee for you in the morning on _____
❑ Dust your desk on _____
❑ Stand in line to pick up your lunch
❑ Take your turn to clean the refrigerator
❑ Give you a ride to and from work
❑ Bring you fresh cut flowers from my yard

Figure 9.3. This recognition insert card was part of a recognition plan developed by a government organization.

time making themselves look good rather than investing the same time collaborating with others for the success of the team as a whole. A possible approach could be to reward all teams based on the level of improvement or savings.

The bottom line: Are people getting rewarded for team efforts? Is the organization celebrating successes?

Planning for the Future

Once initial implementation gets started there will be numerous systems you will want to examine: the organization's compensation system, policies, and procedures and basic systems that get the work done. Often what happens is that an organization will get the basic implementation plan in place, wipe its brow and say, "Whew! Glad that's done!" The truth is, your work has only just begun. If you do not pay attention to these systems, your organization will stay stuck in its initial implementation phase. As you might imagine, this is a great deal of work and organizations hesitate about taking the first step.

Let the following thoughts serve as reminders that you are just starting.

Compensation. Eventually you will want to establish a reward and recognition plan that supports your new culture. This should not be done immediately. The organization will be in the process of learning about itself and what it wants rewarded as it goes through the cultural change that TQM brings. This of course does not mean that it should be ignored.

Reward is an area that requires constant attention, because the tendency is to continue to reward the old results and behaviors that related to success in the traditional controlled environment.

What results have you rewarded? In the past you have probably solely rewarded profits rather than customer satisfaction; budget control rather than process improvement; and/or achieving sales goals rather than achieving quality goals. TQM does not suggest that you should not pay attention to profits or budget or sales. Indeed you won't be in business long if you don't. But, if you only reward these, employees will ensure that they are achieved *at any cost*—including long-term growth and health of the organization.

What behaviors have you rewarded? Some of those old behaviors that you may inappropriately continue to reward include individualism, competitiveness, organizational hierarchy, suboptimization, conformity, compliance, obedience, and over-justification. None of these is bad. But you can easily see that, if solely rewarded, each could prevent a TQM culture from transpiring.

- A team-driven culture can't exist if you reward only individualism and competitiveness.

- A customer-focused culture can't exist if you reward only organizational hierarchy and suboptimization.

- Continuous process improvement can't exist if you reward only conformity and compliance.

- A quality-centered culture can't exist if you reward only obedience.

- A fact-based culture can't exist if you reward only over-justification.

There are numerous compensation plans. The organization needs to decide what behaviors it wants encouraged and take that into consideration as it develops its plan. Experts will advise you about the many new ideas in this area.

In general, competition needs to be discouraged and cooperation encouraged. Team recognition should balance individual recognition. Individual excellence *is* necessary and needs to be recognized as well. One last thought: The goal of the organization should be that the entire organization is working as one team. This means, of course, that total organizational recognition should prevail over even your departmental recognition. Recognition of the dignity of people, their value, their team contributions, and pride in workmanship is paramount.

Quality "is the unforced byproduct of a positive work environment" (Southwest Airlines). To achieve this positive work environment, the behaviors that create that environment must be reinforced. Risk taking, creativity, innovation, and the freedom to satisfy the customer must be allowed and encouraged.

Individuals and teams need a greater voice in who is to give awards, recognition, and rewards and how they are given. The leadership needs to be willing to share the bounty of success with all the people.

Alignment of Policies and Procedures.   Examine policies and procedures for alignment. Some that will probably require examination include recruiting and hiring procedures, customer management policies, benefit policies, policies that address how and when people work each day, and policies surrounding training and education.

Review your organization's compelling reason, vision, strategic imperative, and strategic plan. Then assign a team to examine your organization's policies and procedures. Chances are they have multiplied dramatically over the years. The team needs to ask the following questions:

- Will this policy or procedure help you reach your vision and strategic imperative?

- Will this policy or procedure encourage the behaviors you want from your employees?

- Will this policy or procedure lead to results you want in your strategic plan?

- Does this policy or procedure support the compelling reason for which you implemented TQM?

- Does this policy or procedure serve any worthwhile purpose any longer?

Work Systems.   The systems that are used to get the work done will need to be changed or realigned. Most organizations realize that it is inefficient to organize work around functions. It might be wiser to reorganize around processes, products, product lines, or the customers' needs, thinking in terms of a total systems approach.

> *"Most organizations realize that it is inefficient to organize work around functions."*

You may need to examine specific support systems such as your information systems: how the information comes in, where, when, and how it's available, what's available, and who gets it. The training system will require overhaul as far as what is being delivered and how it's being delivered. (More about the changing role of HRD in Chap. 11.) The planning system is another that will probably require a major redesign to support the changing organization.

If you think about it, you will realize that what you're doing now is easy compared to what's ahead of you.

If You Work with an External Consultant

Most of the quality gurus suggest that you utilize an external consultant to start your change effort. Why would such universal agreement exist? Implementing a change effort of this magnitude isn't easy. But there are more important reasons.

1. Internal experts may be blinded by the paradigms that have become a part of the organization's culture and the "that's-the-way-we've-always-done-it" mentality.

2. Senior management may deny that flaws could exist within the organization; doing so would suggest that their leadership is less than perfect. And of course, no one will mention the flaws since the response will likely be to "shoot the messenger."

3. Let's not forget that most "experts" live 500 miles away; few of us are "prophets in our own land."

You can ensure that the consultant relationship goes smoothly if you have hired the right person for your organization and if you think of the relationship as a partnership.

Choose a consultant who will create your independence within the process. This can be accomplished in several ways. The consultant must provide the tools, skills, and resources to implement TQM. But learning doesn't end in the classroom so the consultant should be available for one-on-one coaching in the workplace (where the action is) to solve problems or coach managers to deal with issues. Will the consultant coach you to continue the coaching? Will the consultant keep you updated with articles and books specific to your needs and with important new concepts?

Will the consultant allow your organization to write its own TQM book? That is, will your approach be customized or will you be forced into the consultant's mold? Will the ownership of the program be kept with the organization, utilizing the organization's employees as much as possible? Will the consultant work as a partner with employees to involve them in the assessment, interviewing customers, training, leading teams, documenting process improvement, running meetings, and designing the training sessions? How soon will you conduct your own training sessions? The sooner an organization can provide its own training the less the implementation costs. How will the consultant bring the HRD Department up to speed in TQM? Will the consultant work as a partner with your training staff to create TQM experts on site? Each of these leads to your independence.

To ensure that you are hiring the right person as a consultant, consider the following questions:

- Will the consultant customize the approach to meet your needs?

- To balance the first point, does the consultant point out potential flaws in your plan based on past experience?

- What relationship does the consultant propose with senior management?

- How will the consultant determine the unique organizational dynamics within the company?

- Has the consultant had actual experience implementing a quality improvement effort?

- How willing is the consultant to share information?

- Will the education and training be customized, using examples from your company?

- What are the objectives of the training?

- Who will be the actual on-site person?

- How does the consultant ensure organizational self-reliance?

- What do the references say about the organization, as well as the specific consultant?

- Can you visualize the consultant working within your organization?

Figure 9.4 identifies the stages that a client-consultant relationship goes through. The client's responsibilities, identified under each stage, will ensure that the client and consultant build a true partnership. A healthy partnership will go through the four stages.

Finding the Right Match.   This is the first stage and may include several consultants as you narrow down your choices and select the one that you believe is right for your organization. You can gather lots of objective data and measure which one appears to be the best choice. But in reality, this stage is a lot like dating as you look for compatibility in the relationship. Subjectivity counts, too.

Getting to Know Each Other.   This is the relationship building stage. Don't be surprised if some misunderstandings occur. The healthy partnership will communicate about them readily and work them out. You will each be learning about your preferences and working out the differences to arrive at what is best for the organization.

Being Productive.   This is the payoff stage for the organization. If a productive relationship has been built, you may at times feel as if the consultant is a part of the organization. The two of you should be on track with what is needed next. It shouldn't surprise you if you greet the consultant with a question and the consultant says, "That's just what I've prepared to discuss with you." The organization truly benefits from the investment in the consultant.

Creating Independence.   In this final stage, both you and the consultant should be strongly focused on transferring everything to the organization. This is also the future-focused stage in which the two of you will plan for ensuring success after the consultant's formal role has been completed.

Any successful consulting relationship will go through stages similar to these.

Client-Consultant Partnership Client Checklist

Finding the Right Match
- ❏ Meet with lead consultants.
- ❏ Request a proposal to ensure the consultant understands the situation.
- ❏ Learn about the company.
- ❏ Contact references and past clients.
- ❏ Obtain information: how long in business, consultants' backgrounds, type of clients served, how much repeat business, general reputation.
- ❏ If possible, observe client in action.
- ❏ Check experience in industry.
- ❏ Identify shared values/differences.
- ❏ Determine capabilities vs. needs.
- ❏ Determine flexibility/availability of company.
- ❏ Clarify specific expectations and who does what.
- ❏ Identify desired time frame.
- ❏ Discuss limitations (money, time).
- ❏ Discuss known/suspected roadblocks.
- ❏ Think in terms of a long-term relationship: Is rapport evident? Is there a personal fit?

Getting to Know Each Other
- ❏ Choose one person as point of contact.
- ❏ Include consultant on the team.
- ❏ Ask the consultant to help identify the problem as well as the solution.
- ❏ Provide telephone directory, rosters.
- ❏ Add to in-house mailing list for newsletters, updates.
- ❏ Add to distribution list for pertinent teams.
- ❏ Provide feedback on initial reactions.
- ❏ Discuss risk factors.

Being Productive
- ❏ Establish regular feedback sessions.
- ❏ Develop tracking system for continuity.
- ❏ Be honest and candid with information and concerns.
- ❏ Communicate, communicate, communicate!

Creating Independence
- ❏ Validate self-sufficiency.
- ❏ Ensure a system of continued communication is in place.
- ❏ Ensure management is aware of next steps.
- ❏ Continue to provide news, success stories.
- ❏ Maintain mailing list status.
- ❏ Be sure to request advice if issues arise.
- ❏ Plan success celebration.

Figure 9.4. The client-consultant partnership checklist identifies the relationship stages from the client's perspective.

What It Takes to Succeed

If you are involved in this change effort, there may be times when you will wonder what you have gotten yourself into. It may be difficult; it may be frustrating. Remember, your organization is steeped in many years of tradition, and our western management style is even more entrenched. It takes the following to succeed:

- A custom-designed approach for your organization.

- Strong, visible leadership and commitment from all levels of management, beginning at the top.

- Clear vision constantly being communicated at all levels.

- A comprehensive strategy for implementation which addresses both the human and organizational responses to change.

- Active participation of the best people regardless of position or experience.

- Effective use of third-party resources.

- Readiness to grow as the need arises.

- Ability to adjust the implementation strategy based on data.

- Discipline to give the TQM implementation effort time to succeed.

For additional guidance and ideas you can find a list of implementation resources in the appendices.

10

HRD's Role in Implementing TQM in the Rest of the Company

Part 2—Training

Quality gurus agree that training is a critical element in every TQM effort. Our caution to you is that training is not enough. Training is a crucial part of the organization's implementation efforts, but it is not the only element, or even the most important element. An entire chapter has been dedicated to the subject of training for the customer—you, the training professional who is reading this book. This is not because it is more important than all the elements in Chap. 9, but because you will be the one who has the primary responsibility to ensure that your organization has an effective training plan and design.

Learning

Learning is the imperative first step for everyone! If there is a doubt in your mind about the importance of learning in organizations of the future, read Peter Senge's *The Fifth Discipline*. New roles will require new skills. It is management's responsibility to see that everyone possesses all the tools, including those skills to do their jobs. Again, training is much broader than TQM training or SPC or diagnostic tools. It is all encompassing: technology, techniques, behavioral, interpersonal, management, leadership, methods, personal development.

HRD has two implementation responsibilities within the training arena. First, to ensure that current training is consistent with the overall TQM philosophy and the organizational strategy. Second, to provide excellent training to learn the TQM tools, methods, skills, and principles.

> *"New roles will require new skills."*

Current Training

Many of the skills needed to implement quality improvement (e.g., effective meeting management, participative management, providing feedback, problem solving, delegation) are not unique. Sometimes this is the reason people think that "we're already doing it." However, often these skills were taught in your classroom, but not implemented in the workplace. This may have occurred because managers and supervisors saw each as disjointed "flavor-of-the-month" concepts and could not see how all of these skills fit together.

TQM provides the broader context to appreciate the various skills' relevance, relationship, and dependence on one another. Think of TQM as the umbrella that brings all of the good management and supervisory skills together under one common strategy. Using good management and supervisory skills may be more meaningful and have a higher perceived value if everyone can see the broader context that TQM provides.

Because TQM does provide this broader context, you will need to examine training offered by your department to determine whether it is consistent with the strategy of the organization and focused toward achieving the strategic imperative. You will need to ensure that all existing training supports the basic principles of TQM and therefore, optimizes the training process and programs. You may need to eliminate classes. As an example, you will probably not teach management by objectives (MBO) as a supervisory development course, while at the same time advocating TQM principles. While MBO is a useful tool, it can thwart a TQM implementation. Here are four reasons why.

First, MBO establishes goals which become the central focus for organizations, departments, and individuals. While setting goals is good, there is little effort made to upgrade or change them. Individuals stay strictly focused on their goals because achieving them is what they will be rewarded for. In addition, setting goals in this way may limit the potential of individuals and ultimately the organization. If you were going to be rewarded for achieving a goal would you set it so high that you might not be able to reach it?

Second, with MBO the focus is on stability. This limits the ability to constantly change and improve processes. TQM brings out the work ethic in each employee. You no longer come to work just to get the job done, but improving your process is a condition of employment. How likely is it that you would change a process if stability is rewarded?

Third, MBO establishes goals and then breaks them down to their smallest level. This prevents people at the bottom from seeing the big picture and encourages suboptimization. With all the emphasis on teamwork and systems thinking you can see how breaking down goals might inhibit the kind of behavior you will want to reinforce in a TQM culture. Even if it was best for the entire organization, would you be willing to give up your goals for the benefit of another department?

Fourth, MBO is generally a short-term effort. New goals and plans are established each year. You will be rewarded if you meet your goals at the end of the year. No one asks *how* you met your goals, just *if* you met them. This may encourage employees to reach goals at any cost—even if the cost is to customers. TQM, on the other hand, is more long-term focused.

You should examine every training program to determine whether discrepancies like this exist.

In addition, some techniques or the terminology in some classes may need to be revised. For example, that project management program your department offers should utilize the same methodology and terminology that is used in the TQM training sessions. Consistency of action is very important, because you can create confusion and doubt about the constancy of purpose. Confusion and doubt create fear.

Training for TQM

What training will be needed?

Everyone needs to understand what TQM is and what it is not, what their roles are, and how they are to achieve them. They need to understand what the organization is about, who the customer is, and what the expectations are. Everyone requires training.

Everyone should receive TQM awareness training to gain an understanding of the basic statistical tools, teamwork, communication, the chosen problem-solving methodology, and the organizational direction.

In addition, specific training should be provided to meet specific needs in a just-in-time (JIT) way such as training for facilitators, team leaders, team members, process action teams (PATs) or any steering groups you may have such as a Lead Implementation Team (LIT), Executive Steering Committee (ESC), Quality Management Board (QMB), or whatever your organization chooses to call them.

Attending a training session does not ensure that people will use their newly learned skills. Everyone will need to be coached, encouraged, prodded, and protected as they try on new skills and behaviors.

You need to be aware of the atmosphere that all class participants

> *"Everyone will need to be coached, encouraged, prodded, and protected as they try on new skills and behaviors."*

will return to. How? If you work within a small organization it should be easy for you to get to know all supervisors and their styles. If you work in a larger organization, you may need to rely on the reputations of people or even the departments. Certainly this isn't the ideal, but it does provide some basis for providing suggestions in class. You will want to build in an "if-this-happens-when-you-return-to-your-work-center" segment in the design.

If you can keep the dialog open between training participants and their immediate bosses, you will take a step in the direction of creating an atmosphere conducive to practicing these skills. Therefore, you should encourage supervisors to visit the classes their people attend. This shows interest as well as support. If it is possible to provide consistency of trainers to one department, division, or branch, do it. The trainers will have a chance to get to know the area better, will be able to predict the issues, and will be able to provide more customized help for each area.

Another thing that will help to ensure that the training is implemented quickly is to be certain that supervisors are trained before their people. This allows the supervisors to learn the skills first so they can support them. Some training departments suggest that meetings be held between the supervisor and the employee before the training to let them know what to expect and to suggest what to look for specifically. A follow-up meeting after the training is also beneficial to both address issues, concerns, and questions, as well as to establish "what's next."

Cascading Training.   Xerox and Motorola popularized the "cascade" training design in which training is cascaded from the top down. This does two things. First, it ensures that everyone learns the information. You'll be a better listener if you know you need to teach this information to your people next week. Second, it is a strong demonstration of commitment. No one can say, "My boss should hear this!"

Other Training Thoughts.   A strong recommendation must be made here about just-in-time training (JIT). Too many organizations have started an implementation effort by training everyone only to learn that the skills were lost because there was nothing to practice with. You need to ensure that the training is JIT so that trainees use the skills immediately either on a team or in a project established with the individual's supervisor.

One last thought before we explore the specifics. We like to encourage organizations to establish a facilitator network that meets at least monthly and preferably every other week. The purpose is to learn from each other, to share ideas with each other, and to give and receive help for difficult problems. A facilitator network can also serve as an important communication link for the entire organization. This could include identifying cultural barriers to the steering committee or being a conduit for information flow between other groups in the organization. This makes the organization more self-sufficient and begins to create a support body for the effort.

Facilitators should receive training and technical assistance as early as possible. They usually receive more training than anyone else in the organization. A facilitator network allows training to continue indefinitely.

Designing Training for Quality

If you are already involved in your quality improvement effort, you have most likely planned, presented, or participated in a training session on quality. Even if you are not yet involved, you can imagine how important it will be for that session to be a perfect example of the content it is teaching. Not only must the content and delivery be top-notch, the total process must be of the highest quality.

Let's explore some of the pitfalls commonly encountered in training for quality improvement. Then let's examine an approach for overcoming and even avoiding these pitfalls. In that approach you will determine how to assess your organization's need for training, how to plan for training, and how to design training. Finally, in the spirit of TQM, let's apply continuous improvement principles to your training sessions so that you, too, are continuously improving.

Pitfalls of Quality Improvement Training Designs

Overcoming the pitfalls of quality improvement training is a matter of knowing what they are and then taking measures to prevent them. This section will summarize the main pitfalls of training and provides suggestions for avoiding them.

Limited Integration of Adult Learning Theory.   Designers and instructors of quality improvement training first stumble when they do not use adult learning theory in their training. Although trainers know and understand how important all the strategies of adult learning theory are, they may be overwhelmed by the huge amount of skills and behaviors that need to be taught. Consequently, they use instructional techniques that are not suited for adult learning. Of all the training you've ever developed, it is probably more important to apply adult learning theory to training for quality improvement than any other.

Adult learning theory as described by Dr. Malcolm Knowles, suggests that when you compare adult learners to children, adults prefer to:

- have control over their learning.

- be involved in active learning experiences.

- set their own pace for learning.

- have more feedback on their learning.

- know why they need to learn the content.

- know how the learning relates to their diverse experiences and their bigger world.

Lack of Upper Management Involvement.   No matter how much quality training you provide, it will have little impact if your organization's top managers are not involved. This includes involvement in both the quality improvement effort and in the training. The more you can get your upper management to participate in the training (both as participants and as instructors), the more likely your training will succeed.

Lack of Tailoring to Your Organization's Needs.   You will most likely encounter this pitfall if you hire a consultant to do your quality improvement training. If participants logically buy in but do not see how to transfer the skills to their work situation, you will be wasting your time. The key to avoiding this pitfall is to use specific organizational examples to integrate your organization's needs into quality improvement training as well as to integrate quality improvement needs into other training programs.

Lacks Integration of Statistical Methods and Team Skills. Many training programs for quality improvement take an unrealistic approach by separating statistical methods and team skills training. Some programs even neglect training in one of these areas in favor of the other. They don't occur separately in real life; why should they in your training session? Team members can't say, "I'll be a good team player for 30 minutes and then I'll put that aside while our team constructs the cause and effect diagram." Effective training for quality improvement provides balance and integration between the statistical methods and the team skills.

> *"...statistics are important, but it takes people to make them work."*

Lacks Application of Skills to Real World Examples. Participants will not find training worthwhile unless it is clear that the concepts being taught can apply on the job. When you design quality improvement training, make sure you base it on your organization's operations. Not only will you ensure that the concepts you teach will transfer to the job, you will also create meaningful training for participants. In addition, activities within the training should apply statistical and team-building skills—just as in real life. After all, statistics are important, but it takes people to make them work.

Poor Timing of Training. Even the best training program will not be well-received if it is ill-timed. Before scheduling quality improvement training, make sure participants will have an opportunity to use the skills soon after the training is complete.

Just-in-time training has several definitions. We take a middle of the road definition and believe that most skills should be introduced in the classroom, and that they need to be reinforced later. In a quality improvement model the skills could be reinforced by the facilitator as the team is about to use a diagnostic tool or team skill. Or the skills could be reinforced by a supervisor when the individual is ready to use the skills on the job. This means that training should be provided as the people are ready to use the skills (in a team situation or on the job) to ensure skill retention and credibility. It also means that the supervisors are prepared to support the use of the new skills.

Lacks Participant Involvement.   Again, because there is so much to teach, trainers panic and move to a "tell" mode rather than an "experience" mode. Participants must experience some of the things that will happen to them once they get into the team. Training designers should think in terms of creating one activity from which participants can glean several lessons about teamwork and quality improvement as well as practice using a tool within the methodology. Designers need to be efficient with their time.

Does Not Address the Future.   If the training you provide is not future-focused, it will lose credibility. The training needs to be candid about what's ahead. Open discussion about the bumps in the road or the possibility of detours needs to occur. Participants need to see that there are challenges ahead and that the skills they learn will help them with those challenges.

Keep these potential pitfalls in mind. They could prevent you from providing outstanding training for quality improvement. Let's turn our attention to assessing the organization's culture, as well as reviewing techniques for designing, developing, and presenting training that avoid these pitfalls.

The Training Process

You have probably used a training process similar to the one in Fig. 10.1 as you deliver services to your company. First you assess your organization's needs. Based on that assessment you develop training objectives. You design the program and present it. Finally, you evaluate the training program and use that data as a portion of your next assessment of needs for the next session or for other programs you may be designing. Look closely and you will see that it is a variation of the PDCA Cycle.

Assess Your Organization's Culture.   An assessment of your organization's culture will tell you whether your training program will be

Figure 10.1. The training process that you have used in the past is actually a variation of the PDCA Cycle.

well-received. Ask questions about both training in general and about the topic area—quality and process improvement.

First, find out which factors in the culture will support training. Are other departments generally supportive of training? How much credibility does the training department have with line management? Have any departments conducted any TQM related training on their own (sometimes large departments bring in guest speakers)? Where do pockets of support exist in the organization? How vocal has top management been in support of training and what actions confirm that? Has the training department been involved in planning your organization's quality improvement strategy? How will it be involved in the future?

Second, learn what obstacles you might encounter. Is this a bad time for training due to a work overload? Have any key individuals left the organization recently (actually this could be either bad or good)? Are budgets slim? Has market share decreased? Have any departments recently experienced a reorganization? Have any damaging rumors about TQM started? What trade-offs have been made when forced to decide between schedules, costs, and quality? Does the incentive system reward quality or cost and schedule? Does the environment encourage employee input?

Last, examine your own department. Do you have the senior talent necessary to produce the level of training required? How responsive have you been to customers' needs in the past? Does HRD have a good profile of the quality improvement skill level of employees and managers in each department? What resources will you need and will they be available to you?

You can obtain this information from your usual informal networks or conduct a more formal written survey. You may also consider bringing someone in from the outside to conduct a focus group with some of your key managers. (See the appendices for a description of focus groups.) Visiting a sample of managers throughout the organization will also provide you with reliable information. Of course, if your organization has been involved in training on a regular and on-going basis, you will already have this information. You might still want to conduct a small amount of data gathering targeted specifically at any changes you expect for this effort. All of this knowledge will help you plan more effective training.

Obtain quality improvement information from all areas of your organization. Find out what your organization is currently doing with respect to quality improvement. Plan to use the positive achievements as case studies and examples in training. Use the weak areas as a basis for setting training objectives.

Measure the amount of support at all levels. This is an important step in your planning. Don't proceed blindly with training without assessing the amount and level of support.

There is one last, but very important initial assessment action your department needs to take: You need to learn senior management's understanding of its role in quality improvement. The best way to do this is to interview each one.

Your assessment will be ongoing in that trainers will hear in class who's committed and who's not. Don't assume that because you have commitment now, you will have it forever. Keep your ears open about the level of management support for quality improvement. Understanding the amount of support at each level and in each area will assist you in providing appropriate guidance to participants and to answer their "what if" questions. But more importantly it may give you an early clue about the health of the effort.

Use Various Assessment Techniques. When you are learning about your organization's quality needs, use a variety of assessment techniques. This will ensure that you capture as many training needs as possible. For example, you might examine past data from your organization to determine where quality, customer service, or employee involvement have been a problem.

You might also conduct a written readiness survey to determine if the people in your organization perceive the same needs. Although the survey in the appendices has been developed specifically for an HRD Department, you could use something similar. The same elements need to be measured: recognition, management skills/leadership, organizational culture/commitment to change, performance management, communication, teamwork, quality improvement readiness, job satisfaction, and creativity/innovation.

A word of caution: A readiness survey will provide you with baseline data from which to measure your progress. Don't plan to conduct a follow-up survey for at least 18 months to two years into your efforts. Even that may be too soon. Remember, TQM is a long-term effort. You may even expect your scores to go down from the baseline. Why? There is a very good chance that the first time employees completed the survey they were unaware of how things could be. After completing awareness training and talking about what could be, their expectations may be raised to a level that actually decreases the survey scores. Believe it or not, even this shows progress! It means employees are more knowledgeable and have higher expectations of the organization.

Even though questionnaires give you a large amount of data in a short amount of time, you still need a method for collecting subjective perspectives about your organization's needs. This is where personal interviews and focus groups are useful. These methods allow you to collect and build into the training first-hand anecdotes, case studies, and role plays. An added value results when you conduct these interviews, because you are also building support for quality improvement training. You can find more information about both techniques, personal interviews, and focus groups, in the appendices.

Planning the Training Design

Let the Organization's Processes Guide Topic Selection.   Don't make the mistake of designing and delivering textbook learning, which ignores an organization's practical training needs. When you conduct the needs assessment to determine where your organization stands with respect to quality implementation, pay close attention. Build training around the topics and issues of most concern to your organization. Find out where your organization is and what it needs, then provide training accordingly.

Plan for Just-In-Time Training.   As you develop the training schedule, build in enough flexibility to train people as they are needed. Be prepared to provide training to team members of a newly-formed process improvement team or to managers in a department that has just embraced the effort. Adults must see the immediate need for training to acquire and retain skills. Skills that are not put to immediate use are lost and that means the training was a waste of time and money. It is important to note that in a quality improvement effort the inability of participants to use their new skills can have even more lasting effects. Participant's hopes may have been raised during the training. That lack of follow through, support, and opportunity for use will lead to frustration and disappointment. Unfortunately, it's one of the fastest ways to change skepticism, or even optimism, to cynicism.

Plan to Spend Time and Money for a Good Design.   Whether you develop quality improvement training in-house or whether you hire a consultant, make sure you budget enough time and money for a good design. A good design means that it is both customized to your organization and that it meets the other criteria identified in this chapter. If you cut corners on training design, you are giving the message that training for quality improvement does not deserve the best investment.

Design Professional TQM Training

Once you have completed your organizational assessment and prepared an initial training plan, you will be ready to design the training.

In doing this, you should rely on the data you collected in your organizational assessment. You have learned your participants' needs and expectations. Build these into your design. Make certain you link their experiences to the importance of quality improvement. Get senior management involved in the design. Check with them at various points in the development to verify you are addressing their expectations to their satisfaction.

Implementing a customized approach means training will go with the grain of the organization—much easier to accept, promote, and maintain.

(*Note:* We don't usually recommend that you purchase off-the-shelf quality improvement training materials. Organizations need to "write their own book" if you want to truly change the culture.)

Our preference is that you design your own training materials. If you lack the time or internal expertise you have two choices. You may hire an external consultant to assist you with the design or you may choose materials that can be customized to your organization. In either case, you must ensure that the design will be compatible with your organization's needs and will address the criteria for good design identified in this chapter. Force-fitting your organization into an incompatible philosophy will be a waste of time and money.

Plan for Participant Involvement.   When you design the training, be sure you design ample opportunities for participant involvement. Participation equals commitment. By involving participants in hands-on exercises and practice, you will provide them with meaningful training experiences that they will be able to apply on the job. Creating a Pareto chart provides much more learning than talking about one.

If you are training teams, they should work in their respective teams and address the real life process they are improving as much as possible. The training session can give them a jump start with real team building and a head start on their process improvement.

Blend Diagnostics and Team Building in Learning Activities.   Build your training plan by integrating the learning of technical and diagnostic skills with the learning of team building and interpersonal skills. There are two reasons for doing this: time efficiency and real-life orientation.

You can be efficient with time if you use one activity to teach both diagnostic tools and team building. For example, you might have participants practice flow charting in a team while having observers watch for specific team dynamics. Or you could have teams construct a Pareto chart and complete a self-evaluation of their team's communication after they have finished. This is realistic since, in a real situation, you will surely be using diagnostic tools in a team setting.

Topic Areas.   There are three general topic areas to consider when you develop training for quality improvement. Let's examine these areas and explore some suggestions for designing training in each.

The first topic area is statistical process tools. This includes training in the diagnostic and technical tools needed for quality improvement. There are some important tips to remember as you develop technical training. First, train only in those tools that apply to your organization. There are many statistical tools and your organization may use only a few. Focus training on those tools your organization uses. Second, give examples, explanations, demonstrations, and practice. This ensures participants get hands-on experience. It also enables you to determine those areas where further training is necessary. Finally, develop quick-reference sheets for participants. These sheets come in handy on the job when participants need a quick refresher or need to construct a specific tool.

The second topic area is process improvement methods and definitions. Whatever approach to quality your organization uses (5-step, 7-step, 14-step, or the basic PDCA), you will want to ensure that participants understand exactly what must be accomplished at each step, what tools will be useful, and what they might encounter along the way. Also, be certain that participants have an understanding of processes, process improvement, customers, suppliers, and other basic concepts.

The final topic area is team development skills. Your design should integrate team development activities with the learning of statistical and process improvement tools. In doing this, you get more valuable use of training time by teaching two sets of skills at one time. Participants are also learning in a more realistic setting since they most often do their technical work in a team setting. Give teams an opportunity to measure their success by using some team skills measurement tools. They should be encouraged to use these to measure their team skills outside of training as well.

Self Improvement.   As important as topic selection is to training design, it is also important that each and every participant experiences growth in the training. Include in your design time for self-analysis, individual reflection, and goal setting. Make use of observers and feedback as methods for giving participants insight into themselves.

For example, individuals could evaluate their listening skills. An observer could count the number of times each team member interrupts the others. A team could compare how well they met the objectives they set as a team in another activity the day before.

Training Delivery Plan

How much training? Who? Here's a typical breakdown.

- *Awareness training:* everyone immediately; 3 hours to 2 days, depending on what else everyone will receive.
- *Team training:* teams that have been assigned a process and are ready to get started; 3 to 4 days (we've seen the most success with this model).
  Or a model that has the team leader attend 4 days and the team members an abbreviated $2\frac{1}{2}$ day training.
  If you can't train in teams you have a decision to make about whether to provide training to one department or to train cross-functional groups. Advantages and disadvantages exist for either model.
- *Management training:* all managers need to know how to support the effort and coach their people before their people attend training; 2 to 3 days.

In addition, senior management should consider spending 3 to 5 days in external training programs to get another view and insight from other organizations and experiences.

Training: Continuous Improvement

The most important part of any training design is making certain it is an example of what it teaches. If continuous improvement is the topic, then the training design itself must undergo continuous improvement. You can use several methods to create continuous improvement in your training session.

> *"The most important part of any training design is making certain it is an example of what it teaches."*

Use the Evaluation.　Your training participants are your customers. Their evaluations of your training constitute their customer input. Pay attention to it and make changes in your training processes accordingly.

Build Continuous Improvement into your Training.　Define the processes you use to deliver your quality training and focus on improving these processes. Be aware that training needs change over time and be prepared to adapt to those changing needs.

✷ Make a commitment to improve your own training skills by trying some of these ideas:

- View someone else conducting training to obtain new techniques.
- Train with a partner and provide feedback to each other.
- As trainers develop new techniques, transitions, introductions, or stories, share them with each other at the next staff meeting.
- Provide demonstrations for certain activities to other trainers.
- Use other trainers to trial run new activities before you do them with a group.

Practical Suggestions for Professional Training.　What practical suggestions will improve your effectiveness or your program's success? These five will give you a start.

1. *Use time efficiently.* Often, the time allotted for training is limited in relation to the amount of material to be learned. Manage training time well. Design training so that one activity contains multiple learning points. Organize the design so that there is a logical flow from one topic to the next. Make transitions smooth and ensure that they add meaning to the two topics you are bridging. Finally, make sure that for everything you teach, you also provide information about how to apply that skill/knowledge on the job.

2. *Model the skills you are teaching.* For example, if you are teaching the team building skill of managing disruptive participants, model how you manage disruptive participants. If you are teaching an analytical tool, model how you use that tool to analyze training processes.

3. *Learn and use a variety of training techniques.* Find ways to use small groups, large group discussion, activities, games, critical incidents, and other training techniques. This keeps your participants involved and interested.

4. *Consider the benefits of team training.* First, you vary the training by varying the instructors. Also, two trainers offer two perspectives on a philosophy or approach. If your senior managers agree to team teach with you, training gets further credibility. Finally, when you team teach, you have an opportunity to learn from participants by watching their reactions.

5. *Make certain you capitalize on teaching moments.* Inevitably in training a question comes up or an incident occurs that is a moment of opportunity for the instructor to make a point. Seize that moment and make it come to life! Do not be so rigid with your schedule that you miss valuable opportunities.

In one classroom there was a thermostat that was so erratic, it seemed that it was placed on the wall as a joke.

One of the teams used the tools they were learning in the session and gathered data about the time of day, the setting, and the actual temperature. By the end of the four-day session they had the thermostat under control! As much learning took place from that activity as any that the HRD Department had designed.

In summary, what key elements will ensure a good training design for your TQM training?

- Integrate adult learning principles.

- Use information gathered in your organizational assessment.

- Customize the training design to your organization's specific needs.

- Provide a plan for educating and involving senior management.

- Maintain a balance between statistical methods and group process skills.

- Integrate statistical training with group process training so learning occurs in a realistic environment.

- Include exercises and examples that show how skills can be applied on the job, in the real world.

- Time the training session so that the learning can be applied immediately after the training session.

- Provide ample opportunity for participants to interact, practice, and exchange ideas.

Be Prepared for Unique Needs Brought on by Change

The training department is often looked to as the change agent when an organization implements TQM. You will need to be prepared for the unique needs and skills that the change will require. The earlier part of this chapter addressed the skill-based requirements of the organization—they are imperative. However, as the organization goes through the phases of change—planning, transition, and vision—your department will be expected to help get through the stressful time. See Chap. 7 for a description of each of the phases.

The transition phase is often fraught with chaos, frustration, and turmoil. The training department should be ready with services that will help the organization move through this uncomfortable phase. These services may include additional training, team building, one-on-one coaching, and consulting.

Additional Training.   When everything is in turmoil, you will more than likely need to provide more skills, not less. Employees will need to be skilled in communication skills such as listening and providing feedback. They will continue to need more and more refined skills in problem solving and more advanced skills in the diagnostic tools.

In addition, you need to ensure that people truly understand the skills they have been taught and are using them. This is not about only checking off the box; people need to *use* the skills. You may even find yourself doing some remedial training. Don't get exasperated and say, "but they had that in the TQM training!" Everyone needs to implement the skills before they really "get it." So although you planned for just-in-time training, this isn't a perfect world. And sometimes you may need to go back and help some people along.

To help people understand what the organization is going

> "This is not about only checking off the box;
> people need to use the skills."

through, you may find yourself setting up informal discussion groups—perhaps a brown-bag lunch discussion between management and employees. Perhaps you'll establish a regularly scheduled Quality Hour within a department or between departments to assist the employees to learn to work together better.

Notice that none of the examples mentions additional *classroom* training—just more training. You will need to become creative in how you provide the additional training and other services. Chapter 11 will give you additional ideas about how.

Team Building.   Better hone your team building skills. People will be told to work in teams. They will have a cognitive sense of what that means from the training sessions, but will have difficulty implementing it. You may be called in by natural work teams or action teams trying to improve a process. Be sure to have trainers on your staff who can conduct team-building sessions or build a relationship with a consultant who specializes in team building.

One-on-One Coaching.   There will be many opportunities for you to make a difference with one-on-one coaching to managers. The manager who talks a great story and says he believes in TQM, but has not yet relinquished all his control will be the focus of many complaints. He may not know what he is doing that is preventing the improvement that he knows can come with TQM. Coaching could make the difference.

There may be a department director who continues to manage, when what is really needed is leadership. You can explain the difference to her, identify specific steps she can take, coach her through the change, and reinforce her as she makes the necessary improvement. Coaching could make the difference.

The coworkers who can't seem to make this "team thing" work may be so caught up in their own styles and what's right and wrong in their own perceptions that they may not see that there is a way to work their differences out. Coaching could make the difference.

Consulting.   As the HRD function changes and grows, it will provide more consulting services at a higher level. At times you may find yourself working at the top of the organization—perhaps developing a "what if" list with your CEO to help both of you be prepared for the future. At other times it may be to simply bring two people together to determine the next steps—perhaps the director of information services with the manager of internal relations to make improvements on the communication plan. In another instance you might be asked to help a department construct an affinity diagram (explained in Chap. 11) as they identify their own quality plans.

So you can see that your training department needs to be ready for more than just training. Prepare yourself.

Resources to Assist with a Trainer's Continuous Improvement

Who trains the trainer? To ensure your own continuous professional improvement, don't forget to take advantage of the resources available to you. You might consider doing some or all of the following:

- Acquire memberships in professional training or quality improvement organizations, such as the American Society for Training and

Development (ASTD), the Association for Quality and Participation (AQP), or the American Society for Quality Control (ASQC).

- Read magazines, periodicals, and journals, such as *Training, Training and Development, Quality Progress, The AQP Journal, The TQM Magazine,* or *Quality Digest.*

- Study books such as those listed in our reading list at the end of this book.

- Participate in community quality organizations or train-the-trainer groups.

- Network with other professionals in your area.

If you continuously improve your skills and knowledge, you will most definitely have an impact on continuously improving the skills and knowledge of your training participants.

✳ TQM coordinators and HRD professionals responsible for developing and delivering training for their quality improvement efforts may feel lost at times, not knowing where to turn for help. One successful solution to this is to introduce those from one organization to those of another. They can then exchange ideas and help to solve problems. It also prevents the feeling of being the only one with a problem.

Bottom Line

The bottom line is that you need a well-developed, people-focused plan for training. The plan must be consistent with the behaviors necessary to allow TQM to flourish. This is one of those places (again) where management needs to "walk the talk." Has enough money been allocated for training? Is the training of the highest possible quality? Are all mangers receiving training before their people so that they can support the atmosphere conducive to change? Is training seen as a priority (and even senior management remains in class and does not attend "more important" meetings)?

Learn, live, and *lead*—all are embodied in this element.

11
HRD's Changing Role

This last chapter could have been the first. That's the way continuous improvement works. It is cyclical in nature. Let's examine HRD's changing role for the future. This will also give you a stronger rationale for implementing a quality improvement effort in both your department, as well as your organization.

HRD's Changing Role

HRD's role is changing. Pulled and pushed by TQM, training departments are facing a new direction, an exciting direction. Gone are the days when you put together a catalog of courses and sent it out to departments. Gone are the days when you developed a time management course and conducted it month after month.

HRD's customers want more. At last check they wanted at least these four:

- Increased customization
- Higher quality
- Decreased turn-around time
- Improved timeliness

Is HRD up to the challenge of meeting these needs?

HRD Is More Highly Respected—Almost

Organizations are beginning to depend more and more on their training departments. They're pulling the training department into decision making. Will training have an opinion? They're asking the training department questions. Will training have answers?

TQM offers a golden opportunity to HRD Departments. Are you ready to grab it?

If you were around the HRD profession 10 years ago you may remember that training was not the most respected department in the organization. In fact, when a recession hit or if massive budget cuts came down, HRD was always the first to get cut. Not so this last recession.

Today organizations recognize the need for changing their cultures to successfully implement their quality improvement effort. Lead teams understand the long-term potential if everyone is involved. Your CEO knows the important role the HRD Department must play in the implementation effort.

TQM is both technically oriented and people oriented in nature. TQM is systems and process improvement oriented and data based. But more important, it is also team driven. A successful effort requires all the statistical tools of improvement but it takes people to make it happen. In many companies it is not "people" people who are driving their companies' quality improvement efforts; the efforts are being driven by technical folks from quality assurance or other related areas. If you believe that the success of your TQM effort depends on people, then HRD must provide the fuel to drive the implementation.

HRD can be a significant player to lead any change effort if the department is prepared.

How to prepare?

- Learn about TQM and identify the skills required to implement a successful effort.

- Clarify the role that HRD can play in the effort.

> "TQM offers a golden opportunity to HRD Departments.
> Are you ready to grab it?"

- Assess your organization's culture (formally or informally) to determine:
  - barriers in the way of success.
  - skills necessary to create the change.
- Develop a training plan that will:
  - teach the skills for both management and nonmanagement.
  - provide a just-in-time strategy to conduct the training so that the skills are used immediately following the training.
  - address the skills employees of the future will need.
  - go beyond mere classroom training and take the training to the people (e.g., brown-bag lunches, one-on-one coaching, CEO information exchanges).
- Identify the HRD Department's assets and liabilities. What skills do people in the department need (consulting, team building, problem solving, change management)?
- Determine the support your department will need to fill in the gaps.
- Be a role model of the behaviors that will be required.

This kind of preparation shows a willingness to take the initiative in an area that is made for HRD.

HRD has an opportunity to play a leading role as change agents. Will you see the potential? Will you jump in and accept the challenge? Or will you hesitate? Will you be cautious or even threatened by the formidable task? The opportunity is there. Your HRD Department will need to make the decision. Will you be the catalysts for change?

Prepare for These Trends

TQM efforts have led to numerous other changes within the organization.

Working at Higher Organizational Levels. The HRD Department will be called on by the highest levels of the organization. It may be asked to provide input to systems redesign. It may be asked to develop a plan to modify the corporate culture. In any case, be prepared to get involved earlier in projects and to be seen as an important element in leading.

Being Seen As a Role Model. Prepare to be an advocate for your organization's quality improvement effort. If the organization cannot look to the HRD professionals as the role models, where will it look? You will be involved in the training and will be expected to model the same skills you are teaching: total employee involvement, teamwork, collaborative efforts, excellent customer service, data-based decisions.

More Creative Delivery of Services. Today employees come to the classroom. In the future you may be expected to take the classroom to the employees. You may find yourself studying processes with employees on the plant floor or observing a staff meeting and then sharing suggestions for improving the effectiveness of that meeting.

And be mindful of the changes that technology is bringing to the training field. Training is changing from how-to-do-it memory skills stored in an employee's head to how-to-access and use job aids stored in a computer. Though you will probably not need to be a computer programmer, you will need to understand the capabilities that exist.

Stronger Emphasis on Organizational Development. Brush off your OD skills. Everyone knows that a TQM implementation requires lots of training. But the truth is that it is really an OD effort. You will find that your organizational development skills will be more in demand than ever before.

> *"Training is changing from how-to-do-it memory skills stored in an employees's head to how-to-access and use job aids stored in a computer."*

New Training Topics. And even when you train, there will be an entirely new set of topics brought on by TQM. Can you help others learn how to read a control chart? Can you explain variation to someone?

Expect to see much more leadership development than before. Coaching, mentoring, facilitation, and empowering will lead the list. They will be followed closely by creative problem solving, decision making, influencing, and negotiating skills.

New Skills for HRD.   You, too, will be in more of a coaching/mentoring role than a training/teaching role.

There will be a great demand for you if you can train others to train. It has been estimated that nearly 80 percent of all skills are acquired on-the-job, not in the classroom. In addition TQM asks managers and supervisors to do more coaching and training. As a result of quality initiatives, the cascade down method of training is used successfully today in many organizations. Expect to see more and more supervisors and managers providing training in all organizations. In fact there's a good chance that more nontraining professionals will soon be training than ever before. If you can help them be more effective you will have a job for life.

Expect to get more requests for interventions of all sorts. You may already conduct team-building interventions (not team skills courses) that assist natural work units to work better together. In the future you may be expected to be more involved in others such as performance or technology interventions.

Work redesign, reengineering, self directed work teams—someone will need to assist your organization to implement these new systems and ways to work. Will it be you? And, even more important, can you explain how they all fit together with TQM so that you are not giving the impression of one more "flavor-of-the-month" management strategy?

Brush up on your problem-solving skills. You will more than likely be called in to assist departments to solve real problems rather than solve cases in class. These will be real survival situations—and they won't be on the moon or in the desert! As an HRD professional you already bring with you problem-identification skills, problem-solving skills, team dynamics knowledge, team-building practice, and an objective outsider's viewpoint.

If you think of yourself as a trainer first and a designer second, better do a quick shuffle. With each department requesting customized products and services, in almost zero turnaround time, you'd better get used to designing on the palm of your hand as you walk down the hall. Hopefully it won't be that difficult, but you will be asked to design more in a shorter amount of time. What will you design? Short experiential exercises, job aids, one-on-one situational learning, supervisory coaching examples, or problem/solution action steps. All customized. All high quality. All short turn-around time. All on time. And of course, all effective.

And of course, don't forget about all the tools that your TQM effort will bring with it. Learn them and use them. As an HRD professional, others will expect you to use the tools since you teach them. Besides, once you use the tools, you will find them to be invaluable.

> *"If you think of yourself as a trainer first and a designer second, better do a quick shuffle."*

What to Do?

The diversity that the HRD Department faces in delivering services requires that everyone become more familiar with not only the business the organization is in, but also all new business practices.

Start reading journals focusing on your particular industry. Read business magazines such as *Fortune* or *Business Week*. Read *The Wall Street Journal*. And get out and talk to the people in the line functions. Learn what they do and how you can help them. They are your customers.

Stay on top of what's new in the HRD profession. For example did you know that three University of Michigan professors are presently conducting benchmarking studies that will measure practices of HR departments and competencies of HR personnel? Soon there will be a way to compare with others or to begin to understand what needs to be improved to attain world-class stature.

Learn what others in your department (both training, as well as the bigger picture of HR) are doing and get involved in as many projects as possible.

Get involved in a professional training organization such as the American Society for Training and Development (ASTD). They can lead you to the information you need to hone your HRD skills in training and development, organization development, and career development.

As mentioned in another place in this book, get involved in a professional quality organization such as the American Society for Quality Control (ASQC) or the Association for Quality and Participation (AQP). Reading their journals, attending their conferences, and staying on top of the many books they have available will keep you abreast of what's happening in the world of quality.

Get yourself up to speed with the newest technology that's on its way. EPSS, IVD, CD-ROM, DV-I, CD-I, PDA, PCA, PCS—just letters to you today? They may be a part of your job in the future and are the acronyms for such things as Electronic Performance Support System, Interactive Video Disc, Compact Disc—Read-Only Memory, Digital Video-Interactive, Compact Disc-Interactive, Personal Digit Assistant, Personal Communications Assistant, and Personal Communications Systems. Technology is changing rapidly and may have a major impact on the training profession sooner than you expect.

Build a relationship with your information systems department. Begin to discuss a plan for the future and how you can work together. Provide a frame of reference for each other by discussing what you each have available now.

Finally, be future oriented. What's ahead for your organization and its industry? Be prepared to help your organization envision its future. Reading books by futurists and journals published by futurist associations will give you a glimpse into the far future and provide you with many new ideas.

＊ Want to develop specific ideas about what your HRD Department could do to explore its future? One of the seven management tools is the affinity diagram. You and your department could use the affinity diagram to organize your thoughts about your changing role and your department's future.

The affinity diagram, in Fig. 11.1 is a tool which allows a team to organize large amounts of data into groupings that share a natural relationship with each other. Follow these simple directions and allow about one to two hours, depending on the size of your group (we've conducted successful groups with as few as six and as many as 30 people).

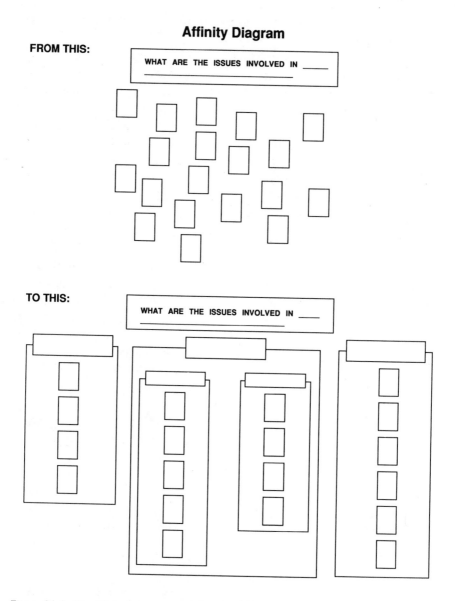

Figure 11.1. The affinity diagram is a tool that is useful for generating and organizing a large number of ideas.

Step 1. Phrase the issue to be considered and post it on a flipchart or wall so that it is visible to the entire team.

- Ensure the phrase is well understood, clearly stated but general enough to be neutral.
- Use the word "issues."
- Example: "What are the issues involved in becoming an HRD Department of the future?"
- Ensure that the team agrees with the phrase.

Step 2. Team members brainstorm ideas to the phrase.

- Brainstorming rules apply: no criticism or discussion, large number desired, full participation.
- Record individual comments on Post-It™ Notes.
- Comment length should be three to seven words.
- Comments should contain a noun and a verb to avoid ambiguous statements.
- Printing on Post-It™ Notes should be large enough so they can be read from a distance.

Step 3. Arrange Post-It™ Notes randomly on a wall.

- Use large enough space for moving the comments.
- Post-It™ Notes may fall off of wallpaper surface. Check it first or use flipchart paper for the backing.

Step 4. All team members go to the wall and arrange the comments into related groups.

- Simultaneously each member of the team moves the comments into groups that share a common relationship.
- This is done in complete *silence.*
- If you don't like where a comment is placed, simply move it. If it gets moved again and you don't agree move it back to where you think it belongs. This is conducted without any discussion.
- Don't force fit loners.

Step 5. Create a header for each grouping.

- A header is a comment that depicts the central idea and ties all of the other comments in the group together.
- It should be concise and make sense standing alone.
- Put it at the top of each grouping.

- Create subheaders if applicable.
- You may also arrange groupings next to each other if related and create a header comment for this relationship.

An affinity diagram can be used for many things. It is most useful in the following instances.

- When data and facts seem to have no structure.
- When issues seem to be too large or complex.
- When the team's thinking needs to be expanded beyond the old solutions and way of thinking.

For more information about the affinity diagram, see *The Memory Jogger Plus+* by Michael Brassard.

One Last Thought

Yes, TQM efforts may fail. Even the most well thought-out plans with the best intentions may go awry—and they have in other organizations. If you know why failure occurred in other organizations, you can prevent failure in your organization and in your department.

Mistakes Made by Others

1. Lack of investment in up-front planning.
2. Insufficient training at all levels.
3. Executive team not leading the effort.
4. Middle management was not involved early.
5. Quality improvement efforts not integrated into the real work of the organization.
6. Communication, reward, long-range planning systems not adjusted to the new way of doing business.
7. Staff driven, rather than line driven.
8. Customer focus is limited.
9. Short-term expectations are too high.
10. Impatience with long-term focus.
11. Fear-based culture is not changed.
12. Implementation becomes the end, rather than the means.

13. Misperceptions that merely implementing a quality improvement effort will ensure survival.

What Is HRD's Role in Preventing These Mistakes?

1. Use your knowledge of OD to ensure that enough time is spent up front to create a corporate vision and a solid strategic plan. Ensure that it is customized.

2. Intensely monitor your organization to know what kind of training will be needed before it is requested. Read more about quality improvement efforts so that you know what to expect.

3. Insist that the executive team is at the helm. And in your own department, ensure that the most senior manager is leading your effort as well. If you have a vice president of HR or HRD, ensure that the individual is involved and committed. Help that process by educating the person. You can send articles or books. (Knowing that your reader may have a limited amount of time, it is always a good idea to highlight the information that is the most important to read.)

4. Use your OD skills to provide suggestions about how middle management could be more involved.

5. Align the HRD Department with line management to ensure that the effort is integrated into the real work of the organization. Become their partner. Remember they are your customer and without them you really don't have a job. How can you exceed their expectations? How can you make implementation easy for them? How can you provide training with the least amount of hassle?

6. You can offer your OD skills to align the systems with the new way of doing business. At the very least, you can align the training system to be more customer-focused.

7. Swallow your pride. Line must lead the effort. Share the work. Give them the credit. Line must maintain the accountability.

8. Start talking customer. Change all training programs to reflect a strong customer focus.

9. Use a combination of your OD skills and your persuasive skills to help the organization understand what is possible and what is not in one year. It is good advice to suggest to small and mid-size companies to focus on a theme for the first year. Perhaps awareness and establishing a clear direction is all that the organization can accomplish. Your company didn't get where it is in one year; it isn't going to get out of it in one year either.

10. To balance impatience, remain steady yourself. Be positive in training sessions or any time you come in contact with other employees. You see more audiences than almost anyone in the organization. Your attitude can make a difference. It's amazing that we Americans are certain that we can accomplish in five months what it took the Japanese 50 years to accomplish.

11. Help every employee understand the relationship between decreasing fear and building trust. "Driving Fear Out" is a good candidate for a new short course or study group. Consider offering it for departments or work units that include both employees and management. (*Note:* Read Chapter 7 in *Driving Fear Out of the Workplace* by Kathleen Ryan and Daniel Oestrich for ideas about what to do.)

12. Do your part to ensure that the company does not lose sight of why it is in business and why it is implementing a TQM effort. To do that, stay focused on the customers and the employees, include the unions, don't start training for training's sake. The implementation is the means, not the end.

13. Not much you can do about misperceptions except educate, educate, educate ... and ... isn't that training's primary responsibility?

Appendices
Index

Learn, Live, and Lead

Learn

Start a Deming Users' Group.

Lead a quality improvement reading group.

Survey positions similar to yours in other companies.

Commit to reading one book per month and providing a synopsis to your work team.

Attend a Deming, Crosby, or Juran seminar.

Agree to provide a great article each month to your department.

Provide a baker's dozen articles for the rest of your team throughout the year.

Visit and interview other managers about their quality improvement efforts.

Survey your management team about the characteristics of a good management team and compare the results to what the experts say.

Visit a Japanese-managed company.

Live

Provide a reward to anyone who "catches" you in the act of *not* walking the talk.

Develop a recognition system in your department for quality improvement efforts.

Conduct an internal customer survey and commit to making the changes that are identified.

Ask peers and subordinates to evaluate you, share results with them, and identify improvement plans.

Lead the effort to create a long-range (10 year) plan for your department.

Break through the class system, how ever that is represented in your organization (lunchroom facilities, parking, dress codes).

Meet with your steering committee and ask how you can support their efforts.

Write an article for the newsletter about quality improvement.

Survey your department about communication and develop a model for the rest of the company.

Benchmark your department against those in other organizations.

Make contact regularly with customers.

Begin to gather data on your personal processes.

Conduct next level training for managers, citing personal examples of quality improvement.

Address groups in your company regarding quality improvement.

Conduct an open forum for managers to discuss "how to lead" concerns.

Determine your most critical process; ask your customers about their satisfaction; set a target and turn your people loose on improving the process.

Add quality improvement to the beginning of every staff meeting.

Plan a Quality Improvement Day to celebrate successes and to showcase teams' successes.

Use a facilitator for your own staff meetings.

Pair up with a colleague to champion a cross-functional process improvement.

Lead a team building effort for your team.

Lead a team building effort for your own management team.

Make a commitment to be the downward communication advocate to ensure all information travels quickly, completely, and honestly throughout your department.

Teach a listening class that is open to all employees.

Survey your department about the processes that need to be improved the most.

Demonstrate interest in others' quality improvement efforts by spending 2 hours per week visiting different areas you manage to discuss quality improvement. (First get coaching for how to ask appropriate questions.)

Start a "listening hour" each month.

Examine and initiate a cost of quality system.

Survey your customers in focus groups; then establish teams to make improvements based on what you hear.

Build quality improvement characteristics into your hiring process.

Evaluate and promote those who support quality improvement.

Evaluate your department against the Baldrige criteria.

Evaluate all training programs for consistency with quality improvement principles.

Lead

Commit to bringing Wheatley, Juran, Covey, or Senge to a company meeting.

Lead the effort to create a quality improvement vision for your department.

Take on one of the lowest rated items on your most recent employee survey and champion it for the year.

Challenge your department to an "improvement-a-pay-period."

Lead a team to improve one of your personal processes.

Be the first to examine your performance appraisal system and link performance to quality improvement.

Conduct a drive-out-fear campaign.

Examine your department's policies and procedures and identify those that do not support the desired culture.

Organize and lead the effort to break through the communication gap, including assigning tasks to the rest of the management team.

Lead your team to develop a plan to reward and recognize team efforts.

Host a luncheon for managers in similar businesses within your geographic area to share what they have learned.

Critically examine the compensation system and whether it supports quality improvement behaviors.

Be patient.

Appendix **II**

Process Identification and Selection

TQM's Bottom Line: Improve Processes

The bottom line to TQM is to change the processes by which work gets done. The changes are made in an effort to better serve the customer.

There are many things that have to be in place before these changes can be identified and achieved. As was mentioned elsewhere in this book: clear achievable goals, involvement, and a climate conducive to TQM are all vital.

However, the one aspect of implementation that seems to be most critical for organizations in the beginning is the proper selection of the first processes to improve. If they are too broad in scope, the teams struggle with politics, generalities, areas of work rather than work itself. If they are too small in scope the teams' solutions and changes are judged to be insignificant and of little value when compared to the amount of time spent by the team. Therefore, the proper size and scope of the process the first teams tackle is important.

Process Identification

A process is a series of steps that are linked together to produce a product or service. There are several ways to identify processes in your department. We've listed six.

1. Start with the customer and work backwards.
   - Identify the product or service in your department.
   - Work backwards chronologically from this product or service listing all of the work that goes into producing this output.
2. Identify what product or service needs to be improved. Then, list what work needs to be investigated that could impact on the product or service.
3. List any backlogs that exist within the department. Then, identify related work procedures that might impact to either increase or decrease the backlog.
4. Ask yourself these questions:
   - Where is the most activity within my department?
   - What work processes are we performing?
5. You may choose an input and follow it through your department until it becomes a product or service in the hands of the customer.
   - What was done to this input to make it change to an output?
   - What value was added to this input?
   - Where were these changes made?
   - When were these changes made?
6. Examine the work that each major section of your department accomplishes each day.
   - What inputs do they work on?
   - What outputs do they produce each day?

Process Selection Guidelines

As you select processes to improve in your department, consider the following guidelines. They are listed in order of importance. However, you will know your department best and should make the selection according to the criteria that is the most important.

1. Customer priorities
   - Which process causes dissatisfaction or complaints?
   - Which complaints are repeated or increasing?
   - How can you be responsive?
2. Recurring problem process
   - Which process causes continuous or repeated problems?

- Could this be a good, early example for other teams to use as a model?

3. Easily correctable process
   - Which process or situation has an easy, fast solution?
   - Will it be reinforcing for other teams to see progress?

4. Early process
   - Which process is nearest the entry point of external supplies?
   - Could this early process have a positive effect down line?

5. Clearly defined process
   - Which process has clear boundaries?
   - Which process is entirely defined within your area?
   - Does the process have a narrow enough scope?

6. Visible process
   - Which process is known by most people?
   - Will this visibility be positive to market the effort?

7. Process within a positive environment
   - Is this process in an area where management supports TQM?
   - Which process has the most positive support for improvement?

8. High return on investment
   - Which process will show a cost decrease or savings?
   - Will this savings affect the bottom line and gain support from nonbelievers?

9. Time-saving process
   - Which process improvement could save time?
   - Which process often faces late deadlines or runs behind schedule?

10. Immediate impact process
    - Which process could show immediate improvement results?
    - Is this process also something that is easily measurable?

Histogram Construction Worksheet

Step 1. Count the number of data points.
N = _____

Step 2. Determine range of data.
R = largest value – smallest value
R = _____

Step 3. Divide range value into classes (K).

Number of data points (N)	Appropriate number of classes (K)
under 50	5-7
50-100	6-10
100-250	7-12
over 250	10-20

K = _____

Step 4. Determine class width (H) and round up.
$H = {}^{R}\!/\!_{K}$
H = _____ rounded up = _____

Step 5. Determine boundary limits (BL).
BL = smallest value +H; +H; +H;... to include the highest value.

Step 6. Determine class boundaries by subtracting 0.5 from each boundary limit except the final (largest) boundary limit. This prevents data points from landing on a boundary limit.

Step 7. Determine frequencies for each class.

	Boundaries	Tally	Frequency
class	_____	_____	_____
	_____	_____	_____
	_____	_____	_____
	_____	_____	_____
	_____	_____	_____

Step 8. Construct histogram and label.

Appendix IV

Additional TQM Tools

Many tools exist that will assist you with process improvement and implementing a TQM culture. Those listed here represent only a few, most of which were mentioned earlier in this book. For ease of location they have been listed in alphabetical order.

Each of the tools is described briefly. These descriptions do not provide enough information for you to construct them and you should use the resources mentioned for additional assistance. In some cases, such as Benchmarking or Quality Function Deployment, entire books have been written about the topic and how to be effective in their use. Therefore, we would be remiss if we suggested that we could give you enough information in a couple of sentences or paragraphs or even pages to make you proficient in their use.

In other cases, we have provided supplemental material following these definitions. We have provided a table that compares the different types of benchmarking and the advantages and disadvantages of each. A step-by-step process for brainstorming and pairwise ranking has been provided. We have also provided you with formats for both force field analysis and pairwise ranking to get you started. If you're wondering how you might use these tools, the examples of possible situations will be useful to you.

Benchmarking

Benchmarking, as defined by Robert C. Camp, is the "search for industry best practices that lead to superior performance." David Kearns, former CEO of Xerox, defines benchmarking as "the continuous process of measuring our products, services, and practices against the toughest competitors or those companies recognized as industry leaders."

As you might imagine there are numerous ways to benchmark and each has its own process and specific number of steps (we've seen the steps in the benchmarking process vary from 5 to 15). Generally you identify what you wish to benchmark and determine who to benchmark against. A table at the end of this description provides an overview of how to choose who to benchmark against. You will collect and analyze benchmarking information and use it to make improvements. This activity is almost always done in a team.

Your HRD department could use benchmarking to study how other departments in your organization work with outside suppliers. You could benchmark how other organizations in your same industry create career ladders for their employees. You could also benchmark against any organization known for its expertise in conducting basic skills training.

Benchmarking

Types	Description	Advantages	Disadvantages
Internal	Same activities within organization Different location or department Similar product, process or service	Easy to identify Easy to share confidential data Good results for diversified organizations	Less likely to find differences Internal bias
Competition	Direct competitor Same customer	Easy to identify Likely to have excellent practices Information will be relevant Similar technology and procedures	Ethical considerations Protective atmosphere Less likely to get crucial data

Functional	Same or similar industry but not direct competition	Strong potential for innovative ideas Easy to make adaptations Average amount of time to transfer ideas Willingness to trade ideas	May not have quality you're looking for May not be able to transfer ideas Harder to identify differences
Generic	Different industry with similar processes	Easier to access confidential data Creative/ stimulating ideas Can choose organization known for best practice in the process	May be difficult to make adaptations Some ideas will not be transferable Time consuming
Third party	Contracting with a third party to research	Neutral intervention Can collect and analyze sensitive data	Costly Must educate person

©1993 ebb associates used with permission

Brainstorming

Brainstorming is a process of free, unrefined thinking used by a group of people to generate many creative ideas without judgment. It is the basis of almost any creativity producing technique. Coined by Alex Osborn, a founder of the advertising firm of Batten, Barten, Durstine, and Osborn, it is the most often used tool to generate ideas. The premise around brainstorming is that quantity will produce quality.

To conduct a brainstorming session, bring together six to ten people (though you may use more or less, six to ten seems to produce the most ideas in the shortest amount of time). Usually you will choose individuals who are familiar with the issue for which you are generating ideas. However, it is often beneficial to bring in someone totally unfamiliar with the issue for a completely new perspective.

These supplemental materials provide a set of nine rules to follow to ensure a productive brainstorming session. Expect the session to last 30 to 60 minutes, but be certain that you do not cut it off too early and before the truly creative ideas are listed.

As an HRD professional you will find hundreds of opportunities to use brainstorming. Some might include brainstorming a list of topics for a new course, ways to recruit new trainers, names for a new course, ways to participate in the TQM effort, how to reinforce employees, or questions to ask on an exam.

Brainstorming Rules

Brainstorming is based on a belief that quantity breeds quality. The more ideas generated, the greater is the chance that one will prove to be a high-quality solution. The key to successful brainstorming is to suspend judgment. All ideas are good. The nine basic rules used to guide a brainstorming session are:

1. Suspend judgment. Failure to follow this rule is the major reason why some brainstorming sessions do not produce the expected results.
2. Freewheeling is encouraged. All ideas that come to mind are valued. The wilder the ideas, the better.
3. Quantity is wanted. The goal is to have many ideas.
4. "Piggybacking" is welcome. Participants are encouraged to build on each other's idea or generate a number of ideas using a previous one as a stimulus.
5. Post all ideas as you go.
6. A member may ask for clarification of a suggestion. However, it is important to avoid any questions that are directed to "how" or "why."
7. Allow enough time.
8. Encourage humor and playfulness.
9. Assign both a facilitator and a recorder.

When conducting a brainstorming session always remind participants of the goals of brainstorming, and of the nine rules of brainstorming. It will be the job of the facilitator to see to it that the rules are enforced.

Brainstorming Variations.   These variations will provide ideas for adapting brainstorming in a number of ways. This will add fun and interest to your idea generating sessions.

1. It is sometimes helpful to send out a statement of the problem to group members a few days before your meeting time and request that they bring ideas with them.

2. Be prepared to offer "stimulators" to the group if they become stuck, or persist in looking at the problem from only one perspective.

3. Push to generate x more ideas.

4. Push to generate as many ideas as possible in x minutes.

5. Structured brainstorming follows the same rules, the only difference is that before the entire group begins to brainstorm ideas, participants write ideas on paper or index cards. The ideas are collected and redistributed. It doesn't matter if participants get their own ideas. The purpose is to add anonymity to the process so participants can bring up ideas with which they may otherwise be uncomfortable. The written ideas are listed in a round robin fashion. When all ideas are out, large-group brainstorming begins.

6. Add-An-Idea is conducted in silence. Each individual gets a stack of index cards. Each writes one idea on a card and passes it to the left. Getting another card, each reads the new card, writes another idea, and passes both cards to the left. Next, each person reads the two new cards, writes a third, and passes all three to the left. This continues until one entire circuit has been completed (10 people means 10 rounds). The only difference is that, if you don't have an idea, you may list a question. Rounds get slower because people need more time to read the ideas and questions. The facilitator collects the cards and categorizes them. This may be done immediately following the brainstorming or at a later time.

7. Sometimes individuals write their ideas on Post-It Notes™. This allows for easier categorizing.

Force Field Analysis

Force field analysis, a technique developed by Kurt Lewin, displays the forces working for and against a predetermined objective. The premise is that any time you face a change there are forces that work for the change and forces that work against the change. These are sometimes called driving and restraining forces.

To construct, first identify the specific objective, challenge, or change. Next identify all the forces working for the objective and those working against the objective. List these on a form similar to the one shown. Next, develop a list of tactics to strengthen the positive forces and a list of tactics to weaken or eliminate the negative forces. Turn these tactics into an action plan with assigned responsibilities and deadlines.

As a trainer you could use a force field analysis anytime you need to identify the principle forces that will support or inhibit a change you or your department are facing. For example, the decision to centralize TQM training, when in the past each division has conducted its own training, is a situation that would produce many forces that would work for, as well as forces that would work against the change. Identifying these and determining how to strengthen the supporting forces and how to weaken or eliminate the inhibiting forces will ensure an easier implementation.

Gantt Chart

Gantt charts come out of project management. They are bar charts used for planning, coordinating, and scheduling the steps required to complete a task.

To construct, you would identify all the steps necessary to complete a project and how much time will be required. List these steps on the left side of the chart in sequential order and draw a bar to represent the amount of time required to complete the step. You then use the Gantt chart to schedule people, order supplies, and request equipment at the appropriate time.

Force Field Analysis

Objective _____

_____

(+) Forces Working for Objective   Forces Working Against Objective (−)

As a trainer you could use a Gantt chart for any large project you are facing. For example, if you are responsible for developing the training for TQM, it would be an excellent tool to coordinate resources and to track the project steps.

Quality Function Deployment

Quality function deployment, more commonly known as QFD or the house of quality, has become synonymous with "listening to the voice of the customer." It is a house-shaped matrix that puts customer requirements on the vertical axis and the methods by which they will be met on the horizontal axis. QFD is a conceptual map that displays the process that turns customer requirements into quality improvements. This ensures that you meet all customer requirements.

The following steps provide an idea of how useful QFD can be. Start with a list of understood and agreed-upon customer requirements. Have the customer rank the requirements. A cross-functional team translates these requirements into design features. Each design feature is weighted to show the correlation between customer requirements and the features. The correlation weight of each feature is multiplied by its respective customer requirement. Add the results for each design feature to determine which require immediate attention. The final steps include establishing targets, comparing a competitor's product, and completing the correlation between features to complete the "roof" of the matrix.

Sounds complicated? It can be. The process is detailed and complex, but well worth the effort. It is not possible to use QFD without extensive further study. Goal/QPC located in Lawrence, Massachusetts is one of the leading companies that train the QFD process. They can provide you with additional resources if you are interested.

HRD can work with others throughout the organization to use QFD to mold customer wishes into product design. You might consider using QFD to plan for the best way to disseminate training and development from your central HRD Department at the home office to the branch offices in other states. You would start with the branches first: what are their requirements?

Seven Management Tools

The *seven management and planing tools* are sometimes called the seven new tools of quality. Michael Brassard explains their use and the construction steps in his *Memory Jogger Plus+*.

The *affinity diagram* can best be described as "organized brainstorming," in which a large group of people can generate and organize 100 or more ideas in less than an hour. It is described in detail in Chap. 11.

The *interrelationship digraph* begins in the same way as the affinity diagram. It too, begins as a brainstorm of ideas, but also displays the logical and cause and effect relationships. A team of people identify all the items that address a particular issue or problem, then draw an arrow from one item to another if a causal relationship exists. Those items with the highest number of outgoing arrows are most likely the items that are root causes. Those items with the highest number of incoming arrows may also be an issue worthy of further investigation.

The *tree diagram* provides a logical sequencing of tasks required to implement a goal. It provides a method to break down the goal into more detailed implementation steps. To construct, a planning team places major items to achieve the goal to the left of a sheet of paper, then asks, "what needs to happen to achieve this?" Those items are posted and then the same questions asked again of them until they reach a detailed enough level of implementation that includes numerous substeps.

The *prioritization matrices* are used to prioritize tasks, options, and outcomes. There are three types. Each of them requires that you determine a method of weighting the options by comparing all options to weighted criteria or comparing all options to themselves.

The *matrix diagram* identifies the correlation of items from one group to another. It also shows the strength of that correlation. It is often used to develop a relationship chart in which items from a tree diagram are compared to specific people to identify who is responsible to implement each step in the plan. To construct a matrix diagram you will list a set of tasks, ideas, or issues vertically, then a second set across the top horizontally. A team will decide on the strength of the relationship (or responsibility or support) and attach a symbol in the appropriate space created by the two lists.

The *process decision program chart*, sometimes called PDPC for short, is used to plan every possible chain of events that must occur when the goal is unfamiliar. It anticipates things that might go wrong and develops potential contingencies. It is useful when the task is new, complex, and on a tight schedule. You can begin with a modified tree diagram, taking it to its first and second level of steps and substeps.

Choose one of the substeps and ask, "What could go wrong at this individual substep?" to identify problems that may occur. Record the responses. Then ask, "How can we respond to this problem?" to generate possible contingencies for those potential items that could go wrong. This process is repeated for each of the tree's "branches" and each substep. To complete, the group will evaluate each possible response and, if necessary, create a contingency action plan. This assures that you are prepared for the alternatives that could happen in any implementation plan.

The *activity network diagram* is used to schedule the implementation of a complex project. To construct, you develop a sequential flow of critical tasks that must be completed for each of the activities. These tasks will form paths and should be connected where appropriate. Times are assigned to each task and the earliest and latest start and finish times are calculated. These calculations provide you with information about the duration and tasks that should be monitored to stay on schedule. It is most useful when the task is familiar.

The seven management tools may be easier to understand if you consider their basic use. Generally, the affinity diagram and the interrelationship digraph are used to generate ideas and to identify relationships among those ideas. The tree diagram, prioritization matrices, and matrix diagram are used to organize and analyze. The process decision program chart (PDPC) and the activity network diagram are used to plan for implementation and to make decisions.

As a trainer you might use the tools to map out a plan for your department's upcoming year. You could bring the department together and use an affinity diagram to identify your key customer needs and the categories they create. You may also want to use the logical approach of the interrelationship digraph to determine the root causes of participant complaints from the past three months. These tools would provide the objectives for the next year and you could use the tree diagram to break these objectives into specific implementation steps. However, after developing the tree diagram you may find that you have an overwhelming number of options, so your department could use one of the prioritization matrices to narrow your options to those that will be most important to achieve your goals.

Your team may use a matrix diagram to determine who in the department will be responsible for each of the new initiatives you have established for the upcoming year. To anticipate and plan for the unexpected problems that may occur as your department rolls out its new plan, you will construct a PDPC to identify contingencies, just in case. Last, your department may construct an activity network diagram to schedule the events that must occur to implement the new training courses you are scheduling. This schedule would integrate instructor training, facilities location, material development, and participant registration.

Storyboarding

Storyboarding is a communication tool. Although there are several definitions for storyboarding, including the technique that Walt Disney used to create animated stories, this definition seems to be the one most often used in quality improvement efforts. The *storyboard* allows an action team to tell its story with pictures. Teams can post the diagnostic tools they used, list the improvements they are suggesting, show the results of any experimentation, identify the team members, and even attach a picture of the team.

Often organizations provide a preformatted foam core or cardboard background on which teams simply need to attach the documentation. The preformatted background may be two to three feet wide by three to five feet high. It usually has large outlined spaces that are printed with the titles of each step in the improvement process. As the team completes each step it inserts documentation to support the step such as the project statement, the cause and effect diagram, or data that supports the improvement plan.

A storyboard can be used for every action team formed. Generally, the organization or a department will make that determination. The storyboard provides a way for a team to communicate within the team, within the department, and out to everyone in the organization. It tracks a team's progress during team meetings and serves as a reminder to the team about where they are in the process. A storyboard can be an excellent visual aid during team presentations to others outside the team. It can speed communication if all teams use the same format, since everyone will know where to look for specific information. The storyboard also advertises the team's activities between meetings to the rest of the department and organization.

Voting Techniques

As a team moves through the improvement process, it will need to make decisions and narrow down potential solutions, remedies, or ideas. These techniques help a team do that in an orderly, equitable way.

If you are narrowing a vary large list to find the top one or two items, it may be better to vote twice. The first time to eliminate a majority of the list and the second time to reach more accurate top choices. The reason you might do this is that team members may choose to use their votes differently when given fewer choices. This also works if the team has a tie after the first vote.

Multivoting is best when there are a large number of choices and it is necessary to bring the list to a more manageable size of less than 15. Each team member chooses the best items from the list and casts one vote for one-fourth to one-third of the items. The team can decide to cut off the list at a particular number (e.g., the top 12), look for the natural breaking point (e.g., where the items have votes that jump from five per item to one per item), or use a combination of both.

The *nominal group technique*, sometimes called NGT, is a technique that allows teams to prioritize a large number of items in a very organized way. NGT was developed by Andre Delbecq and Andrew Van de Ven. It uses a method of ranking and weighting the items that feels equitable to everyone involved. Generally NGT is part of a large process that includes silent brainstorming, combining and eliminating ideas, clarification discussion, and prioritizing.

The voting portion asks each team member to choose the best 3 to 5 items (the exact number is assigned). Team members rank their individual choices with the top priority receiving the highest vote in descending order. For example, if the team decided to rank the top 4, each team member would assign 4 votes to the highest priority, 3 votes to the next, 2 to the next, and 1 to the member's fourth choice. An efficient way to do this is to give each person four Post-Its™. One will have a number "4," one a number "3," one a number "2" and the last a number "1." These numbers provide the weighting.

This technique actually gives you several pieces of data. First, it provides a total number of weighted votes for each item. Second, it tells you how many individuals voted for each item. Third, it tells you which specific items are first choices and for how many team members.

Pairwise ranking, sometimes called "paired comparison," works best for prioritizing a list of less than 10 items. Pairwise ranking is a method in which each item on a list is compared to every other item on the list and rated. It can be conducted as a team in which the team reaches consensus on each of the comparisons. Another method is to have each team member complete a matrix alone and total the scores from all matrices. Step-by-step instructions and a blank form can be found at the end of these descriptions.

Ten-four voting works best when the list of choices numbers 10 to 15. Team members are assigned a total of 10 votes. These 10 votes can be assigned in any combination with a maximum of 4 votes per member per item. For example, one team member might assign 4 votes to two items viewed as top-priority items and the remaining 2 votes to a secondary priority. Another team member might see 10 items as all having equal weight and assign 1 vote to 10 items. The total number of votes distributed must add to 10.

An easy way to conduct ten-four voting, is to have the choices posted on flipchart paper. Give each person 10 Post-It Tape Flags™ (the little colored Post-Its™ that pop up out of a two by three inch plastic container and ask them to distribute appropriately.

Pairwise Ranking Matrix

The *pairwise ranking matrix* is a tool that helps you prioritize a number of alternatives. It can be useful to determine a decision of most importance. By comparing each alternative with every other alternative, you are able to determine your highest priorities. Follow these guidelines to complete the pairwise ranking matrix.

- List each alternative. Assign each a letter (A through H).

- Write each alternative in the appropriate box on the matrix. Except for alternative A, list each alternative both horizontally and vertically.

- Start with alternative A. Go across the page and compare alternative A with each of the other alternatives (B through H). Rate each according to the following descriptors.
  - Put a "0" in the box if the two are of equal importance.
  - If one alternative is more important than the other, put the letter of the more important alternative followed by a "1" if it is somewhat more important or followed by a "2" if it is much more important.
  - Note that each box must have either a zero or both the letter and a weighting for the choice you feel is more important.

- Repeat this process with alternatives B through H.

- Determine the highest priority by totaling the scores for each alternative. For example, add all the scores in boxes where you chose A as the most important alternative. Record the total in the box for A. Repeat this process with all the letters.

- The highest priorities are the ones with the highest scores.

Pairwise Ranking Matrix

	B	C	D	E	F	G	H	
A								A =
B								B =
C								C =
D								D =
E								E =
F								F =
G								G =
H								H =

RATINGS

0 – Equal in importance
1 – Somewhat more important
2 – **Much** more important

NOTE: Each box must have either a zero or both the letter and weighting for the choice you feel is more important.

Appendix V
Focus Groups

Focus groups, first created by Ernst Dichter in the 1930s, are most often connected to marketing research. They provide a method for obtaining subjective information, especially as it relates to your customers. Focus groups come out of the qualitative research field. This means that you will get a feel for important issues, but will not generate any numerical data to support how strong or widespread the issue is.

Generally 8 to 10 participants are brought together for the purpose of gathering information around a particular focus such as "how customers define the quality of a service" or "to compare products of various competitors" or "to provide input to the design of a new product." Sometimes a focus group is used to create a survey or to clarify a survey that's been conducted.

Though the participants may not know each other before the session, they usually have a common thread among them that is tied to the purpose of the session. They may all be users of a particular service or product or may be potential customers. For example, if the training department conducted a focus group, everyone might be potential participants in a new training session. In addition, participants are not provided with details before the focus group begins. Usually they do not know more than the general topic that will be covered.

A focus group usually lasts about two hours and follows a semi-structured format. That is, a list of questions provides the direction of the session, but time is allowed for follow-up and exploring unexpected topics. Ground rules are established at the beginning to ensure flow and a balanced discussion.

The success of the focus group depends on the questions that are asked. A rule of thumb is to ask more "what" questions and to avoid "why" questions. Questions need to be short in length, but need to elicit long answers. Well-worded, open-ended questions will provide the best information.

The moderator of the group should encourage different opinions, remain neutral, and use nonverbals to encourage productive responses, as well as to discourage nonproductive side conversation. A successful moderator is one who is a good listener, understands group dynamics, can encourage participation of quiet participants, and can refocus participants who get on tangents. They must be able to create an atmosphere that feels safe and is conducive to being candid.

The information from a focus group is recorded in some manner. It may be video taped in a special studio with one-way glass, audio taped, or it may be written on flipcharts or paper by recorders.

The final step of a focus group is to analyze the data from the group. Look for themes or categories and determine whether some may be subcategories to be combined with others. Select quotes that best reflect or summarize these themes. Then interpret the information and glean lessons learned from the focus group.

How might the training department use focus groups? Certainly, to identify your customers' needs or to get their opinion about your services or products. You could use focus groups to evaluate training programs, to provide suggestions for revisions, to identify new ways to deliver services, or to select new programs based on available criteria and/or materials.

Focus groups provide several advantages. They are fast, inexpensive, flexible, encourage new ideas, allow for probing, and are enjoyable to most participants. Since they are relatively new to the training field, they will provide an exciting, new method for gathering information for your department.

Personal Interviews

What Is an Interview?

- Verbal interaction between two individuals to gain information.

Standardized

- Answers can be compared and classified.
- Used to obtain specific information.

1. Scheduled
   - Interviewer uses questions verbatim and in order.
   - Best for quantitative analysis.
   - High degree of control.
2. Unscheduled
   - Interviewer has choice in the order of questions.
   - Some choice in the wording.
   - Can probe for more information.

Nonstandardized

- Interviewer doesn't pose the same questions in each interview.
- Low degree of quantitative analysis.
- High degree of flexibility.
- Success dependent on skill level of interviewer.

How to Interview

Preparation

- Establish purpose and objectives.
- Develop a question outline.
- Use open-ended questions.
- Group questions according to topics.
- Schedule interviews at the individual's convenience.
- Practice questions with your team.

Conducting an Interview

- The interviewer is responsible for the quality of the interview.
- Deal with issues first then focus on the subject matter.
- Use silence to let them think and provide additional information.
- Taking notes: listen while writing, capture quotes, do not write word for word.
- Note-taking encourages the individual to talk.
- Don't interrupt unless absolutely necessary.
- Ask clarifying questions but don't get involved in a discussion.
- Show respect and be attentive at all times.
- Be flexible.
- Conclude the interview by thanking the person and telling them what you will be doing with the information.

Compiling and Analyzing

- Clean up quotes to ensure accuracy.
- Summarize important points.
- Quantify where possible.
- Compare to other interviews.
- Compile and analyze as soon after the interview as possible.

Be prepared to handle the following:

"I'm too busy now."

"Why are you conducting these interviews?"

"I don't know enough to give you good answers."

"Why are you taking notes?"

"Why do you want to know that?"

"I don't remember."

"I don't want my answers recorded."

"Why don't you interview someone else?"

HRD Quality Improvement Readiness Survey

HRD Quality Improvement Readiness Survey

Please check the box which applies to you:

☐ Management

☐ Non-Management

For each of the 57 statements you will be asked to give two ratings: how much you believe exists now and how much you believe there should be. Low numbers represent low amounts and high numbers represent high amounts for each factor. Please circle only one number in each column.

	How much exists now?	How much should there be?
	low high	low high
1. Amount of recognition top performers can expect from management.	1 2 3 4 5	1 2 3 4 5
2. Amount of pre-planning by management for changes that might impact HRD's ability to perform.	1 2 3 4 5	1 2 3 4 5
3. Level of commitment to improving procedures in HRD.	1 2 3 4 5	1 2 3 4 5
4. Your understanding of the vision and strategic plans of HRD.	1 2 3 4 5	1 2 3 4 5
5. Amount of encouragement for people in your department to be open and candid.	1 2 3 4 5	1 2 3 4 5
6. Level of effort by people in your department to improve processes.	1 2 3 4 5	1 2 3 4 5
7. Your level of agreement that an organizational wide effort to improve methods and processes in HRD is needed.	1 2 3 4 5	1 2 3 4 5
8. Opportunity to improve your skills in your present job.	1 2 3 4 5	1 2 3 4 5
9. Willingness of management to reward taking risks.	1 2 3 4 5	1 2 3 4 5
10. Amount of credit management gives to people when they deserve it.	1 2 3 4 5	1 2 3 4 5
11. Degree that senior management sets an example of quality performance in day to day activities.	1 2 3 4 5	1 2 3 4 5
12. Level of acceptance of new policies and procedures within your department.	1 2 3 4 5	1 2 3 4 5
13. Level of agreement among all employees concerning HRD's vision, strategic plan, and day to day operational priorities.	1 2 3 4 5	1 2 3 4 5
14. Level of communication between departments.	1 2 3 4 5	1 2 3 4 5
15. Your desire to be involved in HRD's Quality Improvement Process.	1 2 3 4 5	1 2 3 4 5
16. Opportunities for improvement that exists with HRD today.	1 2 3 4 5	1 2 3 4 5
17. Opportunity to make a worthwhile contribution to the goals of HRD.	1 2 3 4 5	1 2 3 4 5
18. Your willingness to take risks on the job.	1 2 3 4 5	1 2 3 4 5
19. Level of opportunity for people to receive promotions because they earned them.	1 2 3 4 5	1 2 3 4 5
20. Management's ability to create and convey a vision for the future.	1 2 3 4 5	1 2 3 4 5
21. Willingness of senior management to accept improvement suggestions.	1 2 3 4 5	1 2 3 4 5

	How much exists now?		How much should there be?	
	low high		low high	
22. Your understanding of how your work contributes to HRD's goals.	1 2 3 4 5		1 2 3 4 5	
23. Level of feedback you receive on how well you do your job.	1 2 3 4 5		1 2 3 4 5	
24. Amount of time the people in your department spend regularly together planning for the future.	1 2 3 4 5		1 2 3 4 5	
25. Level of possibilities to improve procedures within your department.	1 2 3 4 5		1 2 3 4 5	
26. Level of satisfaction you have for career advancement in HRD.	1 2 3 4 5		1 2 3 4 5	
27. Level of acceptance within HRD for creative thinking.	1 2 3 4 5		1 2 3 4 5	
28. Amount of recognition you receive for doing a good job.	1 2 3 4 5		1 2 3 4 5	
29. Level of opportunity you have to provide your input to your manager before final decisions are made.	1 2 3 4 5		1 2 3 4 5	
30. Willingness of management within your department to be receptive to your ideas and suggestions.	1 2 3 4 5		1 2 3 4 5	
31. Your willingness to support goals set by management.	1 2 3 4 5		1 2 3 4 5	
32. Amount of information you receive through official communication channels to do your job.	1 2 3 4 5		1 2 3 4 5	
33. Amount of responsibility the people in your department accept for the success or failure of the products or services they produce.	1 2 3 4 5		1 2 3 4 5	
34. Your understanding of external customers' needs.	1 2 3 4 5		1 2 3 4 5	
35. Level of pride the people in your department have in their work.	1 2 3 4 5		1 2 3 4 5	
36. Likelihood of new ideas quickly being approved for trial implementation.	1 2 3 4 5		1 2 3 4 5	
37. Amount of increased responsibility you can expect for being a top performer in HRD.	1 2 3 4 5		1 2 3 4 5	
38. Amount of coaching provided by management to prepare you for future responsibilities.	1 2 3 4 5		1 2 3 4 5	
39. Your trust and confidence in management in leading HRD's Quality Improvement Process.	1 2 3 4 5		1 2 3 4 5	
40. Your level of knowledge of short term objectives set by management concerning quality and/or productivity improvement.	1 2 3 4 5		1 2 3 4 5	
41. Level of opportunity for people in your department to exchange information with their supervisor.	1 2 3 4 5		1 2 3 4 5	
42. Level of cooperation between co-workers to get the job done.	1 2 3 4 5		1 2 3 4 5	
43. Level of flexibility within HRD to change management methods.	1 2 3 4 5		1 2 3 4 5	
44. Your level of satisfaction with the working environment in HRD.	1 2 3 4 5		1 2 3 4 5	
45. Amount of emphasis by management for all HRD staff to develop new ideas for improving procedures.	1 2 3 4 5		1 2 3 4 5	

	How much exists now?		How much should there be?	
	low high		low high	
46. Amount of concern management has for people who do not perform well.	1 2 3 4 5		1 2 3 4 5	
47. Ability of management to guide a department wide change effort in HRD.	1 2 3 4 5		1 2 3 4 5	
48. Level of commitment your manager has for implementing HRD's Quality Improvement Process.	1 2 3 4 5		1 2 3 4 5	
49. Your understanding of the performance measures set by management to monitor progress toward reaching short term objectives and goals.	1 2 3 4 5		1 2 3 4 5	
50. Frequency with which supervisors of similar work units share information about their work methods and practices.	1 2 3 4 5		1 2 3 4 5	
51. Opportunity for you to participate in setting goals or objectives related to your work.	1 2 3 4 5		1 2 3 4 5	
52. Level of satisfaction with the products and services you receive from your internal suppliers, who provide you with information, materials or other services required to get your job done.	1 2 3 4 5		1 2 3 4 5	
53. Your level of satisfaction with your present job.	1 2 3 4 5		1 2 3 4 5	
54. Amount of time allowed during work hours for people to work together to develop new ideas.	1 2 3 4 5		1 2 3 4 5	
55. Level of effectiveness of the appraisal system.	1 2 3 4 5		1 2 3 4 5	
56. Amount of responsibility people in your department take for improving your work group's productivity and quality.	1 2 3 4 5		1 2 3 4 5	
57. Number of innovative ideas regularly implemented by senior management.	1 2 3 4 5		1 2 3 4 5	

This space is for your comments regarding the preceding statements and questions or any other issues you think are significant.

Implementation Resources

Books

Moran, J.W., Collett, C., Cote, C. *Daily Management–A System for Individual and Organizational Optimization*, GOAL/QPC, 1991.

Tunks, Roger. *Fast Track to Quality–A 12 Month Program for Small-to-Mid-Sized Businesses.* McGraw-Hill, Inc., 1992.

Griffiths, David N. *Implementing Quality–With a Customer Focus.* ASQC Quality Press, 1990.

Jablonski, Joseph R. *Implementing TQM: Competing in the Nineties Through Total Quality Management,* Second Edition. Technical Management Consortium, Inc., 1992.

Slater, Roger. *Integrated Process Management: A Quality Model.* McGraw-Hill, Inc., 1991.

Cocheu, Ted. *Making Quality Happen.* Josey-Bass, Inc., 1993.

Berry, Thomas H. *Managing the Total Quality Transformation.* McGraw-Hill, Inc., 1991.

Sashkin, Marshall, and Kiser, Kenneth J. *Putting Total Quality Management to Work.* Berrett-Koehler Publishers, 1993.

Brocka, Bruce, and Brocka, M. Suzanne. *Quality Management–Implementing the Best Ideas of the Masters.* Business One Irwin, 1992.

Organizations

American Society for Quality Control
611 East Wisconsin Avenue
Milwaukee, WI 53201-9488
414/272-8575

Association for Quality and Participation
801-B West 8th Street
Cincinnati, OH 45203
513/381-1959

American Society for Training and Development
1640 King Street Box 1443
Alexandria, VA 22313-2043
703/683-8100

Reading List

Adair, John. *Not Bosses But Leaders*. Kogan Page Limited, 1990.

Beckhard, Richard, and Pritchard, Wendy. *Changing the Essence*. Jossey-Bass Publishers, 1992.

Berry, Thomas H. *Managing the Total Quality Transformation*. McGraw-Hill, Inc., 1991.

Biech, Elaine, and Danahy, Mike. *Diagnostic Tools for Total Quality. INFO-LINE*, American Society for Training and Development, September, 1991.

Block, Peter. *The Empowered Manager: Positive Political Skills at Work*. Jossey-Bass Publishers, 1987.

Brassard, Michael. *The Memory Jogger: A Pocket Guide of Tools for Continuous Improvement.* GOAL/QPC, 1988.

Brassard, Michael. *The Memory Jogger Plus+*. GOAL/QPC, 1989.

Brocka, Bruce, and Brocka, M. Suzanne. *Quality Management–Implementing the Best Ideas of the Masters*. Business One Irwin, 1992.

Camp, Robert C. *Benchmarking*. ASQC Press and Quality Resources, 1989.

Chang, Richard Y. *Continuous Process Improvement, INFO-LINE*. American Society for Training and Development, October, 1992.

Cocheu, Ted, *Making Quality Happen*. Jossey-Bass, Inc., 1992.

Cocheu, Ted, DeJater, Gerald, et al. *Training for Quality, INFO-LINE*. American Society for Training and Development, May, 1988.

Covey, Stephen R. *The 7 Habits of Highly Effective People*. Simon & Schuster, 1989.

Covey, Stephen R. *Principle Centered Leadership*. Summit, Division of Simon & Schuster, 1991.

Deming, W. Edwards. *Out of the Crisis*. Massachusetts Institute of Technology, 1986.

DePree, Max. *Leadership is an Art*. Doubleday, 1989.

DePree, Max. *Leadership Jazz*. Doubleday, 1992.

Feigenbaum, Armand V. *Total Quality Control*. McGraw-Hill, Inc., 1991.

Gilley, Jerry W. *Strategic Planning for Human Resource Development, INFO-LINE*. American Society for Training and Development, June, 1992.

Griffiths, David N. *Implementing Quality–With a Customer Focus*. ASQC Quality Press, 1990.

Jablonski, Joseph R. *Implementing TQM: Competing in the Nineties Through Total Quality Management*, Second Edition. Technical Management Consortium, Inc., 1992.

Juran, J.M. *Juran on Leadership for Quality: An Executive Handbook.* The Free Press (a division of Macmillan), 1989.

Kinlaw, Dennis. *Developing Superior Work Teams.* Lexington Books, 1991.

Moran, J.W., Collett, C., and Cote, C. *Daily Management–A System for Individual and Organizational Optimization.* GOAL/QPC, 1991.

Neave, Henry R. *The Deming Dimension.* SPC Press, Inc., 1990.

Olivetti, L. James, Editor, *ASTD Trainer's Toolkit: Mission Statements for HRD.* American Society for Training and Development, 1990.

Poirier, Charles C., and Houser, William F. *Business Partnering for Continuous Improvement.* Berrett-Koehler Publishers, Inc., 1993.

Roberts, Harry V., and Sergesketter, Bernard F. *Quality Is Personal.* The Free Press, 1993.

Ryan, Kathleen D., and Oestrich, Daniel R. *Driving Fear Out of the Workplace.* Jossey-Bass Publishers, 1991.

Slater, Roger. *Integrated Process Management: A Quality Model.* McGraw-Hill, Inc., 1991.

Sashkin, Marshall, and Kiser, Kenneth J. *Putting Total Quality Management to Work.* Berrett-Koehler Publishers, 1993.

Senge, Peter M. *The Fifth Discipline.* Doubleday, 1990.

Tunks, Roger. *Fast Track to Quality–A 12 Month Program for Small- to Mid-Sized Businesses.* McGraw-Hill, Inc., 1992.

Walton, Mary. *The Deming Management Method.* Dodd, Mead & Company, 1986.

Wheatley, Margaret. *Leadership and the New Science.* Berrett-Koehler Publishers, 1993.

Pull Quotes
Index

Chapter 1

"If it's just common sense, why aren't we doing it?" (p. 2)

"TQM creates an opportunity for employees to improve processes which make a meaningful contribution to the organization." (p. 6)

"It will be more difficult than you expected." (p. 8)

Chapter 2

"Always think of your customers as suppliers first. Work closely with them so that they can supply you with the information you need and, in turn, you can supply them with the products and services that meet their needs and expectations." (p. 15)

"You will want your measurements to go beyond a mere head count and tell you what the heads think and feel." (p. 20)

"Your challenge in this should be to know your customers' next needs before they do!" (p. 23)

Chapter 3

"Quality is the measure of satisfaction that occurs between a customer and supplier that only they can define." (p. 25)

"Don't be surprised if your customers respond with, 'It's about time someone asked me!'" (p. 29)

"If you don't improve things, someone else will." (p. 33)

Chapter 4

"A process is a series of steps that when combined produce a result." (p. 37)

"Variation is the result of the unique combination of the five components of a process: people, materials, methods, machines, and environment." (p. 37)

"Over time nonvalue added work creeps into your processes in the form of duplication, errors, rework, outdated procedures, and double inspection." (p. 41)

"The most fundamental change that must occur during this decade is that we must begin to manage processes." (p. 48)

Chapter 5

"Be wary of people who believe that 'the tools' are all there is to TQM." (p. 52)

"You are surrounded by data." (p. 65)

Chapter 6

"TQM teamwork. Teamwork TQM. You can hardly mention one without the other." (p. 68)

"Empowering employees means to stop stopping them!" (p. 69)

"Teams need to break paradigms that tend to hobble them." (p. 71)

"When teams face up to their awesome responsibility unbelievable things happen." (p. 72)

Chapter 7

"TQM will be most successful in a department that has both a need and a desire to implement TQM." (p. 77)

"Only if you have a vision of the future will you be able to create it." (p. 80)

"TQM becomes the way things are done, rather than something else to do." (p. 83)

"The amount of time invested is often the first sign of commitment to the rest of the department." (p. 86)

"As management plans to support and coach teams, there is a fine line between support and moddling, between coaching and interfering." (p. 93)

"Communication is a major reason for the success or failure of TQM efforts." (p. 97)

Chapter 8

"Processes are wrapped in the culture. It is not possible to change one without the other." (p. 103)

"The fact that you as a leader didn't know that there was dissent before, doesn't mean it didn't exist." (p. 104)

"Leaders must recognize and accept their role to learn, live, and lead the transformation. They need to set the example—to exemplify the new principles in their own actions and reactions." (p. 111)

Chapter 9

"If you want the effort to succeed get someone from line management to lead the effort and complement that individual with your skills." (p. 118)

"Remember, the plan must be customized. Someone else's plan will fail." (p. 119)

"... keep tracking mechanisms simple. Your TQM effort should not deplete another forest." (p. 122)

"... people do or will continue to do what gets rewarded." (p. 124)

"Most organizations realize that it is inefficient to organize work around functions." (p. 128)

Chapter 10

"New roles will require new skills." (p. 136)

"Everyone will need to be coached, encouraged, prodded, and protected as they try on new skills and behaviors." (p. 138)

"... statistics are important, but it takes people to make them work." (p. 142)

"The most important part of any training design is making certain it is an example of what it teaches." (p. 151)

"This is not about only checking off the box; people need to *use* the skills." (p. 154)

Chapter 11

"TQM offers a golden opportunity to HRD Departments. Are you ready to grab it?" (p. 158)

"Training is changing from how-to-do-it memory skills stored in an employee's head to how-to-access and use job aids stored in a computer." (p. 160)

"If you think of yourself as a trainer first and a designer second, better do a quick shuffle." (p. 162)

Index

About the Author

Elaine Biech is president and managing principal of *ebb associates*, a human resources development firm that creates custom-designed training programs and provides management consulting to clients in the private and public sectors. The firm has offices in Portage, Wisconsin, where Ms. Biech is based, and in Norfolk, Virginia. The author is a graduate of the University of Wisconsin-Superior and holds an M.S. degree in Human Resources Development. A frequent speaker at regional and national conferences, Ms. Biech is a member of the National Board of Directors of the American Society for Training and Development. In addition, she is active in the American Society for Quality Control and the Association for Quality and Participation.

QUEST
FOR PEACE

The Story of
the Nobel Award

by
Mortimer Lipsky

South Brunswick and New York:
A. S. Barnes and Co.
London: Thomas Yoseloff Ltd

To the memory of Ruth

Foreword

by Norman Angell

If we are to avoid repetition of the errors of the past, which are proving so disastrous in the political conditions of the twentieth century, then we must have some sense of the nature of those past errors and some fairly clear notion of the cultural failure which explains them. The understanding of where and in what way our culture failed us has suddenly assumed a life-and-death urgency it never before possessed.

This is the most educated century that history has known, with more schools, more universities, a longer period for the mass of men at school and greatly increased access to the university; yet this most educated of all centuries has known two world wars, many minor ones, and episodes worse than war, like the Hitlerian abomination of Belsen and Buchenwald. War is as ancient as history yet mankind has survived it. But technology has now given armies access to instruments which, if used with recklessness, will destroy mankind. Heretofore, men could afford war in the sense of surviving it, but if we go on simply repeating the past, mankind will perish.

This book examines the outstanding features of that past. Because it does so with a cultivated judgment, it will greatly help the reader understand why the mass of men have through-

7

out the ages behaved as they have behaved, and still display a political judgment inadequate to the problems confronting us. We have gone through two world wars, many minor ones and have witnessed the most "educated" of the nations organize the massacre of ten million men, women, and children for the sole offence of belonging to the race which was the race of Jesus Christ. It is a book which helps us to understand why the mass of men yielded to self-evident fallacies — self-evident because the cultural failure which they revealed is manifest in the daily lives of the mass of mankind.

Early in the history of Christendom, the Christian church, then a political as well as a theological power, set out to carry the message of the Prince of Peace to the whole of mankind. In the effort to carry that message to mankind, the church managed to provoke some of the most destructive wars of history; the burning alive of the heretic became a public exhibition, the occasion of public holiday.

This, like many other features of theological behavior, has disappeared. Not merely have we stopped burning the heretic but we have made the discovery that heretic and orthodox can live in peace and do so. Theological tolerance has reached a point where it is possible for a Protestant Archbishop to visit the Pope and have a friendly talk with him about their common problems. As recently as half a century ago this would have been impossible. If at the beginning of this century a Protestant Archbishop had paid friendly visits to the Pope, there would have been a Protestant explosion of wrath. But the intolerance which once marked theological differences seems to have been transferred to the political field, and the major problems of our time arise from differences in social and political doctrines, not in theological differences. What we have managed in the theological field we must somehow transfer to politics.

This book presents features of past experience in the political field which should be of incalculable value in facing those dangers which political theories engender.

NORMAN ANGELL

Contents

Illustrations

The illustrations appear as a group after page 128.

Joseph Austen Chamberlain
Aristide Briand
Gustav Stresemann
Ferdinand Buisson
Ludwig Quidde
Frang B. Kellogg at the signing of the Peace Pact
Nathan Söderblom
Nicholas Murray Butler
Jane Addams
Norman Angell
Arthur Henderson
Carl von Ossietzky
Carlos Saavedra Lámas
Edgar Algernon Robert Cecil
Cordell Hull
John R. Mott
Emily Greene Balch
Lord Boyd-Orr of Brechin
Ralph J. Bunche
Léon Jouhaux
Albert Schweitzer
George C. Marshall
The U.N. High Commissioner for Refugees, Dr. G. J.
    van Heuvren-Goedhart
Lester B. Pearson
Rev. Dominique George Pire
Philip J. Noel-Baker
Albert John Luthuli
Dag Hammarskjold
Linus Carl Pauling
Dr. Martin Luther King
UNICEF emblem
Henry R. Labouisse
Nobel Peace Medallion

Quest for Peace
The Story of the Nobel Award

1 Introduction

Here is the greatest story of the twentieth century. It is a tragedy performed in the great classical tradition with the entire earth as its stage, and the human race as its protagonist. Here is the gravest problem confronting mankind — the problem of survival or extinction for everybody — compared with this all other problems are unimportant. Here is what Philip J. Noel-Baker, laureate for 1959, considered "the greatest honor a man can receive in this world."

Search the shelves of your local library; you will find books about the winners of the Nobel prize for physics, chemistry, medicine, and literature. The probability is that you will not find any books concerning the winners of the Nobel *peace* prize.

Alfred Hermann Fried, laureate for 1911, remarked that the events at an international bicycle race are described in greater detail by the press, and more eagerly swallowed by the readers, than the events pertaining to the international struggle for peace. This is to be expected in the age when we want happy stories about happy people with happy problems. An age which worships the bitch-goddess success, naturally has little patience for an endeavor which can only report failure. Alfred Nobel himself recognized that "nobody nowadays reads essays about other people other than actors or assassins — preferably the latter, whether they committed homicide on the battlefield or at home." Thus, the books in our libraries about wars and generals crowd out the few forlorn volumes about peace.

The story of the Nobel peace prize is thus not one of success, but of failure. In reading it, however, we must never forget that this is our story, and that the failures are our failures, and the lack of success is our death sentence. Perhaps the mistake lies in accepting the criterion of Adolf Hitler, that "the only earthly criterion of whether an enterprise is right or wrong is its success." Perhaps Arnold Toynbee was closer to the truth when he postulated that "nothing fails like wordly success."

Man, in his infinite wisdom, has succeeded in harnessing the vast powers of the atom. In the midst of man's greatest triumph, at the apex of his supremacy over the forces of nature, what is his only question? William Faulkner, laureate for literature for 1950, formulated it most eloquently with his question, "When will I be blown up?"

We live in an apocalyptic age where the daily newscasts carry overtones of eternity, and the people are filled with a sense of great and impending events. President John F. Kennedy stated that we "happen to live in the most dangerous time in the history of the human race." Fear haunts the world.

Even so, in this age of absurdity, the ageless lament for a "pax orbis" will not be still. Let us give ear, in the words of Pope John XXIII, "to the anguished cry of 'peace! peace!' which rises up to Heaven from every part of the world praying for this blessing, which for the human family is a blessing greater than any other."

Dr. A. Powell Davies has truly stated that "the world is now too dangerous for anything but the truth." Mankind is in desperate need of a great dialogue on the issues of war

and peace. In the words of Murray D. Lincoln, president of
CARE :

Let's face it then. There is the possibility that we will not survive.
There is the real and present danger that in our ignorance, in our
pettiness, in our greed, in our distrust we might turn this new
force against ourselves. There is the real possibility that the same
awesome power which could make this an earth of milk and
honey will instead reduce it to radioactive rubbish. This, too, is
one of the facts of life in the mid-twentieth century and we can
hardly forget it.

There is no better approach to the problem of peace than
the study of the story of the Nobel peace prize. Here is the
mirror of our age — of the naïveté of the Hague period of
arbitration; of the holocaust of two world wars; of the hope
of the League of Nations; of the blackest depths of Hitlerism;
of the cautious wariness of the United Nations; of the Cold
War; of the ominous shadow cast by the bomb's mushroom
cloud. Here is reflected the hopes and aspirations of our times
— the rapprochements, the retreats and the despairs. Even the
omission of the award 16 times in its 65 year history is eloquent
commentary on our new Dark Age.

Like Diogenes who cast about the light of his lamp at noon
in the market place, in his search of an honest man; so does
the Nobel prize committee of the Norwegian Storting focus its
searchlight into the highways and byways, where men trod,
in its quest for an elusive peace. The "greatest honor" in the
power of man to bestow, sought the answer to its quest for
peace in the seats of the mighty, and the obscurity of neglect;
in the ink-stained printing shops, and the courts of justice.
It is sought in the pulpit, the cloistered halls of learning, and
the frozen North, in the jungles of Africa, the fortress of the
military, and the workshops of labor. Yes, the search has even
penetrated the banishment of exile, detention in South Africa
and — even the concentration camp.

For, the first obligation of each man is to support himself and his family so as to be beholden to none. And no man, in this materialistic world, has ever earned his crust of bread as a hero of peace carrying its white banner. He cannot afford to work full time at what Albert Einstein called "the greatest of all causes." At best, the cause of peace can only be a part-time vocation. Thus, our heroes come from many walks of life. They are statesmen, lawyers, scholars, labor leaders, churchmen, journalists, social workers, humanitarians, international civil servants—even a professional soldier. Who will show the way down the road to peace—the practical politician, the professional pacifist, the man of God, the proselytizing journalist or the humanitarian?

Peace will not fly in like a dove, or sprout up like an olive branch, without the united and dedicated efforts of human beings. The power of the military-industrial complex is much too formidable, to permit an easy victory by the legions of peace. To quote Ralph Waldo Emerson, "Peace has its victories but it takes brave men to win them." Peace is primarily a matter of people, so our story is not only about a gold medal or a large sum of prize money. Rather, our tale is a great human interest story. As it unfolds, we will meet the great and the humble: the man called the "Thirteenth Apostle"; the woman called "America's uncrowned queen"; and Germany's most militant anti-war evangelist. We will see the most beloved man in northern Europe, the man for whom the whole world mourned, the Moses of our time, and many other inspiring workers for peace.

Primarily, however, our story is a story of great romance, for here is the stuff from which epic novels are created. There is romance in the very concept of a prize for peace which was spawned in destruction. Imagine the anachronism of Alfred Nobel, merchant of death, the creator of the most powerful weapons of war up to his day, who turned his face away from

the scourge of war and toward the works of peace, in one of
the strangest paradoxes that has ever occurred in the history
of human nature. We shall meet this "richest vagabond" of
Europe who wrote in his torturous English poetry :

> You say I am a riddle—it may be,
> For all of us are riddles unexplained.

There is romance also, in the story of the penniless noble-
woman who inspired the prize, married her baron, and lived
happily ever after. There is romance also in the mystery of
the prize money that was embezzled, of the bankrupt who had
disappeared from public view for over 40 years, and who was
thought dead, of the Dominican who founded the "Europe of
the Hearts," and of the many others to be dubbed heroes
of peace.

What has been the effect and influence of this gift to mankind that was bequeathed by the inventor of dynamite? Some
commentators have stated that it "is like fighting a city fire
with a gilt-tipped bottle of rose water." Others have hailed
it as a beacon light to the pursuit of sanity by man. Some
critics would divert the fund to other uses and purposes. On
occasion, the awards have stuttered like an uncertain trumpet;
at other times they have reverberated like the grand amen of
a stately organ.

One thing is certain. As Pope John XXIII has so rightly
said :

Between two words, war and peace, are entwined the anguish
and the hopes of the world.

In that sense, with the awareness that a foreboding roll of
drums is marking the retreat of mankind to the caves of our
Mousterian and Aurignacian ancestors, we shall attempt to
evaluate the role that the Nobel peace prize might play in

the new human habitat created by the thermonuclear bomb. In this task we shall keep before us the dictum of Socrates that "an unexamined life is not worth living."

2 Spawned in Destruction

There are many competent biographies which give the main facts of the life of Alfred Nobel. They will inform you that he was born October 21, 1833, in the northern outskirts of Stockholm, Sweden; that he was a sickly child (and man), who suffered from headaches, colds, poor digestion and a weak back; that he was very close to his mother who strove so desperately to preserve the breath of life in that weak body; that he enjoyed only one year of formal schooling in his life, the first grade of elementary school in St. Jakob's Higher Apologist School; and that his father Immanuel was an unsuccessful architect and inventor who went bankrupt in Sweden and set off to Finland and Russia to seek his fortune, leaving his family behind. The biographies will go on to relate how Immanuel made his fortune in Russia by manufacturing mines and munitions to be used against the English in the Crimean War; how the father brought his family to St. Petersburg; how young Alfred traveled in foreign lands, including the United States for two years; how Immanuel again went bankrupt after the death of Nicholas I; and how the parents and two of the four brothers returned to Heleneborg, Sweden.

At this point the chronicle will take up Alfred's work where, in building upon his father's failures, he developed Nobel's

23

blasting oil, blasting gelatin, blasting cap, and dynamite — 355 patents in all. Nor, was this hammer of Thor fashioned without travail and anguish. Explosions occurred all over the world, in scattered locations such as Panama, San Francisco, and Kümmel, Norway; causing deaths to hundreds and great damage to property. On September 3, 1864, the home workshop at Heleneborg exploded, killing his younger brother Emil and four workers. The father never recovered from this tragedy, but the stubborn Alfred transferred his own workshop to a raft, where police power could not reach, and continued his experiments.

To exploit his inventions, Alfred Nobel opened ninety-three factories in his lifetime. These were located in Sweden, Belgium, France, the United States, Scotland, Germany and fifteen other countries which yielded a production of 66,500 tons of explosives in the year of his death, 1896. His brother Robert discovered the great petroleum resources of Baku in Russia, and he created a great industrial complex there which Alfred assisted financially. These works eventually became the founding stones for I. G. Farben, the Hermann Goering Works, Imperial Chemical Industries, the Putiloff Works and the Russian oil trust. Yet in all these vast enterprises, employing over 100,000 workmen, there never was a strike in a Nobel industry. The Nobels were always model employers. "Nobel by name, noble by nature," was the reputation which they enjoyed among their workers.

Alfred Nobel traveled extensively in pursuit of his business interests; fought, won and lost many law suits in defense of his patents, and ably administered his far-flung establishments. From Sweden he moved to Paris and still later to San Remo on the Italian Riviera.

One or two books will even enlighten you about Nobel's sex life, and tell you about his mistress Sophie Hess, whom he called The Troll, a flighty, empty headed salesgirl twenty-three years his junior, whom he first met in a flower shop in Baden bei-Wien, Austria, and who led our benevolent misanthrope upon a merry chase for many years.

Nobel is described as being below medium height with a slight stoop, dark of complexion with blue eyes under bushy eyebrows, high forehead, prominent nose and a full beard. He died at 2 a.m., December 10, 1896, at his estate Il Nido at San Remo, "surrounded only by hired servants and without any dear one close by, whose gentle hand can one day close my eyes and who can whisper a soft and sincere word of comfort," leaving an estate of 33,233,792 kroner (8 to 9 million dollars) and a famous will. Funeral services befitting so rich a man were held on December 29, 1896, in Storkyrka, the great church of Stockholm, and the ashes were finally interred in the Nobel family plot at Stockholm Northern Cemetery near the remains of his parents, and of Emil. Reverend Nathan Söderblom, whom we shall meet again as a laureate in 1930, officiated at the solemn services although it was known that the deceased was an avowed agnostic.

Unfortunately, in this volume we shall have to gloss over most of the events in the life of Alfred Nobel and concentrate on only those matters which influenced his thinking on the subject of peace, and which resulted in the creation of the peace prize.

We have already noted that Nobel traveled extensively, lived in many places, had world-wide business interests, and was known as Europe's richest vagabond. He spoke and wrote Swedish, Russian, German, French, and English, and carried on a vast international correspondence in all these languages without utilizing the services of even a secretary. Little wonder then, that such a man should say, "I am a cosmopolitan. My home is where I work and I work everywhere."

Nobel, early in life, was fascinated by the poetry of Shelley, and he wrote many verses in imitation. No doubt, the completely pacifist views of this poet influenced the later thinking of the founder of the peace prize.

Psychologists have tried to analyze what might have taken place in the mind of this great merchant of death to obsess him so with the quest for peace. It has been postulated that Nobel was primarily a creative spirit, and only to a lesser extent a personality born to acquire a dominating position because of his talent for organization. As such, he held a high regard for the free personality and an aristocratic contempt for democracy and the masses.

In this connection, we have the testimony of Leonard Hwass, a witness to the will and an old associate. He said Nobel was "a quiet, high-minded, Teutonic aristocrat, an individualist of the first water, who never fixes his hopes upon the elevation of the masses, but upon the encouragement of individuals of high social value. He recognized that they are the real dispensers of blessings and happiness to mankind." Nobel believed that a new order could be built upon the foundation of the higher knowledge of the gifted individual. For the great bulk of humanity, however, Nobel held only distrust and voiced fears that "A new tyranny, that of the dregs of the population, is looming up; one fancies one detects its approaching murmur." He thought that stupidity was world enemy number one.

Herta E. Pauli, one of Nobel's biographers, attempts this explanation:

Like so much in his character, his pacifism always bore a Russian stamp; it was abstract, fatalistic, undemocratic, contemptuous of human life. It was a sterling paradox, as odd a thing in itself, as was the fact that it was harbored by the producer of one-half the world's high explosives and it could have been spawned only in Russia, in those years when for the first time his job was to furnish men with the means of killing their fellows.

Although Nobel may have held a contemptuous disregard

for life in the mass, he fully appreciated the value of the gift of life to the creative individual. One of his poems in English reads as follows:

> I look upon life as a noble gift,
> A gem from Nature's hand for man to polish
> Till sparkling beams repay him for his toil.

As a hard businessman, Nobel was fully aware of the nature of the product he manufactured. He once wrote, "Well, you know, it is rather fiendish things we are working on." The death of his own brother Emil, and of many others in the handling of dynamite, never deterred Nobel from the continuation of his work. Contrast Nobel's attitude with that of Asconio Sobrero, the first discoverer of nitroglycerine, who abandoned his experiments because he could not put his heart into a type of work the primary aim of which had to be greater destruction, when the whole idea of destruction was so repugnant to him. (It should be noted, however, that these sentiments didn't stop Sobrero from later going to work for Nobel.)

Unwilling to forsake his will toward peace, Nobel at first tried to rationalize away the fodder he was creating for the jaws of Mars. He wrote to Baroness von Suttner in 1892:

My factories may well put an end to war sooner than your congresses. The day when two army corps can annihilate one another in one second, all civilized nations, it is to be hoped, will recoil from war and discharge their troops.

A few years earlier, in 1890, Nobel had stated, in a similar vein:

War must be made as deadly for all the civilians back home as for the troops on the front lines. Let the sword of Damocles hang over every head and you will witness a miracle.

This theme kept recurring in his earlier letters and conversations. To one friend he wrote that war would stop instantly if war meant death to generals as well as soldiers and if death "hovered impartially over every man, woman and child." He concluded by writing, "The only thing that will ever prevent nations from beginning war is terror." Baroness von Suttner quotes Nobel as having stated, "I wish I could produce a substance or machine of such frightful efficiency for wholesale devastation that wars should thereby become altogether impossible."

Perhaps Nobel was reflecting the influence of his compatriot John Ericsson whom he had met in New York and who had said, "The art of war is still in its infancy; brought to perfection, it will force men to live in peace."

But the march of events forced the inevitable conclusion upon Nobel, that more perfect weapons would lead not to a peace of terror, but to bigger and more terrible wars. There is no record of his mentioning the horror theory of peace subsequent to 1892. M. E. Schneider-Bonnet published a recollection of conversations held with Nobel in 1895, and quoted the inventor of dynamite as having said :

My hope was that the terrible effects of dynamite would keep men from war, but now I see to my utter dismay that my life work amounts to nothing . . . High explosives will not deter men from waging war . . . Nobody will profit by my inventions except manufacturers of war materials, some generals, admirals and diplomats. Mankind on the whole will be the loser.

Realizing the fallacy of his former theories, but unwilling to abandon his vision of peace, Nobel was forced to turn to more conventional approaches to peace, such as arbitration and collective security. It may be imagined that Nobel did not feel very comfortable in these spheres because of his low opinion of governments and his still lower opinion of the people.

Although he termed himself a social-democrat, but a moderate one, he saw little value in free speech or a free press and believed that "giving the same suffrage rights to the educated and the uneducated inevitably leads to corruption and all kinds of other abuses." He saw "the governments as striving to calm the idiotic passions of a public roused by pernicious newspapers." He said, "If the nations are still nearly mad, the governments are no more than half-mad."

Yet, in his political writings, he enumerated three forms of government : Hereditary autocracy, constitutional monarchy, and republic, all equally bad. He called parliament a "House of Bluster and Braggarts," and stated that "the main occupation in it is to talk and, in some countries, to take bribes. Its members are, therefore, recruited chiefly from lawyers and other red-tape parasites."

He hired a former Turkish diplomat, Gregoire Aristarchi Bey, to advance the cause of peace by urging arbitration upon the governments and the peoples through the press and other means. It was Nobel's idea to have each government agree by compact to a cooling off period of one year, during which it would agree not to resort to arms in settlement of disputes. During this period, if a dispute should arise, seconds would be appointed, as in a duel, to make a preliminary inquiry to determine if grounds existed for the peaceable arbitration of the dispute. It was hoped that this cooling off period could be extended from year to year until the climate of peace could be established. The relationship with Aristarchi Bey lasted only one year when it became evident that no nation-state would agree in advance to arbitrate in a world of fear and insecurity, where the timing of the initial attack and the state of preparedness were of first importance. Wilhelm II best expressed this reservation when some years later he refused to sign the Bryan arbitration treaty, stating, "Our strength lies in being always prepared for war at a second's notice. We will not resign that advantage and give our enemies time to prepare."

Nobel, in essence, advocated what later became Article XVI of the Covenant of the League of Nations when he wrote to Baroness von Suttner:

We could and ought to reach the point where all States will mutually pledge themselves to fight whatever State attacks another. This would make war impossible and would force even the most brutal and senseless Power to address itself to a tribunal or to keep quiet.

He thus favored:

a convention by which the governments engage jointly to defend any country that is attacked. A peace ensured by the power of the united armies would inspire respect in any disturber of the peace and would soon lead to a relaxation.

In a letter dated January 7, 1893, to Baroness von Suttner from Paris wherein he first outlined his ideas for a peace prize, Nobel had written:

I do not refer to disarmament which can be achieved only by very slow degrees. I do not even necessarily refer to compulsory arbitration between the nations; but what I have in view is that we should soon achieve the result and undoubtedly a practical one—that all states should bind themselves absolutely to take action against the first aggressor.

It would seem that Nobel, in the last decade of his life, after a lifetime of thought and contemplation on the subject of peace, lacked a definite idea as to how peace might be accomplished. This uncertainty is reflected in the general terms of his will. Nobel had written to his dear friend, the baroness, "Inform me, convince me, then I will do something great for the movement." In replying to a request for money from the baroness, Nobel exhibited his own lack of a program while chiding her similar lack. He wrote:

What you need, I think, is not money but a program. Good intentions alone will not assure peace—nor, I might say, will great dinners with great speeches. You must have an acceptable plan to lay before the well-intentioned governments. To demand disarmament means simply to make yourself ridiculous without gaining anything. By calling for the immediate establishment of a court of arbitration you hurl yourself at a thousand prejudices and turn every man of ambition into an obstructionist. To achieve success, one has to be content with more modest beginnings.

The realist Nobel told his friend, M. Schneider-Bonnet, "I am pessimistic about mankind. I greatly fear that the perpetual peace of which Kant has spoken will be preceded by the peace of the cemetery . . . The twentieth century will be an epoch of great unrest."

Thus, burdened, if you will, by a guilt complex, and realizing that his life work contributed to war and militarism, which was the most dangerous menace to the personal freedom that he valued so highly, Nobel, with characteristic stubbornness, persisted in his quest for peace. In the words of Albert Einstein :

Nobel's soul might have been depressed because his most important creative achievement benefited those powers which, as a human being, he considered hostile and destructive.

It is not certain when the idea of a peace prize first occurred to the inventor of dynamite. Baroness von Suttner, no doubt, was a very great influence in this regard, but it is doubtful whether she should receive the entire credit. Alfred Nobel was a man of independent and searching mind, and was not easily led down a designated path.

Nobel first mentioned the idea of a peace fund in an interview he gave in 1890 :

I intend to leave after my death a large fund for the promotion of the peace idea, but I am skeptical as to its results. The savants will write excellent volumes. There will be laureates. But wars will continue just the same until the force of circumstances renders them impossible.

In the January 7, 1893 letter to Baroness von Suttner, Nobel wrote :

Dear Friend : May the new year prove prosperous to you and to the noble campaign which you are carrying on with so much power against human ignorance and ferocity. I should like to allot part of my fortune to the formation of a prize fund to be distributed in every period of five years (we may say six times, for if we have failed at the end of thirty years to reform the present system we shall inevitably revert to barbarism). This prize would be awarded to the man or woman who had done most to advance the idea of general peace in Europe.

The first drafts of Nobel's will were written in 1889 and 1893. The latter contained a bequest to the Austrian Society of the Friends of Peace (the organization of which Baroness von Suttner was president) "to be expended in the promotion of pacific ideas." That draft also created a fund for the awarding of prizes to persons stipulating that it was the testator's wish "that such persons should be especially considered as are successful in word and deed in combatting the peculiar prejudices still cherished by peoples and governments against the inauguration of a European peace tribunal."

The final draft of the will is dated November 27, 1895. It reads :

I, the undersigned Alfred Bernhard Nobel, hereby do declare after mature consideration my final will regarding the property I may leave at the time of my death to be as follows—

The whole of my remaining realizable property shall be dealt with as follows :

The capital, which is to be invested by the executors in stable securities, shall constitute a fund, the annual interest on which shall be awarded as prizes to those persons who during the previous year have rendered the greatest services to mankind. The interest shall be divided into five equal parts : One part shall be awarded to the person who has made the most important discovery or invention in the realm of physics; one part to the person who has made the most important chemical discovery or improvement; one part to the person who has made the most important discovery in the realm of physiology or medicine; one part to the person who has produced the outstanding work of literature, idealistic in character; and one part to the person who shall have done the most or the best work for fraternity among nations, for the abolition or reduction of standing armies and for the holding and promotion of peace congresses.

The prizes . . . shall be awarded . . . for the promotion of peace by a committee of five persons to be selected by the Norwegian Storting. It is my express wish that the prizes be distributed without regard to nationality, so that the prize may be awarded in every case to the worthiest, whether he be Scandinavian or not.

Thus, again in the words of Albert Einstein, "his testament appears as a heroic attempt to place his life work at the feet of the good and life-giving gods, and in this way to dissolve a painful discord in his soul — a deed of the most noble self-liberation."

Here is the lasting memorial created by the man who had written, "I have no family to furnish the only kind of survival that concerns us, no friends for my affection or enemies for my malice." Rather, the bequest of Alfred Nobel was made to mankind to further its development, promote its welfare and serve its idealistic purposes. It is probably the most magnificent gift a private person has ever had both the desire and the ability to make. Nobel succeeded in his wish "to create a spiritual family which, down through the years, shall be enabled to give their best services to humanity through the agency of my money."

In the words of one commentator, "Could we have believed it possible that Mammon, Mammon sprung from dynamite should be so ennobled?"

3 Nurtured in Norway

The probate of the last will and testament of Alfred Nobel developed into one of the greatest estate contests of any age. Several countries claimed jurisdiction over the assets. Miss Hess and the children of Nobel's brothers claimed their shares. The loose construction of the will added to its vagueness and the lack of compliance with legal requirements all combined to complicate the issues.

Because the will, consisting of four handwritten pages, was in Swedish, because it had been deposited for safekeeping in a Swedish bank, because Nobel had returned to Stockholm regularly to visit his mother while she was alive, and because Nobel had never renounced his Swedish citizenship and domicile, the will was entered for probate before the Karlskoga County Court, in Sweden. The able executors smuggled the Nobel securities out of France and other countries. A settlement was reached with Miss Hess. Nobel's nephew, Emanuel, persuaded the family to withdraw their claims. The various Swedish cultural and scientific institutions accepted their responsibilities under the will for the literary and scientific awards. The Norwegian Storting on April 26, 1897, accepted its responsibility for the peace prize. The necessary regulatory statutes were promulgated, and the Nobel Foundation was set up to administer the fund. The entire structure was ratified by King Oscar II.

Why was the Norwegian Storting, and not the Swedish Riksdag, selected for the honor of awarding the most coveted prize—the peace prize? Here is another riddle and one can only speculate. After having been united with Denmark since 1381, Norway, in 1814, formed the Swedish-Norwegian Union, with a common king and common administration of foreign and consular affairs. Because of the large Norwegian merchant marine, and because she felt that consular affairs were not being adequately handled by Swedish representatives, the Storting in 1892 passed legislation providing for a separate Norwegian consular system. This law was promptly vetoed by the Swedish Crown, and the consular and other similar issues agitated the two countries until 1905. On June 6 of that year, after an all-night session, the Storting voted to dissolve the Union. This decision was ratified by the people in a plebiscite held August 13, 1905, by a vote of 368,208–184. The crown was offered to Prince Charles of Denmark who ascended to the throne of Norway as King Haakon VII. Could it be that Nobel had been sympathetic to the Norwegian cause?

The Storting was originally constituted in 1814. It functions as both a unicameral and bicameral legislative body. Its members are elected for a three year term. They, thereupon, select one-quarter of their number for a sort of upper house called the Lagting, while the remainder constitute the lower house called the Odelsting. Although most of the business is transacted by the Storting acting as a single body, certain specified matters require bicameral procedures.

Perhaps because of the influence of English Quakers who had settled in the Stavanger area during the Napoleonic wars, there had long been a strong peace tradition in Norway. The Storting was the first national assembly to go on record in favor of the settlement of international disputes through the orderly processes of arbitration. By a vote of 89–24, the Storting on March 5, 1890, adopted an address to the King stating that :

The idea of arbitration as applied to the relations between peoples is beginning to win favor. Just as law and justice have long ago replaced fist-law in disputes between man and man, so the idea of settling disputes among peoples and nations is making its way with irresistible strength. More and more, war appears to the general consciousness as a vestige of prehistoric barbarism and a curse to the human race. The King is, therefore, requested to try to arrange with foreign powers treaties to decide by means of arbitration, disputes which may arise between Norway and these powers.

Also, the Storting was the first official body to have attempted to organize an international peace union, and to have appropriated funds for international peace work. It was an active sponsor of the Inter-Parliamentary Union.

Once having accepted its role as the arbiter of the Nobel peace prize, the next step for the Storting was to proceed with the adoption of rules for the selection and tenure of the Nobel peace prize committee. Beyond stipulating " a committee of five persons to be selected by the Norwegian Storting," the provisions of the Nobel will had set forth no qualifications for the members of the committee. Should they be members of the Storting? Should they be Norwegians? Or might they be foreigners in view of the will's mandate that nationality be ignored in the awarding of prizes?

Ferdinand C. Prahl contended that the committee should be international. As was to be expected, this proposal attracted little support. John T. Lund, a member of the aggressive Left, voiced the prevailing opinion of his legislative colleagues. He declared that the suggestion to appoint foreigners to the committee could not be regarded "otherwise than almost as an insult to Nobel's memory that we Norwegians who have received this honorable mandate, this distinguished commission, which has brought a flattering attention to our fatherland from elsewhere in Europe, should now hand ourselves that vote of lack of confidence which a decision to include foreigners would imply."

Having determined that the committee should be Norwegian, the next question was whether it should be a standing committee of the Storting, as advocated by Björnstjerne Björnson, or one more representative of the Norwegian people. The regulations, as finally adopted in August, 1897, provided for a more representative committee. Its members were to be elected at the last session of each Storting term, that is, once every three years. To give a revolving character to the committee, two of the first members chosen were to serve three years while the others were to serve the full six-year term.

The first committee chosen was composed of three politicians of the Left: John T. Lund, Johannes Steen and Jorgen Lovland; one poet of the Left, Björnstjerne Björnson; and one neutral scholar, Bernhard Getz. Getz, a Christiana jurist, was the first president of the committee.

The regulations provided that nominations for the peace prize had to be submitted before February 1st of each year, together with supporting papers and documents. The nominees may be forwarded by members and former members of the Nobel committee of the Storting, advisers appointed by the Norwegian Nobel Institute, members of the various national parliaments, members of the governments of the different nation-states, members of the Inter-Parliamentary Union, members of the International Court of Arbitration at the Hague, and members of the Council of the International Peace Bureau. Also, members and associates of the Institute of International Law, university professors of political science, law, history, and philosophy, and persons who had previously received the Nobel peace prize.

Article Four of the Rules prescribes that the award may only be made to a living person with the exception that a nominee might still be considered if death occurred between the nomination and award dates. Under this rule, Erik A. Karlfeldt received the literature prize posthumously in 1931 and Dag Hammarskjold the peace prize in 1961, while Count Folke Bernadotte was disqualified for the peace prize in 1948. However, an artificial person, such as an organization or institution, was declared eligible. And the prize might be distributed among three recipients. When in 1901, the first prize was split between Jean Henri Dunant, and Frédéric Passy, Baroness von Suttner commented, "I observe that the division of the prize corresponds neither to the letter of the will nor to the testator's intention, which I know well."

Under Article Two of the Rules, consideration may be given to works of peace performed in the previous year, or to earlier works of peace whose significance later becomes evident. The committee usually meets twice a year : in the spring to review the nominations, and in November to either make the award or withhold it. But, the prize must be awarded at least once every five years.

To assist the committee in its deliberations and to handle administrative matters, the Norwegian Nobel Institute was established in 1902. The Institute follows the development of international relations and works for peaceful fellowship between nations through its publications, its lectures, its meetings, and its library. Twenty-five per cent of the annual income is set aside for administrative expenses. Christian C. Lange, laureate for 1921, said in a magazine article, written in 1907, while he was secretary to the Nobel committee, "Thus twenty-five per cent is paid as an insurance premium that the seventy-five per cent is worthily bestowed." He explained that the objective of the Institute was :

to follow the development of international relations, especially the work for pacific settlement of them, and thereby counsel the committee with regard to the distribution of the prize. The Institute shall moreover work to promote mutual friendship and respect, peaceful intercourse, justice and fraternity among nations.

With the ground rules established, Gustav Vigeland was commissioned to sculpt a Nobel medallion carrying the image of Alfred Nobel on one side, and depicting on the reverse side, three men joined in the embrace of brotherhood bearing the legend, "Pro Pace Et Fraternitate Gentium." The stage is now set for the chosen laureate to proceed in solemn procession down the aisle of the Storting (later the Hall of the Norwegian Nobel Institute or the assembly hall of the University of Oslo), to receive in the presence of the King of Norway, his gold medal, and a check, (depending upon the rate of exchange), varying between $30,802–$54,600.

4 Jus, Ergo Pax

The twentieth century opened on an optimistic and hopeful note. The usually dour Alfred Nobel on November 21, 1896, had written in his last letter to Baroness von Suttner: "I am enchanted to see that the peace movement is gaining ground. That is due to the civilizing of the masses."

In her turn, the Baroness was to say in her Nobel speech in December, 1905:

What the immediate future will bring in our field must in importance and effect rise above the modest and hidden beginnings. The movement has gone far beyond the circle of private societies, resolutions and the individual effort; it has become a fight for a world outlook and a world order. From the hands of the so-called apostles it has passed into the hand of those in power and into the minds of the awaking peoples. It is a process taking its course with the force of nature, a slowly growing reorganization of the world. The next stage lies before us as something quite concrete, quite attainable—the formation of a United States of Europe. Terrible warlike relapses may yet occur, but the future will confirm my faith : the peace of nations is on the way.

Yes, there was a peace ferment in the air. Beginning with 1889, an International Peace Congress was held annually in a different city — Paris, London, Rome, Berne, Budapest, Chicago, Boston, Milan and elsewhere. In 1891, a "Bureau Internationale permanente de la paix" was established at

Berne, to give continuity to the work of the peace congresses. Similarly, beginning in 1889, the Inter-Parliamentary Union also began to hold annual international conferences, also establishing a permanent information office called the "Bureau Interparlementaire."

Most important of all was the action of Czar Nicholas II of all the Russians. Following in the tradition of Czar Alexander I, who had proposed in 1804 that no war be begun "until all the resources which the mediation of a third party could offer have been exhausted," he issued on August 24, 1898, a magnificent appeal to all the nations of the world, inviting them to assemble at the Hague, in order to organize a world of law and order. Whether the Czar was influenced by Baroness von Suttner's book, *Die Waffen Nieder,* or by his lack of funds to compete in the arms race doesn't matter. The important thing is that 26 states sent representatives to the First Hague Peace Conference which was held from May 18, to July 29, 1899. Nothing was done about disarmament, despite the warning of the Czar. If the pace of arming "were prolonged," he declared, "it would inevitably lead to the very cataclysm which it is desired to avert, the horrors of which make every thinking man shudder in advance." Although compulsory arbitration was rejected, hopeful conventions were adopted to establish a permanent court of arbitration and to humanize the rules of war.

A Second Hague Peace Conference was to follow in 1907, where the machinery for voluntary arbitration was enlarged, the rules of war further humanized, and conventions adopted setting forth the rights of neutrals, and regulating the actions for collection of international debts.

The first decade of the twentieth century was not quite free of wars. The Boer War, The Russian-Japanese War, the Boxer Rebellion, the Tripolitan War, and the two Balkan Wars disturbed the relative tranquility of the era. But, at the same time, over one hundred treaties providing for arbitration of international disputes were being filed with the Permanent Court at the Hague. During a good portion of this period, the Peace Palace was under construction in the same city as a tangible symbol of the hope of humanity to substitute the rule of law for that of war. If any slogan can be adopted as representative of the spirit of an age, the watchword for the Hague period of good feeling would be "Jus Ergo Pax" — Law, therefore, peace. So, convinced of the inevitability of Darwinian linear progress toward perfection, mankind entered with hope and confidence upon the threshold of the twentieth century.

This was the international setting for the announcement on December 10, 1901, by the Nobel committee of the Norwegian Storting of the first winners of the Nobel peace prize. The committee had compromised by bestowing recognition on each of the two outstanding lines of peace work. One school of thought contended that only through works of charity and humanitarianism could a foundation be formed for reverence of life and, therefore, for peace. The other school of thought claimed that peacefare had to be waged like any other struggle, and that only the professional fighters deserved recognition.

Of the two laureates for 1901, Jean Henri Dunant (1828–1910), represented the humanitarians and Frédéric Passy (1822–1912), the professionals. The work of Dunant, founder of the Red Cross, will be discussed in a later chapter.

Passy qualified as a true professional — he was universally hailed as "le doyen des pacifistes." Baroness von Suttner, who was in a position to know, commented, "The oldest, the most deserving and the most highly regarded of all, the prize was a great satisfaction to us — only the whole amount should have gone to him." It is indicative of the public status of professional pacifists to note that he was also known as the national bore.

Passy was 79 years old at the time of the award. Trained in the law, he had served as a government clerk for several years before turning to journalism, and then to lecturing in the social sciences at the University of Montpellier. Intellectually, young Passy had been influenced by the free trade theories of Richard Cobden but his thinking became crystalized during the Crimean War. It was then that he perceived the difference between the calloused public reaction to the horrors of the man-made catastrophe of war, and their sympathetic reaction to a natural catastrophe, such as the Loire flood.

Passy resolved to "make war on war." In a letter written to "Le Temps" in 1867, he suggested formation of a French peace society. The response was so great that the "Ligue internationale et permanente de la paix" was formed the same year, with Passy as the general secretary. The work of this organization was interrupted by the Franco-Prussian War but resumed after 1871 as the "Société francaise des amis de la paix." It was reconstituted in 1889 as the "Société francaise pour l'arbitrage entre nations" with Passy as president.

In 1871, Passy had published an appeal, *Revanche ou Relèvement,* in which he pleaded for a real peace settlement between France and Germany. It was based on voluntary arbitration and national sovereignty, with Alsace-Lorraine as an independent neutral area. He represented the Seine department in the Chamber of Deputies from 1881 to 1899. As such, he was instrumental with Sir William Randal Cremer in forming the Inter-Parliamentary Union in 1888.

Passy was host to, and presided over, the first International Peace Congress which was held in Paris in 1889. A lecture he delivered in 1891 illustrates the immediacy of Passy's awareness of the perennial state of Europe. He said :

I need hardly describe the present state of Europe to you. The entire able-bodied population is preparing to massacre one another; though no one, it is true, wants to attack and everybody protests his love of peace and determination to maintain it, yet the whole world feels that it only requires some unforeseen incident, some unpreventable accident for the spark to fall in a flash, as Lord Palmerston put it, on these heaps of inflammable material which are being foolishly piled up in the fields and on the highways and blow all Europe sky-high.

Passy was a sensitive man who burst into tears when he was shown a photograph by a *New York Times* reporter of a wasted and disfigured Boer child. He summed up his life's work in an 1896 article: "I have labored unceasingly in the cause of peace for thirty years. The future shall belong to peace, to work and to arbitration."

The prize for 1902 was divided between Elie Ducommun (1833–1906), and Charles Albert Gobat (1843–1914). Ducommun was the first international civil servant, author, orator, and administrator, who performed the day to day ministrations required to keep the faint flicker of peace alive. Ducommun rose to eminence in many positions. Beginning as a teacher in the public schools of Geneva, he achieved an important position in the "Geneva Departement de l'instruction publique" and in the municipal government of that city — becoming Vice-Chancellor, and then Chancellor of Geneva. Ducommun also became the editor-in-chief of the *Revue de Geneve*.

Moving to Berne, Ducommun assumed the editorship of *Der Fortschritt*. There he served on the Grand Council of Berne, was translator to the national council, and became secretary-general of the Jura-Simplon Railroad. He had conducted the press organ *Les Etats-Unis d'Europe* for Passy's "Ligue international de la paix."

The third international peace congress held in Rome, in 1891, resolved, at the suggestion of Frederik Bajer, to set up an administrative and information office to collect information about institutes, organizations and individuals working for peace, and to improve contacts among them. The office was instructed to examine and prepare material for discussion at the sessions of the international peace congresses; to organize the congresses themselves; to implement its resolutions, and to keep informed on peace publications and international events, especially arbitration. The natural choice for secretary-general was Elie Ducommun. The "Bureau internationale permanente de la paix" began its activities at Berne on December 1, 1891. Without pay and almost without assistance, Ducommun managed to keep the Bureau operating as a vital force in the world peace movement.

Upon the death of Ducommun in 1906, his position with the Bureau internationale passed down to Charles Albert Gobat. Trained in the law, like so many of the laureates of the Hague period, Gobat had taught law at the Sorbonne, and had practiced in Berne and Delément. He held several government offices, including that of superintendent of instruction, before becoming a member of the Swiss federal council in 1890. As a member of the council, he was instrumental in adopting the agreement to submit all disputes between Switzerland and other countries to the Permanent Court of Arbitration.

Gobat was president of the fourth conference of the Inter-Parliamentary Union held at Berne in 1892, and was one of the founders of the "Bureau interparlementaire de la paix." Like the "Bureau internationale permanente de la paix," the "Bureau interparlementaire" was established as a permanent information and administrative office. Its function was to list the parliamentary groups of the various countries, to initiate formation of groups where none existed, to act as a link between national groups, and to keep abreast of activities in the peace movement and in the field of arbitration. Gobat was the first secretary-general of this Bureau, and he served as such for twenty years, like Ducommun, without remuneration, and almost unaided.

The prize winner for 1903, Sir William Randal Cremer (1838–1908), was also associated with the Inter-Parliamentary

Union. We have already noted that he and Passy were in 1888 the founders of this organization. Cremer served as its secretary from 1889. Beginning with representatives of only England and France, this oldest of all world organizations now boasts membership by legislators of sixty-four nations. The goal of the Union is to unite members of all parliaments in order to promote, peace and cooperation, "particularly by means of a universal organization."

Cremer was the first of the very few labor leaders who have won the coveted peace prize. He had gone to work at the age of 12 as a pitch boy in a shipyard. He was later apprenticed as a carpenter, and worked at this trade until 1860, when he became one of the founders of the Amalgamated Society of Carpenters and Joiners. Cremer was chosen secretary of the British section of the First International, but resigned because of dissension over his non-socialist convictions and because his pacifist program was turned down by the Geneva conference of the International in 1866.

Although Cremer led the campaign for the nine hour day and conducted many strikes for his union, his convictions as a Quaker persuaded him that, "warfare between those who are dependent on each other is madness." He, therefore, came to the conclusion that the only practical answer to industrial and international strife was arbitration.

During the Franco-Prussian War of 1870–1871, Cremer formed a working men's committee for the advocacy of neutrality. This committee developed into the Workmen's Peace Association, and was later renamed the International Arbitration League. Cremer was editor of its publication, *The Arbitrator,* and secretary of the League until his death. He agitated actively, but in vain, for an arbitration treaty between the United Kingdom and the United States, making three stumping tours of the latter country. Cremer donated the bulk of his Nobel prize money to the International Arbitration League.

Cremer was elected to represent the Haggerston district of London in the House of Commons from 1885 to 1895, and 1900 to 1908, and he was knighted by King Edward VII in 1908. It is typical of the home-spun nature of the man that he appeared for the dubbing ceremony in his frock coat, rather than in the prescribed fancy dress suit complete with sword.

It was wholly natural for an age whose slogan was "Jus, Ergo Pax" to award the 1904 prize to the "Institut de droit international" of Ghent. This institute was founded in 1873, in the tradition of the great Grotius, by G. Rolin-Jaquemyns, T. M. C. Asser, J. K. Blumtschle, G. Magnier, and F. Lieber as a private association of prominent scholars of all nations for the study and codification of international law. The academy functions through sixty "membres effectifs" and sixty "membres associes" who carry out their work through periodic congresses, publications, and the regular *Revue de droit international*.

The Institute worked out general rules for certain sections of private international law. It also formulated codifications of maritime law; of extradition rules; of uniform treatment of marriage, divorce and trusteeship; of rights of citizenship; of rights of neutral countries in wartime; and of treatment of private property during wartime. During the 1880 annual meeting at Oxford, a resolution was passed inviting governments to include in their legislation rules formulated by the Institute. Most of the countries of the world took this advice, and their various statute books are a tribute to the constructive work of the Institute.

The academy also discussed urgent international problems and suggested ways and means of solving them. For instance, in the case of the Suez Canal controversy, the Institute proposed at its 1875 meeting that the canal be declared neutral and placed under international protection.

During the Russo-Turkish War, the Institute issued an appeal to the belligerents in 1877 reminding them of the existence of rules of warfare. A "Handbook of the rules and observances of warfare" was issued in 1880 stating:

War occupies a considerable place in the pages of history and it is not reasonable to suppose that man will be capable of breaking away from it so soon, despite the protests it arouses and the disgust it inspires. For it proves to be the only possible solution to the conflicts which jeopardize the existence, the freedom and the vital interests of nations. But the gradual raising of accepted standards and morals should be reflected in the way war is conducted. It is up to the civilized nations, as has so rightly been said, to try to restrict the horrors of war while at the same time recognizing its inexorable demands.

A set of regulations for arbitration of international disputes was one of the first tasks of the Institute, and the earliest formulation dates back to 1875. The Institute was charged with most of the burden of preparing for the First International Arbitration Conference, at the Hague in 1899.

Unfortunately for mankind, the law did not go forth out of Zion, nor did the word of the Lord from Jerusalem. Chang Hsin-hai's description of international law, "like a bee with the sting extracted which does not hurt, having no vital hold on the conscience of nations" is still a truism.

We have already encountered the 1905 laureate many times in the course of this narrative. The next chapter will be devoted to the romance of Baroness von Suttner.

In 1906 the prize was awarded for the first time to an American. Theodore Roosevelt (1858–1919), President of the United States. He was selected in recognition of his efforts to bring the Russo-Japanese War to an end through the Treaty of Portsmouth in 1905. Here was a departure from the old pattern in that the award was made to a statesman, not because

of continuous work in the service of peace, but for an isolated
act. The role played by statesmen generally, and Theodore
Roosevelt in particular, in the quest for peace will be discussed
in a subsequent chapter.

The 1907 award was divided between Ernesto Teodoro
Moneta (1833–1918), and Louis Renault (1843–1918). Moneta, the president of the "Societa internazionale per la pace :
Unione Lombarda," which he had founded in 1887 along the
lines of the International Arbitration and Peace Association of
Hodgson Pratt, had presided over the fifteenth annual peace
congress held at Milan in 1906. As a boy of fifteen he had
participated in "le cinque giornate," the revolt of the people
of Milan against Austria. After Austria crushed the uprising,
Moneta fled to Piedmont where he entered the military
academy of Ivrea. When the war broke out again in 1859,
Moneta and his four brothers enlisted in the corps of the
mountain troops organized by Garibaldi. He remained in the
regular army until 1866 after the unification of Italy.

Leaving the army, he took up journalism and became editor
of *Il Secolo,* a democratic newspaper published in Milan. In
1898 he began publication of the organ of the Unione Lombarda *La Vita Internazionale.* Moneta supported disarmament and arbitration. After winning the prize, he supported
Italian occupation of Libya in 1911, and Italian entry in
World War I.

Renault, one of the most eminent jurists of his day, was
largely responsible for the positive results of the Conference
of Private International Law of 1904 and the revised Red
Cross Convention of 1906. He had taught Roman, commercial,
and international law in the Universities of Dijon and Paris,
and in the Sorbonne. He was among the first members (1875),
of the "Institut de droit international," and among the first
judges (1899), of the Permanent Court of Arbitration at the
Hague. Renault was appointed juris consultant to the French

foreign ministry in 1890, and represented France at both Hague conferences in 1899 and 1907, at the London naval conference of 1908–1909, at the conference of private international law, and various other international conferences and inquiries.

Renault's talents as a jurist were universally acknowledged and he was selected as arbitrator in many famous international cases. He was arbitrator for the Japanese House Tax case of 1905, the Casa Blanca case of 1909, the Sawarker case of 1911, the Carthage case of 1913, and the Manouba case of 1913. Here was a truly distinguished man of the law.

The 1908 peace prize also was divided — again between two professionals of the peace movement: Klas Pontus Arnoldson (1844–1916) and Fredrik Bajer (1837–1922), the first Scandinavians to be so honored. The award to Arnoldson was not favorably received in his native Sweden. Because Arnoldson had sympathized with Norway on the secession question, the Stockholm Dagbladet termed the award a "bloody outrage against Sweden," a "dishonor to every Swedish man who takes pride in his national honor," and a "misuse of the prize to insult Sweden."

The designation of Arnoldson may, in part, be traced to the influential position of Björnstjerne Björnson on the Nobel committee of the Storting. Arnoldson, Bajer, and Björnson were active in the movement to set up a Nordens Fristatssam fund (Free State Government of the North), a sort of romantic pan-Scandinavian republic of the North. They felt that the big nations had come into possession of too much "unjust territory" to be interested in a genuine democratic and peaceful universe. The initiative for world peace, therefore, must, of necessity, come from the smaller states. It was hoped that if a few smaller countries formed a small federation in order to apply the principles of arbitration and disarmament, this area of calm would take root, and grow.

Björnson, as a popular poet and winner of the Nobel prize for literature in 1903, had given wide publicity to the works of Arnoldson. He had written an introduction to the latter's pacifist novel, *Mary Magdalene,* declaring that war, instead of being held in honor, must lose its glamor "like brass that is not to be polished." Arnoldson was further identified with the Norwegian cause by his advocacy of the arbitration address to the King by the Storting in 1890. He toured Sweden and Norway speaking in favor of the principles of the petition, and was popularly called the father of the address.

Arnoldson worked as a railway clerk and had risen to the post of stationmaster. His interest in the peace cause having been originally awakened by the Danish-Prussian and Austrian War of 1864, Arnoldson finally quit the railroad in 1880 to devote himself entirely to the cause. He took up newspaper work and became a publicist and agitator. He was elected to the Riksdag in 1882, and helped form the "Svenska Freds-och Skiljedomsförening" (Swedish Peace and Arbitration Union) in 1883. He also campaigned for other causes, such as religious liberty, and equality of women before the law. "How beautiful upon the mountains are the feet of him that bringeth good tidings that publisheth peace."

We have already seen how the third international peace congress, based upon a suggestion originally made by Bajer in 1890, at the second congress in London, had established the "Bureau internationale permanents de la paix." Bajer was chosen as its first president, and he served from 1891 to 1907, when he became honorary president. We have also reviewed his advocacy of a "Nordens Fristatssamfund." Based upon his experience as a lieutenant of dragoons in the 1864 war of Denmark against Prussia and Austria, Bajer was convinced that Nordic security lay, not in armaments and fortifications, but in international recognition of a Scandinavian neutrality similar to that of Switzerland. Thus, in a series of travel letters which he wrote for publication in 1886, Bajer ended each letter with the Cato-like admonition : "For the rest I am of the opinion that the fortifications of Copenhagen should be destroyed."

After his Army service, Bajer studied languages and worked as a translator and teacher. He devoted himself to politics and the peace movement. In 1869 he assisted in founding the first Liberal association in Copenhagen, and in 1872 he was elected as a left-wing Liberal member of the Folketing, where he served until 1895. In 1882 he was one of the founders of the Dansk Fredsforening (Danish Peace Union) and served as its first president from 1882 to 1891. Bajer was active in organizing the first Scandinavian peace conference in 1885, and in founding the Danish Inter-Parliamentary Union in 1907. Bajer was a lifetime advocate of arbitration of international disputes and of the emancipation of women.

The year 1909 saw another division of the award — between Auguste Marie Francois Beernaert (1829–1912), and Paul Balluet, Baron D' Estournelles de Constant de Rebecque (1852–1924).

We have alluded many times to the Inter-Parliamentary Union — Beernaert served as its president for many years. He also had been trained in the law, and he served as president of the International Law Association for more than 35 years. Beernaert devoted most of his life to public service, beginning in 1874 with his election to the Belgian Chamber of Deputies as a member of the Clerical Party. He joined the government in that year as minister of public works, a portfolio which he held until 1878. In 1884 he became prime minister and minister of finance, positions he held for ten years. In his last year of office, he was instrumental in enacting constitutional reforms including universal suffrage and the list system of election. Beernaert was president of the Chamber of Deputies from 1895 to 1899, and headed both Belgian delegations to the Hague conferences. In a later chapter we will discuss Beernaert's position on international matters as a member of the Belgian government.

Baron d'Estournelles also was identified with the Inter-Parliamentary Union, having been one of the leaders of the French group.

In preparation for a career in the diplomatic service, he had studied oriental languages and traveled widely in the Orient. Once in the foreign service of France, his experiences there convinced him that the conventional methods of professional diplomacy were incapable of bringing about peace. Thereafter, he worked both within, and outside, the formal governmental framework.

He was elected to the Chamber of Deputies from the Sarthe department in 1895, and to the Senate in 1904. He was a member of the French delegation to both Hague conferences, and served as a judge of the Permanent Court of Arbitration at the Hague.

In 1902, he persuaded President Theodore Roosevelt to refer the dispute between the United States and Mexico to the Hague Tribunal. In 1903, he headed a French parliamentary delegation to the British parliament in a bid for the adoption of voluntary arbitration by the two governments. Also in 1903, he founded a Franco-German friendship association in Munich. In 1905, he was one of the founders and became the president of the "Ligue de la conciliation internationale." In 1909, he lectured in the Prussian House of Peers on the "Franco-German rapprochement as a basis for world peace." He was among the pioneers in the search for a European Union.

As the organ for the Conciliation Internationale, in 1905 Baron d'Estournelles founded the pamphlet *International Conciliation*. Publication of this periodical was later taken over by the Carnegie Endowment for International Peace and

Baron d'Estournelles became the head of the Endowment's organization in Europe. He continued his efforts on behalf of international conciliation for many years after he received the Nobel peace prize. For example, in 1921 he made a laudable, but vain, attempt to have the French Inter-Parliamentary Union group meet jointly with the German section.

The precedent set in 1904, of awarding the prize to an artificial person was followed in 1910 when the "Bureau internationale permanente de la paix" was named. The initial organization of the Bureau as the administrative link to keep the lamp of peace lit between sessions of the international peace congresses has already been discussed. By 1910, the one-man organization of Ducommun and Gobat had grown into the clearing house of the pacifist organizations of the world, a combination of institutions, associations and individuals directed by a commission of 35 members from many nations.

The commission included such famous members as Henri Lafontaine, Lord Darby, Alfred Fried, Ludwig Quidde, Baroness von Suttner, Moneta, and Passy. The office had been moved from Berne to Geneva. Regular subventions were received from the governments of Switzerland, Denmark, Sweden, and Norway. A library of peace publications was established to preserve the archives of international peace gatherings, and to maintain an up-to-date bibliography. An *Annuaire du mouvement pacifiste* and *Correspondence bimenuelle* were published regularly.

The two prize winners in 1911 had little in common except their mutual desire for international amity. One, Tobias Michael Carel Asser (1838–1913), held the highest office his nation could offer to one not of royal blood, while the other, Alfred Hermann Fried (1864–1921), was accused of high treason by his native land, and lived in exile for many years.

Asser, a collaborator with Renault at many international law conferences, was another of the international lawyers who almost monopolized the prize during this period. After receiving his law degree at the University of Leyden, Asser in 1862 became professor of commercial and private international law at the University of Amsterdam. He was one of the founders in 1868 of the *Revue de droit international et de législation comparée* and in 1873, of the "Institut de droit international" which we have discussed elsewhere. On his initiative, the Dutch government summoned four conferences at the Hague for unification of international private law, in 1893, 1894, 1900 and 1904. Asser was in the chair at each of the sessions.

Asser's government service began in 1874, with his appointment as an adviser to the ministry of foreign affairs. In 1893, he was elected a member of the Dutch Council of State, later becoming prime minister and a member of the Privy Council. He represented the Netherlands at both Hague conferences, and was one of the foremost advocates of the Permanent Court of Arbitration to which he was himself appointed, in 1900.

Fried belonged to the line of publicists, "sounding brass and tinkling cymbals" which was later to include Carl von Ossietzky. As a bookseller in Vienna, he was inspired by Baroness von Suttner's great peace novel to begin publication of a monthly peace magazine, *Die Waffen Nieder*, and he even persuaded the Baroness to act as editor. The next year found him selling books in Berlin where he was one of the organizers of the "Deutsche Friedensgesellschaft" (German Peace Society). Two years later, he was in Stuttgart publishing the *Monatliche Friedenskorrespondenz*.

In 1899 Fried returned to Vienna to found the peace publication *Die Friedensworte,* a periodical still in existence although its headquarters had to be moved to Zurich in 1933. Because of his opposition to Austrian participation in World War I, he was forced to flee to Switzerland where he lived during the war years.

Fried frequently criticized the publicists who were employed as lackeys to beat the drums of war. He had written in 1901 in *Unter den weissen Fahne,* "The priests of Philistinism, the newspaper editors, had the pleasant task of mocking and making ridiculous the work of the Hague conference according to the spirit of their mandates. They performed that task." To counteract this influence, Fried was one of the founders of and general-secretary of the "Union internationale de la presse pour la paix."

To further the cause, in 1917 Fried published a collection of Baroness von Suttner's smaller pacifist writings. He also wrote the monumental work *Kriegstagebuch* (The Struggle to Prevent War). His writings on peace were designed to arouse interest in intellectual circles. He was opposed to the idea of disarmament because he believed that armaments and war were only symptons of the unhealthy state of international life, a condition caused by the absurd architecture of international anarchy, created by the existence of sovereign nation-states. These conditions could only be removed by the establishment of an effective international organization. Disarmament would then follow automatically.

The 1912 prize was awarded to another American, Elihu Root (1845–1937), in recognition of his efforts on behalf of arbitration of international disputes. The work of Root will be discussed in a later chapter.

The laureate for 1913, Henri Marie Lafontaine (1854–1943), was another international lawyer and the successor to Bajer as president of the "Bureau internationale permanente de la paix." One of the founders of that organization, he was the last president to hold office, serving from 1907 until his death. An expert on Richard Wagner and an alpinist, he was professor of international law at the Université Nouvelle in Brussels. He had founded the "Société Belge pour l'arbitrage et la Paix" in 1889, and had helped organize the sixth "Congres internationale de la Paix" at Anvers in 1894. In 1895, he was elected to the Belgian Senate as a Socialist representative for Liege, and later served on the Brussels council and the Belgian cabinet. Jointly, with Paul Otlet, Lafontaine in 1895 founded and became the director of the "Institut bibliographique international" as an exhaustive clearing house for pacifist literature. He also founded the review *Le vie internationale*, and in 1902 wrote a complete historical account of international arbitration cases from 1794 to 1900.

Again with Otlet, he founded in 1907, the "Bureau centrale des associations internationales" in Brussels, as a different sort of clearing house which is still in existence — for the registration and cooperation of international organizations. Now known as the Union of International Organizations, it was granted consultative status by the Economic and Social Council of the United Nations in 1951. The Union published its first yearbook of International Organizations in 1908–09; it described the 297 then existing international organizations. The 1964–65 edition covers 1,897 organizations.

Lafontaine was an active delegate at many Inter-Parliamentary conferences. He was one of the first to advocate a sort of Oxford Oath, where pacifists pledge themselves to refuse to take up arms in a war of aggression undertaken by their respective countries. At the nineteenth peace congress at Geneva in 1912, Lafontaine pushed to adoption a resolution against aerial warfare.

Lafontaine continued his efforts after he had won the Nobel peace prize. He was a member of the Belgian delegation to the Paris Peace Conference in 1919. When Belgium was represented at the First Assembly session of the League of Nations in 1920 and 1921 by a representative from each of the three major parties (Catholic, Liberal and Socialist), Lafontaine was the Socialist delegate.

Many of the concepts of the specialized agencies of the League of Nations, and of the League of Nations Institute for

Intellectual Cooperation may have come from the "Centre intellectual mundial" which had been founded by Lafontaine. Through the medium of this center, he had proposed a world school and university, a world library, an international auxiliary language, international offices for labor, trade, statistics and immigration, an international parliament, an international court of justice, and a central monetary office. Here was a true internationalist.

Thus ended the Hague period of hope. Except for the 1917 grant to the International Red Cross of Geneva, the Nobel peace prize was not to be awarded again until 1919. To quote Viscount Edward Grey of Fallodon :

The lamps are going out all over Europe : we shall not see them lit again in our lifetime.

5 Peace Bertha

Upon notification that he had been awarded the first Nobel peace prize in 1901, Dunant dispatched the following letter to Baroness von Suttner: "This prize, gracious lady, is your work: for through your instrumentality Herr Nobel became devoted to the peace movement and at your suggestion became its promoter."

The award of the Nobel peace prize to Bertha von Suttner (1843–1914) in 1905 was a nostalgic occasion. Many workers in the cause of peace were of the opinion that the final will of Alfred Nobel had been drafted to fit the Baroness. There was a good deal of dismay, therefore, when her name was passed over by the committee of the Storting on four successive years. Thereupon, Emanuel Nobel, the nephew who had refused to join the suit to break the will, felt compelled to intervene. He called upon committee member Björnson in order to inform him that from remarks made by his uncle, Emanuel knew for certain that the prize was intended for the Baroness. One of the witnesses to the will, Lieutenant Ehrenburg, wrote similarly to Björnson who himself declared at the Nobel award ceremony that the designation of the Baroness was "a duty to Nobel's memory."

It all began with a famous help-wanted advertisement

that Nobel had inserted in the Vienna newspapers in 1876. The advertisement read, "Elderly, cultured gentleman, very wealthy, resident of Paris, seeks equally mature lady, linguist, as secretary and supervisor of household." The elder Baroness von Suttner read this notice to Bertha Kinsky, the governess for the four daughters of the family. Bertha was a penniless aristocrat, the daughter of Field Marshall Count Franz Kinsky of the Austrian Army who had died before she was born. Unhappily, she had had the poor fortune and judgment to fall in love with the scion of the house, the future Baron Gundaccar Arthur von Suttner, a youth seven years her junior. She had written, "When he entered the room it grew bright and warm." Such a match was naturally out of the question and it was, therefore, necessary that Bertha leave the household as soon as possible.

After some correspondence between Herr Nobel and Bertha, the applicant was invited to come to Paris for a personal interview. The elderly Nobel, 43, seemed to be quite enchanted with the wit, charm, linguistic ability and wisdom exhibited by the mature lady of thirty-three. She was described then as a statuesque woman with finely chiseled features and big dark eyes. Bertha was thus hired and installed in a Paris hotel while her quarters at the Nobel ménage were made ready. Her employer had several long conversations with Bertha and took her riding in his carriage before leaving town on a business trip.

But, poor Bertha pined for her Arthur and would not be consoled even when her new employer advised her to forget the past and to let time heal the wounds. Thus, when Arthur wrote to her, she pawned her only piece of jewelry to buy a railroad ticket to Vienna and rushed back to the arms of her beloved. She had remained in Paris only five days.

The couple was married and eloped to Mingrelia, a Caucasian principality, for a honeymoon that was to last for nine years. At first they were guests at the estate of the old Princess

Dadiani. Later, they fended for themselves and came to know poverty and privation. Bertha gave piano and voice lessons while Arthur worked as a bookkeeper in a wallpaper factory. With the outbreak of the Russo-Turkish War, they both worked for the Red Cross. Arthur wrote articles about the progress of the war which he sent back to the Vienna papers where they were published. After the war ended he continued to write descriptive articles about the Caucasus and its people. Bertha, too, began to write for the periodicals back home and her work was also published. Together they wrote six novels. The prodigal children had proven their mettle and they were welcomed back to Vienna in 1885.

While Bertha was on a visit to Paris in 1886 Max Nordau interested her in the work of the International Arbitration and Peace Association which had been founded by Hodgson Pratt in 1880. Influenced by her membership in this organization and drawing upon her own association with the Austrian military hierarchy, Bertha began writing an anti-war novel which was to be called *Die Waffen Nieder* (Ground Arms). The manuscript was rejected by every publishing house in Europe and finally was printed in 1889 when Bertha threatened to sue her regular publisher.

Die Waffen Nieder was translated into twelve languages and sold over one and one-half million copies. Leo Tolstoi compared the book to Harriet Beecher Stowe's *Uncle Tom's Cabin*. Nobel wrote that the book would carry further than new guns "and all the other implements of hell." It is claimed that Czar Nicholas II was inspired to issue the call for the first Hague conference by his reading of the novel. *Die Waffen Nieder* is generally considered, second only to Mrs. Stowe's work, as the most influential novel of the nineteenth century.

Bertha von Suttner sets the theme of her book: "Are there not enough catastrophes of nature? Must men on their own arbitrarily create new ones by their wars? They bring death instead of preserving life." The introduction written by Alice Asbury Abbott in 1899 to the English edition brought out by A. C. McClurg Co. catches the spirit of the work:

> This book is written with a hot heart and a burning pen. The book is a crusade against war and its whole object is to present the claims of the individual and the family as superior to those of the state; as an individualist she presses the claim of every human being to the ownership and control of his own life. Then, regarding the family as the social unit, she emphasizes the claim of wife and child as far superior to that of church or state.

Upon reading the novel even today, one's soul cannot fail to be kindled by the "hot heart and the burning pen." The plot is concerned with the tribulations visited upon Countess Martha, the daughter of a retired Austrian general, by wars and their aftermath. Her first husband, Arno Dotzky, is killed in battle leaving her with an infant son. After a long period spent in numb grief, she remarries a Lieutenant-Colonel Baron Frederick Tilling. Once again, her father and the elders and the organs of public information begin to talk about the glory of the fatherland and the need to arm themselves against threatened aggression. She recognizes the melody. Her husband Frederick is mobilized while the Countess Martha is in labor and her baby dies. When she learns that Frederick has been wounded, she goes searching for him through the unspeakable horror of military hospitals. A cholera epidemic following the war between Prussia and Austria-Hungary in 1866 causes the deaths of her two sisters, and her brother and father. With Frederick, she moves to Paris to blot out the memories, only to be embroiled in the Franco-Prussian War. On February 1, 1871, Frederick is seized by a Paris mob. They find a German letter that he is carrying. For this, Frederick is hauled before a patriotic drumhead tribunal. He is accused of treason and summarily shot.

In the words of Baroness von Suttner, "How the nations

will be relieved when the command Ground Arms is heard around the world."

Bertha renewed her acquaintance with Alfred Nobel in 1887 and we have seen how this flowered into that historic comradeship between the wealthy inventor of dynamite and his baroness and friend. In 1891, she founded and became the first president of the "Verein der Friedensfreunde" (Austrian Peace Society). It was the same year that she headed the Austrian delegation to the third world peace congress in Rome. She was the only woman among ninety-six delegates from twenty-six countries, and was given a great ovation. Her fellow delegates dubbed her pacifism's "Joan of Arc"; the man in the street called her "Peace Bertha." She was to write, "What I experienced here was like the fulfillment of a lofty ambitious dream."

Her editorship of the monthly publication *Die Waffen Nieder* from 1892 to 1899 has already been mentioned. She was designated one of the thirty-five members of the governing commission of the "Bureau internationale permanente de la paix," becoming its vice-president in 1899. She wrote and lectured widely, appearing in France, Belgium, Holland, Denmark, and the United States.

Baroness von Suttner suffered a deep personal loss when, in 1902, her co-worker and beloved Arthur died prematurely at the age of fifty.

Like so many other professional pacifists, Bertha von Suttner opposed attempts to humanize war and to alleviate its horrors. She wrote, "St. George rode forth to kill the dragon, not to trim its claws." Yet, her approach to peace was bourgeois, and not revolutionary. In an article written in 1896 she said, "We do not say that this or that must happen, or this or that class come into power and then war will certainly disappear of its own accord, but we say : first the world must be released from the threat of world war and the armaments race, then the other social questions can be solved more easily and more justly."

She favored compulsory arbitration of international disputes, disarmament, and a United States of Europe. She said in her Nobel lecture, "The peace movement has become a fight for a world outlook and a world order."

Bertha died on June 20, 1914, in Vienna. A kindly providence spared her the agony of World War I. The Archduke Franz Ferdinand and his wife were assassinated just eight days later at Serajevo by Gavrilo Princip.

An era had ended. The vials of wrath were boiling over.

6 The War to End All Wars

Thus, in the words of David Lloyd George, the world "stumbled and staggered" into war and the horsemen of the Apocalypse, with all their attendant horror, rode over the blackened fields of Europe.

For the first time since its creation in 1901, the Nobel peace prizes were not awarded for the years 1914, 1915, 1916, and 1918. For 1917 the citation went, appropriately enough, to the International Red Cross of Geneva. The work of this organization will be discussed in a later chapter.

The Nobel committee naturally felt that there was no cause for celebration in a world plunged into the depths of war. However, the committee's failure to respond positively on behalf of the cause of peace — even if only a gesture — has evoked considerable criticism. It was maintained that it is better to light a candle than to curse the darkness. It was difficult to convince these critics that mankind had sunk to so low a level of depravity that nowhere could there be found at least one person or one group who was trying to keep the flicker of peace burning.

As Jacques F. Ferrand, secretary of the American Nobel Anniversary Committee, was to say in a later era:

Failure to make the award is a lost opportunity for talking up for peace. This is particularly regrettable in view of the urgent need in our time to face up to the fact that it is the eleventh hour in mankind's race for self-destruction. The Nobel peace prizes are one of the most effective means for bringing this message to the peoples of the world. They should be awarded especially when the international situation seems darkest—to help in supplying a beacon of hope for all mankind.

The award of the Nobel peace prize in 1919 to Woodrow Wilson marked a new direction for the Nobel committee of the Storting. Perhaps it was the trauma of World War I which caused the committee to veer from its former course. The new direction was not so much a complete turnabout as a change of emphasis.

As we have seen, the winners of the coveted prize during the Hague era were predominantly international lawyers and professionals of the peace movement. With the world in a shambles, the Nobel committee was ready to turn its back upon the earlier heroic period marked by idealistic pacifism, and to grimly embrace a more practical approach to peace. Beginning with Wilson, the trend turns toward the professional politician. Or should we use the term statesman instead to avoid the derogatory connotation of the word politician? One is reminded of the story about Boss Tweed who, upon being apprehended in Spain, was asked his profession. He drew himself upright and proudly answered, "Statesman." Thus, in this work the words will be used interchangeably and will be used to designate a person who holds a high executive office in the government of his country.

Of course, several statesmen had been awarded the laurel wreath, even during the Hague period : Gobat was a member of the Swiss federal council; Theodore Roosevelt, President of the United States; Beernaert, premier of Belgium; Asser, prime minister of Holland; and Root, Secretary of War and Secretary of State in the American cabinet. Gobat, Beernaert, and Asser, as representatives of smaller countries, could obviously have little impact upon the course of world history. But, the role of the smaller nations in the cause of peace should be neither deprecated nor minimized. As Renault stated in his Nobel lecture, "They most often represent justice, precisely because they are not able to impose injustice."

It should be pointed out that Beernaert, who had previously spoken out for compulsory arbitration, pushed for a much vaguer formulation and a more cautious approach at the Hague 1907 conference because his government was loathe to apply the principles of arbitration to the Congo dispute.

In designating Theodore Roosevelt as laureate for 1906, the Nobel committee for the first time, as has been stated, made the award in recognition of a single act (the Treaty of Portsmouth), rather than for continuous work in the service of peace. In his own evaluation of his term of office, Roosevelt had ranked the Russo-Japanese peace treaty as third, behind the strengthening of the navy and its circumnavigation of the globe, and the rape of the Panama Canal, "I took Panama," he said in his *Autobiography*.

It is difficult to explain how the peace prize was awarded to a man who is on record as having eulogized war "as a necessary means of settling great national and international differences and problems."

Roosevelt was a man who had been eager for a war throughout the 1890's and didn't care much whether it be with Chile, Spain, or England. He "wanted to give our people something to think of that isn't material gain." He feared that America would grow soft and "an easy prey for any people which still retained those most valuable of all qualities, the soldierly virtues." He was a man who had convinced himself that "all the great masterful races have been fighting races." He proclaimed before the Naval War College in 1897, "No triumph of peace is quite so great as the supreme triumphs of war . . . It may be that in some time in the dim future of the race the

need for war will vanish; but that time is yet ages distant."
He once said he was "not in the least sensitive about killing
any number, of men if there is adequate reason."

Theodore Roosevelt was against disarmament and in favor
of large standing forces. He stated, "We need to keep in a
condition of preparedness, especially as regards our navy, not
because we want war but because we desire to stand with
those whose plea for peace is listened to with respectful attention." His well-known motto was "Speak softly and carry a
big stick," while he felt that, "It is only the warlike power of a
civilized people that can give peace to the world." William
Jennings Bryan had said of Roosevelt's New Nationalism,
"This is an exalting of the doctrine of brute force. It darkens
the hope of the race . . . It is a turning backward to the age
of violence." Roosevelt called sending the navy around the
world to show the flag "the most important service that I
rendered to peace."

Yes, Roosevelt could be ruthless in foreign relations as is best
illustrated by his action towards Columbia during the con-
trived Panama revolt. Christian Lange, laureate for 1921,
while secretary of the Nobel committee had written that if one
lifted the veil of Theodore Roosevelt's pan-Americanism, one
would find American imperialism. On the credit side of the
ledger it should be noted that Roosevelt was among the first
of the heads of state to submit disputes to arbitration at the
Hague; negotiating treaties with France, Germany, Portugal,
and Switzerland. At the same time, however, he could call
President Eliot of Harvard University, "A futile sentimentalist
of the international arbitration type."

During the American neutrality period prior to its entrance
into World War I, Roosevelt was one of the leaders of the
jingoist group favoring an immediate declaration of war against
Germany. He proclaimed, "I shall never accept the view that

all wars are to be condemned alike or that all kinds of peace are to be glorified."

Theodore Roosevelt had a very low opinion of professional peace advocates, stating :

There is no more utterly useless and often mischievous citizen than the peace-at-any price, universal arbitration type of being who is always complaining either about war or else about the cost of armaments which act as insurance against war.

On another occasion he said of pacifists :

The trouble comes from the entire inability of these worthy people to understand that they are demanding things that are mutually incompatible when they demand peace at any price and also justice and righteousness.

Even Roosevelt's Nobel lecture at Christiana was pugnacious and one newspaper commented, "Some may find the peace lecture of Mr. Roosevelt rather warlike."

A student of the peace movement must come to the conclusion that the award to Mr. Roosevelt must have been motivated, to some extent, by the desire of the Norwegian Storting to enlist powerful friends on its side in the separation dispute with Sweden.

Elihu Root was a somewhat different kind of politician (or statesman). We have the opinion of Nicholas Murray Butler, laureate for 1931, that "the source of Root's power was intellectual. No American in the last half-century has equalled him in the field of constructive statesmanship or in intellectual grasp and power of exposition." The editors of the *New York World* agreed that Root was "one of the few living statesmen of the first intellectual rank."

Yet the peace laureate for 1912 had served as the Secretary of War from 1899 to 1901 in the cabinets of William McKinley and Theodore Roosevelt. In this post he was, we must assume, more occupied with the pacification of Cuba and the Philippines, and the building of a military machine, than with reduction of standing armies and the outlawing of war. In the Philippines he was instrumental in repudiating the commitments that had been made and in crushing the republic that the Philippine people had set up for themselves. He helped to install, with American power, a government in which the people had no part — this, at a cost of 250,000 Filipinos dead from disease, starvation and exposure. The final act of betrayal came with Funston's capture of General Emilio Aguinaldo in the Luzon jungle on March 27, 1901. In Cuba Root was one of the first advocates of the Platt Amendment permitting American intervention.

Elihu Root returned to the Roosevelt cabinet as Secretary of State in 1905, holding that post until almost the very end of the administration in 1909. It does not appear likely that the man who held the key cabinet post under Roosevelt for so many years could have differed materially in viewpoint from his chief. Root, who is so identified with the Roosevelt Latin-American policy, thus also becomes suspect of the charge of American imperialism leveled by Lange.

In connection with his attendance at the Pan-American Congress at Rio de Janeiro in 1906, Root toured throughout Latin-America. At the congress, he emphasized New World solidarity and objected to interference by European nations. In the subsequent year, Root took the initiative in convoking a Central American Peace Conference at Washington which resulted in the establishment of a permanent court of arbitration for Central American states at Carthage, Costa Rica.

The interest of Theodore Roosevelt in arbitration of international disputes has already been mentioned. Root negotiated the first general arbitration treaties entered into by the United States — twenty-four in all. In 1906 he mediated the dispute between the United States and Japan concerning immigration into California, which resulted in the Immigration Law of

1907. He had served as one of the four American members of the Permanent Court of Arbitration at the Hague.

The point is, that when the road to peace happens to coincide momentarily with the maneuvers and gyrations of the politician, such a coincidence is strictly accidental. The tactics could just as easily have coincided with war. The exigencies of the moment control.

Is it honest to award the Nobel peace prize to a statesman for a single act which incidentally aided peace while withholding the award from a peace worker who has devoted his life to the cause? Under present conditions of international organization the statesman occupies a position similar to that of coach to an athletic team. His job is to win victories. The statesman who conducts foreign policy can concern himself with values of justice, fairness and tolerance only to the extent that they contribute to, or do not interfere with, the power objective. They can be used instrumentally as moral justification for the power quest but they must be discarded the moment their application brings weakness. The search for power is not made for the achievement of moral values; moral values are used to facilitate the attainment of power.

Machiavelli's famous quotation puts it thus: "When the bare safety of the country is at stake no consideration of justice or injustice, of mercy or cruelty, of honor or dishonor, can find a place. Every scruple must be set aside and that plan followed which saves the country's life and preserves her liberty." Translating Machiavelli into modern idiom, David Lloyd George stated that "If you want to succeed in politics, you must keep your conscience well under control."

These statesmen, not as individuals, but by virtue of their political position, have incidentally mediated an armed conflict or have contributed by coincidence to the prevention of hostilities. But a statesman can never work unconditionally against war because his first obligation is not to mankind, but to his own country. That is why we will find not one uncompromising pacifist among the statesmen winners of the prize either before or after World War I. The statesmen won the Nobel peace prize for the effect of their official actions; their intent and motivation probably would not have made them eligible.

Perhaps that is why politics has been called an obscene conspiracy of opportunists. For politics is the projection of a personality upon the body politic. We turn now to a man who epitomizes the axiom of Baroness von Suttner, "In statescraft, egoism is the main principle."

The Nobel prize for 1919, which had been previously withheld, was awarded on December 7, 1920, to Woodrow Wilson (1856–1924), President of the United States. David Loth published a book in 1941 entitled, *Woodrow Wilson:The Fifteenth Point*. The fifteenth point was the personality of Wilson. Here was a man who, in the words of Herbert Hoover, "had reached the zenith of intellectual and spiritual leadership of the whole world." Here was a man who was hailed as the modern prince of peace. Candles were burned beneath his picture. Streets were named for him. Mankind has never witnessed the equal of the ovation that was accorded Mr. and Mrs. Wilson from the moment the old Hamburg-Amerika liner George Washington docked at Brest on the morning of December 13, 1918.

Serried straining ranks of blue uniformed police could hardly restrain the millions who surged forward to wildly hail their hero. The Wilson procession moved through the triumphal arches of Brest; along the tracks to Paris in the private car of President Poincaré while thousands lined the rails in homage during the chilly night; under the Arc de Triumphe (whose chains had been removed for the first time since 1871) with Poincaré, and up the Champs Elysées between the lines of captured German cannons and the fluttering flags, to the Hôtel de Murat while flowers rained down on the open victoria until the occupants could hardly be seen. The din raised by the cheering multitude broke about their heads like claps of thunder. The placards proclaimed "Wilson le juste" and "President Wilson a bien merité de l'humanité!" Similar overwhelming receptions faced Wilson in other countries. He addressed a vast populace from the balcony of Buckingham Palace in London. In Italy women fought to kiss his clothes.

Here was a man who had been "too proud to fight" and who, only a few months before, had been reelected on the platform : "He kept us out of war." This was no party hack. This was a trained scholar who had proclaimed, "I have no enthusiasm for war," and who was aware that, "Once lead this people into war and they'll forget there ever was such a thing as tolerance. The spirit of ruthless brutality will enter into the very fiber of our national life infecting Congress, the courts, the policeman on the beat, the man in the street."

Beset by irresistible pressures, Wilson finally found himself being escorted by two troops of cavalry towards the Capitol building on that gusty, rainy night of April 2, 1917. Crowded galleries were waiting to hear the President's war message to the special session of the 65th Congress. To cheers and acclamation, he declared, "There is one choice we cannot make, we are incapable of making : we will not choose the path of submission." He declared that the nation had no alternative save to fight "for the things which we have always carried nearest our hearts — for democracy, for the right of those who submit to authority to have a voice in their own governments, for the rights and liberties of small nations, for a universal dominion of right by such a concert of free peoples as shall bring peace and safety to all nations and make the world at last free."

"For the ultimate peace of the world and the liberation of its people," Wilson asked that America "dedicate our lives and our fortunes, everything that we are and everything that we have, with the pride of those who know that the day has come when America is privileged to spend her blood and her might for the principles that gave her birth."

Back at the White House, Wilson said to Joe Tumulty, "Think of what it was they were applauding. My message today was a message of death for our young men. How strange it seems to applaud that." Then Tumulty reported, "As he said this, the President drew his handkerchief from his pocket, wiped away great tears that stood in his eyes, and then laying his head on the cabinet table, sobbed as if he had been a child."

No longer could the world say to America, "You kept your heads when we lost ours." Thenceforth the rule of the day was to be, "Force, Force to the utmost, Force without stint or limit."

Thus, reluctantly maneuvered into war and having waged that war successfully, Wilson arrived in Paris to make that peace, in obedience to the "mandate of humanity." Wilson had pledged a peace "without victory" and had acknowledged that, "only a peace between equals can last," and that "a victor's terms imposed upon the vanquished would leave a sting, a resentment, a bitter memory upon which terms of peace would rest, not permanently, but only as upon a quicksand." Had not Wilson, in his very war message, promised to "set up such a peace as will satisfy the longing of the world for disinterested justice and make the world safe for democracy?"

Had he not pledged in a speech launching the Fourth Liberty Loan that "it will be necessary that all who sit down at the peace table shall come willing and ready to pay the price, the only price that will procure it. That price is impartial justice on every item of the settlement, no matter whose interest is crossed."

Wilson had disdained the dictum of Baroness von Suttner that, "Every war, whatever the result may be, contains within itself the seed of future wars." He ignored the Cassandra-like prediction of Jane Addams, laureate for 1931, when she observed, "It seemed to me quite obvious that the processes of war would destroy more democratic institutions than he could ever rebuild however much he might declare the purpose of war to be the extension of democracy." Of the doctrine that the world's greatest war was to make an end to all wars, she went on to state, "It was hard for some of us to understand upon what experience this pathetic belief in the regenerative results of war could be founded; but the world had become filled with fine phrases and this one, which afforded comfort to many a young soldier, was taken up and endlessly repeated with an entire absence of the critical spirit."

Wilson had brushed aside the advice of Colonel Edward M. House and others against his going to Europe. "This trip will either be the greatest success or the supremest tragedy in all history," he had said to Joe Tumulty. He had also disregarded the statement of David Lloyd George to the House of Commons that he would squeeze Germany "until the pips squeak" and that of Georges Clemenceau to the Supreme War Council that "The only thing we aren't taking from Germany are the Kaiser's pants."

What sort of a man was this one, who carried the hopes of mankind as he faced the tiger of France, and the Welsh terrier? Here is a man who had come to a sad and ugly end in every single endeavor which he had undertaken in his lifetime: as a lawyer in Atlanta, as a professor at Bryn Mawr, as president of Princeton, as governor of New Jersey. Wilson was stubborn, vain, arrogant, paranoically ambitious, frequently hypocritical, without human warmth. William Allen White commented that Wilson's handshake was "like a ten cent pickled mackerel in brown paper. He had a highty tighty way that repulsed me. When he tried to be pleasant he creaked." This savior of mankind did not have much use for man, the individual. He admitted, "seeing people exhausts me." William Howard Taft mentioned Wilson's "angular disregard of other people's feelings." Wilson evidently had not read Henry Adams who had said, "Knowledge of human nature is the beginning and end of political education."

This scholar of government and history rejected all counsel and advice. Colonel House, in his diary, noted an occasion when Wilson had remarked that he was always eager for advice. The terse commentary of Wilson's closest associate was, "I almost laughed at this statement." One of Wilson's many biographers, John A. Garraty, concluded, "He was always far better at reaching large groups than small. Where he could stand as acknowledged leader, where communication flowed only outward from him, he was at his best — and incomparably effective." Professor Arthur S. Link has written about Wilson's handling of the Republican legislative majority in the New Jersey legislature of 1912 :

Wilson revealed his temperamental inability to cooperate with men who were not willing to follow his lead completely; he had not lost his habit, long since demonstrated at Princeton, of making his political opponents also his personal enemies whom he despised and loathed. He had to hold the reins and do the driving alone; it was the only kind of leadership he knew.

Eugene V. Debs and some 2,000 Socialists, syndicalists, and pacifists, were jailed during the war so that their voices would not jar George Creel's propagandistic waging of the war to make the world safe for democracy.

Nor was Wilson known for loyalty to his convictions or his commitments. He began as a political conservative. Senator Henry Cabot Lodge had commented during the 1912 campaign concerning Wilson's embracing of liberalism, "A man can change one or two of his opinions for his own advantage and change them perfectly honestly, but when a man changes all the well considered opinions of a lifetime and changes them all at once . . . it seems to me that he must lack in loyalty of conviction." In the course of a dispute with Dean Andrew West of the Princeton graduate school, Wilson had once remarked, "We must not lay too great stress on commitments."

One must wonder to what extent Wilson's switch from neutrality to belligerency was influenced by his ambition to transfer his acknowledged talents from the limited American stage to the world stage. It was rationalized that America, as a neutral, could, at best, call through a crack in the door. She could not sit at the peace table and plan the peace unless she had been a participant in the hostilities. While at Bryn Mawr, Wilson had written, "I constantly feel the disadvantages of the closet. My ambition is to add something to the statesmanship of the country." He had escaped from the closet into the widest possible arena — the world.

Henry Adams had written earlier in a prophetic vein :

Power is poison. Its effect on Presidents has been almost tragic, chiefly as an almost insane excitement at first and a worse reaction afterwards; but also because no mind is so well balanced as to bear the strain of seizing unlimited force without habit or knowledge of it; and finding it disputed with him by hungry packs of wolves and hands whose lives depend on snatching the carrion.

Wilson sat down with Lloyd George and Clemenceau to redraw the globe. Clemenceau immediately recognized the messianic complex in Wilson. He called him Jupiter and said, "talking to Wilson is something like talking to Jesus Christ." Clemenceau did not have to know the story of Wilson's comment when notified by William McCombs that the democratic nomination had been won after forty-six ballots. Wilson said, "You know I am a Presbyterian and believe in predestination. It was Providence that did the work at Baltimore."

Wilson had boasted to the 1918 Convention of the American Federation of Labor in Buffalo, "What I am opposed to is not the feeling of the pacifists, but their stupidity. My heart is with them, but my mind has contempt for them. I want peace but I know how to get it and they do not." Unfortunately, however, Providence could not prevent the victory that had been won at such a cost on the battlefield, from being squandered at the conference table. Clemenceau had said, "God gave us the Ten Commandments and we broke them. Wilson gives us the Fourteen Points. We shall see." Wilson broke himself to pieces against Lloyd George and Clemenceau during the long months at Versailles.

The treaty as it emerged from the hands of the "dawdlers of Paris," who dallied while the blockade continued and Europe faced the worst famine since the Thirty Years' War, bore no resemblance to the Fourteen Points. It was a vindictive document imposed by the will of the victors upon the vanquished. It divided the globe into indefensible little chunks that would make true the prediction of Robert Lansing, Wilson's Secretary of State and a member of the delegation to Versailles, who said of self-determination, "What a calamity that the phrase was ever uttered! What misery it will cause." Besides, Wilson's newly found regard for sovereignty did not square with his earlier adventures in Mexico, Haiti, Nicaragua and Santo Domingo.

"These ignorant and irresponsible men," in the words of Harold Nicolson, had cut the world into little bits, "as if they were dividing a cake" and the results were "immoral and impracticable." The flaws in the Treaty of Versailles were immediately perceived. Herbert Hoover commented, "Hate and revenge ran through the political and social passages." John Maynard Keynes expressed the criticism which was later to be formalized, in *Economic Consequences of the Peace,* that the treaty was "abhorrent, detestable . . . there are few episodes in history which posterity will have less reason to condone — a war ostensibly waged in defense of the sanctity of international agreements ending in a definite breach of one of the most sacred possible of such engagements on the part of the victorious champion of these ideals." The treaty makers had ignored the fundamentals set forth by Jan Christian Smuts in a letter to Lloyd George:

> To my mind, certain points seem quite clear and elementary:
> 1. We cannot destroy Germany without destroying Europe.
> 2. We cannot save Europe without the cooperation of Germany.
> Yet, we are now preparing a peace that must destroy Germany, and yet, we think we shall save Europe by so doing. The fact is the Germans are, have been and will continue to be the dominant factor on the continent of Europe, and no permanent peace is possible which is not based on that fact. The statesmen of the Vienna Congress were wiser in their generation; they looked upon France as necessary to Europe.

"In the end," as Smuts observed, "not only the leaders but the people themselves preferred a bit of booty here, a strategic frontier there, a coal field or an oil well, an addition to their population or their resources—to all the faint allurements of an ideal."

The International Congress of Women, which was meeting in simultaneous session in Zurich, passed the following resolution of censure:

> This International Congress of Women expresses its deep regret that the Terms of Peace proposed at Versailles should so seriously violate the principles upon which alone a just and lasting peace can be assured and which the democrats of the world had come to accept.
> By guaranteeing the fruits of the secret treaties to the conquerors, the Terms of Peace tacitly sanction secret diplomacy, deny the principles of self-determination, recognize the right of the victors to the spoils of war, and create all over Europe discords and animosities which can only lead to future wars.
> By the demand for the disarmament of one set of belligerents only, the principle of justice is violated and the rule of force continued.

By the financial and economic proposals a 100,000,000 people of this generation in the heart of Europe are condemned to poverty, disease and despair which must result in the spread of hatred and anarchy within each nation.

The story has been told many times as to how Wilson carried the Treaty of Versailles back across the Atlantic aboard the George Washington, in order to secure ratification by two-thirds of the Republican controlled Senate. In this battle for ratification the true enemy was as much Wilson's inability to compromise as the so-called "Battalion of Death" led by the majority leader, Senator Lodge. Wilson had not changed from the Princeton president who had declared during the quadrangle fiasco of 1908, "A Scotch-Irishman knows that he is right and will see who is master." It was the opinion of qualified observers that Wilson could have had his treaty, with only minor reservations but even a stricken Wilson was clenching his fist and proclaiming, "Better a thousand times to go down fighting than to dip your colors to dishonorable compromise." The treaty was rejected by the Senate 55 to 49, 15 votes short of the two-thirds required. Wilson had turned his back on his political mentor Edmund Burke who had cautioned, "All government — indeed every human benefit and enjoyment, every virtue and every prudent act — is founded on compromise and barter."

A politician is engaged in a practical art and his worth can only be judged by results. To paraphrase Joseph Fouché, failure in politics is more than a fault; it is a crime. In Wilson's case it was a crime measured by the untold millions of casualties of World War II. The play of a personality upon the world politic had left a legacy of disaster. A crusader's sword is emblazoned on Wilson's tomb in the National Cathedral at Washington. But a crusade founded on the concept of a war to end war is an absurdity.

Aware of the nature of the Treaty of Versailles, aware that

the pact and the League had been rejected by the United
States, the Nobel committee still chose to award the prize to
Wilson. The Berlin clerical newspaper *Germania* commented :

President Wilson is the man who gave Germany the right to hope
and then robbed the Germans of their peace. If hypocritical
peace ambitions are to be crowned with the Nobel prize, then
each succeeding recipient of the award must carry a share of his
shame.

The Nobel committee never gives its reasons for its awards,
but perhaps it was motivated by the fact that the League
of Nations — a League without the United States but still a
League — had come into being through the efforts of Woodrow
Wilson and his stubborn insistence that the League must be an
integral part of the peace treaty. Wilson himself had called
the League, "the key to peace."

7 Collective Security

The watchword for the Hague period was, "jus, ergo pax"; the watchword for the League of Nations era was to be collective security. Wilson's fourteenth point had demanded that a "general association of nations must be formed under specific covenants for the purpose of affording mutual guarantees of political independence and territorial integrity to great and small states alike."

Despite the shambles left by the Paris peace conference, there emerged one gleaming hope—the League of Nations at Geneva. Here was one dream of mankind fulfilled. The preamble to the Covenant expressed the most noble sentiments:

The High Contracting Parties
In order to promote international cooperation and to achieve international peace and security
By the acceptance of obligations not to resort to war,
By the prescription of open, just and honorable relations between nations,
By the firm establishment of the understandings of international law as the actual rule of conduct among governments,
And by the maintenance of justice and a scrupulous respect for all treaty obligations in the dealings of organized peoples with one another
joined to form the League.

The principle of collective security is embodied in Article

16 of the Covenant: "Should any member of the League resort to war in disregard of its covenants under Articles 12, 13 or 15, it shall ipso facto be deemed to have committed an act of war against all other members of the League, which hereby undertake immediately to subject it to the severance of all trade or financial relations, the prohibition of all intercourse between their nationals and the nationals of the covenant breaking state and the preventing of all financial, commercial or personal intercourse between the nationals of the covenant breaking state and the nationals of any other state, whether a member of the League or not."

The Assembly of the League of Nations met for the first time on November 15, 1920. On December 9, 1920, the winner of the 1920 Nobel peace prize was announced. He was Léon Victor Auguste Bourgeois (1851–1925), the president of the French Association for the Society of Nations, the French member of the peace conference committee which had drafted the Covenant, the first chairman of the League of Nations Council and the permanent French delegate to Geneva.

In a sense, Bourgeois was a bridge between the Hague and the Geneva eras. Educated in the law, he had entered the civil service in 1876 and risen to the position of police prefect of Paris in 1887. The next year he was elected to the Chamber of Deputies. Then followed a long series of portfolios in successive French cabinets, including a term as premier of a Radical ministry in 1895. He was a representative at the Hague conference of 1899, and headed the French delegation to the 1907 conference. He was appointed to the Permanent Court of Arbitration at the Hague in 1903. Bourgeois was elected to the French Senate in 1905 and served as president of that body between 1920–1923. He served as minister without portfolio in Briand's war cabinet.

In 1917, Bourgeois was appointed chairman of a French commission to study the possibilities of the creation of a

"Societé des Nations." This commission proposed a League which would function only in time of crisis with its sole objective the preservation of peace. To that end, arbitration of international disputes was to be compulsory and an international apparatus of justice was to be established to enforce sanctions. Bourgeois had advocated an international armed force and an international general staff long before Lester B. Pearson (laureate for 1957).

It is an interesting footnote to the role of the nation-state politician on the international scene that Bourgeois' first public speech after the award attacked any limitation on armaments.

The 1921 prize was divided between two Scandinavian delegates to the League of Nations: Karl Hjalmar Branting (1860–1925), and Christian Louis Lange (1869–1938).

Branting, prime minister in Sweden's first Social-Democratic government in 1920, and again in 1921–1923 and 1924–25, was Sweden's first delegate to the League of Nations and attended the Assembly sessions of 1920 and 1921. He was chairman of the Assembly committee on disarmaments. Branting served on the League Council in 1922 and was a member of that body's commission on armaments.

Strangely enough, Branting had begun his working career in 1883 as an assistant in astronomy at the Stockholm observatory after having pursued his studies at Uppsala. In 1884 he switched to journalism and became editor first of the radical paper *Tiden* and later of *Sozialdemokraten*. He was active in the formation of the Swedish Social Democratic Labor Party, which was organized in 1889, and became leader of the party in 1907. He was elected in 1896 as the first Social-Democrat in the Riksdag, and was the only Social-Democrat in the second chamber from 1897 to 1902. He was minister of finance in the Eden Liberal cabinet of 1917–1918, and was the Swedish delegate to the Paris Peace Conference.

Although Branting chaired the first post-war conference of

the Socialist International, he was a stout supporter of state sovereignty, declaring, "A nation's right to shape its own destiny, free from external pressure, shall be as incontestable for all democrats as it should be worth a sacrifice to maintain." While in public office, Branting had advocated peaceful settlement of the question of separation of Norway from Sweden's crown, general suffrage, national insurance, and more democratization.

Branting's peace prize lecture is one of the most eloquent on record. He said, "The brotherhood of nations touches the deepest springs of men's nature. It has been the ideal of the highest minds for thousands of years."

Lange was an international bureaucrat in the tradition of Ducommun and Gobat. A graduate in languages from the University of Oslo, Lange first came into prominence as the secretary to the arrangements committee of the ninth Inter-Parliamentary Union conference held in Oslo in 1899. He became the first secretary to the Storting Nobel committee, serving until 1909. In this position he was instrumental in founding the library of the Norwegian Nobel Institute in 1904. He represented Norway at the second Hague peace conference.

Lange was offered the paid position of secretary-general of the Inter-Parliamentary Union in 1909 as successor to Gobat. Lange occupied this post until 1933, keeping the organization alive during the war years with Nordic meetings when he had to flee the Brussels headquarters. During these years he was also a professor of history at the Norwegian Nobel Institute. From 1934 to 1938 he was a member of the Nobel peace committee.

At the League of Nations, Lange criticized the League Council for its lack of action on disarmament. He declared that weapons must be taken out of the hands of the neurasthenics and that it was not enough to humanize war; war had to be suppressed. Lange was a member of the Norwegian delegation to the Conference of Neutrals in Stockholm in 1916 which sought an early end to World War I.

As one who had received his doctorate for a thesis on the history of internationalism, as the author of the classic *Histoire de la l'Internationalisme*, as a life long employee of international organizations, Lange was well qualified to set forth the salient features of internationalism as compared with pacifism. In his Nobel lecture, he explained :

I speak of internationalism, not pacifism. The latter word has never appealed to me—it is a linguistic hybrid and it leads one to think merely of the negative side of the peace movement, the struggle against war; and for this side of our efforts the term antimilitarism is a more fitting name. Not that I disagree with pacifism or antimilitarism; they are necessary links in our struggle. But to my mind these words have the special significance—though not everyone agrees about this—of a moral theory; by pacifism I mean the moral protest against the use of violence and war in international relations. A pacifist will usually be an internationalist and vice versa. But history shows us examples which prove that the pacifist need not think internationally; he may be apolitical. Internationalism is a social and political theory, a definite conception of how society should be organized, especially a conception as to how the nations should settle their mutual relations.

Like so many other bureaucrats, however, Lange came to believe that the movement existed for the benefit of the bureaucracy and not vice versa. He believed that a larger proportion of the Nobel endowment should be devoted for the functions of the Norwegian Nobel Institute and its library and that the peace prize should be awarded less frequently. It was Lange's opinion that it ill served the prestige of the prize if it were awarded to some one who was not worthy merely because he seemed the best of a meager herd. The president of the Norwegian Peace Union, Bonnevie, commented that in Lange's view the peace prize existed for the purpose of providing an elegant Nobel Institute with its library and its staff of committee members, secretaries, alternates and counsellors.

The 1922 award went to Fridtjof Nansen (1861–1930), the president of the Norwegian League of Nations Society, Norway's first delegate to the League and the League's high Commissioner for Refugees. Nansen's life is the sort of stuff from which the Norse sagas were fashioned; Lord Cecil (laureate for 1937), called him, "almost the only man I have ever met who deserved to be called heroic."

Nansen was a famous scientist and explorer who had been curator of zoology at the Bergen museum, professor of zoology and oceanography at Christiana University, and who crossed Greenland by dog sled and had drifted on ice floes. Nansen became interested in politics during Norway's struggle to win freedom from Sweden. He later became his country's first ambassador to London.

Nansen supported Norwegian neutrality during the war declaring, "For what are they fighting? Power—only for power." At the award ceremony years later, Nansen voiced his lifetime conviction, "No more war. That is the greatest movement of the age." After the war he urged Norway's early entry in the League claiming that the organization could be, "a protection for the weak and oppressed, a judge in the disputes of its members, a force for peace and justice." As League commissioner, Nansen was instrumental in repatriating two million prisoners of war. He organized the transfer of population between Turkey and Greece. When the Soviet Union would not recognize the League office, he formed the Nansen Relief Organization and made a world-wide appeal for funds for Russian famine relief. He initiated the Nansen passport which was recognized by fifty-two nations. The Danish journalist Jens Marinus Jensen commented, "The Nobel peace prize has in the course of the years been given to many different sorts of men. It has surely never been awarded to anyone who in such a short time has carried out such far reaching practical peace work as Nansen."

At the League, Nansen advocated the admission of Germany. In his desire to secure rapprochement of the Western Allies with Germany, Nansen even brought about personal contact between Aristide Briand and Gustav Stresemann, the foreign ministers of France and Germany. When Nansen, the conscience of the League of Nations, died in 1930 at Oslo, the whole world mourned. In the words of his biographer Jon Sörenson, "Seldom or never has the sorrow of a nation been so much a sorrow of love and it was more than a national grief. A whole world mourned."

No awards were made for either 1923 or 1924. The 1925 prizes were originally withheld and later announced simultaneously with the 1926 prizes. Ostensibly, the 1925 accolade was divided between Charles G. Dawes (1865–1951), vice-president of the United States and head of the committee which drafted the Dawes plan; and Sir Joseph Austen Chamberlain (1863–1937), British foreign secretary; and the 1926 award between Aristide Briand (1862–1932), and Gustav Stresemann (1878–1929). Actually, however, the awards were made to the Treaty of Locarno as we shall see in a subsequent chapter.

The 1927 prize money was divided between two old professionals: Ferdinand Buisson (1841–1932), and Ludwig Quidde (1858–1941). Buisson, 87 at the time, was called the "world's most persistent pacifist." His activities dated back to 1867 when he had taken part in the formation of Passy's "Ligue internationale et permanente de la paix." Since then he had written thousands of articles on the peace question and lectured from countless lecterns. Moved by the injustices of the Dreyfus case, Buisson helped found in 1898, the "Ligue des Droits de l'Homme," of which he became president in 1914.

Upon graduation from the College D'Argente, Buisson could

not take up his chosen profession of teaching in France because his conscience would not permit him to take an oath of loyalty to Napoleon III. He thus was forced to teach in the schools of Neuchatel, Switzerland, from 1866 until 1870. In the latter year, with the establishment of the Third Republic, he returned to France where he was appointed inspector of elementary education. However, this post was not destined to be his for long because the rightest government which came to power after the defeat of the communards looked with disfavor upon Buisson's advocacy of secularization of schools. The political situation relaxed after the crisis of Seize Mai and the fall of the De Broglie ministry, and Buisson came back into service as inspector general of elementary education in 1878. The next year he became director of elementary education; a position he was to hold until 1896. In that year he joined the faculty at the Sorbonne as professor of the science of education. He wrote many books on pedagogy.

He was elected in 1902 by the Radical-Socialist Party to the Chamber of Deputies as a representative of the Seine department, serving until 1914, and again from 1919 to 1924. In the Chamber, he worked for separation of church and state; for support of the League of Nations; against the French Ruhr policy, and for Franco-German reconciliation. To that end, he lectured extensively in Germany.

The work of Quidde will be discussed in a later chapter.

The award was omitted again in 1928. The 1929 prize was not announced until November 27, 1930, when it was given to Frank B. Kellogg (1856–1937), former Secretary of State in the Coolidge cabinet. Kellogg and the Kellogg Pact will be discussed in a later chapter. The winner of the 1930 prize, Nathan Söderblom (1866–1931), Lutheran Archbishop of Sweden, will also be considered in a subsequent chapter.

The 1931 award was shared between Nicholas Murray Butler (1862–1947), president of Columbia University; and

Jane Addams (1860–1938), of Hull House and the Women's International League for Peace and Freedom. Butler, who had been on intimate terms with Kaiser Wilhelm II and had been closer than any other American scholar with the ruling classes of Germany, received a statement from German intellectuals shortly after the outbreak of World War I. He refused to even read the document and proceeded to ruthlessly purge the faculty and student body of Columbia of any vestige of Teutonism in a witch hunt that must have been the envy of A. Mitchell Palmer. He had declared, in no uncertain terms, in his June, 1917 Commencement Day address, "This is the University's last and only word of warning to any among us, if such there be, who are not with whole heart and mind and strength committed to fight with us to make the world safe for democracy."

Yet, Butler had done yeoman service in the field of international relations. After receiving his baccalaureate and graduate degrees from Columbia in the fields of education and philosophy, Butler joined the faculty of that university in 1885 as an assistant in philosophy, rising to a full professorship in five years. He became first dean of the faculty of philosophy in 1890 and president of the college in 1901.

Butler made famous the term, "the international mind." This term was the title of a book embodying the addresses made by Butler to the summer Lake Mohonk Conferences on International Arbitration which were held annually from 1907 to 1912, and over which Butler presided each year except for 1908. The "international mind " is defined as "nothing other than that habit of thinking of foreign relations and business and that habit of dealing with them which regard the several nations of the civilized world as friendly and cooperative equals in aiding the progress of civilization in developing commerce and industry and in spreading enlightenment and culture throughout the world."

As a representative of the doctrine of, "the international mind," Butler traveled extensively throughout the Western world. He was accepted everywhere in the highest circles and his travels read like a round of receptions, convocations, dinners, soirées and audiences. An intimate of presidents and kings, Butler became known as, "America's unofficial ambassador." He favored, "cooperation in the task of building some form of federal world, which seemed an absolute essential if economic prosperity and international peace were to be brought within the range of practical political action."

Butler was closely associated with Baron d'Estournelles in the work of the Carnegie Endowment and the "Ligue de la conciliation internationale," of whose American branch, the educator was president.

Butler played a leading role in proposing and securing the adoption of the Kellogg Pact. In his memoirs, *Across the Busy Years,* Butler writes that he conceived the idea of a pact to renounce war as an instrument of policy while reading a chapter entitled, "War as an Instrument of Policy" in the third volume of Karl von Clausewitz's *Vom Kriege.* Butler states that he passed this idea on to Briand in June, 1926. The story of the Kellogg Pact will be discussed in detail in a later chapter. Butler focussed public attention on Briand's proposal by a letter to the *New York Times* on April 25, 1927, and then campaigned vigorously about the country for its adoption. As a prominent Republican who had been a delegate to many national conventions, Butler's views commanded respect from the people and from the solons in Washington.

In a sense, the 1931 award was also made to another outstanding peace organization, the Carnegie Endowment for International Peace. As early as 1900, Herbert Spencer had suggested to Andrew Carnegie, "I wish very much that you would spend some thousands out of your millions in employing a few capable men in the United States and Great Britain to war against war."

Butler had finally influenced Andrew Carnegie in 1910 to donate ten million dollars to establish the endowment with Elihu Root as head of the board of trustees and Butler as head of the division of intercourse and education. The other two divisions of the endowment were international law and economics and history. Butler later succeeded to the presidency of the endowment. In his letter of presentation, December 14, 1910, to the twenty-six distinguished trustees, Carnegie had set forth the purpose of the Endowment:

> to hasten the abolition of international war, the foulest blot upon our civilization. Although we no longer eat our fellow men nor torture prisoners, nor sack cities killing their inhabitants, we still kill each other in war like barbarians. Only wild beasts are excusable for doing that in this, the Twentieth Century of the Christian era.

The Carnegie Endowment financed visits of "intellectual interpenetration" (a sort of early Fulbright plan), of professors, economists and newspaper men, "making peoples hitherto strange and remote more familiar with each other through personal contact on the part of outstanding representatives of the life and thought of each one of them." Over nine hundred "international mind" alcoves were set up in libraries in smaller cities in the United States. Over a thousand international relations clubs were financed in the United States where students and faculty advisers could meet at frequent intervals to discuss matters of international interest. Similar clubs were organized in Britain, Australia, Canada, South Africa, India, China, Japan, Phillipines, and in various South American countries. After the war, the ravaged libraries of Rheims, Belgrade, and the University of Louvain were rebuilt. It is interesting to note that a proposed inscription for the Louvain library, "Destroyed by Teutonic fury, rebuilt by American generosity," was dropped at Butler's insistence.

The Carnegie Endowment also financed the reconstruction of the commune of Fargniers in Aisne which had been designated by the French government as the village which had suffered most during World War I. The endowment also underwrote the administrative costs of several international conferences, notably the Balkan conferences of 1930 to 1934. It sponsored studies of international law, of the history of World War I, of the Saar conflict, and of international relations generally. The Endowment maintains a large library and has compiled treaty texts and diplomatic documents. It also issues a periodical *International Conciliation*.

The contributions of Jane Addams to the cause of peace will be discussed in a subsequent chapter.

The Nobel committee again could not find a worthy recipient in 1932. The 1933 award was at first passed over with the explanation that the year "was lacking a deserving enterprise in the cause of peace" but the Nobel committee relented on December 10, 1934, and belatedly named Norman Angell, (born in 1874).

Dr. Christian Lange called Angell the "great educator of public opinion." The winner of the 1933 prize had spent over thirty years trying to convince the world that war is foolish, that trade cannot be won by force of arms, that war does not pay, and that advantages supposedly to be gained from war are an illusion. These revolutionary ideas were set forth in a book published in 1910 and called *The Great Illusion*.

Professor Gilbert Murray commented, "It is a magnificent crown to at least twenty years of continuous and concentrated work. I think that the Nobel committee have done themselves credit in selecting a real peace worker who is not a cabinet minister or a general or a head of state." Philip Noel-Baker (laureate for 1959) wrote, "It is of course twenty years overdue.

Other people have battered on the walls of hell, but you have undermined the foundation."

As was the case with *Die Waffen Nieder* and as was to be expected, the manuscript of *The Grand Illusion* was rejected by every publisher in the British Isles. The English youth had abandoned his studies and set about the task of finding a meaning in life for himself, as a cowboy, in the American West. Angell went on to become a miner, prospector, farmer, reporter for the *San Francisco Chronicle,* and the *St. Louis Globe-Democrat;* and then returned to Europe to work on English newspapers and then take up the editorship first of the *Paris Daily Messenger,* and then of the *Paris Daily Mail.* Finally, he had to personally finance the publishing of his book.

It was Angell's purpose in his work to strip away the prejudices and emotions that obscure popular thinking in the area of international affairs, and expose these matters to the open-eyed scrutiny of common sense and rational thought. In Angell's words :

The purpose of this book is to suggest that, in a vitally important field of human activity—the relations between states which are daily becoming more closely concerned with the maintenance of an orderly civilization—we proceed upon assumptions which prove, on examination, to be utterly unsound; often in plain violation of self-evident fact, of common sense, of arithmetic, of any decent workable code of conduct.

He states elsewhere :

the tendency of human judgment in social and political matters to be utterly distorted, warped and twisted, both in its interpretation of objective fact and in its estimate of the means by which a given policy can be carried into effect; distorted by emotional forces within ourselves, forces of whose nature, of whose very presence, indeed, we seemed for the most part to be unaware. Events showed that these emotions could on occasion make us completely blind to what ought to be self-evident, to simple facts of the external world beneath our noses.

War is not due to evil intention, is not made by wicked men knowing themselves to be wrong, but usually by good men passionately convinced—on both sides—that they are right. It is a problem of understanding. Without that understanding the will to peace may be sincere and genuine and yet be defeated by failure to realize the inevitable outcome of the policies which we pursue.

Angell contended that a rational analysis would disclose that the whole theory of the commercial basis of war was wrong, that no modern war can make a profit for the victors. The *Great Illusion* is that war is profitable. Actually, however, modern war is as economically outdated as religious wars, piracy, and dueling. The costs of war have become so great that both the victor and the vanquished are defeated in terms of lives, markets, trade, and general welfare.

In Angell's words :

It cannot throughout this discussion be too often repeated that the world has been modified and that what was possible to the Canaanites or the Romans, or even to the Normans, is no longer possible to us. The edict can no longer go forth to slay every male child that is born in the conquered territory, in order that the race may be exterminated. Conquest in this sense is impossible.

Also :

less and less can war be made to pay; that all those forces of our world which daily gain in strength make it as a commercial venture more and more preposterous.

Angell thus traces the causes of war, not to "commercial venture," but to the drive of competing nationalism for naked power. The subtitle to the *Great Illusion* is, *A Study of the Relation of Military Power to National Advantage.* Angell states near the very beginning of his book :

No one, it will be said, believes today for a moment that war pays; which comment would illustrate the way in which a phrase may kill understanding and put an all but complete stop to thought . . . . Every nation sincerely desires peace and all nations pursue causes which if persisted in, must make peace impossible.

Angell sees the world, "Wrecking itself on the rocks of nationalist fallacies, passions and retaliation."

He asks us to :

see nationalist morality for what it is—an opportunity to indulge vicariously, in national policy, the savage instincts which personal life in organized society within the nations affords no opportunity to indulge. Power, the struggle for it, the fear of it in others, is the ultimate fact explaining the political chaos in the international field.

Thus, "Until we are taught to recognize — what our history books do not teach — that the fault is usually ours as much as some other nation's, we have not taken the first step to that wisdom which alone can save us." Then as we now "see that it is irrelevant and unworthy to fight about religion, we would as readily come to see that it is irrelevant and self-defeating to fight about our nationalisms." Angell pleaded for a "world philosophy," and a "world conscience" where nationalisms would give way to a "community of nations." "We can still make a cosmos out of this chaos by taking thought."

Angell noted the "gulf between private and public opinion," and stressed that, in the final reckoning, the choice between war and peace rested with each individual in the "sense that the fate of the world depends on the individual good judgment of each of us since the world is made up of individuals."

Angell maintains :

A decision has to be taken. It has to be taken, not only by the experts, the trained economists, the academic specialists, but by the voting millions of over-driven professional men, coal heavers, dentists, tea-shop waitresses, parsons, charwomen, artists, country squires, chorus girls who make and unmake governments, who do not hesitate, as we have seen, again and again to override the specialist or expert and impose their opinion upon him. With them rests the final verdict.

The war traders can only act through the public mind—its beliefs, fears, cupidities, prejudices, hates, pugnacities, animosities. So long as these lie beneath the surface of the ordinary man's thoughts, he will be an easy victim of the war trader's exploitation. If we would reduce the war traders to . . . powerlessness . . . there is only one means of so doing—to bring home to the public, which they exploit, the . . . sense of futility of war. A few score officials—or capitalists—cannot by their physical power compel hundreds of millions year after year to go on paying taxes, taking vast risks, jeopardizing prosperity, if those millions are persuaded that the taxes, the risks, the sacrifices are quite unnecessary and, indeed, mischievous.

The *Great Illusion* sold over two million copies and was translated into twenty-two languages. Norman Angell Leagues sprang up all over England; a *Norman Angell Monthly* journal was started; and a movement for peace called "Angellism" began. Angell felt impelled to leave Lord Northcliff's organization in 1912, and to associate himself as director with the Garton Foundation for Encouraging the Study of International Polity which had been endowed in order to utilize Angell's talents.

By this time, the war clouds over Europe were becoming quite ominous and Angell was instrumental in forming a Neutrality League. But, he never identified himself as a pacifist, writing :

at the opposite end of the Blimps were the non-resisters who were against all force and who perhaps did not see very clearly that the refusal to endow law with power did not diminish the total amount of force in the world but left it in the hands of the lawless, the most violent.

Thus, when Britain entered World War I, Angell had no conscientious scruples against dropping his policy of neutrality and supporting the war effort. He explained, "no nation can any longer remain neutral as against any wilful disturbance of the peace of the world." He went to the United States to preach and write against the American policy of neutrality. Angell returned to England in 1916 and tried to enlist in the Army, but was rejected for physical reasons. There he found his articles barred and censored, and his passport picked up. He was finally accepted by the ambulance corps, and he drove an ambulance in France.

Yet, Angell was revolted by those who "saw the German not as a person at all, but as an abstraction." To him, rather, Germany was "an entity which included underfed children, old women and ignorant peasants as well as besotted high collared officers." Therefore, he, together with Ramsay Mac-Donald, Arthur Henderson, Bertrand Russell, and others, formed the Union for Democratic Control in order to try to prepare for a just and equitable peace. Angell believed that "physical force is a constantly diminishing factor in human affairs; the increasing factor is cooperation." He felt that the closer relation between nations caused by modern business and modern communication made international cooperation necessary and that such cooperation would result in increased prosperity, progress, and peace.

Angell was one of the earliest proponents of a League of Nations founded upon the principles of collective security. In a statement of principles which he prepared in 1918 for the Foreign Policy Association, he wrote:

Under any system in which adequate defense rests upon individual preponderance of power, the security of one must involve the insecurity of another.

He was later to declare:

If we will not defend other nations their right to life, then inevitably the time will come when it is impossible to defend our own nation, our right to life. If each is to be his own and sole defender, then any minority which can make itself stronger than one nation can place not one but all at its mercy. A little gang of ruthless men could overcome twenty nations because when one was attacked, the others remained indifferent.

This was to be the story of the fall of the League of Nations.

Angell held only one official post in his life—that of Labor member of Parliament for one term from 1929, to 1931. In summing up his life in his autobiography, Angell wrote :

The end I chose—elimination of war—I would without any hesitation whatsoever choose again. No other single task would be more worth the efforts of a lifetime.

8 Collective Security Crumbles

Nobel's will charges the prize committee to consider, "the person who shall have done the most or the best work . . . for the abolition or reduction of standing armies." It is altogether proper, therefore, that the 1934 award should have gone to Arthur Henderson (1863–1935), president of the World Disarmament Conference at Geneva from 1932 to 1934.

Kant had presented the classical case for disarmament in his *Preliminary Articles to Perpetual Peace* :

Standing armies must in time entirely cease to exist. They are a continual menace to other states and by their apparent preparation will incite neighboring nations to range themselves in arms, a condition of things which will know no limits and which, through the increased cost of maintaining peace, will become more oppressive than a short war; thus becoming a cause of war to escape this burden.

Lord Grey of Fallodon, in his review of the causes of World War I, set down in *Twenty-Five Years* :

The enormous growth of armaments in Europe, the sense of insecurity and fear caused by them—it was these that made war inevitable. This, it seems to me, is the truest reading of history and the lesson that the present should be learning from the past in the interests of future peace, the warning to be handed on to those who come after us. The increase of armaments that is intended in each nation to produce consciousness of strength and a sense of security does not produce these effects. On the contrary, it produces a consciousness of the strength of other nations and a sense of fear. Fear begets suspicion and distrust and evil imaginings of all sorts till each government feels it would be criminal not to take every precaution; while every government regards every precaution of every other government as evidence of hostile intent.

Woodrow Wilson's Point Four wanted "adequate guarantees given and taken that national armaments will be reduced to the lowest point and consistent with domestic safety."

It was to be expected, therefore, that Article VIII of the Covenant of the League of Nations should require the Council to formulate plans for arms reduction. Germany's greatest misgiving against affixing its signature to the Treaty of Versailles concerned her required unilateral disarmament. In a formal letter to the Paris Peace Conference, the German delegation wrote : "Germany is prepared to agree to her proposed disarmament provided this is a beginning of a general reduction of armaments."

Clemenceau replied :

The Allied and Associated Powers wish to make it clear that their requirements in regard to German armaments were not made solely with the object of rendering it impossible for her to resume her policy of military aggression. They are also the first step toward that general reduction and limitation of armaments which they seek to bring about as one of the most fruitful preventatives of war and which it will be one of the first duties of the League of Nations to promote.

Lloyd George, in his *The Truth about the Peace Treaties,* agreed "Disarmament would be regarded as the real test of whether the League of Nations was a farce or whether business was meant."

Thus, one of the first independent agencies created by the League was the "Temporary Mixed Commission for Disarmament" which was constituted in 1920 and charged with the formulation of a definite plan for disarmament. The commission held meetings, made studies, condemned the private manufacture of munitions, pressed for control of the traffic in arms, and recommended the creation of a section of the League Secretariat to deal with disarmament. But, the commission was doomed to failure from the beginning because it provoked the opposition of the various national bureaucracies in that the commission members were appointed by the League and were not official representatives of the various governments.

The work of the "Temporary Mixed Commission" finally came to an end in 1925 when Britain refused to have anything further to do with it. Was it Count Talleyrand who stated that the principal task of statesmen was to devise new and better sounding titles for policies which have become discredited, without changing the practices in any way? In any event, a new Preparatory Commission was created by the League to work toward an international conference on disarmament. The efforts of the new commission dragged along desultorily for five years before the League announced that the "World Disarmament Conference for the Reduction and Limitation of Armaments" would convene at Geneva on February 2, 1932.

Why was Arthur Henderson chosen as the presiding officer of the conference? He was not a pacifist. In contrast to the pacifist views of his fellow labor member of Parliament, Ramsay MacDonald, Henderson had strongly supported the munitions bill, the registration bill and compulsory service. He was chairman of the National Advisory Committee on War Output, and a member without portfolio of the Lloyd George war cabinet. In 1917 he had gone to Russia to urge the revolutionary government to continue in the war against Germany.

Henderson first achieved prominence in the Newcastle trade union movement. After having held a number of local governmental positions, he was elected to Parliament as a Liberal member in 1903. He changed to the new Labor party, becoming its parliamentary leader from 1908 to 1910, and from 1914 to his death. He held several portfolios in the war coalition cabinets, having joined the first coalition government under Lord Asquith, in June, 1915, as President of the Board of Education. Thus, he became the first Labor member of Parliament to sit in the cabinet. He was Home Secretary in the first Labor government, and Foreign Secretary in the second (1929–1931).

Lord Cecil offered the following appraisal of Henderson :

the most successful Foreign Minister we have had since 1918, with no brilliant and shiny qualities, but with that faculty for being right which Englishmen possess. His political courage was great—almost the rarest and most valuable quality for a statesman.

"Uncle" Arthur was a member of the Salvation Army, a methodist preacher, and an anti-communist.

The world realized that the fate of mankind depended upon the work of the disarmament conference. The Women's Societies presented a monster petition with twelve million signatures, declaring that the delegates must choose between "world disarmament or world disaster." In his opening address to the conference at which sixty nations were represented, Henderson declared, "I refuse to contemplate even the possibility of failure; but if we fail, no one can foretell the evil consequences that might ensue."

The dismal failure of the disarmament conference which Winston Churchill called "a solemn and prolonged farce," is a matter of history. Its deliberations were drowned out by the beat of hob-nailed Nazi boots and the cacaphonic melody of Europe rearming. The world had chosen disaster.

Yet, at a time when the British Conservative government had lost interest in the disarmament conference, and when the life of the parley was oozing out ignominiously, the stout Scotsman maintained in his Nobel lecture on December 10, 1934:

There is no greater human issue upon which hope concentrates than the cause of disarmament. There is no greater achievement to be realized than that of securing the world's peace. There is no greater action in the world than that of leading the people to peace, freedom and security.

Why did this great disarmament conference, why did the naval conferences of the 1920's, why have all disarmament conferences come to naught? It is the old question of which comes first — the chicken or the egg. Some students of the problem maintain that armaments are only a symptom of the absurd anarchy of our system of nation-states, and that disarmament will be achieved only when the underlying disease is cured. That was the opinion of Arthur Henderson who attributed the lack of success of the disarmament conference to "the failure to tackle security effectively before we started on disarmament."

The other viewpoint, that armaments are an evil per se, is set forth by Lord Cecil:

saying that armaments did not lead to war is very much like saying that alcohol does not lead to drunkenness. In one way that is true, but without alcohol there would be no drunkenness and without armaments there would be no war.

In all fairness to Lord Cecil, it should be noted that he made the above statement before the final outcome of the American prohibition experiment.

Whatever the viewpoint, the failure of the League of Nations to come to grips with the disarmament issue proved its undoing. In a debate with Austen Chamberlain in 1927, Dr. Carl Joachim Hambro, last president of the Assembly of the League, made a prophetic prediction as he argued vainly for real disarmament among the great powers. He said, "outlaw nations will overrun the world and all humane civilization will be crushed." He lived to see that almost come to pass.

Because of a policy dispute within the Nobel committee which will be discussed later, the 1935 award was not announced until November 24, 1936. The 1935 designee Carl von Ossietzky (1889–1938), will be considered together with Quidde.

The year 1936 found the prize going for the first and only time to a South American, Carlos Saavedra Lamas (1878–1959). Lamas had been president of the 1936 session of the Assembly of the League of Nations.

Lamas received his Doctor of Laws degree from the University of Buenos Aires summa cum laude in 1903. After holding a series of municipal and minor posts, he became national minister of justice and public education in 1915, and minister of foreign affairs in 1932. He presided at the Geneva International Labor Conference in 1928. As foreign minister he initiated the 1932 declaration in which the American republics agreed not to recognize any change of territory in the Americas resulting from the force of arms. In 1933 he authored an anti-war pact which was adopted by the seventh Pan-American conference in Montevideo.

After the League of Nations had failed to terminate the Gran Chaco war, Carlos Saavedra Lamas helped set up a mediation commission of six neutral nations which persuaded Bolivia and Paraguay to lay down their arms in 1935. A warm supporter of the League, Lamas had brought Argentina back into the fold after a thirteen year absence. After retiring from public office, he held the chair of international law at his alma mater and later became rector of the university.

In making its choice the Nobel committee had evidently not taken into consideration the fact that Lamas, as foreign secretary, served the ruthless dictator President Augustin Justo under whose regime the common people were ground into the

dust by the landowners, industrialists and militarists. The
Nobel committee also overlooked the fact that the aristocratic
diplomat who wore frock coats, white waistcoats and high stiff
collars had been awarded and had accepted, in 1935, the
German Iron Cross, for work on behalf of peace from the
Hitler government.

The laureate for 1937, Edgar Algernon Robert Cecil,
Viscount Cecil of Chelwood (1864–1958), the last natural
person to win the award during the League of Nations era was
one of the initiators of the League and the man who had most
justly earned the title Mr. League of Nations. Even Lord Cecil
modestly regarded the award as, "a feather in the cap of the
League." Woodrow Wilson had written to Lord Cecil on
May 2, 1919:

I feel, as I am sure all the other members of the commission
feel, that the laboring oar fell to you and that it is chiefly due
to you that the Covenant has come out of the confusion of
debate in its original integrity.

In a unique tribute to the "Don Quixote of Geneva," a
letter to the editor of the London *Times,* dated October 25,
1930, and signed by three British prime ministers, representing
the three British parties, Ramsay MacDonald, Stanley Baldwin
and David Lloyd George, stated:

The formation and maintenance of the League of Nations are
due to the labours of many distinguished men of many nationali-
ties, but it has fallen to Lord Cecil to devote himself single-
mindedly to strengthening the League and promoting an intelligent understanding of its work among all classes of his fellow
citizens.

Born into an old and noble British family and the third son
of the Third Marquess of Salisbury, Britain's prime minister
from 1890 to 1902, Cecil was afforded the finest available

training for his future career. He finished Eton and University College at Oxford and was admitted to the bar at Inner Temple in 1887. He served for a period as his father's private secretary before being elected to Parliament in 1906 as the Conservative member for East Marylebone. He represented this constituency until 1910, and the Hitchin division of Hertfordshire from 1911 to 1923.

With the outbreak of war, Cecil joined the Red Cross and went to Paris to organize the Department of Wounded and Missing. Of these experiences he was to write later, "Altogether my work with the Red Cross made me hate war even more bitterly than I had done before." This feeling did not keep Cecil from joining Asquith's first war coalition cabinet in 1915 as under-secretary for foreign affairs in charge of the Blockade Department. It was the job of this department to starve the military machine—and the civilians—of the Central Powers into submission. One of Cecil's most demanding tasks in this position was to cope with the constant protests of the United States against harassment of American shipping.

Cecil continued in his post under the Lloyd George government of 1916 where the status of his department was promoted to that of Ministry of Blockade with Cecil as its first minister. Early in 1918 Cecil handed over this ministry to Leverton Harris and became the assistant secretary of state for foreign affairs.

In 1918, upon Cecil's suggestion, Lord Grey, the foreign secretary, appointed a commission with Lord Phillimore as chairman. They were to draw up a first British draft of a Covenant for the proposed League of Nations. Cecil was the driving force behind this commission and, together with Smuts, composed most of the draft. Cecil was the originator of the plan to have the League handle humanitarian, social and economic functions, while Smuts first suggested the Secretariat and the concept of mandates. Cecil and Smuts were both designated

British representatives to the Paris Peace Conference and both served on the committee charged with the responsibility of drafting the Covenant for the League. When Wilson arrived in Paris, he found that the British draft covered comprehensively the aims of the proposed League and this became the working draft of the peace conference. Cecil, Smuts, and Wilson are generally considered as the authors of the Covenant of the League of Nations.

Cecil and Smuts attended the first Assembly of the League in 1920 as representatives of South Africa. Cecil quickly assumed an important role on the Assembly disarmament committee. He was appointed first to the "Temporary Mixed Commission," and later to the Preparatory Commission. He joined the first Baldwin government in 1923 as Lord Privy Seal, in charge of League of Nations affairs and headed the British delegation to the League in that year. However, he found it difficult to go along with Conservative policy toward the League and late in the year requested elevation to the peerage.

Cecil's final break with the Conservative party came in 1927. He was the British representative at the Geneva naval disarmament conference which had been called by President Coolidge. After Cecil had worked out an Anglo-American-Japanese agreement, London repudiated his signature because he had accepted a drastic cut in the British cruiser ratio. Cecil railed at "those idiots in the cabinet," and complained, "It was quite wrong to treat the question as if we and the Americans were enemies, if not actual, at least possible."

He had said, "Right through the centuries there have always been the two currents of opinion, those who believe that patriotism must have a moral basis and those who do not." There was very little question as to which current Cecil belonged. He was later to write :

Thenceforward the effort to abolish war seemed to me, and still seems to me, the only political object worthwhile. As time went on I became increasingly conscious that that view was not really accepted by most Conservative politicians and was, indeed, hotly and violently rejected by large numbers of the right wing of the party. Not only, indeed, did they reject in their hearts the League of Nations, but they did not propose to take any step for getting rid of war. Clearly then, I could not honestly belong to the same party.

Cecil was to officially represent Britain at Geneva again in 1929 as the delegate of the MacDonald Labor government and in 1931 as the representative of the MacDonald coalition ministry. Cecil was president of the "British League of Nations Union," from 1923 to 1945, and head of the international federation in 1932–1933.

He organized the Peace Ballot of 1934–1935 in which eleven-and-a-half million Britons, over 40 per-cent of the electorate, voted in favor of the following five proposals:

    a. British continuance in the League.
    b. Arms reduction by international agreement.
    c. Outlawing of military aircraft by international agreement.
    d. International agreement for the prohibition of private manufacture and sale of armaments.
    d. Collective security through economic and military sanctions.

With the spread of aggression in Asia, Africa and Europe, Cecil was one of those who tried to rally the forces of resistance against international gangsterism through the "Rassemblant Universel pour la Paix," which was organized in 1936. Despite charges in fascist and isolationist quarters slandering him as a warmonger, Cecil called for, "collaboration of the community of nations to prevent the triumph of violence." He maintained, "That any ambitious Power, dominated by a tyrannical government, should be able to plunge the nations into war and inflict incalculable suffering on mankind, is intolerable."

At the same time, however, he was realistic enough to recognize that the old order had changed, that Britannia could no longer hope to rule the world, and that the whole colonial idea required revision. He favored, "abolition of the whole conception of individual ownership of these underdeveloped territories."

Cecil's work had previously received recognition when he was named the first winner in 1924 of the Woodrow Wilson Foundation's $25,000 award for having, "striven for world peace through justice."

There was to be one more peace award to be made, before the lamps of civilization were to be extinguished again. The 1938 prize was awarded to the "Bureau International Nansen pour les Réfugés," whose excellent work will be discussed in a later chapter.

By this time it was evident that the League of Nations had failed. Germany, Japan, and Italy had withdrawn; Austria, Czechoslovakia, and Albania had been erased. The Soviet Union had been expelled. Only forty-six of the sixty-three member states remained. Or perhaps it was not the League, but as Cecil contended, the governments which had failed. It is the opinion of the Earl of Avon (Anthony Eden) that the Council of the League was, "as serviceable a piece of diplomatic machinery as I have ever known." Winston Churchill expressed the opinion to Cecil during World War II that :

This war could easily have been prevented, if the League of Nations had been used with courage and loyalty by the associated nations.

Perhaps Professor Gilbert Murray's analysis is more correct when he wrote :

The international anarchy of a world administered by some 60 sovereign independent states with no authority over them, admitting no reciprocal duties and nursing unlimited national ambitions, was a disease carrying the seeds of death.

Cecil and Angell had warned the League of the consequences that would follow upon the failure to quarantine the aggressors and to impose sanctions upon lawless nations. By ignoring the aggressions against Manchuria, China, the Ruhr, Ethiopia, the Sudetenland, and Austria, the nations earned for themselves not Neville Chamberlain's "peace with honor, peace in our time" — but war. The horsemen of the Apocalypse were again mounting their stirrups. The "tragedy of disappointment" which Wilson had foreseen had come true.

9 Those Brittle Treaties

Although the 1925 prizes went to Dawes and Austen Chamberlain and those for 1926 to Briand and Stresemann, the honor was actually intended for the Treaty of Locarno.

It would be somewhat difficult to fit General Dawes into any of the criteria for the peace prize as set forth by Alfred Nobel in his will. Dawes had never attended a peace congress; he had never had anything to do with promoting fraternity among nations; he had never spoken out for the abolition or reduction of standing armies. Charles Dawes had been the general purchasing agent for the American Expeditionary Forces in France during World War I. Dawes was in the habit of entrusting his inmost thoughts to his voluminous journals. One can scour his diaries without discovering anything but a genuine admiration for Black Jack Pershing and a passive, unthinking acceptance of the necessity for wars.

Dawes had closed his law office in Lincoln, Nebraska, to enter the manufactured gas business. After achieving success there, he entered the banking business and became the president of the Central Trust Company of Illinois in Chicago. With American entrance in the war, Pershing helped his old friend Dawes to secure a commission as a major in the Engineers. Pershing soon arranged for the transfer to the purchasing job with the general staff. After the war, Dawes became the first budget director of the United States in 1921.

The designation of Charles Dawes for the Nobel prize arose from his chairmanship of the Expert Commission on German Finances and Reparations. It will be remembered that Wilson and Lloyd George had disclaimed any desire for indemnity as a result of World War I. In a masterful application of Talleyrand's dictum concerning "better-sounding titles," Article 231 of the Treaty of Versailles compelled Germany to abjectly accept her war guilt and to undertake to pay "reparations" (never indemnities) for the "damage done." Fifty-two per-cent of these reparations were to go to France, 22 per-cent to Britain, 10 per-cent to Italy, 8 per-cent to Belgium, and 8 per-cent to various other injured nations.

The amount of the reparations was left to be determined later and in 1920 was finally fixed at 269 billion gold marks, payable at 3 billion marks annually. Although this amount was successively reduced, the Germans found themselves unable to continue the payments and eventually defaulted altogether in 1923. Thereupon, French and Belgian troops occupied the Ruhr in retaliation. This was the spark required to set off a complete collapse of the German economy. Inflation ravaged the country like a plague until billions of marks could barely buy a postage stamp.

This was when the Allied Reparations Commission screamed for help, and pleaded for the assistance of a committee of experts. Belgium, France, Great Britain, Italy, and the United States each sent two experts, with Dawes and Owen D. Young as the American delegates. The recommendations of the commission, generally referred to as the Dawes Plan, were submitted in 1924. Based on the slogan of, "business, not politics," they suggested reorganization of the Reichsbank, the establishment of a transfer commission to supervise reparation payments, and arranged for an open loan of eight-hundred million gold marks to Germany. They recommended mortgaging of German industry to raise sixteen billion gold marks, and scaled down the amount of future reparation payments. These payments were to be fixed at one billion gold marks per year subject to an upward sliding scale. The Reichstag in the same year accepted the Dawes Plan for stabilizing the German economy and the level of reparations. It is interesting to note that only a small percentage of the reparations was ever paid, and that the amounts advanced as loans substantially exceeded the reparations paid.

In any event, the Dawes Plan was an important prerequisite for the readmission of Germany into the European fraternity. Nansen termed adoption of the plan the first light shed in the darkness of postwar Europe. The Dawes Plan paved the way for, and made Locarno possible.

Locarno is a town in Switzerland. Delegates from Belgium, France, Germany, Czechoslovakia, Great Britain, Italy, and Poland assembled there in October, 1925 to bind up the ugly scars left on the map of Europe in the wake of World War I. As a result of these negotiations, France made defensive alliances with Poland and Czechoslovakia, and Germany entered into arbitration treaties with several of the participants. But the important result of Locarno was the Rhineland Security Pact. In this pact the parties guaranteed the inviolability of the borders which had been fixed and guaranteed and made inviolable by the Treaty of Versailles, and wherein Germany again promised not to try to recover Alsace-Lorraine. The pact then recited the pledges of Germany, Belgium and France never to attack, invade, or wage war against each other except in "legitimate defense," or in response to a mandate of the League of Nations and the further commitment of these nations to come to the aid of the aggrieved party if this pledge were breached.

Briand stated, "The Locarno Agreement is not an end but

a beginning. To each his own—to every one his place in the sun." Germany was afforded its place in the sun and was admitted to the League of Nations in September, 1926. The award of the Nobel peace prizes to Briand, Chamberlain, and Stresemann was announced on December 10, 1926.

M. Scialoja, the Italian member of the Council of the League, commented, "They did practical things." Other critics did not deal so kindly with the triumvirate of laureates. A. O. Normann described them as follows in the *Bergen Tidende* :

Austen Chamberlain, who resembles his father, the imperialist, in everything except in intelligence; Stresemann, who would willingly belong to the German Nationalists if he were not too canny; and Briand who can belong to anything at all if he believes that France and he himself stand to win by it.

Von Ossietzky's *Weltbühne* commented :

While Briand, Chamberlain, and Stresemann were just wrangling over military controls, the news came, somewhat strange in this situation, that they had been awarded Nobel's peace prize. If there were writers of political comedies, they should find here a subject of overwhelming humor.

The careers of Chamberlain, Briand, and Stresemann were remarkably similar in many respects. Each was a professional politician who had worked and fought his way up to the position of foreign secretary after having held a series of less influential portfolios in a succession of ministries. None had played a notable role in the peace movement. Briand had broken early with the pacifist Jaurès wing of the French socialist party. Chamberlain had been opposed to the peace ballot. Stresemann was involved in the secret rearming of Germany.

In fact, Locarno was based on practical international politics. It was beginning to appear as if the Soviet government of Russia would survive and the Western allies were anxious to wean Germany away from the process of rapprochement with the Eastern power which had begun with the Rapallo agreement of 1922. Nansen recognized this situation in his speech at the award ceremonies:

What inspires our confidence is the fact that it was neither idealism nor altruism which compelled men to make this attempt; it was the feeling of necessity.

At the same ceremonies, in his acceptance speech, Briand declared, "my ambition is that ten years hence the people will say that we deserved this award." Ten years hence, Japan had raped Manchuria and China; Germany, Italy, and Japan had withdrawn from the League of Nations; Germany had formally and unilaterally repudiated the Treaty of Versailles; Italy had ravaged Ethiopia; Germany had violated the Locarno Treaties by reoccupying the Rhineland; and the Berlin-Rome axis had invaded Spain. Perhaps the events of that decade prove that Locarno failed precisely because it was a practical work of necessity; perhaps idealism and altruism cannot be ignored. To give Briand his due, however, it was he who made the most eloquent appeal during the Manchurian crisis to save the League of Nations as "the most precious thing that mankind had ever created."

In the so-called spirit of Locarno, Briand and Stresemann continued private discussions at Thoiry, but without results. It is the opinion of certain international observers that the history of that decade would have been different if Briand and Stresemann had lived longer. For instance, Nicholas Murray Butler maintained in 1939:

It will always remain my firm conviction that had Stresemann and Briand been spared for another decade to maintain and to strengthen their mutual confidence and their commanding leadership in their respective countries, conditions in Europe and the world would be very different today from what they so unhappily are.

Butler evidently was not aware that Stresemann had gone on record in declaring:

The vital interests of the great powers cannot suffer the straight jacket of legal paragraphs. If they are violated, these vital interests will burst the bonds which are imposed by international agreements. This has been the situation as long as the world has lasted and thus it will remain.

It would seem typical of Butler's personal approach to international affairs, that he would gamble world peace on the heartbeat of a handful of leaders rather than entrust the continued life of the planet to a broad-based public opinion.

In another sense, the awards for 1925 and 1926 were made in recognition of the traditional method of handling international relations since time immemorial; to wit, diplomacy. The dictionary defines diplomacy as the "conduct by government officials of negotiations and other relations between states." A more caustic lexicographer, Ambrose Bierce, defines the term as, "the patriotic art of lying for one's country."

If one accepts the picture of Hobbes, as one must, that:

in all times, Kings and Persons of Sovereign authority, because of their independency, are in continual jealousies and in the state and posture of gladiators; having their weapons pointing and their eyes fixed on one another, that is, their forts, garrisons and guns upon the frontiers of their kingdom; and continual spies upon their neighbours; which is a posture of war; then one can understand why diplomacy is merely a continuation of war by other means.

In the words of Emery Reves:

Diplomacy, like military strategy, consists of hoodwinking, tricking and outwitting the other party . . . . In every other field of human activity, we call this man a liar, a deceiver, a cheat.

One might also better understand Frederick the Great's

truism that diplomacy without armaments is like music without instruments. It must therefore follow that inferior armed strength is reflected not only on the battle field, but also at the council table; and that the outcome of international conferences is determined more by the respective size of the military establishments, than by the eloquence or logic of the arguments advanced. Thus, also, one might better understand why treaties are considered only temporary truces and temporary waiving of sovereignty until such a time as the power situation might change.

With such a stress upon sovereignty and power, one can sympathize with Rousseau's description of international conferences as places, "where we deliberate in common council whether the table will be round or square, whether the hall will have more doors or less, whether such and such a plenipotentiary will have his face or back turned toward the window." Count Metternich actually cut three additional doors in the conference room at Belvedere Palace during the Congress of Vienna so that each of the mighty potentates might make a simultaneous entry.

Over the centuries the art of diplomacy has become as stylized and formalized in performance as the ancient Japanese "kabuki" drama. Despite the call of Wilson and others for "open covenants, openly arrived at," the public witnesses only the stylized postures. The actual work of any international meeting is always conducted under conditions of secrecy. To quote Baroness von Suttner again:

Quite right; secrecy is the kernel of all diplomacy. The people must not know anything of the differences; if matters come to blows they have the right to shed their blood. Why they shed it is of no consequence to them.

No other human endeavor in the long history of civilization has had as unbroken a record of failure as diplomacy. Alexander Hamilton wrote how "triple and quadruple alliances were formed; but they were scarcely formed before they were broken." Baroness von Suttner coined the phrase "Those brittle treaties"; Hitler called them "scraps of paper." Let us consider another scrap of paper, the Kellogg-Briand Pact.

Several individuals—Senator Borah, Salman O. Levinson, Butler, James T. Shotwell, Briand—might, with some degree of justice, have taken credit for the ideas finally embodied in the Kellogg Pact. It was Levinson, a Chicago lawyer, who had first used the phrase "outlawry of war." Certainly, Kellogg, the winner of the 1929 prize, had the least claim to authorship of the pact which, by an ironic twist of history, was to bear his name. In his memoirs, *Across the Busy Years*, Butler writes:

It is not a little amusing to have this Pact of Paris so frequently referred to as the Kellogg Pact. When it was proposed, Kellogg was violently opposed to it and sent me word through my intimate friend and his, the late George Barton French, that he did not think I was such a fool as to favor an impossible treaty of that kind.

Events proved Kellogg to be right; the treaty was impossible.

Kellogg was a prominent lawyer who had been raised in the midwest and had built a reputation for himself as a trust buster. After a term in the United States Senate, he had served as ambassador to Britain and later as secretary of state in the Coolidge cabinet. He had stated, "I am not an internationalist. I believe in national pride and patriotism."

It was to Kellogg then, that Briand, on April 6, 1927 (the tenth anniversary of American entry into World War I), addressed the following appeal:

France is willing publicly to engage itself with the United States to put war as between the two countries outside the pale of law.

Because of a certain aloofness existing at that time between the two nations on account of the question of outstanding debts, there was little immediate public response to the Briand proposal. In a preceding chapter we described the campaign led by Butler to secure adoption of the pact.

He had written in his letter to the *New York Times* :

We have been celebrating, and justly celebrating, the tenth anniversary of the entry of the United States into the World War. Where and how could we find a more fitting tribute to the memory of those, whose lives were given in that stupendous struggle than by making a solemn compact with that nation most severely stricken by that war, for the formal and definite renunciation of war itself as an instrument of policy? M. Briand, speaking the voice and expressing the soul of France, has called out to us across the ocean. What answer is he to hear? What evidence is he to have that these noble words have been heard and understood?

This campaign was crowned with success when the pact was ratified by the United States Senate on January 15, 1929, by a vote of eighty-five to one.

In all, sixty-three nations eventually adhered to the Pact of Paris whose key clauses declared.

Article I—the high contracting parties solemnly declare in the names of their respective peoples that they condemn recourse to war for the solution of international controversies, and renounce it as an instrument of national policy in their relations with one another.

Article II—The high contracting parties agree that the settlement or solution of all disputes or conflicts of whatever nature or of whatever origin they may be, which may rise among them, shall never be sought except by pacific means.

Kellogg became a judge at the Permanent Court of International Justice at the Hague. The ink was hardly dry on the pact which renounced war but did not provide sanctions for enforcement before Butler was lamenting :

No sooner had it been ratified by 63 governments than at least one-half of them began arming for war, under the pretense of arming for defense, at a rate that had never been equalled in all history . . . The disastrous and humiliating result is written on the pages of time.

10 Two German Traitors

Commenting on the award of the 1927 prize to Quidde, the *Frankfurter Zeitung* editorialized, "Men who sacrifice themselves for an idea are scarce." The two men we will meet in this chapter are not of the butterfly chasing, harmless parlor pacifist type of whom Baroness von Suttner wrote :

It was, in truth, discouraging whenever one broached the subject to be met by shrugs of the shoulder, a sort of pitying smile and even condemnation. The world prefers, it seems, to be not only deceived, but made unhappy. When one proposes a means to put an end to misery and suffering, one is met by utopia, "a childish dream" and no one will listen.

The subjects of this chapter were militant firebrands of peace whose clamor could not be ignored and who demanded to be heard. They rejected what they considered the faulty strategy of the idealists who have too many illusions when they face realists who have too little conscience. They realized that the nation-state whose first business was murder would not look with tolerant forebearance upon a group of trouble makers whose antimilitarism threatened the very mainsprings of national power. No leader could afford to permit pacifist propaganda that would dull the nation's fighting edge.

These militant pacifists exhibited a courage that no government could forgive; they were a menace to the inward untruth-fulness of the sovereign state. Thus, Quidde and the fighters of peace like him had to be denounced as enemies of the State and harassed and hounded ruthlessly and cruelly by the awesome power of the nation-state. Great heroism was required for service in the ranks of the army of peace, and the hazards confronted were much greater than those in the regular army. Those who made war on war found themselves arrayed against the overwhelming strength of the vested system of things. All too often, these crusaders were crushed by the Leviathan.

The *Vossische Zeitung* was aware of this situation in its comment on the Quidde award : "Shunned by his countrymen, he carried on the fight for peace without murmur or thought of reward." Hugenberg's organ, the *Deutsche Allgemeine Zeitung,* was also aware of the real situation when it asked sarcastically :

Who is Herr Quidde? More than thirty years ago he gained cheap fame by the publication of the pamphlet "Caligula" in which he rudely attacked the Kaiser. Since then he has played certain roles as a Democratic deputy, pacifist writer and leader in peace societies dominated by the Foersters, Schoenaichs and Martens.

Who is Herr Quidde? He had studied German medieval history at the Universities of Strassbourg and Göttingen and then taught history at the University of Munich. He founded the *German Review of Historical Sciences* in 1888 and directed its publication until 1896. He was secretary of the Prussian Historical Institute from 1890 to 1892. It has already been mentioned that he was a member since 1901 of the directing commission of the "Bureau internationale permanente de la paix," at Berne.

Quidde followed an anonymously published attack on German militarism issued in 1893 with a lampoon on Wilhelm II. This was contained in a pamphlet published in 1894 entitled,

Caligula, A Study in Roman Caesarean Madness, which was ostensibly a biography of the dissolute Roman emperor but actually a neatly veiled presentation of the foibles of the Kaiser. The pamphlet ran through thirty editions in the short space of a year and the author was jailed for his temerity.

He was acquitted, however, and went on to found the Munich Peace Society in the same year, serving as its president until 1918. He was president of the German Peace Society from 1914 to 1929 and participated actively in the international peace conferences. He was elected a member of the Bavarian Landtag in 1907, and took part in the work of the Inter-Parliamentary Union.

Because of his pacifist activities, Quidde was forced into exile in Switzerland shortly before the outbreak of World War I. He maintained an extensive communication with other pacifists in belligerent and neutral nations and was the German delegate at the 1915 Hague meeting which was arranged by the Anti-Orloog Raad in an effort to secure an early end to the war. He agitated against the German drive for annexation and published a pamphlet in 1915, *Sollen wir annektieren,* which tried to show how impractical the Greater German movement was.

With the end of the war, Quidde returned to Germany and was elected in 1919 to the Weimar National Assembly of the Reichstag. There he made violent speeches against acceptance of the Treaty of Versailles because of his unwillingness to recognize German war guilt. However, he did favor German entrance into the League of Nations.

In 1924 he wrote an article concerning Weimar's secret rearming in violation of the Treaty of Versailles. He was arrested again and accused of treason but was released after an investigation. With the advent of National Socialism in 1933, Quidde was forced to flee to Switzerland again. He died there in Geneva in exile.

The announcement of the 1935 award was held up for almost one year because of an internal wrangle within the Nobel committee. The leading candidate for the prize, Carl von Ossietzky, was then incarcerated in a Nazi concentration camp. Certain members of the committee led by Halvdan Koht, the Norwegian foreign minister, were reluctant to do anything that might place Norway in an awkward position in relation to Germany and they were sincerely apprehensive of the consequences that might follow if the Nazi regime were offended.

While the argument raged within the split committee, a world wide movement was organized under the slogan, "Send the Peace Prize into the Concentration Camp." Twenty-one nations and hundreds of eminent persons filed petitions urging the designation of von Ossietzky. Norway itself was split on the issue, with Sigrid Undset leading the pros and Knut Hamsun the anti-von Ossietzky factions. At the same time the German government was exerting pressure with the *Schwarze Korps* warning the committee "not to provoke the German people by rewarding this traitor to our nation. We hope that the Norwegian government is sufficiently familiar with the ways of the world to prevent what would be a slap in the face of the German people."

Finally, it was announced on November 16, 1936, that Koht and Johann Ludwig Mowinchel, former premier and foreign minister and leader of the opposition, were resigning from the Nobel committee. The official notice explained that since :

the prize awarding might affect foreign nations' feelings and interests and since the official position of these members causes doubt as to the political integrity of the prize awarding body, the rules of the Nobel committee were being changed to exclude persons who hold positions in the Norwegian government.

A little over a week later the award to von Ossietzky

was announced. The prize had penetrated the barbed wire of the concentration camp. The Angriff fumed that, the "German people have been publicly insulted through a brazen burlesque." An official German government communiqué declared :

The award of the Nobel prize to a notorious traitor is such a brazen challenge and insult to the new Germany that it will be followed by an appropriate unequivocal answer.

The appropriate answer came from Hitler himself :

In order to avert such shameful occurrences for all future time . . . Acceptance of the Nobel prize is herewith forbidden to all Germans for all future time.

The supporters of the man whom John Dewey called, "the outstanding hero of peace of modern times and perhaps of any time," were also making themselves heard. Dr. Samuel McCrea Cavert, general secretary of the Federal Council of Churches of Christ in America, termed the award "one of the most articulate and crushing indictments of the Nazi regime." Oswald Garrison Villard sang :

All honor to the government of Norway and the Nobel prize committee ! That government deserves the highest credit for refusing to bring any pressure to bear upon the committee; its representatives resigned so that Hitler could not charge an official governmental action.

In announcing the award, Professor Frederik Stang, chairman of the Nobel committee, had declared :

A symbol may have its value; but Carl von Ossietzky is not only a symbol. He is something quite different and something more. He is a deed and he is a man.

Who was this man von Ossietzky, who was called Germany's, "most militant anti-war evangelist," and the "very incarnation of pacifistic idealism?"

Von Ossietzky was called from his desk as a clerk in the Hamburg municipal service to serve as an infantryman on the Western front during the entire four years of World War I. He was appalled at what he saw there, writing later:

What I saw of war only confirmed my earlier opinion of it—that war brings terror and despair to mankind and that there is nothing heroic about it.

He returned to Hamburg after the war to edit the radical pacifist review, *Die Revolution,* and to become chairman in 1920 of the Hamburg branch of the German Peace Society. Quidde was so impressed with the young man that he appointed him secretary of the German Peace Society with headquarters in Berlin. He co-founded the world movement "Nie wieder Krieg—guerre à la guerre—No more War" and proposed an international anti-war day. But von Ossietzky was essentially a writer, not an organizer, and so he resigned his post in 1921 to become foreign editor of the *Volkzeitung.* He began contributing political articles to *Die Weltbuehne* and became its editor in 1927.

Von Ossietzky was a "pamphleteer with a mordant pen," and he had little use for the parlor pacifist. "Cursed are the meek," he scorned, "for they are beaten to earth by their enemies, jailed by the state's attorneys, ridiculed as weaklings by the ignorant mob and when they are among themselves they devour each other." He was a realist; he sensed that the nature of war had changed:

It is the misfortune of old-line pacifism that everything for which it strove for long years has now been fulfilled beyond the boldest expectations—and yet the smell of fire has not lessened in the world. League of Nations, Locarno, Kellogg Pact—whoever would have believed in such impending possibilities? But the danger of war has nevertheless not diminished but rather increased . . . If at the moment of a declaration of war colossal air squadrons cross the border dropping gaseous death what will it mean to call out "I object—I won't play" . . . No, mere refusal to bear arms will not do any good. The hell-holes, where the instruments of war are manufactured, ought to be smoked out while there is peace.

Wilson had expressed the same thought in another way with his usual eloquence :

In the sense in which we have been wont to think of armies, there are no armies in this struggle. There are entire nations armed . . . It is not an army that we must shape and train for war; it is a nation.

The *Weltbuehne,* with its pinkish red cover, and printed on cheap paper, leveled a weekly broadside against the forces of militarism. Von Ossietzky was arrested early in 1931 for publishing an article by Kurt Tucholski in which the author had stated :

Soldiers are murderers; little murderers are hanged, but big ones are crowned with laurel wreaths.

Von Ossietzky was acquitted but he was back before the court later that year, this time on charges of having published an article in 1929 entitled *Windy Things in German Aviation.* The story, written by Walter Kreisler, but published anonymously, revealed that German fliers were being secretly trained on Soviet flying fields, at Lipetsk, that German commercial airlines were being reorganized along military lines, and that a scheme was afoot to set up factories to manufacture arms for the Reichswehr in Fili, Russia. The *Weltbuehne* showed that the Brüning government was not living up to its Policy of Acceptance and that the Reich was arming clandestinely, in violation of treaty pledges. The magazine wrote, "At Versailles we gave our word . . . When pledges are made, they should be kept."

Von Ossietzky was tried in secret on charges of treason,

Alfred Nobel.

Nobel Institute in Oslo, Norway. (Courtesy Norwegian Nobel Institute)

Jean Henri Dunant at the time of the founding of the Red Cross. (Courtesy International Committee of the Red Cross)

Frédéric Passy.

Elie Ducommun.

Charles Albert Gobat.

Sir William Randal Cremer. (Courtesy British Information Service)

Bertha von Suttner. (Courtesy Austrian Information Service, New York)

Ernesto Teodoro Moneta.

Theodore Roosevelt. (Courtesy Theodore Roosevelt Foundation)

Louis Renault. (Courtesy International Committee of the Red Cross)

Klas Pontus Arnoldson.

Francois Beernaert.

Fredrik Bajer. (Courtesy Danish Information Office, New York)

Paul Balluet, Baron d'Estournelles de Constant de Rebecque.

Tobias Michael Carel Asser. (Courtesy the Netherlands Information Service)

Alfred Hermann Fried.

Elihu Root. (Copyright by Harris & Ewing)

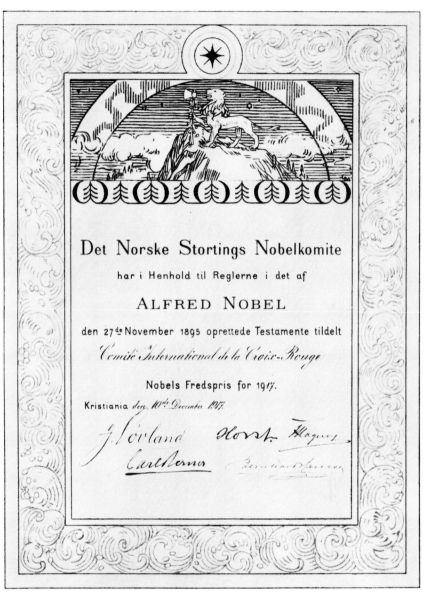

Det Norske Stortings Nobelkomite

har i Henhold til Reglerne i det af

ALFRED NOBEL

den 27de November 1895 oprettede Testamente tildelt

Comité International de la Croix-Rouge

Nobels Fredspris for 1917.

Kristiania den 10de December 1917.

Nobel Prize Certificate awarded to the International Committee
of the Red Cross in 1917. (Courtesy International Committee
of the Red Cross)

The International Prisoners of War Agency in Geneva. (Courtesy International Committee of the Red Cross)

Leon Bourgeois

Henri Marie Lafontaine.

Karl Hjalmar Branting. (Courtesy American Swedish News Exchange)

Woodrow Wilson with the other representatives of the Big Four at the Paris Peace Conference in 1918. (From the Collections of the Library of Congress)

Christian Louis Lange.

Fridtjof Nansen. (Courtesy United Nations High Commission for Refugees)

Charles G. Dawes. (From the Collections of the Library of Congress)

Joseph Austen Chamberlain. (Courtesy British Information Services)

Aristide Briand

Gustav Stresemann. (Courtesy German Information Center)

erdinand Buisson.

Ludwig Quidde.

Frank B. Kellogg (to the left of President Coolidge signing the
Kellogg Peace Treaty). (From the Collections of the Library of
Congress)

Nathan Söderblom. (Courtesy World Council of Churches, Geneva)

Nicholas Murray Butler. (Courtesy Carnegie Endowment for
International Peace)

Jane Addams. (From the Collections of the Library of Congress)

Norman Angell. (Courtesy British Information Services)

Arthur Henderson. (Courtesy British Information Services)

Carl von Ossietzky.

Carlos Saavedra Lámas.

Edgar Algernon Robert Cecil. (Courtesy British Information Services)

Cordell Hull.

John R. Mott. (Courtesy World Council of Churches, Geneva)

Emily Greene Balch. (Courtesy Swarthmore College Peace Collection)

Lord Boyd-Orr of Brechin (Courtesy United Nations)

Ralph J. Bunche. (Courtesy United Nations)

Léon Jouhaux

Dr. Albert Schweitzer. (Courtesy French Embassy Press and Information Division)

George C. Marshall. (Courtesy George C. Marshall Research Foundation)

Gunnar Jahn (left), Chairman of the Norwegian Nobel Committee, handing the Peace Prize to Dr. G. J. van Heuven Goedhart, the U.N. High Commissioner for Refugees, who accepted the prize for the Office of the United Nations High Commissioner for Refugees. The gold medal is in the small box, the diploma in the large one. (Courtesy United Nations)

Lester B. Pearson (right), accepts the gavel from Dr. Luis Padilla after his election as President of the U.N. General Assembly. (Courtesy United Nations)

Rev. Dominique Georges Pire. (Courtesy Belgian Government Information Center)

Philip J. Noel-Baker. (Courtesy United Nations)

Albert John Luthuli.

Dag Hammarskjold. (Karsh, Ottawa)

Linus Carl Pauling

Dr. Martin Luther King (left), with his wife, is congratulated by his fellow Nobel laureate, Ralph Bunche. (Courtesy United Nations)

UNICEF emblem. (UNICEF Photo)

Henry R. Labouisse, Executive Director of the United Nations Children's Fund, about to make a statement to the press on the award of the 1965 Nobel Peace Prize to UNICEF. (Courtesy United Nations)

Nobel Peace Prize medallion.

convicted, and sentenced to eighteen months imprisonment. Over fifty thousand Germans signed petitions asking for his freedom but he was finally freed under the amnesty of Chancellor General Kurt von Schleicher. He had been in prison for seven months—from May to December, 1932.

As is to be expected, von Ossietzky was an implacable foe of the Nazis and he attacked the "spinelessness" exhibited by the Weimar republic in its dealings with its political enemies. When the National Socialists came to power, his friends urged von Ossietzky to flee the country along with Quidde, but he refused. "A man speaks with a hollow voice from across the border," he said. "If you wish to fight effectively against rottenness in a nation, you must do it on the inside."

He was seized by storm troopers on February 27, 1933, the night of the Reichstag fire, and shipped to the notorious Sonnenburg concentration camp. The proud fighter for peace would not sign a pledge to Goebbels to confine his future writings to non-political subjects in exchange for his freedom. For five interminable years he was moved from one Nazi hell hole to another—to Papenburg, Esterwegen, and Spandau. Finally, with the announcement of the prize, von Ossietzky was transferred first to the Berlin Police Hospital and then to the Berlin West End Hospital. There he was visited by a delegation of five men appointed by the Norwegian parliament. They found a broken man dying from tuberculosis and kidney trouble brought on by five years of torture and abuse.

The poor man was even cheated of his prize money. The money had been deposited in escrow at the Kristiana Banking and Credit Co., in Oslo. On January 15, 1937, a Mme. Alexandra Kreutzberger presented herself at this bank, identified herself as the secretary of a Berlin lawyer, Dr. Kurt Wannow, and offered a power of attorney signed in favor of her employer by Mme. von Ossietzky. Payment was held up while Norwegian consular officials in Berlin checked the authenticity of the power of attorney. Apparently the officials were satisfied because the prize money was paid to Mme. Kreutzberger on January 18th.

It was later learned that Dr. Wannow had met Frau von Ossietzky, who had become a habitual drinker, at a bar and had duped her into signing the power of attorney. Using this power, Wannow secured the necessary permits from the Reichsbank. Of the 103,000 marks prize money, Wannow had loaned 40,000 marks to his mistress to purchase a Berlin movie theater and had used most of the rest of the money so that only 16,500 marks were left when he was arrested for embezzlement. The Gestapo confiscated this balance and neither von Ossietzky nor his wife ever received one pfennig. In 1954 the West German government awarded their daughter Mrs. Rosalinde Ossietsky-Palm an indemnity of 5,000 Deutsche marks ($1.192.50).

11 Two Brooding Mothers

Mrs. Caroline O'Day has truly stated that "women best know the cost of human life." It is understandable, therefore, why so many persons held the keenest hopes that women's groups would be in the forefront of the quest for peace. It is also a source of deep disappointment that women have not provided the hoped-for leadership.

In all only three women have earned the Nobel peace prize. The great contribution of Baroness von Suttner has already been reviewed. In this chapter we shall discuss the work of the remaining two women. Living the half life of unmarried women, without children, these two women adopted the whole of humanity. Unlike the sentiments expressed in Margaret Gibb's poem *I Have No Time,* these women cared; they cared like hell. These women, if you will, were two American traitors but they persisted in their conviction that a person's "primary allegiance is to her vision of the truth and she is under obligation to affirm it."

One hesitates in awe before dipping his pen into the life stream of the first of these women, the co-winner of the award for 1931. In the words of Emily Balch, laureate for 1946:

Of all my experiences the greatest and dearest was the being privileged to know Jane Addams. It is as impossible to evoke her for those who did not have the happiness of knowing her as to evoke the fragrance of a ripe strawberry or of a water lily for some one who has never smelled one. She was so unlike anyone else that I have known—so utterly real and first hand; so subtle, so simple and direct; so free from any pre-occupation from self, as free from asceticism as from self-indulgence; full of compassion without weakness or sentimentality . . . . loving merriment while carrying the world's woes in her heart—both the many which pressed upon her in immediate personal shape at Hull House and those of the nameless, unseen millions whose fates are part of our own personal fate. A great statesman, a great writer, one of the world's rarest spirits, how can I or any one evoke her?

Jane Addams was probably the greatest American who ever lived; certainly she was the greatest American of her Age. Dr. John Haynes Holmes said of her:

The name of Jane Addams is destined to be remembered and adored when the names of nearly all other members of her generation are forgotten. . . She was in her own right one of the greatest women of all time.

At the ceremonies in which the prize was presented to her in absentia, she was referred to as, "the foremost woman of her nation," and the "spokesman for all the peace loving women of the world." Professor Frederik Stang, chairman of the Nobel committee, called her, "America's uncrowned queen." The Chicago City Council hailed her as the "greatest woman who ever lived," and Sidney Webb, Sir John Gorst, John Burns, and Samuel Barnett offered a joint testimonial to the "greatest man in America."

Charles E. Merriam best expressed her position:

More than any other woman in America, she has caught the brooding spirit of the mother and understood how to appeal to what Lincoln called the better angels of our nature. If you say it is not possible for any one to be at once a statesman without portfolio, a professor without a chair and a guiding woman in a man-made world, I answer that it is not possible but—here she is!

She was born in Cedarville, Illinois, the eighth child in the family. Her mother died when Jane was only two years old and she became very much attached to her father who was the local miller. He had served in the Illinois state Senate and had been a friend of Lincoln. This small, frail, pigeon-toed girl who carried her head to one side because of a spine curvature was to grow into a radiant beauty whose comeliness was to be expressed not by her face but by her works.

At Rockford College she was graduated as class president, class valedictorian and editor of the college magazine. In October, 1881, she entered the Women's Medical College of Philadelphia but she stayed only seven months because her depression over the death of her father would not permit her to concentrate on her studies. Then followed one of the many periods in her life when she was sick and confined to hospitals. She underwent an operation for the spine curvature and learned that she could never have children. As part of her convalescense she left for Europe, in 1883, staying twenty-one months. There she was inspired by the example of London's Toynbee Hall settlement house and decided upon her life's work. A period of intensive study and preparation followed, including a second trip to Europe in 1887.

Hull House was opened at 335 (renumbered later as 800 S.) Halsted Street, Chicago, in September, 1889. It is most difficult to refrain from writing at length concerning Jane Addams' work in that Cathedral of Compassion that is called Hull House and her impact upon the city of Chicago which is best typified by her humble, self-effacing service as garbage inspector of Ward 19 at a salary of $1,000 per annum. But our subject here is peace and the life of Jane Addams is intertwined with the woman's peace movement of the United States and of the world.

The settlement house fulfilled Jane Addams' search for :

the mere foothold of a house, easily accessible, ample in space, hospitable and tolerant in spirit, set in the midst of the large foreign colonies which so easily isolate themselves in American cities, would be in itself a serviceable thing.

Hull House acted as a springboard to catapult its director into wider fields of activity such as the women's suffrage movement, the Women's Trade Union League, and the peace movement. Jane Addams learned her internationalism in Chicago where Hull House, with its polyglot of national origins, afforded a companionship which naturally expanded itself from the neighborhood until it encompassed the world.

She wrote several works on peace, and was one of the founders in 1914 of the Women's Peace Party. This organization was the outgrowth of a speaking tour in the United States of Mrs. Emmeline Pethic-Lawrence of England, and Mme. Rosika Schwimmer of Hungary. In response to the plea of these European pacifists for an indigenous American women's peace movement, Carrie Chapman Catt issued a call for a convention to convene at the grand ballroom of the New Willard Hotel in Washington on January 10, 1915. Three thousand women responded to the call. Jane Addams presided over the sessions of what was to become the Women's Peace Party. She later became its president. The organization adopted the following platform proclaiming that :

As women, we are especially the custodians of the life of the ages :
   1. Immediate calling of a convention of neutral nations in the interest of early peace.
   2. Limitation of armaments and the nationalization of their manufacture.
   3. Organized opposition to militarism in our own country.
   4. Education of youth in the ideals of peace.
   5. Democratic control of foreign policy.
   6. The further humanizing of governments by the extension of suffrage to women. .

7. The concept of a Concert of Nations to supersede the principle of Balance of Power. [It was Baroness von Suttner who had written, "O, this balance of power! What blood-thirsty diplomatic hypocrite invented this hollow phrase?"]
8. Action towards the gradual reorganization of the world to substitute Law for War.
9. The substitution of economic pressures and of non-inter-course as sanctions against belligerents instead of the building of rival armies and navies.
10. The removal of the economic causes of war.
11. The appointment by our government of a commission of men and women with an adequate appropriation to promote international peace.

It was at this convention that Julia G. Wells of the University of Wisconsin first proposed her plan for continuous mediation. By 1916 the Women's Peace Party could boast forty thousand members.

The Women's Peace Party was one of the organizations to issue a call for the International Congress of Women to be held at the Hague from April 28 to May 1, 1915. Forty-seven American women — with Jane Addams, Grace Abbott, Emily Balch, Madeleine Z. Doty, Professor Sophinisba Breckenridge, and Alice Hamilton as the chief delegates, who were promptly dubbed Peacettes, by the press — sailed on the Noordam from Hoboken to participate. In Holland they met delegates from fourteen other countries — neutrals and belligerents alike. It was the first entrance of women, acting together as women, into international politics. At the first session the assembled audience cried and cheered as the representatives of Belgium and Germany shook hands and as Dr. Aletta Jacobs welcomed them with the admonition:

that above the interests of one's country stand the interests of humanity, by serving which, a still higher duty is fulfilled.

The congress, with Jane Addams again presiding, adopted the following resolution:

We, women in International Congress assembled, protest against the madness and horror of war, involving as it does a reckless sacrifice of human life and the destruction of so much that humanity has labored through the centuries to build up.

The congress conceived a plan for a mediation board of experts from neutral countries to sit in continuous session in order to collect and evaluate mediation proposals and forward the more likely ones to the governments concerned. To this end, the Women's International Committee for Permanent Peace was established with headquarters in Amsterdam.

In addition, it was resolved to send committees of women delegates to the political leaders of fourteen countries with a message urging the termination of the war through continuous mediation by a neutral conference. As Catherine Marshall remarked :

Surely never since Mary Fisher, the Quakeress, set out on her mission to preach Christianity to the Grand Turk was such an adventure undertaken by women.

As Emily Balch was to report :

They were received gravely, kindly, perhaps gladly, by 21 ministers, the presidents of two republics, a king and the Pope. All, apparently, realized without argument that an expression of the public opinion of a large body of women had every claim to consideration in questions of war and peace.

Jane Addams, traveling with Rosa Genoni and Dr. Aletta Jacobs, saw eight heads of state or prime ministers and nine foreign secretaries, including Herbert Asquith, Sir Edward Grey, German Chancellor Theobold von Bethman-Hollweg, and French Premier Réné Viviani.

German Foreign Secretary Gottlieb von Jagow had told the delegation, "It was the right of women to do this sort of thing, he was surprised that they had not done it sooner."

Miss Addams relates her meeting with Count K. Stürgkh of Austria-Hungary :

We told him our little story and he said nothing. I never have a great deal of self-confidence—I am never so dead sure I am doing the right thing and I said to him : "It perhaps seems to you very foolish that women should go about in this way; but after all, the world is so strange in this war situation that our mission may be no more strange nor foolish than the rest."

He banged his fist on the table. "Foolish," he said, "not at all. These are the first sensible words that have been uttered in this room for ten months. That door opens from time to time and people come in to say, 'Mr. Minister, we must have more armor, we must have more money or we cannot go on with this war.' At last the door opens and two people walk in and say, 'Mr. Minister, why not substitute negotiation for fighting?' They are the sensible ones.

Only the American representatives abroad, echoing the views of President Wilson, scoffed at the peace mission. The Ambassador to Berlin, James W. Girard, wrote in his memoirs, "Early summer brought also a number of cranks to Berlin : Miss Addams and her fellow suffragettes." The Ambassador to London, Walter Hines Page, had nicknamed the Women's Congress the "Palace of Doves." It was the opinion of Secretary of State Robert Lansing that Miss Addams had been more or less imposed upon.

Colonel E. M. House wrote to President Wilson from Manchester, Massachusetts, on July 17, 1915 :

Dear Governor :
Jane Addams comes on Monday.
She has accumulated a wonderful lot of misinformation in Europe. She saw von Jagow, Grey and many others and for one reason or another they were not quite candid with her, so she has a totally wrong impression.

Secretary Lansing summed up the American position in a memorandum to President Wilson :

I would strongly favor discouraging any neutral movement toward peace at the present time because I believe it would fail and because, if it did fail, we would lose our influence for the future.

Wilson's response was "I entirely agree."

Miss Addams' meeting with President Wilson and her mission came to naught because without the United States a conference of neutrals would have been of little use.

Mme. Schwimmer had persuaded Henry Ford to sponsor a conference of neutrals that would offer to mediate the issues of the war. With the same showmanship utilized to merchandise Model T's, a Norwegian ship Oscar II was chartered as the Peace Ship to transport the American delegates to Europe. Despite misgivings concerning the saturnalia into which the mission would be converted by the newspapers, Jane Addams agreed to sail. She had always felt that, "nothing could be worse than the fear that one had given up too soon and had left one effort unexpended which might have saved the world."

With the reporters turning the event into a carnival, the peace ark, America's first venture in knight-errantry, sailed on December 4, 1915, with a banner nailed to its masthead proclaiming, "Get the boys out of the trenches by Christmas." Aboard were eighty-three delegates, fifty staff members, and sixty-four newsmen. But Jane Addams was not among those sailing. She was in a Chicago hospital seriously ill with pleuropneumonia. One of her kidneys had to be removed and she was invalided for a period of two years. Emily Balch was to join the conference in Stockholm later as her substitute.

The Oscar II was detained for a while in British waters while the editorials mocked the "ship of fools"; "the folly in petticoats"; "the shipload of hysterical women"; "the pro-Hun Peacettes"; and "the women peace fanatics." The ship was finally permitted to proceed to Stockholm where a neutral conference was convened on January 20, 1916, with representatives from the United States, Denmark, Holland, Norway, Sweden, and Switzerland. The conference set up an international commission of neutrals at the Hague which functioned until Henry Ford withdrew his financial support, upon America's entry into the war.

That entry came on April 6, 1917 — Good Friday. As Emily Balch wrote to Representative Isaac R. Sherwood :

So, nearly 1900 years after the death on the cross this is to be the celebration of Good Friday.

Congresswoman Jeanette Rankin expressed the viewpoint of the Women's Peace Party when she stood up in the well of the House of Representatives and declared, with tears streaming down her face, "I want to stand by my country but I cannot vote for war." The House vote for war was 373–50; the Senate 82–6.

Jane Addams, whose feelings were governed by "the sentiment of nonresistant love," refused to be swept away by "the wave of hate that engulfed" the United States. She stated :

That the United States has entered the war has not changed my views of the invalidity of war as a method of settlement of social problems one particle and I can see no reason why one should not say what one believes in time of war as in time of peace.

She rebelled at the realization that :

the nation was demanding worship and devotion for its own sake similar to that of the medieval church, as if it existed for its own ends of growth and power irrespective of the tests of reality.

But she was to find out how difficult it was to sponsor :

that most unpopular of all causes—peace in time of war. . . Our portion was the odium accorded those who, because they are not allowed to state their own cause, suffer constantly from inimical misrepresentation and are often placed in the position of seeming to defend what is a mere travesty of their convictions.

She found that :

even to appear to differ from those she loves in the hour of their affliction or exaltation has ever been the supreme test of a woman's conscience.

She was reviled, jeered and spat upon and told to go back to Germany. She was accused by the Daughters of the American Revolution of : "operating a world revolutionary movement whose goal was nothing less than 'to destroy civilization and Christianity.' "

In conformity with Angell's dictum that "poets sing, orators declaim and patriots assassinate," patriots demanded that Jane Addams be "hanged to the nearest lamp post."

Of this difficult period, Miss Addams was to write in *Peace and Bread* :

The force of the majority was so overwhelming that it seemed not only impossible to hold one's own against it, but at moments absolutely unnatural, and one secretly yearned to participate in the folly of all mankind. . . The misunderstanding encountered by the pacifist brings him very near to self-pity, perhaps the lowest pit into which human nature can sink. . . We never ceased to miss the unquestioning comradeship experienced by our fellow citizens during the war, nor to feel curiously outside the enchantment given to any human emotion when it is shared by millions of others. . . In the hours of doubt and self-distrust the question again and again arises : has the individual, or any small group, the right to stand out against millions of his fellow countrymen? . . . Even if one were right a thousand times over in conviction, was he not absolutely wrong in abstaining from this communion with his fellows?. . . On the other hand, there were many times when we stubbornly asked ourselves, what after all has maintained the human race on this old globe despite all the tragic failings of mankind, if not faith in new possibilities and courage to advocate them?. . . the ability to hold out against mass suggestion, to honestly differ from the convictions and enthusiasms of one's best friends did in moments of crisis come to depend upon the categorical belief that a man's primary allegiance is to his vision of the truth and that he is under obligation to affirm it.

The International Congress of Women, which had since

become the Women's International League for Peace and Freedom, had resolved that the second women's congress be convened to meet simultaneously with the peace conference. Accordingly, the congress was called for May 12, 1919, in Zurich and met with 137 delegates in attendance from twenty-one countries. The resolutions of that congress criticizing the proposed treaty of Versailles have already been discussed.

Jane Addams again presided and she was elected first president of the organization, a post she was to hold until the 1929 convention at Prague when she became honorary president, and the actual direction was taken over by a presidium of three. Jane Addams was to explain that :

the Women's International League for Peace and Freedom joins a long procession of those who have endeavored, for hundreds of years, to substitute law for war, political processes for brute force. [It sought] to unite women in all countries who are opposed to every kind of war, exploitation and oppression and who work for universal disarmament and for the solution of conflicts by the recognition of human solidarity, by conciliation and arbitration, by world cooperation and by the establishment of political and economic justice for all without distinction of sex, race, class or creed.

The constitution of the Women's International League for Peace and Freedom adopted by the Zurich Congress of 1934 sets forth as its goal :

The Women's International League for Peace and Freedom aims at bringing together women of different political and philosophical tendencies united in their determination to study, make known and abolish the political, social, economic and psychological causes of war and to work for a constructive peace.

The primary objectives of the Women's International League for Peace and Freedom remain : total and universal disarmament, the abolition of violent means of coercion for the settlement of conflicts, the substitution in every case of some form of peaceful settlement and the development of a world organization for the political, social and economic cooperation of peoples. Conscious that these aims cannot be attained and that a real and lasting peace and true freedom cannot exist under the present system of exploitation, privilege and profit, they consider that their duty is to facilitate and hasten by non-violent methods the social transformation which would permit the inauguration of a new system under which would be realized social, economic and political equality for all without distinction of sex, race or opinion.

They see as the goal an economic order on a world-wide basis and under world regulation, founded on the needs of the community and not on profit.

Jane Addams was in the president's chair again when the third Congress convened in Vienna in 1921 with thirty countries represented. She had been haunted by the "Weltschmertz" of poverty ever since her experience at a London East End food auction, where she saw "myriads of hands, empty, pathetic, nerveless and workworn, showing white in the uncertain light of the street and clutching forward for food which was already unfit to eat." To her, peace was "not merely an absence of war but the nurture of human life." Her compassion was outraged that millions of men, women, and children (Sir George Paish estimated a hundred million) in Europe were starving, while the statesmen were jockeying for political advantage. Since her great cause was that of life itself, she was sorely disappointed that the limited accomplishments of the League of Nations did not measure up to her hopes that the League would be founded, "not upon broken bits of international law, but upon ministrations to primitive human needs."

The third congress called for a Conference for a New Peace to convene at the Hague in December, 1922, and 111 national and international organizations were invited to send representatives. At this conference, resolutions were adopted calling for the withdrawal of the armies of occupation from Germany;

for the referral of the question of reparations to an international court; and for the convening of a world economic conference.

Jane Addams was to preside over later congresses in Washington, Dublin and Prague. She had given a portion of her Nobel prize money to the Women's International League for Peace and Freedom. Although she continued as the director of Hull House, her breadth of vision had truly expanded to embrace the whole world. In her introduction to the *Second Twenty Years in Hull House* she wrote:

The modern world is developing an almost mystic consciousness of the continuity and interdependence of mankind. It lies with us who are here now to make this consciousness—as yet so fleeting and uncertain—the unique contribution of our time to that small handful of incentives which really motivate human conduct.

But she was aware that:

this determination, as we well know, cannot be aroused by a mere choice between expediencies nor made effective by political machinery alone. It demands active devotion to the vision of a world of peace, justice and friendliness—in which life, not death is honored; humanity not wealth, is valued; love not hate, prevails.

A plaque hanging at Hull House honors Jane Addams:

Not the heroism connected with warfare and destruction but that which pertains to labor and the nourishing of human life.

Her tombstone can bear no more heroic inscription than its:

Jane Addams of Hull House and the Women's International League for Peace and Freedom.

It is necessary to run a little ahead of our narrative in order to consider the second of the brooding mothers. She was Emily

Greene Balch (1867–1961) co-winner for 1946. Although a good part of her work on behalf of the peace cause falls within the period under discussion, recognition by the Nobel committee came somewhat late.

Like its Chicago counterpart, Boston, too, had its female aristocracy of goodness and public spirit who sallied forth daily from luxurious homes to do battle with human filth, misery, ignorance, and strife.

Emily Balch had entered Quaker Bryn Mawr College in 1886 and was a member of its first graduating class in 1889. Although she had majored in the classics, she had studied economics under Franklin H. Giddings in her senior year. As the winner of the European Fellowship for European Study for one year, Miss Balch spent her lehrjahr at the Sorbonne in Paris.

Back home again, she entered the first of her three careers : social work, college teaching, and peace. She became associated with the Denison House settlement in the South Cove District of Boston as headworker. She also became acquainted with early trade unionism and was one of the founders in 1903, and later, the president of the Women's Trade Union League of America.

She continued her economics studies at Harvard Annex (now Radcliffe), the University of Chicago, and the University of Berlin (1895–96). A chance meeting with Miss Katharine Coman, then teaching economics single-handedly at Wellesley, led to an offer for Miss Balch to join that faculty.

Thus did she enter upon her second career in 1896; a career she later described as "my happy profession for more than twenty years till in 1918 my teaching came to a sudden end." A pupil described her as "an utterly unpretentious woman, spare of figure, unmindful of clothes and fripperies." She was tall, unstooped, angular with an air of crispness.

In 1913 .she became head of the department of economics

and sociology at Wellesley. As such, she introduced new courses in socialism and labor problems. She served on the Massachusetts Factory Inspection Commission. Also, she was chairman of the Massachusetts Minimum Wage Commission where she was instrumental in drafting the first minimum wage law in the country.

She became active in the Boston and Wellesley branches of the Women's Peace Party, and a disciple of Jane Addams. She wrote :

It is to Jane Addams, too dearly loved for words, that as a pacifist I owe the most of all and in every respect immeasurably much.

We have already mentioned her name as one of the American delegates to the International Congress of Women held at the Hague in 1915. While Jane Addams headed one of the two delegations dispatched to intervene with the rulers of Europe in the hope of halting World War I, Miss Balch led the second group consisting of Chrystal Macmillan, Rosika Schwimmer, and Cor Ramondt-Heischmann. She went to Russia and the Scandinavian countries. She was later to comment, "For one brief, accidental moment in my life I consorted with men in the seats of power."

On her return to her country, Miss Balch met with President Wilson and Secretary Lansing. She wrote to Jane Addams on August 19, 1915, reporting on her audience with the President:

I wonder if it would have been better if my interview had been postponed. I feel such a babe in judgment in all these things. . . I had many qualms after the interview as to my manners and my management of the golden moments.

Of her interview with Secretary Lansing, she wrote to Oswald Garrison Villard on September 28, 1915 :

The talk with Secretary Lansing was a disheartening experience. I hate to think of his representing our country. What he said to us was on an unspeakably lower moral level than what was said by any of the European statesmen with whom we talked. Of course, words are not everything, but to openly take an absolutely amoral and cynical attitude and defend it seems to me to unfit him for any large or constructive action in international affairs, however shrewd and capable he may be as an international lawyer.

We have already also noted that Miss Balch substituted for the ailing Jane Addams as the alternate American delegate, together with Rev. Charles Aked, among the twelve delegates from six neutral lands at the Neutral Conference on Continuous Mediation held in Stockholm from April to July, 1916. Miss Balch, who was to join the Religious Society of Friends in 1921, vehemently opposed, like Jane Addams, American entry into World War I.

With Jane Addams, Lillian Wald, Paul U. Kellogg, Rev. John Haynes Holmes, George Kirchwey, and Rabbi Stephen S. Wise, she had been one of the founders of the American Union Against Militarism which was headed by Miss Wald. The organization held giant mass meetings, peace parades and inserted newspaper advertisements declaring, "War is Not Necessary." Emily Balch spoke at many of these meetings and at rallies of the later People's Council. The New York *Evening Sun* called these activities "doing the work of sedition and treachery."

Although Emily Balch's primary allegiance was also to her vision of the truth, she too was not spared the doubts and self-distrust that are the lot of a pacifist in time of war. She was to write in the Bryn Mawr Alumnae Bulletin of May, 1933 :

It is needless to say that to me, as to every one else, the war years brought pain. . . It is a hard thing to stand against the surge of war-feeling, against the endless reiteration of every printed word, of the carefully edited news, of posters, parades, songs, speeches, sermons. In spite of a consciousness at times as clear as Luther's Ich kann nicht anders, at other times one staggered. To the question, "What if Germany wins and militarizes the world?" I had no answer ready. Bitterest of all was the sense that if America kept out of the war it would be largely, perhaps mainly, not for noble reasons, but from greed for profits. Conscience was uneasy, as well it might be. Where is the line dividing inner integrity from fanatical self-will?

Miss Balch had been on sabbatical leave until Spring, 1918. By a coincidence her five year appointment expired at the same time. As a result of her "too notorious efforts to try to prevent the United States from entering World War I," and her "outspoken views on pacifism and economics," her reappointment was held up by the Board of Trustees of Wellesley.

Emily Balch had written to President Ellen F. Pendleton on April 3, 1918 :

I believe so deeply that the way of war is not the way of Christianity, I find it so impossible to reconcile war with the truth of Jesus' teachings. . . I care because it appears to me to be very dangerous in a democracy for citizens—day laborers or professors or any one else—to feel that they are controlled in their decision as to joining or not joining a political organization by considerations as to retaining their opportunity to work.

The minutes of the Trustees meeting of April 23, 1918 read :

While recognizing the sincerity of the views expressed by Miss Balch and her essential nobility of spirit, the Trustees decided to postpone further consideration of her appointment.

A unanimous statement by the members of the economics department to the Trustees emphasized the serious loss to the college.

A cable from Miss Pendleton the next year informed Miss Balch of the final decision of the Trustees not to reappoint her. The Wellesley Alumnae Magazine of July, 1919, carried a tribute to Emily Balch signed by fourteen members of the faculty and staff :

We desire, therefore, to express our belief that Wellesley College has incurred a grave loss. Those of her colleagues whose names are given below, of various opinions and habits of mind, take this occasion to express their esteem for Miss Balch as economist, teacher and woman.

Emily Balch's only comment was "I overstrained the habitual liberality of Wellesley."

Emily Balch was only one of many educators who were purged in the wave of intolerance which followed in the wake of the outbreak of World War I. Bertrand Russell who was dismissed from Cambridge and Charles Beard who resigned in protest from Columbia were others. When Professor Beard protested that she "had made things too easy for the Trustees," Miss Balch insisted that she had not acted "wantonly nor lightly," and she refused to make a cause celèbre of her dismissal or to utter a single word of censure or recrimination. She had always said, "The creature in me does hate controversies." Little wonder that Dr. Alice Hamilton could say, "her disposition is for the Kingdom of Heaven."

Upon her dismissal, she wrote, "This left me at fifty-two with my professional life cut short and no particular prospects."

Oswald Garrison Villard, another outstanding pacifist, offered her a position on the staff of the *Nation* magazine. She was a delegate to the Second Women's Congress held in Zurich in 1919 and stayed on as its international secretary-treasurer and a member of the permanent staff of the Women's International League for Peace and Freedom which was planned to be established in Geneva. In this position, she helped organize conferences on drug control and disarmament.

She later wrote :

Here for a dozen years or so I spent much of my time, absorbed by the peepshow that Geneva afforded of the events of that fateful period during which there was complete failure to make any intelligent or adequate effort to check the growing aggression that began in Manchuria and swept on its triumphant way to Pearl Harbor and beyond; during which the noble experiment of the League of Nations failed, so far as its function of preserver of the peace went, because the governments were not in earnest in using it to that end and during which consequently the peace was lost for a time.

She had supported the League of Nations because she felt that even enlightened public opinion had to work through existing political organizations capable of dealing with concrete issues. She wrote :

With all its limitations, the League was a going concern, an instrument for dealing with a multitude of international problems. In the course of these activities, the League could develop habits of cooperation that might be extended to wider political relations.

This was the functional theory of internationalism whereby world government would evolve out of the "complex interweaving of functional arrangements for common interests."

In 1925, she represented the Women's International League for Peace and Freedom as a member of a committee of six in a mission to Haiti to investigate the conditions of that country's occupation by the United States marines who had been there since 1915. She and Paul H. Douglas then campaigned and lectured with great vigor in a drive to secure withdrawal of the occupation troops.

When Jane Addams resigned as president of the Women's International League for Peace and Freedom at the 1929 convention at Prague, Miss Balch was elected to the three member presidium together with Gertrude Baer and Clara Ragaz. In 1939 she became honorary international president as successor to Jane Addams.

In a gesture of reconciliation, Miss Balch was invited back to Wellesley in 1935 as the Armistice Day speaker. During the Second World War she abandoned her pacifist stand and gave reluctant approval to the war effort because she believed that the sword had become a necessity in order to defend fundamental human rights against those who would, "fasten a curse on mankind." She realized that her position was, "neither very definite nor very consistent." She became very much interested in the refugee question, publishing, *Refugees as Assets,* in 1939 in which she wrote : "They are bringing to us more than they ask of us. May we ourselves be worthy of the refugee !" She opened her Wellesley home to Jewish and other refugees and aided Japanese-American evacuees.

Miss Balch was at the Wellesley-Newton Hospital with a bronchial infection when the Nobel award was announced. She was unable to be present at the presentation to hear Gunnar Jahn say :

She has shown us that the realization we seek must be won through hard work in the world in which we live, but she has shown us more than this; that one does not become exhausted and that defeat gives new courage for the struggle to those who have within them the holy fire.

Miss Balch turned most of the prize money over to the Women's International League for Peace and Freedom.

Her many years of living abroad had turned Emily Balch into a true internationalist. She had written :

Wherever there are men I am indeed not only at home but among my own. I am no alien, no outsider; this is my dear familiar family——Deeply and happily I feel myself a citizen of the world. I am at home wherever there are people. Wherever I go, I know I shall find cruel, sly, dishonest, unpleasant people and everywhere I shall find magnanimous and generous people with keen minds, friendly, honest, open, serviceable . . . I am a patriot and my fatherland is this dear, dear, earth, sole home of life in infinite space.

The historian William Ernest Hocking best summed up the work of Miss Balch :

No other life known to me has been so consistently and almost exclusively devoted to the cause of peace and with such pervasive good judgment and effect . . . Her own thought was recognized as responsible in the best sense and without self-advertisement won its way to the minds of those who were making decisions. It will be long before the sum of her labors can be gathered, but when it is done, its achievements will be recognized as the more remarkable because its methods have been so much the quiet ways of friendly reason.

It may be interesting to note that the Women's International League for Peace and Freedom is still a functioning organization. Six hundred delegates from 34 countries attended the 50th anniversary congress at The Hague in the summer of 1965.

12 Reverence for Life

One would expect a chapter of this sort to be full of stories of martyrs of the church who bared their breasts against the savage superstition of nationalism and built cathedrals of humanity to bring peace on earth to men of good will. It is a keen disappointment to have to report that only four clergymen and one religious organization have been awarded the Nobel peace prize and that the awards in only two of the instances were actually directly concerned with the work of the church. Very few persons representing religion have even been nominated for the coveted prize.

Popes Benedict XV and Pius XII made eloquent and sincere pleas for peace in each of the two world wars, and Pope John XXIII in his encyclical *Pacem in Terris* movingly voiced the hunger of the masses during the Cold War for the greatest of all blessings, Pax Orbis. Pope Paul VI made a dramatic one-day trip to the United Nations to plead "no more war, war never again." But the fact is that the church had lost its battle with Caesar centuries ago and Caesar, in the form of the nation-state, has pre-empted to himself the whole sphere of human life. The clergy has been reduced to the function expressed by Erasmus in his *Praise of Folly*:

Learned sycophants will be found who will give to this manifest madness (war) the names of zeal, piety and fortitude, devising a way whereby it is possible for the man to whip out his sword,

152

stick it into the guts of his brother and nonetheless dwell in that supreme charity which, according to Christ's precept, a Christian owes to his neighbor.

As a matter of fact, a good number of the Nobel peace laureates, such as Bertha von Suttner, Hjalmar Branting, Fridtjof Nansen, and Carl von Ossietzky, were unbelievers. Nobel, himself, had little respect for organized religion. He had written :

Priestcraft leads to the worst abuses. True, royal power also is badly misused and the whole of so-called Christiandom still resembles a slaughterhouse, but compared to the horrors of priestcraft all this is trivial. Christ preached the rights of mankind and universal brotherhood; his ministers and their hypocritical following practice every kind of torture and baseness that the human animal can devise.

Yet, Nobel was friendly with and rarely turned down any request for assistance from the rector of the Swedish church in Paris, Nathan Söderblom, the Nobel laureate for 1930. And, it was Söderblom who officiated later at the Nobel funeral. Söderblom served as chaplain of the Swedish delegation to Paris from 1894 to 1901 after having received his degree from the University of Uppsala in classical and oriental languages and theology. He left Paris to become professor of theology at his alma mater. In 1914 he was designated archbishop of Uppsala and Lutheran primate of Sweden.

That same year, the Archbishop, at a congress in Constance, helped found a General World Union of Churches for International Understanding but the outbreak of the war forced a suspension of the organization's activities. Söderblom tried several times during World War I to rally Christians for peace but his efforts brought little response.

In 1925 he organized an ecumenical conference in Stockholm called the Universal Christian Conference on Life and Work, with over six hundred protestant and orthodox delegates in attendance from thirty-seven countries. Over the years the conferences of this Organization united with the conferences of World Faith and Order, in order to form the World Council of Churches.

It was said of Söderblom that he was the, "best loved man in Northern Europe."

The other person recognized by the Nobel committee for his church work was John R. Mott (1865–1955), co-winner with Emily Balch in 1946. While a student at Cornell University, he organized the Christian Student Union. Upon his graduation in 1888 he joined the Inter-Collegiate Young Men's Christian Association as student secretary, a post he held until 1915. In this position, he toured the colleges of the United States and Canada. He also was chairman of the executive committee of the Student Volunteer Movement for Foreign Missions whose slogan was "The evangelization of the world in this generation."

With Karl Fries, Mott was responsible for organizing the World's Student Christian Federation at Dodstene Castle, Sweden, in 1895, with himself as general secretary, and later as chairman, until 1928. A Methodist, he presided over the World Missionary Conference at Edinburgh in 1910 and became chairman of its Continuation Committee, a position he held until 1920. When the work of this group was assumed by the International Missionary Council, Mott became its chairman, serving until 1942.

In 1915 he became general secretary of the International Committee of the Young Men's Christian Association. As such he was active in welfare work among allied troops and prisoners of war during World War I. For these activities he was decorated by the United States government with the Distinguished Service Medal. He was one of the first persons to visualize the World Council of Churches, and he became its honorary president in 1948.

The award to Mott was severely criticized because he had strongly supported the entry of the United States into the First World War, and because he had been a member of an American commission to Russia which had attempted to persuade the Soviets to continue that war after the revolution. Norman Thomas, in a letter to the Christian Century, voiced this criticism. "Whatever one's judgment of these activities, they scarcely constitute a claim to be considered a leader in the cause of peace."

Religious leaders nominated for the Nobel peace prize included Pope Pius XII and Frank Buchman, the founder of the International Moral Rearmament Movement.

This chapter will deal with those individuals and organizations whose works of charity and compassion have earned recognition by the Nobel prize committee. We have already delineated the two main lines of peace work : humanitarianism, and active peacefare.

As we have seen, the professional crusaders for peace like Baroness von Suttner, opposed attempts to humanize war and alleviate its horrors. She said, "St. George rode forth to kill the dragon, not to trim its claws." She wanted the monster war to be let alone to develop all its hideous features so that the evil would die from the excess of evil. Even Florence Nightingale openly opposed the Geneva Red Cross convention because she feared that it would encourage belligerent nations to go to war.

The opposite school of thought is epitomized by the Norwegian poet Nordahl Grieg who was killed while on a bombing raid of Berlin during World War II. He wrote, "In creating human worth, we are creating peace." Dr. Schweitzer expresses the proposition in the simplest possible terms, "It is good to maintain life. It is evil to destroy it." Following Dr. Schweitzer's theory that, "no ray of sunshine is ever lost," it is hoped that the indication of a feeling for other people; the desire to help them, the expression of human sympathy, the respect for the dignity of every human being despite differences in nationality and race, must, in time, form a basis for a lasting peace.

In essence, this distills down to Tolstoy's doctrine of universal love : "who loves his neighbor loves peace." Dr. Schweitzer calls love the highest form of reason. He goes on to state :

Only such thinking as establishes the sway of the mental attitude of reverence for life can bring to mankind perpetual peace. The ethics of reverence for life . . . . force everyone without cessation to be concerned with all the other human destinies which are going through their life-course around him, and to give himself, as man, to the man who needs a fellow man. They will not allow the scholar to live only for his learning, even if his learning makes him very useful, nor the artist only for his art, even if by means of it he gives something to many. They do not allow the busy man to think that with his professional activities he has fulfilled every demand upon him. They demand from all that they devote a portion of this life to their fellows.

Evidently, the Nobel committee believes that both lines of peace work will ultimately converge to accomplish the desired goal. In its very first selections, in 1901, the committee designated Dunant who desired to remedy the worst excesses of war, and Passy, who was the leader of the constructive peace professionals.

Dunant had trained for the banking business and had become the representative of a Geneva bank in North Africa. While there, he had bought a tract of land in Algeria. It so happened that his land was arid but adjacent land owned by the government had a supply of water. After the usual frustrating attempts to secure some sort of action from the local officials, the brash Dunant resolved to go to Paris to press his claims directly with the Emperor of Louis Napoleon. Unfortunately, when Dunant arrived at the city of light, he learned that the Emperor was pursuing military adventures in Italy. Undaunted, the future founder of the Red Cross followed in the path of the armies, determined to gain a royal audience. That was how Dunant happened to run across the battle of Solferino on June 24, 1859. He was deeply touched by the need of the wounded soldiers of the French, Sardinian and Austrian forces for medical care. In contrast to the usual practice of leaving the wounded unattended, Dunant converted a Roman Catholic church in Castiglione into an emergency field hospital and did what he could to succor some of the forty thousand casualties of that battle. Three years later he published *Souvenir de Solferino*, which quickly became an international best seller.

The book ends with this plea :

Would it not be possible, in time of peace and quiet, to form relief societies for the purpose of having care given to the wounded in wartime by zealous, devoted and thoroughly qualified volunteers?

In response, four influential members of the Geneva Welfare Society joined with Dunant on February 17, 1863, to form what became known as the International Committee of the Red Cross.

In addition, Dunant travelled widely all over Europe advocating the organization in each country of a voluntary Red Cross society to serve as a humane adjunct of war for, "the amelioration of the condition of the wounded in armies in the field." He also favored an international agreement to formulate rules for the protection of the victims of war. An international congress was held in 1864 and the Geneva Convention for the Amelioration of the Condition of Wounded in Armies in the Field was adopted. The convention was originally ratified by sixteen nations and, at this writing, eighty-nine countries have ratified it.

Because his work with the Red Cross absorbed so much of his time and energy, Dunant neglected his business and was

forced into bankruptcy in 1867. In order not to embarrass the
Red Cross, he resigned his position as secretary and left
Geneva. In obscurity, he drifted off to Paris, London, Stuttgart, and back to Heiden, Switzerland, barely subsisting on
odd jobs. He was to write :

I, too, have belonged to those who on the streets gnaw at a roll
which they have hidden in their pocket, who darken their clothes
with ink and whiten their collars with chalk and fill out a shabby,
formless hat with papers.

When a Swiss journalist published an interview with Dunant
in 1895 the world was surprised to learn that the founder of
the Red Cross was still alive. By that time his memory and his
faculties were already fading. If you visit the cemetery in
Zurich where he is buried you will find his grave marked by a
white marble monument of a man kneeling to offer water to
a fallen soldier. Dunant's birthday, May 8th, is celebrated as
World Red Cross Day.

Appropriately enough, Dunant's International Committe of
the Red Cross was awarded the Nobel peace prize during each
of the two world wars and during the Cold War—in 1917,
in 1944 and in 1963. This committee, with headquarters at
Geneva, now consists of twenty-five members —all Swiss, who
serve without compensation. The International Committee
works with, but is not controlled by, the League of Red Cross
Societies, which shared the award in 1963 and which is composed of 102 national Red Cross societies of the various
countries with 170,000,000 members. It is this unique position
of neutrality and independence which has enabled the International Committee to carry on its functions during the
great wars.

With the outbreak of war in 1914, the committee established
the "Agence internationale de secours et de renseignements
en favour des prisonniers de guerre," to establish communica-

tion between prisoners of war and their relatives. The committee arranged for the inspection of prisoner of war camps and handled the exchange, via Switzerland, of seriously wounded non-commissioned soldiers. It protested strongly against inhumane acts of war; such as the German sinking of hospital ships, and the Turkish massacre of the Armenians.

The International Committee, which had been given official standing by the Prisoner of War Convention of 1929, resumed its work during the Second World War. During this conflict it shipped over forty million items to prisoners of war and civilian internees. With the assistance of between four thousand to five thousand aides; one million incoming and nine hundred thousand outgoing messages were handled each month. A pile of over twenty-five thousand index cards was established to help in the tracing of displaced persons.

In peace time and during the Cold War, the International Committee and the Red Cross League extended disaster relief, helped evacuate and resettle civilians, reunited dispersed families, assisted political detainees, and distributed relief supplies on both sides of the iron and bamboo curtains.

At the time of the granting of the second award, Dr. Max Huber, a professor of international law, a former president of the International Court of Justice at the Hague, and acting president of the International Committee, was able to state with pride that his organization had been, "able to keep alive some shred of human decency, some spark of humanity, some hope in the heart of mankind that all good has not vanished from the earth." He goes on to say:

The Red Cross ideal stands as the embodiment of the notions of worth and dignity of the human being. In this respect, the Red Cross transcends by far the concepts of international law and of war. In the deepest sense of the term, this ideal is the preliminary condition for any community of man.

However, in any study of the history and work of the Red Cross movement, there is one gnawing question that will not permit itself to be stilled : Why has the Red Cross always accepted the inevitability of war and never concerned itself with how wars might be prevented?

Strange as it may seem, the symbol of the twentieth century is not the automobile, or the jet plane, or the sputnik, or even the mushroom cloud of the exploded atom bomb. Rather, the symbol is that of the refugee, fleeing along the clogged roads, clutching his meagre belongings, huddled over a fire in the open fields, picking his way through the mine field and the barbed wire, and then rotting away in the displaced persons camps. Like the prisoners in Beethoven's "Fidelio" who emerge from the bowels of the earth, the refugee comes forth, from ruthless Turkey, Hindu India, Moslem Pakistan, Red China, Nazi Germany, Bahutu Ruanda, communist Indo-China, communist Hungary, communist East Germany, Castro Cuba, and Portuguese Angola. They flee before the advancing German, Japanese, and Russian armies. Young and old, male and female, threadbare, hungry, destitute, unwanted, distrusted, they are, in the words of Dr. G. J. Von Heuven-Goedhart, "one of the greatest human tragedies of the twentieth century."

The "Bureau internationale Nansen pour les refugés " had been constituted by the League of Nations in 1930 as the central refugee service of the League. The agency was named in honor of the 1922 Nobel peace laureate who had been the League's first high commissioner for refugees, and who had just died. When the Nansen agency was announced as the winner of the peace prize for 1938, it had already helped to resettle over eight hundred thousand refugees, including Armenians, Saarlanders, and Jews. The agency also collected information on the material and moral welfare of the refugees, which was reported through the League, and gave general direction to relief institutions which were helping the displaced persons.

In its turn, the United Nations also found it necessary to set up an agency similar to the Nansen office. It was set up in 1951 as the United Nations Refugee Emergency Fund, with headquarters in Geneva under the administration of a United Nations High Commissioner for Refugees. The 1954 Nobel peace prize was awarded to this office.

To this agency had been assigned the task of resettling the 350,000 residual refugees who had been left in Europe by World War II. Scattered in camps throughout Germany, Austria, Italy and Greece, these unfortunates represented "one of the painful legacies of the last war." It also provided legal and social safeguards for two million refugees throughout the world.

The 1958 award was also made in recognition of work on behalf of refugees. The recipient was Reverend Dominique George Henri Pire, born in 1910, a member of the Dominican order, who had organized the Europe of the Hearts movement in an attempt to have displaced persons "rejoin the human race."

As a boy, during World War I, Reverend Pire had watched as the German troops stood his grandfather against a barn and shot him. Thus, during the Second World War, the priest, who had been educated at Bellevue College (Dinant), Rome, and Louvain, and taught, for ten years, moral philosophy and sociology at the Huy, Belgium, monastery, became the chaplain of the Belgian underground and an intelligence officer assisting in the escape of downed Allied flyers. He received the Belgian War Cross with palms, the French Legion of Honor, the Resistance Medal with Crossed Swords, and the National Recognition Medal.

Father Pire had begun his charitable work, in 1938, with the founding of a "Service d'Entraide de la Familiale" to help needy families, and of "Stations de Plein Air de Huy" to provide fresh air vacations for poor children. After the war he became concerned with the plight of the hard core of refugees from Eastern Europe, "people who have been sitting for twelve years on their suitcases in a railroad station waiting for a train that will never arrive." He set up a system of sponsors or godparents who were encouraged to correspond with and help refugee children and families. Eventually, a hundred thousand letters a year were being exchanged among the correspondents.

Operating under the theory that "it is better to get one little apple tree well planted than a thousand trees in a dream orchard," European villages were built in Aix-la-Chapelle, Germany; Augsberg, Germany; Bregenz, Austria; Brussels, and in the Saar. The population of each of these villages is limited to 150 persons, with the intention that the rehabilitated displaced families might be reintegrated into the human community. Four homes for aged displaced persons were also established in Belgium.

In the face of these good works, the communist press of Czechoslovakia could, with characteristic totalitarian disregard of the individual, condemn the award to Reverend Pire as "an insult to all true lovers of peace."

Interviewers who sought out Reverend Pire after the award was announced, found this quotation from Anne Frank's diary framed on his desk :

Things will change and men become good again and these pitiless days will come to an end and the world will once more know order, rest and peace.

In his presentation, Gunnar Jahn, the president of the Nobel committee, had commented, "What counts much more than figures is the spirit which has animated Georges Pire's work, what he has sown in the soul of man and which in the future will, we hope, blossom in the shape of disinterested work for our fellow men plunged in misery."

In accepting the Nobel Peace Prize, Father Pire had pledged :

I should like to use the moral credit of the Nobel Peace Prize in such a way that when I die this credit will return to you, not only whole and intact, but increased, augumented by the way in which I have used it, so that later on, your successors will be able to offer in the Nobel Peace Prize even greater moral credit, because your 1958 laureate has borne it well.

He considered the award "not as a reward, but as a responsibility." A Belgian newspaper greeted Father Pire on his return from Oslo: "From now on you are a part of every man's dream of peace."

In furtherance of this pledge and responsibility, Father Pire helped found the University of Peace at Tihange-lez-Huy on April 10, 1960, to which five hundred participants from forty countries had come in the first five years. They came to acquire training in the Fraternal Dialogue. He organized World Friendships to incarnate the Fraternal Dialogue either by friendly exchange or correspondence; and World Sponsorships where individuals are encouraged to act as godfathers or godmothers, undertaking to provide financial aid for a godchild (a refugee from Ruanda, Angola or Tibet) for one year to enable him to continue his studies. The Island of Peace was founded in February, 1962, at Gohire, East Pakistan, to help the disadvantaged "to walk alone."

All these activities make up the work of the Heart Open to the World, founded June 5, 1959, as an extension of the Europe of the Hearts movement. The principal object of the new movement was the diffusion of the practice of the Fraternal Dialogue as the true path leading to peace.

Fraternal Dialogue is defined by Professor Dondeyne of

Louvain University as "a mutual effort to understand what is in the other's mind and how he feels."

Man begins with a personal opinion; this is the monologue stage. This opinion comes up against the opinion of others. Monologues may clash and one may attempt to impose his opinion upon others by force and violence. But, instead, men may compare and discuss opinions. This is the transition from monologue to dialogue, from barbarism to civilization, from pre-man to truly human being. The object of true dialogue is to open the mind to the understanding of those who differ from ourselves, to listen and to harmonize those differences which are, in themselves, a richness. Father Pire quotes Antoine de St. Exupéry: "If I differ from you, far from doing you wrong, I augment you." Father Pire concludes, "Those who are not men of the Dialogue are fanatics."

13 Balance of Terror

Norway did not escape the ravages of World War II. On April 9, 1940, German sea and airborne divisions invaded Oslo, Bergen, Trondheim, Stavanger and Narvik. The Norwegians rallied from the surprise attack and offered growing resistance, but the small nation and her brave people were overwhelmed. On April 30th, King Haakon VII and his cabinet were forced to flee to London. The Germans installed Vidkun Quisling as minister president, whose rule was to become synonymous with betrayal and treachery.

Halvdan Koht and the other members of the Nobel committee had to flee for their lives: the committee didn't even meet during 1940, 1941, and 1942. The next prize was to be announced in 1944 and, as we have seen, it went, for the second time, to the International Committee of the Red Cross at Geneva.

The end of World War II witnessed the establishment of another organization of victors—this time called the United Nations—with the signing of the Charter by the plenipotentiaries of fifty nations at San Francisco on June 26, 1945. Japan was finally admitted to membership in December, 1956, while the truncated portions of Germany and Red China are still denied membership. The written constitution is now called the Charter of the United Nations and is another high-sounding document. Its preamble reads as follows:

> We the peoples of the United Nations
> Determined to save succeeding generations from the scourge of war, which twice in our lifetime has brought untold sorrow to mankind, and
> To reaffirm faith in fundamental human rights, in the dignity and worth of the human person, in equal rights of men and women and of nations large and small, and
> To establish conditions under which justice and respect for the obligations arising from treaties and other sources of international law can be maintained, and
> To promise social progress and better standards of life in larger freedom, and for these ends
> To practice tolerance and live together in peace with one another as good neighbors, and
> To unite our strength and to maintain international peace and security, and
> To insure, by the acceptance of principles and the institution of methods, that armed force shall not be used, save in the common interest, and
> To employ international machinery for the promotion of the economic and social advancement of all peoples, have resolved to combine our efforts to accomplish these aims.

The era of the United Nations is being lived in the shadow of poisonous radio-active dust clouds spewed into the atmosphere; at Alamogordo July 16, 1945; Hiroshima August 6, 1945; Nagasaki; Nevada; Eniwetok; Johnston Island; Novaya Zemlya; Sahara; Christmas Island; Semipolatinsk; and the Taklamakan Desert. The masthead, "balance of terror," is the only possible slogan for an age with a stockpile of bombs sufficient to over-kill every inhabitant of the earth thirty-two to thirty-five times, which, in the words of John Steinbeck, is a prolonged "tragedy of universal physical fear."

The political catchwords; brinkmanship, cold war, overkill, second strike, massive instant retaliation, total annihilation, megadeath, escalation, and pre-emptive war, strike terror into the heart of every man and woman. In writing about this "peace through mutual terror," Winston Churchill describes how "by a process of sublime irony," the world has reached a stage "where safety will be the sturdy child of terror and survival the twin brother of annihilation."

In times gone by, there could be confidence in the future because even the worst disasters could not destroy mankind — some would be spared. But a new ingredient has been added, since July 16, 1945, to the witches' brew which is international relations: the ability of man, imperfect man, to completely obliterate life on this planet. To quote Steinbeck again:

We have usurped many of the powers we once ascribed to God. Fearful and unprepared, we have assumed lordship over the life and death of the whole world, of all living things.

Man's understanding and his political and social institutions have not kept pace with the surge in knowledge and mechanical manipulation in the physical sciences. Mankind since Alamogordo has lived under the Damocles sword of momentary and instantaneous annihilation through deliberate act, accident, miscalculation or madness.

This, then, is the age of the United Nations. Throughout this period, however, the Nobel committee continued to grope with its Diogenes lantern through the thick blanket of fear and suspicion, in its never ending quest for that elusive peace. It was to be expected, therefore, that the prize for 1945 should go to the man who was known as the father of the United Nations, Cordell Hull (1871–1955). Frankin D. Roosevelt had characterized Hull as "the one person in all the world who has done the most to make this great plan for peace (the United Nations) an effective fact."

Hull, as United States Secretary of State, had gone to Moscow for the conference of foreign secretaries which had drafted the Declaration of Moscow of October 30, 1943. This declaration had pledged the four big powers to cooperate until the surrender of the Axis nations, and then to establish a general international organization open to all peace loving states for the maintenance of international peace and security.

Hull's internationalism was a natural development of his work as a congressman, and as a member of the cabinet on behalf of lower tariffs and reciprocal trade. He also actively promoted the good neighbor policy in Latin America, but, he has been criticized for his support of dictatorships in that region and especially for his friendship with Generalissimo Rafael Trujillo of the Dominican Republic. The main street of Santo Domingo was renamed by that dictator to honor Cordell Hull. It was the letter that Hull wrote to Speaker Sam Rayburn that is credited with having won the extension of the draft law by one vote in August, 1941. He falls in the typical pattern of national politician thrust upon the world scene as previously exemplified by Beernaert, Root, Lamas, Briand, Chamberlain, and others.

We have already discussed the contributions of the co-winners of the 1946 award, John R. Mott, and Emily G. Balch.

The 1947 prize was won by 140,000 persons, the members of the American Friends Service Committee in Philadelphia, and of the Friends Service Council in London. In announcing the choice, Gunnar Jahn, the chairman of the Nobel Committee, had commented that the "reason is so obvious that further comment ought to be unnecessary. . . . It is the silent help from the nameless to the nameless which is their contribution to the promotion of brotherhood among nations."

Norman Angell had written :

The dedication and abnegation which is so commonplace with Quakers should reduce us ordinary mortals to silence and humility in their presence.

The Religious Society of Friends had first been formed in

1647 by that inspired weaver, George Fox. Upon being offered a captaincy in Cromwell's army, that good man Fox wrote in his Journal:

> I told them I knew from whence all wars arose, even from the lust, and that I lived in the virtue of that life and power that took away the occasions of all wars.

In 1660 the Society sent the following manifesto to Charles II:

> We utterly deny all outward wars and strife, and fightings with outward weapons, for any end, or under any pretence whatever; this is our testimony to the world . . . . and we certainly know and testify to the world, that the Spirit of Christ, which leads us into all truth, will never move us to fight and war against any man with outward weapons, either for the kingdom of Christ, nor for the kingdom of this world. Therefore, we cannot learn war anymore.

From that day, Quakers will not fight or recognize war; they recognize that in every human being there is an "inner light" which no man has the right to extinguish. These witnesses for peace preach a positive idea of peace—not as opposite to war—expressed in good works performed selflessly and offered entirely on the basis of need, without regard to creed, nationality or political belief.

To accomplish these ends, the Service Council of the British Society of Friends was formed in 1850, and the American Friends Service Committee in 1917. At the time of the award, these groups, as a practical expression of social concern, had administered over $60,000,000 for relief in more than twenty devastated countries. They had fought typhus epidemics in Poland and Serbia, had cooperated with the Hoover relief administration from Belgium to Russia, had distributed food and clothing in Austria, Germany, Hungary, Poland, Japan, Spain, and China, had organized community service projects in France and Finland, had helped students in Italy, strikers in Southern United States, and stateless refugees in Spain, had inaugurated medical and industrial rehabilitation programs in China and India, and had helped with Negro job placements in the United States. And, in each country, the Friends had sponsored conferences, and seminars, and educational programs.

The Friends were the first to establish a Peace Corps. They also sponsored peace intern programs and courses of peace education as witness of their convictions. Clarence E. Pickett, the secretary emeritus, defined bearing witness as "any and all pacifist actions, and means standing up for one's conscience with the purpose of influencing others to do the same."

A newspaper editorial summed up the practically universal reaction as:

an award richly deserved. These indefatigable Friends have quietly and persistently confronted strife and starvation with peace and mercy, pestilence and death with healing and life, the dehumanization of man with redemption and personal love.

Yet, some critics even termed these humanitarian groups "well known transmission belts for the Communist apparatus."

The year 1948 witnessed the omission, once again, of the peace prize award.

The award to the service organizations of the Friends had dramatized one of the greatest problems facing the United Nations—eradication of disease and hunger. These twin scourges have been spectres haunting mankind since the dawn of history. Until now they have been patiently accepted as the lot preordained for man. What makes these curses particularly horrifying now is the fact that now there exists the wherewithal to end all hunger and most diseases.

Two current reports of the United Nations Food and Agricultural Organization list one-half of all humanity as suffering either outright hunger or weakening malnutrition. Almost all of the people of Asia, most of those in the Middle East, parts of Africa, Central America, and north and northwest South America receive less than two thousand calories a day, while in other parts of the world food is plowed under and farmers are paid to not grow. For five successive years, through July 15, 1964, population growth increased faster than food production. According to Dr. Binay Ranjan Sen, United Nations director-general of the Food and Agricultural Organization, more people were starving to death in 1963 than at any other time in history.

Alfred Nobel had said, "As a rule, I'd rather take care of the stomachs of the living than the glory of the departed in the form of monuments." The winner of the peace prize for 1949 qualified under this rule, for he was Lord Boyd-Orr of Brechin, born in 1880, the first director-general of the United Nations Food and Agricultural Organization. He was also qualified for this position on the basis of his training and experience.

A doctor of medicine from Glasgow, who had switched from the study of theology to that of nutrition, Boyd-Orr became the director of the Institute of Animal Nutrition of Aberdeen University in 1914, and the founder of the Rowett Imperial Bureau of Animal Nutrition in 1919. In 1932 he was appointed to a government committee charged with surveying the nutrition status of the various income groups. The result of that study was *Food, Health and Income,* published in 1936, which demonstrated that the cost of a diet fulfilling the basic nutritional requirements was beyond the means of one-half of the British people, and that ten percent of the British population was suffering from actual malnutrition. To correct this condition, Boyd-Orr favored subsidies to farmers and to low income consumers.

In the same year of 1936, he was appointed to a League of

Nations committee to investigate world nutrition. It was to be expected, therefore, that Boyd-Orr would be unanimously elected director-general at the first UNFAO conference at Quebec, in October, 1945. He has been professor of agriculture at Aberdeen University, has been the rector of Glasgow University since 1945, and has been the member in Parliament for the Scottish universities. He was knighted by his king in 1935 and made a baron in 1949.

Pointing out that the Chinese word for peace is ho-ping which means food for all, Boyd-Orr believed that cooperation by the nations in a common war against want would be the key to ultimate collaboration on international political issues. In a statement upon retiring from FAO in April, 1948, he said:

It is difficult to get nations to cooperate on a political level. The world is torn by political strife. But through the FAO the nations are cooperating. Here at the council table, representatives of governments are not talking about war, not thinking about war. They are planning for the greatest movement that will make for peace—increased food production, the strengthening of agriculture and food for the people of the world.

As a scientist he knew that "Modern science has the answer to Malthus," and that "with known methods the earth could support a population of six billions." To put the question in his words:

so we come back to the fundamental question upon the answer to which the future of mankind depends: Will governments cooperate to apply science to promote the welfare of the peoples of the world, or, in rival groups, apply it to their mutual destruction? The aggression of hunger and poverty which causes the premature death of two-thirds of the people of the world, is a greater menace to health and happiness than either communist or capitalist aggression. Apart from moral principles, intelligent self-interest should induce the highly industrialized countries to cooperate in abolishing hunger and poverty, for these are a growing threat to the security of the prosperous third of the world population and to world peace. [He continues], The all-important

question is whether the relatively few men who control the
destiny of the present changing world have the political maturity,
the wisdom and the goodwill to initiate the great international
creative effort needed to bring the new epoch into being, or
whether in their short-sighted pride of power, they will attempt
to apply absolute means which will destroy the present civilization.

He notes that :

The world would be a much safer place for our children if there
were fewer soldiers thinking of armaments for the next war and
more statesmen thinking of food for the next generation.

Boyd-Orr observes that :

freedom from hunger must come first. It would be foolish to
eliminate disease and cause a sudden increase in the population
when there is not sufficient food for the present population.

The logical units to direct the battle against malnutrition
and disease are, in Boyd-Orr's opinion, the specialized agencies
of the United Nations and he deplored the niggardly granting
of authority and funds by the nations to these agencies.

In his Nobel address, Boyd-Orr declared :

If the 60 governments which adhere to these specialized agencies
and have given them a great deal of cooperation and lip service,
would agree to devote to them one unit of their currency for
every one hundred they are devoting to preparation for war and
allow them freedom of action, I venture to predict that within a
few years the political issues which divide nations would become
meaningless and the obstacles to peace disappear.

Boyd-Orr continued his work on behalf of peace as president
of the British Peace Council, of the World Federalist Association and the World Peace Association.

The award for 1948 had been omitted because the Nobel
committee had intended to name Count Folke Bernadotte, the
United Nations mediator in Palestine. This intention was

thwarted by his assassination by terrorists of the Stern group in September, 1948. Instead, the prize for 1950 went to Ralph J. Bunche, born in 1904, who had been the count's assistant for five months and who had become acting mediator upon his death.

Bunche was superbly qualified by training and experience to supervise the eighty-one days of difficult negotiation on the island of Rhodes between Israel and her four Arab neighbors. The son of a barber and the grandson of a slave, he had been orphaned at the age of fourteen and been required to move from Detroit to the Watts district of Los Angeles where he was raised by his grandmother. He laid carpets in order to pay his way through high school, and then received a partial athletic scholarship to the University of California. There he worked as a janitor during the school year and as a messenger for a shipping line during the summers, starred in basketball, baseball and football, was elected to the Phi Beta Kappa, and received his B.A. in 1926. He went on to receive his M.A. from Harvard University in 1928, and the same year joined the faculty of Howard University (a Negro university), as an instructor in the political science department.

Bunche continued his graduate studies at Northwestern University, The London School of Economics, and the University of Capetown and finally earned his Ph.D. from Harvard in 1934 with a thesis on French administration in Togoland and Dahomey. He also worked on Gunnar Myrdal's staff in their comprehensive study of the American Negro, sponsored by the Carnegie Corporation. In the meantime, he had become chairman of the political science department at Howard.

He received a leave of absence from that university in 1941 so that he could become Chief of the African section of the United States Office of Strategic Services (intelligence corps). In 1944 he moved to the State Department as associate chief of the division of dependent area affairs. He served as a technical expert with the United States United Nations delegation to San Francisco in 1945.

Bunche joined the United Nations in 1946 as director of the Department of Trusteeship and Information from Non-Self Governing Territories. It was from this job that he was detailed to assist Count Folke Bernadotte and thereby became acting mediator in Palestine. In this position, he literally worked around the clock in order to achieve the armistice among practically irreconcilable enemies. Moshe Sharett, the minister of foreign affairs for Israel, praised Bunche's "herculean efforts to put an end to the fighting in Palestine," and commented on how all the emissaries had "learned to admire his inexhaustible patience, resources and ingenuity in the complex armistice negotiations between Israel and her four neighbors." Dean Acheson, the United States Secretary of State, recognized that :

Dr. Bunche's achievement in bringing about armistice agreements between Israel and the neighboring Arab states stands as one of the first and foremost contributions of the United Nations to the peaceful settlement of international disputes.

Dr. Bunche was the first to acknowledge that responsibility for his achievement lay with the United Nations team of about seven hundred military observers and international civil servants, and to the organization itself. When informed of the award, he stated : "I, more than any one, recognize the extent to which my peace efforts in the Near East flowed from the strength of the United Nations." In his Nobel address he reiterated : "If the United Nations cannot ensure peace, there will be none."

A permanent employee of the United Nations, Dr. Bunche has advanced to the position of Under Secretary for Special Political Affairs.

The award of the 1951 peace prize to Léon Jouhaux (1879–1954) will be discussed in a subsequent chapter.

It would be impossible, indeed impudent, to discuss, within the confines of this small volume, the Olympian breadth of the work of Albert Schweitzer (1875–1965), the winner of the 1952 peace prize. As an organist, musicologist, philosopher, theologian, physician, and writer — many books have been written about this man who has been called the thirteenth apostle and the twentieth century's matchless human being.

Yet, the student is puzzled to understand the basis upon which Dr. Schweitzer qualified for the peace prize unless the Nobel committee was seeking to clothe itself with some of the aura that surrounds the man. True, he came out against atomic testing, but so have millions of other people and it didn't put them in line for the Nobel peace prize. The fact is that Dr. Schweitzer, during a very long life, had never been associated with the international peace movement. In this regard, an editorial in the *Christian Century* commented :

The award to Dr. Schweitzer can hardly have been recognition for any direct contribution he has made to the organized peace movement, for he has never taken a conspicuous part in it. Rather, it is recognition, well merited, that what a man is can be more far-reaching in its effects than what he says or even what he does.

The editorial is undoubtedly referring to Dr. Schweitzer's identification with the doctrine of "reverence for life." As he put it :

It is good to maintain life. It is evil to destroy it. Only such thinking as establishes the sway of the mental attitude of reverence for life can bring to mankind perpetual peace.

This, he has extolled, is the "highest form of reason — love, the first principle of civilization."

Implicit in this ethic is the concept of service. Dr. Schweitzer counseled, "You must give some time to your fellow man. Even if it's a little thing, do something for those who have need of a man's help, something for which you get no pay but the privilege of doing it." Dr. Schweitzer heeded the biblical injunction to, "Heal the sick, cleanse the lepers, raise the dead, cast out devils: freely, ye have received, freely give."

Dr. Schweitzer described the origin of the phrase "reverence for life": "Slowly we crept upstream laboriously feeling—it was the dry season—for the channels between the sandbanks. Lost in thought, I sat on the deck of the barge, struggling to find the elementary and universal conception of the ethical which I had not discovered in any philosophy. Sheet after sheet I covered with disconnected sentences merely to keep myself concentrated on the problem. Late on the third day, at the very moment when, at sunset, we were making our way through a herd of hippopotamuses, there flashed upon my mind, unforeseen and unsought, the phrase, 'Reverence for Life.' The iron door had yielded: the path in the thicket had become visible."

The whole world is familiar with the story of the brilliant scholar who renounced the blandishments of Western Europe and set sail in 1913 for the Paris Evangelical Mission station and hospital in the Ogooue River at Lamberéné, Gabon, French Equatorial Africa. In time, the original broken-down hen coop grew to encompass more than seventy buildings, 350 beds and a leper village of 200. Over a million and a half sick people have been treated there. Although his medical practices may have been termed somewhat outdated, no one will question that this remarkable missionary performed extraordinary humanitarian deeds of charity on behalf of the natives. But do we witness a life governed in its daily routines by the expressed philosophies of "reverence for life" and love of humanity, or are these abstract formulations, which have not been permitted to apply to the individual African?

Except for internment as an enemy alien during World War I, Dr. Schweitzer spent most of the last fifty years of his life in the black continent. This half-century coincided with the period of great ferment among the subject colonial peoples and the emergence of a score of new African nations. Yet, in his southwest African hospital, he remained largely insulated from the main current of events gripping this restive continent. One would imagine that the impact of such a giant over the course of such a span of time would percolate down and make itself felt in the limbs and extremities of that dark continent. But, one would have to search hard to find any bearing or influence upon Africa that could be traced to Dr. Schweitzer. He has had no effect upon the position of the black man or upon the headlong drive of Africa's current history.

Dr. Schweitzer was sitting there in the African jungle, right smack in the middle of one of the most burning questions of the United Nations era—the emancipation of the depressed and exploited black people, and their preparation for self-government and for a position of human dignity; economically, socially, and politically. But the good doctor remained aloof from the swirl of the seething maelstrom. He never learned to speak any African dialect. Although he found time to travel extensively throughout the white man's world, he never visited any other part of Africa nor had he even been to Brazzaville, the former capital of French Equatorial Africa.

One begins to understand the, "Schweitzer, Go Home," signs which often plastered his compound.

Perhaps this lack of identification with the black man and the black man's hopes and aspirations is due to the basic approach of Dr. Schweitzer to international and racial questions, which is that of the nineteenth century imperialist. He would not understand Patrice Lumumba's lament of the, "ironies, the insults, the blows that we had to submit to morning, noon, and night because we were Negroes." Dr. Schweitzer would not agree with Pope John XXIII's contention that : "it is not true that some human beings are by nature superior and others inferior. All men are equal in their natural dignity."

In a sense, the ramshackle, dirty, primitive, tin-roofed village hospital is a manifestation of a nostalgic desire to hold back the tide of change, to perpetuate the imperialist notion of the savage. Dr. Schweitzer said, "simple people need simple healing methods."

Dr. Schweitzer stated, "You don't live in a world all your own. Your brothers are here, too." But he hastened to qualify this broad embrace by adding a postscript : "I am the Negro's brother, but his elder brother." John Gunther reported that the Doctor had "scarcely ever in his life talked with an adult African on adult terms." This deprecating attitude can be illustrated by any number of quotations from Dr. Schweitzer :

One arranges at once in Africa that the blacks shall be in the white people's quarters as little as possible; that is a necessary part of one's care for one's self.

One's servants are so unreliable that they must not be exposed to the slightest temptation; this means that they must never be left alone in the house.

One can never rely on the natives here, not even in things which they understand from long practice.

In Africa we learn not to be too exacting.

The Negro is a child and with children nothing can be done without the use of authority.

In dealing with the native one must combine in right measure firmness and kindness, avoid unnecessary talk and find a jocular remark at the right moment.

Inability to exert themselves and adapt themselves to difficult circumstances is typical of the natives and makes them pitiable creatures.

Africa would be beautiful without its savages.

At this stage (1963), Africans have little need for advanced training. They need very elementary schools run along the old missionary plan, with the African going to school for a few hours every day and then going back to the fields.

The Africans have not learned to understand what we really mean by continuous work.

The zeal of my colored folk to provide for those who come after them for better quarters than they have themselves is very small; they do not work for those they do not know.

Perhaps this is why Dr. Schweitzer never tried to train any Africans to enable them to carry on his healing work at Lambaréné after he had gone.

Such a patronizing attitude casts suspicion on Dr. Schweitzer's entire concept of humanitarianism. Can we really term charity that act of giving where a self-supposing superior bestows largesse upon those whom he considers his inferiors? Or must we look for the true meaning of charity to Jane Addams and to the blessed Friends who give in a spirit of humility and abnegation which ties them with an identification of brotherly love and understanding to the recipient?

An African nationalist leader once said of Dr. Schweitzer, "He is doing things for us and not with us." Another African observed, "I'd rather die unattended than be humiliated in Dr. Schweitzer's hospital."

Dr. Schweitzer once commented to Pablo Casals: "It is better to create than to protest." Replied the great cellist and protester: "Why not do both?"

The winner of the 1953 prize, General George C. Marshall (1880–1959), will be discussed in a later chapter.

The work of the Office of the United Nations Commissioner for Refugees, the recipient of the 1954 award, has already been reviewed.

No awards were made for the years 1955 and 1956.

The designee for the 1957 prize was a man who has been termed the diplomat of the atomic age — Lester B. (Mike) Pearson, born in 1897.

Mike Pearson had left the University of Toronto during World War I to enlist first in the Canadian Army, and later in the Royal Air Force. After the war, he returned to finish his studies at the university. After graduating in 1919 he tried working in the Armour meat packing plant in Chicago but finally decided that he was better suited for an academic life. He quit Armour to accept a fellowship in history at St. John College, Oxford, where he also played Olympic ice hockey and lacrosse. He returned to teach history at his alma mater from 1924 to 1928, and to coach its football and hockey teams.

Pearson changed careers again in 1928, after topping all applicants in a civil service examination, and joined his country's foreign service. After experience as secretary to royal commissions on grain futures and price spreads, he was assigned to the London office of the Canadian High Commissioner from 1935 to 1941 (the blitz) and to the embassy in Washington from 1942 to 1945. In 1945 he was advanced to ambassador, serving until 1946 when he was called to Ottawa as under-secretary of state for external affairs. He entered politics in 1948 and was elected as a Liberal Member of Parliament from the northern Ontario uranium area of Algoma East. Later that year he achieved cabinet status with his promotion to Secretary of State for External Affairs, a position he was to hold until the Conservative Party victory in 1957.

As the author of the first Western statement leading to the establishment of that organization, Pearson played an active role in the affairs of the North Atlantic Treaty Organization and served for a term as chairman of its Council. He was one of the three wise men who, with Halvard Lange of Norway and Gaetano Martino of Italy, were charged with studying ways of expanding the functions of NATO to non-military fields. Pearson's tart comment was "three blind mice is more likely." Perhaps that is why he was known as a "strictly non-stuffed shirt diplomat."

He was involved in the activities of the United Nations from its very beginnings, having been a senior advisor to the Canadian delegation at San Francisco. After the United Nations began functioning, Pearson made many valuable suggestions which were decisive in influencing the course of that organization. He was chairman of the conferences which organized the FAO and the United Nations Relief and Rehabilitation Administration (UNRRA). He was chairman of the General Assembly fifty-five-nation special committee on Palestine, and was the architect of the plan that made possible the partition of that former colony into Jewish and Arab states in 1947; with the blessing of both the United States and the Soviet Union. He was one of the three statesmen who brought about a truce in the Korea-Peking prisoner of war dispute. He was elected president of the General Assembly's seventh session in 1952–1953.

Pearson's greatest contribution to the United Nations was made during the course of the Suez crisis. In the debate on the evening of November 2, 1956, he had taken the initiative of proposing a "United Nations force, a truly international peace and police force," in the following terms:

I would like to see a provision authorizing the Secretary-General to begin to make arrangements with member states for a United Nations force large enough to keep these borders at peace while a political settlement is being worked out.

France, Britain and Israel seized this suggestion as the peg upon which they might base their withdrawal from Egypt with a minimum loss of face. Accordingly, Pearson offered the key resolution on the Suez crisis the next day. It directed the Secretary-General to submit:

within 48 hours, a plan for the setting up, with the consent of the nations concerned, of an emergency international UN Force to secure and supervise the cessation of hostilities in accordance with all the terms of the aforementioned (November 2 cease-fire) resolution.

The resolution was adopted 57–0 with nineteen abstentions and the United Nations Emergency Force (UNEF) came into being.

At the time of the Berlin crisis, Pearson, in an extension of his proposal of a United Nations force, had regretted the absence of a force in existence and questioned why the middle and smaller powers, "whose credentials and whose motives would be above reproach," should not agree without waiting for a General Assembly resolution to, "earmark, train and equip certain of their forces for UN action," on a standby basis and available upon call. This suggestion was to bear fruition at the time of the Congo crisis. Pearson had also originally suggested OPEX, which was a pool of experienced administrative, operational and executive personnel that was available for assignment to the service of the governments requesting them, and who would be responsible solely to these governments.

On accepting the peace prize from King Olav V on December 10, 1957, Pearson urged the world to "work for an empire of peace," and declared that weapons of mass destruction must be junked or "they will destroy us all." Although Pearson is not an orator, his Nobel lecture delivered the next day at Oslo University, entitled the *Four Faces of Peace,* was widely hailed as a masterful exposition of the status of peace in the atomic age. He enumerated the faces of peace as, "peace and trade, peace and power, peace and policy or diplomacy and peace and people." Although he admitted that :

it would be folly to expect hostility and fears suddenly to vanish . . . it is an equal or an even greater folly to do nothing, to sit back, answer missile with missile, insult with insult, ban with ban. That would be the complete bankruptcy of policy and diplomacy.

He conceded that each nation wants its "own kind of peace brought about in our own way." But, he continues, "The choice, however, is as clear now for nations as it was once for the individual : peace or extinction." He repeats the lesson that Angell had sought to teach an earlier generation :

We know now that in modern warfare, fought on any considerable scale, there can be no possible economic gain for any side. Win or lose, there is nothing but waste and destruction.

As a product of the nation-state system, Pearson accepts that, "every state has not only the right but the duty to make adequate provisions for its own defense in the way it thinks best." He then goes on to say that "if the United Nations were effective as a security agency—which it is not," then these provisions might conceivably become, "unnecessary, therefore, undesirable." However, he is forced here to acknowledge concerning his own proposal : "Certainly the idea of an international peace force effective against a big disturber of the peace seems today unrealizable to the point of absurdity." Yet, he insists that :

the best defense of peace is not power, but the removal of the causes of war and international agreements which will put peace on a stronger foundation than the terror of destruction.

In discussing this terror of destruction, he notes that, "the warrior is the man with a test tube or the one who pushes the nuclear button." He explores the mystery of why :

even people with generous and understanding hearts, peaceful instincts in their normal and individual behavior can become fighting and even savage national animals under the excitement of collective emotion. Why this happens is the core of our problem of peace and war.

Pearson finally comes to the cold war :

Our policy and diplomacy, as the two sides in the cold war face each other, is becoming as rigid and defensive as the trench warfare of 40 years ago, when two sides dug in, dug deeper and lived in their ditches. The time has come for us to make a move, not only from strength, but from wisdom and from confidence in ourselves, to concentrate on the possibilities of agreement, rather than on disagreements and failures, and the evils and wrongs of the past.

Following the pattern which we have come to expect from national politicians, Pearson, after the defeat of the Liberal party, rejected the offer of positions with several international organizations in order to return to Canada in January, 1958, and take over the leadership of the Opposition from Louis St. Laurent. As one of his biographers explained, "First, last and always Lester Pearson is a Canadian and proud of it."

Pearson, who had deplored that "the grim fact is that we prepare for war like precocious giants and for peace like retarded pygmies," in an amazingly complete reversal of the position which he had taken in 1960, stood for election as leader of the Liberal Party in 1963 on a platform advocating acceptance of nuclear warheads from the United States. His wife, the former Maryon Elspeth Moody, rounded out the reversal of position by resigning as honorary sponsor of the Voice of Women, Canada's feminine pacifist organization.

The 1958 award to Reverend Dominique Georges Pire has already been discussed.

As laureate for 1959 the Nobel committee chose Philip J. Noel-Baker, born in 1889, whose activities on behalf of international understanding and, especially, disarmament spanned both the League of Nations and the United Nations eras.

The diplomats of the balance of terror era were still talking disarmament and approaching no nearer to an agreement than the disarmament conferences and the diplomats of all the ages of history. The United Nations era was to see numbered disarmament commissions and committees of twelve, twenty-five, eighty-two, five, ten, eighteen, and seventeen meeting both under and outside the roof of the international organization. At times, it appeared that perhaps an understanding was near but one or the other of the great powers could always be trusted to kick over the chess board and require the game to begin anew. In his book *The Arms Race — A Programme for World Disarmament* Noel-Baker is particularly critical about what he calls the "Western volte face" of May 10, 1955, when the Western powers under the leadership of Harold Stassen backed away from agreement after the Soviet Union had fully accepted the Western disarmament proposals, including inspection. What he called a "moment of hope " slipped away, never to be regained.

Noel-Baker prepared for his career by attending a Quaker school, Haverford (Pennsylvania) College. He then read international law at Cambridge and at the University of Munich. As a Quaker, he joined the ambulance corps during the first World War, served on the Belgian, French, and Italian fronts and received several decorations.

The end of the war found him at the Paris Peace Conference as secretary to Cecil. After taking time out to captain the British Olympic team and to run the 1500 meters at Antwerp in 1920, Noel-Baker returned to Geneva as the personal assistant to Cecil who was then a delegate at the League of Nations. Service with the League Secretariat followed in 1924 before Noel-Baker returned to England to become first Cassell professor of international relations at the University of London.

He entered politics in 1929 and was elected as Labor member of Parliament from Coventry. He was a member of Britain's delegation to the 1929–1930 sessions of the League of Nations Assembly, and served from 1929 to 1931 as parliamentary private secretary to Arthur Henderson, the foreign secretary. Noel-Baker was Henderson's personal assistant during the ill-starred Disarmament Conference at Geneva.

During most of the Second World War he served as parliamentary secretary to the Ministry of War Transport. In the Labor government that took office in 1945 he held several posts of cabinet rank including those of Minister of State, Secretary of State for Air, and Secretary of State for Commonwealth Relations. He was one of the British delegates who helped draft the United Nations charter at San Francisco in 1945 and was a delegate to the first United Nations General Assembly in 1946.

His Quaker origins and the long years spent in the hubs of international affairs have crystallized Noel-Baker's political philosophy :

War is a damnably filthy thing that has destroyed civilization after civilization—that is the essence of my beliefs.

Concerning disarmament, he states :

I think the great danger at the present moment is the incredibly fatalistic apathy of people who say, "Oh, well, there will always be armaments and governments will go on talking about it and never do anything." If the opinion of the people could only be mobilized into an active movement, I believe we could have disarmament in a week. The trouble is, of course, that armaments produce fear and fear produces more armaments.

Despite this deadly spiral, Noel-Baker feels that the "governments, the general staffs, the peoples simply have not grasped what the modern armaments mean."

How then can we reconcile increased armaments with the fact that, as Noel-Baker said : "the very employment of the word defense to describe modern military preparations is an extreme example of how language can deceive."

14 We Shall Overcome

The 1952 prize had been awarded to one who represented the "white man's burden" approach to the grave problem of colonialism. The Nobel committee balanced accounts by giving the delayed 1960 award to Albert John Luthuli, born about 1898, a black man who had felt the whip lash of baasskap.

Here again, Luthuli was not active in any peace movement. But he was an outstanding representative of the realization, as he himself expressed it, that "any situation where man must struggle for his rights is a threat to peace." At a time when, in the words of Sir Roy Welensky, there was "a savage fist pounding on the door " of white Africa, the Nobel committee saw fit to give recognition to Luthuli, "because in his fight against racial discrimination he has always worked for non-violent methods." Luthuli himself had written that he was "not by temperament a very aggressive person."

In his introduction to Luthuli's autobiography, *Let My People Go,* Charles Hooper describes the African leader as having the "humility of a man who cannot be humiliated." Luthuli was born in Rhodesia where his father had enlisted in the Rhodesian forces. However, his father died when Albert was only six months old and, after he had reached boyhood, his mother sent him to school at the ancestral home in Groutville, where his grandfather Ntaba had been chief and where his uncle Martin was the present chief.

Four years in the Groutville School were followed by two terms at a boarding school at Oklange. He then attended a Methodist secondary school at Edendale. His white teachers were so impressed with the youth that he was given a scholarship for a two year teaching course. This training was rewarded by appointment to a school in Blaeuwbosch where he taught for two years. It was here that he was confirmed in the Methodist Church and he remained an active and devout church member. The district educational authorities were impressed with Luthuli's ability as a teacher and he was given a scholarship to a higher teachers' training course at Adams College. He studied there for two years, and then served on the faculty for the next thirteen years. There, too, he displayed his organizational abilities and became secretary of the African Teachers Association in 1928 and president in 1933.

A new direction was given to Luthuli's life when in 1936 he was elected chief of the Umvoti Mission Reserve with headquarters in Groutville. Now he was face to face with the economic facts of life in the Union of South Africa. Ten million blacks worked to support three million whites. The average South African farm owned by white persons averaged 375 acres and the average black farm four to five acres. To strengthen the economic position of the farmers in his reserve, Luthuli helped organize the Groutville Cane Growers Association which later expanded to the Natal and Zululand Bantu Cane Growers Associations.

He also joined the African National Congress which has been called the "watchdog of the African people." The Congress launched a Defiance Campaign against the "pass," and other discriminatory laws. In Luthuli's words:

the intention was to disobey these laws, suffering arrest, assault and penalty if need be, without violence. The method was to send in groups of carefully trained volunteers to disobey publicly.

Luthuli was jailed and fined for burning his pass. Because of his activities in the Defiance Campaign, he was dropped as chief by the Native Affairs Department.

Election as president of the Natal branch of the Congress in 1951 was followed by his election as president-general of the national Congress in 1952. He was one of the original 155 persons accused of treason in 1956. The trial dragged on for years and charges against Luthuli were finally dismissed, but he was confined to Groutville for five years, from 1959, by administrative order under the anti-subversive act, for having engaged in "activities furthering the cause of communism." In 1964, this order was renewed for another five years. In effect, the Chief is confined to his home and two narrow corridors, leading to his store four miles away and to his nearby sugar plantation. He is barred from the adjoining town of Stanger. No one, not even his doctor, may visit him without a permit. No word of his may appear in any South African newspaper or magazine, or be broadcast or reproduced in any way.

Announcement of the Nobel prize found this Gandhian-like father of seven children chained to his front yard. Alan Paton commented that the Union of South Africa government had believed that Luthuli was "chained like a backyard dog," but now they discover that "they are chained and you are free." An official spokesman railed (as the Hitler regime did against von Ossietzky and the Soviets against Pasternak):

The government fully realizes the award was not made on merit and must necessarily rob the Nobel peace prize of all its high esteem in the judgment of objectively minded people.

At first Luthuli was denied a passport altogether but in the face of a world-wide outcry he was finally given a ten day pass restricted solely to Oslo.

Thus it was that a black man dressed in his chief's regalia was able to step before the rostrum in the hall of the University of Oslo to accept his prize and to deliver the most heart-rending lecture ever recorded in the annals of the Nobel prize. He tried to describe how it felt:

to be plucked from banishment in a rural backwater, to be lifted out of the narrow confinement of South Africa's internal politics [a South Africa which is] a museum piece in our time, a hangover from the dark past of mankind, a relic of an age which everywhere else is dead or dying.

He stressed the paradox that the prize be given to a man from a country where "the brotherhood of man is an illegal doctrine, outlawed, banned, censured, proscribed, prohibited." He mentioned another paradox pointing out that "peace and revolution make uneasy bed fellows," but insisted that "there can be no peace until the forces of aggression are overthrown." He closed with the enunciation that:

our goal is a united Africa in which the standards of life and liberty are constantly expanding, in which the ancient legacy of illiteracy and disease is swept aside, in which the dignity of man is rescued from beneath the heels of colonialism which have trampled it.

Luthuli returned to his forced confinement in his rural backwater where even Prime Minister Harold Macmillan of Britain could not get permission to see him. From there, he continues to spend the years cʳ his life "knocking in vain, patiently, moderately and modestly at a closed and barred door." Luthuli stresses the existence of a police state in South Africa:

Far more significant than the color ban in South Africa now is the bar which stands between those who place their faith in rule by force and violence and those who repudiate the police state. [He insists], what we have aimed to do in South Africa is to bring the white man to his senses, not slaughter him [because] the progressive isolation of the men who live by the apartheid creed is desirable, if only because they are sick with a loathesome disease.

[However,] the minds of Dr. Verwoerd and his company are already preoccupied with their last bunker, with the picture they will make as they go down—martyrs to what? Why must they continue to destroy when so much lies ready for the hand that will create?

Unfortunately, despite the non-violent intentions of the Bantus, the Defiance Campaign ended in riots, and the burn-the-pass drive ended with the fatal shooting of eighty-nine natives on March 21–22, 1960, in Sharpeville, Langa, and, elsewhere.

On April 1, 1965, John Harris stood on the gallows of Pretoria Central Prison and sang, "We Shall Overcome."

Thousands of miles away, the same song was being sung in Selma, Alabama, for this, "loathesome disease," of discrimination, unfortunately, is not peculiar to dark South Africa. It is endemic throughout the world; appearing in such scattered places as India, Australia, the Soviet Union, Britain, and the United States. A particularly virulent form of that malady afflicts the United States, the leader of the free world.

In the South of that country, nearly one hundred years after emancipation, the Negro still found himself oppressed by the most vicious manifestation of white supremacy. He could not be served in the restaurants, admitted to the movie theaters, accommodated in the inns, educated in the schools, employed in the factories, allowed in the churches, treated in the hospitals, or buried in the cemeteries with the white man. He was not permitted to vote nor was he even extended the normal courtesies of every day address. This second class citizenry for the Negro was enforced by the callousness and timidity of the average white man, the connivance of the police and courts, the full use of economic sanctions, the terror instilled by the Ku Klux Klan, and, very often, the brutality of the whip, the lash, the cattle prod, the torch, the dynamite stick, and the gun.

In the process of degradation and intimidation, the racists did not stop at murder and the list of martyrs is long : Medgar Evers, Emmett Till, William L. Moore, Cynthia Wesley, Addie Mae Collins, Denise McNair, Carol Robertson, James E. Chaney, Andrew Goodman, Michael Schwerner, Jimmie Lee Jackson, Reverend James J. Reeb, Mrs. Viola Gregg Liuzzo, James L. Coley, Virgil L. Ware, Lemuel Penn, O'Neal Moore, and Jonathan Daniels.

Nor was the discrimination less oppressive or less brutalizing in those citadels of hypocrisy in the North where lived forty-eight percent of the 18,871,381 Negroes counted in the 1960 census. The racial setup was not very different from that in the South — only the etiquette. The Negro wound up with a mouthful of civil rights laws and an empty stomach. Crammed into rat infested teeming ghettoes, ignored in segregated schools, locked out of jobs and opportunities and into a permanent condition of poverty, cast off by broken families, rootless, bitter, disillusioned and without hope, the Negro found freedom to have "a dull ring, a mocking emptiness." It was necessary for the President of the United States to point out on June 11, 1963, that the Negro has; only about one-half as much chance of completing high school as a white, twice as much chance of becoming unemployed, a life expectancy which is seven years shorter, and the prospects of earning only half as much.

Beneath the surface seethed a slow fire of discontent fed by the continuing indignities, inequities, humiliations, "wounds, gouges, amputations, scars endured " in three hundred years of slavery. What James Baldwin called a "rage in the blood, a kind of blind fever, a pounding in the skull and a fire in the bowels " erupted into the civil rights movement on Thursday evening, December 1, 1955, at Montgomery, Alabama.

Montgomery was known as the cradle of the Confederacy. It was here that Jefferson Davis had taken the oath on February 18, 1861, and here that the first Confederate flag had been sewn and unfurled. Out of a population of 120,000, about 70,000 were whites and 50,000 Negroes. Of the 30,000 Negroes of voting age in the city only about 2,000 were registered. The 1950 median income of the whites amounted to $1,730, of the Negroes $970. Sixty-three percent of the Negro female workers were domestics and forty-eight percent of the Negro male workers were either laborers or domestic workers. Ninety-four percent of white families had housing with inside flush toilets, only thirty-one percent of the Negro families.

At the same time that Luthuli was leading the struggle of the African National Congress, Mrs. Rosa Parks was finishing her day's work as a seamstress at the Montgomery Fair and was boarding the Cleveland Avenue bus in downtown Montgomery. Tired, she sat down in the first seat behind the section reserved for whites. After a while the bus driver ordered her and three other Negro passengers to stand to accommodate white passengers who were boarding the bus. The other three complied ; Mrs. Parks politely refused. She was removed from the bus by police, and taken to the police station. She was charged with violation of the city segregation ordinances. Later she was fined ten dollars plus four dollars in costs.

Mrs. Parks had been a former secretary of the National Association for the Advancement of Colored People's local branch. But she was to deny that she had been planted on the bus and the incident staged by the NAACP. The Reverend Dr. Martin Luther King, Jr., the Nobel peace laureate for 1964 explained :

Eventually the cup of endurance runs over and the human personality cries out, "I can take it no longer" . . . her intrepid affirmation that she had had enough. It was an individual expression of a timeless longing for human dignity and freedom . . .

she was planted there by her personal sense of dignity and self-respect. She was anchored to that seat by the accumulated indignities of days gone by and the boundless aspirations of generations yet unborn.

The news of the arrest of Mrs. Parks spread like wild-fire through the Negro community. The discourtesies of the bus drivers; and the absurd rules of the transit company, The Montgomery City Lines, which required colored passengers to board the front of the bus, pay their fare and then leave the bus and reenter the rear door (often being left minus their fares) had built up a good deal of ill will toward the company. The leaders of the Negro population, led by E. D. Nixon, a pullman porter and the president of the local NAACP, met the next evening at the Dexter Avenue Baptist Church and called for a one day boycott on Monday, December 5th, and for a mass meeting the same evening at 7 P.M. at the Holt Street Baptist Church.

Present at the planning meeting was the pastor of the church and the man who was to emerge as the leader of the American Negro's drive for civil rights, the Reverend Dr. Martin Luther King, Jr., born in 1929, the winner of the Nobel Peace Prize for 1964.

By the grace of God's good fortune, Montgomery witnessed one of the few instances in history where the man, the hour, and the environment met and merged into a beautiful and fruitful harmony toward the pursuit of a great cause. As we have seen, the bus boycott was not premeditated; it happened. King did not create it; he was at first its creature and later its spokesman, philosopher and symbol. King was uniquely equipped by upbringing and training to perform this role. Consciously or unconsciously, his whole life had been a preparation for this moment.

He had been born on January 15, 1929, at the crossroads of Negro America — 501 Auburn Avenue, N.E. Atlanta,

Georgia. His father was the minister of the Ebenezer Negro Baptist Church, and King's early life was that of the middle class Negro child. He completed his undergraduate studies at Morehouse College, Atlanta, in 1948, and then enrolled in the Crozer Theological Seminary at Chester, Pennsylvania. When he received his Bachelor of Divinity degree in 1951, he carried off all the honors as class valedictorian, president of the student government, and the recipient of the Pearl Plafkner award for scholarship.

The Lewis Crozer Fellowship of $1200 for two years of graduate work enabled King to pursue his graduate studies at Boston University. He was awarded his Doctor of Philosophy degree in systematic theology there in 1955. During this time he was also serving as assistant pastor in his father's church. He was also courting Coretta Scott who was studying voice at the Boston Conservatory of Music. They were married and there are now four children.

After a good deal of soul searching, the Kings accepted, on September 1, 1954, the call to serve as minister in the South, at the Dexter Avenue Baptist Church in Montgomery. This place of worship was known as the silk stocking or big folks church. But King had definite ideas about the functions of a pastorate. He recognized the danger that the church might become little more than a social club with a thin veneer of religiosity. He has written :

A religion true to its nature must also be concerned about man's social conditions. Religion deals with both earth and heaven, both time and eternity . . . Any religion that professes to be concerned with the souls of men and is not concerned with the slums that damn them, the economic conditions that strangle them and the social conditions that cripple them is a dry as dust religion. Such a religion is the kind the Marxists like to see—an opiate of the people.

King translated his ideas into action. He became a member

of the executive committee of the NAACP, formed church social and political action committees, pushed the drive for Negro registration, and became vice-president of the Alabama Council on Human Relations, the only operating inter-racial group in the state.

On that crucial Monday, December 5, 1955, the buses rolled in Montgomery but only a handful of the usual 17,500 daily Negro passengers were aboard. For the meeting at the Holt Street Baptist Church, every seat had been filled at least two hours before the appointed time. Thousands more stood outside. Dr. King's speech struck the keynote of the evening :

But there comes a time that people get tired. We are here this evening to say to those who have mistreated us so long that we are tired—tired of being segregated and humiliated; tired of being kicked about by the brutal feet of oppression. We have no alternative but to protest. For many years we have shown amazing patience. We have sometimes given our white brothers the feeling that we liked the way we were being treated. But we come here tonight to be saved from that patience that makes us patient with anything less than freedom and justice. . . . One of the great glories of democracy is the right to protest for right . . . in our protest there will be no cross burnings. No white person will be taken from his home by a hooded Negro mob and brutally murdered. There will be no threats and intimidation. We will be guided by the highest principles of law and order . . . Our method will be that of persuasion, not coercion. We will only say to the people, 'Let your conscience be your guide' . . . Love must be our regulating ideal. Once again one must hear the words of Jesus echoing across the centuries : "Love your enemies, bless them that curse you and pray for them that despitefully use you." If we fail to do this our protest will end up as a meaningless drama on the stage of history and its memory will be shrouded with ugly garments of shame. In spite of the mistreatment that we have confronted we must not become bitter and end up by hating our white brothers.

The Negro civil rights movement had come of age. There had been previous demonstrations including even a bus boycott in Baton Rouge, Louisiana in 1953. But now the Negro had a voice, a philosophy—non-violence—and a leader with the stature of a Luthuli.

King had always had good stage presence. He had begun singing in churches and at church conventions at the age of four. He had taken second prize in the oratorical contest while a senior at the Booker T. Washington High School. At college he made the glee club and chorus and won second prize in the Webb Oratorical Contest during his sophomore year. Mrs. Almena Lomax described his oratory :

the impact of Martin Luther King is in his delivery, which is all of a piece, like a narrative poem . . his elocution has the beauty and polish of Roland Hayes singing a spiritual.

King's biographer, L. D. Reddick, lists the laureate's heroes as Jesus, Thoreau and Gandhi. In his student days, King had read and been impressed by the works of the latter two. Mohandas K. Gandhi had come to the conclusion that non-violence was the only morally and practically sound method open to oppressed minority peoples in their struggle for freedom. This philosophy was not so much passive resistance as it was civil disobedience; a withdrawal of cooperation with evil, a mass violation of immoral laws. Gandhi had termed this satyagraha, meaning truth firmness or soul force—the faith that it is better to be the recipient of violence than the inflicter of it since the latter only multiplies the existence of violence and bitterness while the former may develop a sense of shame in the opponent, thus bringing about a transformation and a change of heart. "Conquer hate by love, untruth by truth, violence by suffering." In this sense, to refrain from striking back requires more will and courage than the automatic reflex of returning the blow. Non-violence is ultimately the way of the strong man. King has stated, "From my Christian background I gained my ideals and from Gandhi my operational techniques."

Despite police brutality and molestation, despite indictments for criminal conspiracy, despite arrests and jailings, despite bombings, despite economic reprisals, the demonstrating Negroes, throughout the 381 days of the bus boycott, did not permit themselves to be provoked into violence.

Nor was King, the head of the Montgomery Improvement Association which sponsored the boycott, spared the agonies of harassment. His phone jangled all night with foul threats; he was charged with all sorts of traffic violations; he was indicted for conspiracy with 114 others; he was convicted and jailed as convict number 7089; his home was bombed one winter night while his family slept. Shortly after the bombing, King stood on his shattered front porch and told an angry group of his followers who had surrounded the city's mayor and police commissioner :

Please be peaceful. We want to love our enemies. Be good to them. Love them. Christian love can bring brotherhood on earth. We must love our white brothers no matter what they do to us. There is an element of God in every man.

Thus did the bus boycott drag on for 381 interminable, but glorious days. The Negroes of Montgomery made do with makeshift car pools and by walking; some trudging as much as twelve miles a day. Mother Pollard summarized that uplifting of the spirit which accompanied the rebirth of Negro dignity :

My feets is tired, but my soul is rested.

It was more honorable to walk the streets in dignity than to ride the buses in humiliation. As King had stated after the first planning meeting, "The clock on the wall read almost midnight, but the clock in our souls revealed that it was daybreak."

King himself explained the roots of the resurgence of self-respect : the old corroding sense of inferiority often expressed itself in a lack of self-respect. Many unconsciously wondered whether they actually deserved any better conditions. Their minds and souls were so conditioned to the system of segregation that they submissively adjusted themselves to things as they were. This is the ultimate tragedy of segregation. It not only harms one physically but injures one spiritually. It sears the soul and degrades the personality. It inflicts the segregated with a false sense of inferiority while confirming the segregator in a false estimate of his own superiority.

By the time the Supreme Court decision striking down the Montgomery segregation ordinance was delivered on November 13, 1956, the Negro had acquired a new estimate of his own human worth. The official end of the boycott came on December 21, 1956, with the receipt of the court order. The Montgomery Negroes had won a complete victory but history has never recorded such a victory. There was not a single white home in Montgomery that had lost a loved one, for there had not been a single white casualty. The last leaflet read :

If pushed, don't push back; if cursed, don't curse back.

Montgomery is one of the great sagas of our heritage. It is a story that will rank alongside the heroism of the old American frontier. As for its guiding spirit, the Reverend Martin Luther King, Jr.; at the age of twenty-seven, he stood forth as the acknowledged leader of his people. He was hailed as the Moses of our time. *The Afro-American* of Baltimore proclaimed in headlines, "King is King." In a sense, whatever followed after Montgomery was to be anti-climactic.

With the local courts and all other avenues of protest closed to the Negro, Dr. King was to lead many another crusade into the streets in the tradition of the Boston Tea Party, the American suffragettes, and the trade union movement. Wave after wave of Negroes were to march peacefully into the teeth of red-necked sheriffs like Laurie Pritchett, Bull Connor, Al

Lingo, Jim Clark, and their possemen in riot helmets with nightsticks, cattle prods, and guns hanging from their belts. Everywhere, King preached his message :

So listen to me children : Put on your marching shoes; don't 'cha get weary; though the path ahead may be dark and dreary; we're walking for freedom, children.

After Montgomery, King moved back to Atlanta to become associate pastor of his father's church. In 1957 he founded the Southern Christian Leadership Conference to spearhead the civil rights movement. On May 17th of that year, King led twenty-five thousand demonstrators in the first prayer pilgrimage to Washington. After his long recuperation required by the Harlem stabbing incident, King returned to the struggle in 1960 to lead lunch counter sit-ins in Atlanta, Greensboro, Raleigh, Durham and other communities. In 1961 and 1962, the non-violent army of King's organization moved into Albany, Georgia, in the first attempt to bring the full resources of the Negro community to bear in an across the board attack on the system of color caste. More than a thousand Negroes marched to jail with Dr. King in Albany on July 27, 1962. Led to believe that an arrangement to desegregate public facilities was acceptable to the white power elite, King accepted bail two days later. But the victory turned out to be a hoax and segregation continued.

The next move came in 1963, in Birmingham, Alabama, the most segregated of all major Southern cities. The resultant police brutality, and the use of fire hoses and police dogs against the peaceful demonstrators, shocked the conscience of mankind. Newspapers around the world printed pictures of the atrocities and the mass arrests. But the relentless marchers continued until the wheels of Birmingham ground to a standstill with the jails filled and the downtown streets, sidewalks, and store corridors clogged with standing, squatting, and singing demonstrators. Here, too, the local capitulation of the whites was largely a hoax to be crowned with the horrible bombing on September 15, 1963, of the Sixteenth Street Baptist Church and the killing of four young girls who were attending Sunday school.

In atonement for these horrendous deeds, the guilt-ridden nation enacted into law the Civil Rights Act of 1964. President Johnson had told the Congress:

We have talked long enough about equal rights. We have talked for 100 years or more. Yes, it is time now to write the next chapter—and to write it in books of law.

Birmingham finally had its victory.

A call had gone out for a march on Washington on August 28, 1963, as "a living petition in the flesh." The outpouring of over two hundred thousand citizens of all races dwarfed the previous pilgrimage of 1958 and was the greatest demonstration in the nation's history. The principal address on that day was delivered from the foot of the Lincoln Memorial by Dr. King. With the faith of a man of God, he cried:

I have a dream . . it is a dream deeply rooted in the American dream. . . . it is a dream that one day in the red hills of Georgia, sons of former slaves and the sons of former slave-owners will be able to sit down together at the table of brotherhood.

Dr. King knew that freedom was not something that one can be given; that it had to be earned over and over again. So 1964 found him in Philadelphia, Mississippi, conducting the first freedom rally ever held in the town where three civil rights workers were murdered; in St. Augustine, Florida, seeking service in segregated motels. In 1965 he was in Selma, Alabama, leading the march of disenfranchised Negroes to the courthouse, and to the State Capitol, to seek registration for voting. The march to Montgomery has been compared to

Gandhi's march to the sea at Dandi, in 1930, in protest against the salt tax. It is interesting to note that out of fifteen thousand Negroes of voting age in Selma, only 335 were registered to vote while 9,543 out of 14,440 whites had been registered. The memorial to the excesses of the storm troopers of Selma is the Voting Rights Act of 1965 so that Negro citizens will no longer be denied the right to vote by every device of which human ingenuity is capable. Henceforth, they will, at last, be permitted to partake of what H. G. Wells called "democracy's ceremonial, its feast, its great function — the election."

Reverend King often quotes the following passages from the Scriptures:

Blessed are ye, when men shall revile you and persecute you and shall say all manner of evil against you falsely, for my sake. Rejoice and be exceedingly glad for great is your reward in heaven; for so persecuted they the prophets which were before you. (Matthew 5:11–12).

Also from Matthew 5:10:

Blessed are they which are persecuted for righteousness sake for theirs is the kingdom of heaven.

The reward accorded to all prophets of peace by our world of violence has also been visited upon Reverend King. He has been reviled and persecuted and all manner of evil said against him. Four attempts have been made against his life. His home has been dynamited. Crosses have been burned on his lawn. He has been physically kicked and assaulted. On September 20, 1958, while autographing his book *Stride Toward Freedom* at Blumstein's department store on 125th Street in New York's Harlem, a demented woman, Mrs. Izola Ware Currey, plunged an eight inch Japanese letter opener into his chest, narrowly missing the aorta. At Harlem Hospital it was necessary to remove one rib and part of the breast bone.

Dr. King's recovery was further complicated by pneumonia.

Fellow clergymen have protested his participation in demonstrations as "unwise and untimely." Militant Negro leaders have called him an "Uncle Tom" and pelted him with rotten eggs. The chief law enforcement officer of the United States, J. Edgar Hoover, attacked King as "The most notorious liar in the country," and labeled him a communist. Leaflets circulated throughout the country by a so-called Alert Americans Association, pictured King at an alleged communist training school. A former President of the United States called King a "troublemaker," and termed the Selma to Montgomery march "silly."

As battle ribbons to mark his campaigns, Dr. King can point with pride to his seventeen jailings: in Montgomery, Atlanta, Albany, Birmingham, St. Augustine, and Selma. Thoreau had said:

Under a government which imprisons any unjustly, the true place for a just man is also prison.

At the same time, King has been a consultant and advisor to Presidents. Two Presidents, Kennedy and Johnson, have sought his counsel on civil rights and related matters. During the 1960 presidential election, Kennedy phoned Mrs. King to express his concern over her husband's jailing in Albany. The call may have won Kennedy the election. As President, he again phoned Mrs. King in April, 1963, when King was jailed and he was kept in solitary confinement in Birmingham.

It was to be expected, therefore, that the announcement of the award to King would be greeted with a mixed reception. On the one hand, it was denounced as "one of the biggest jokes of the year," as "scraping the bottom of the barrel." On the other hand, it was hailed as "richly deserved," as "an award that exalts the prize as much as it does this brave crusader for human understanding and brotherhood."

So it was that the Reverend Dr. Martin Luther King, Jr., the third man of his race, stepped forward in the marble hall of Oslo University to receive the Nobel medal and diploma from Dr. Gunnar Jahn, chairman of the Storting's Nobel Committee, and the audience of several hundred distinguished guests stood and applauded. So it was that King Olav and Crown Prince Harald stepped forward to congratulate Dr. King.

But did the award of the peace prize to Dr. King, or to Chief Luthuli for that matter, conform to the conditions of Nobel's will? What work had King, or Luthuli, done toward the "fraternity among nations, for the abolition or reduction of standing armies and for the holding and promotion of peace congresses?"

True, civil wars have often been more bloody and more bitter than wars between nations: witness the American Civil War, the Spanish Civil War, the Thirty Years War, and the War of the Roses. But evidently, Nobel was not concerned so much with internecine strife as he was with truly international conflict. The *Norwegian Journal of Commerce and Shipping,* the *Aftenposten* and the *Morgenbladet,* with good cause, raised the question concerning the use of domestic problems of a single country as the yardstick for the award of the prize.

Obviously, neither King nor Luthuli had become involved with what has been termed the greatest challenge of our age — disarmament. Neither has been active in peace organizations. King explained at some length why he had never joined a pacifist organization: that Reinhold Niebuhr's

theology is a persistent reminder of the reality of sin on every level of man's existence. These elements in Niebuhr's thinking helped me to recognize the illusions of a superficial optimism concerning human nature, the dangers of a false idealism. While I still believe in man's potential for good, Niebuhr made me realize his potential for evil as well. Moreover, Niebuhr helped me to recognize the complexity of man's social involvement and the glaring reality of collective evil. Many pacifists, I felt, failed to see this. All too many had an unwarranted optimism concerning man and leaned unconsciously toward self-righteousness. It was my revolt against these attitudes under the influence of Niebuhr that accounts for the fact that in spite of my strong leaning toward pacifism, I never joined a pacifist organization. After reading Niebuhr, I tried to arrive at a realistic pacifism. In other words, I came to see the pacifist position not as sinless but as the lesser evil in the circumstances. I felt then, as I feel now, that the pacifist would have a greater appeal if he did not claim to be free from the moral dilemmas that the Christian non-pacifist confronts.

What then is the significance; what is the lesson to be learned from the awards to King and Luthuli? Dr. Jahn spelled out the meaning in his presentation speech, introducing King as one who although he :

has not personally committed himself to the international conflict, his own struggle is a clarion call for all who work for peace.

King was hailed as an "undaunted champion of peace," and the "first person in the Western world to have shown us that a struggle can be waged without violence."

King and Luthuli bring home to us the realization that freedom is indivisible, that true positive peace is impossible as long as injustice exists anywhere.

King and Luthuli may be indicating to us the only answer left to the great question of our time — war or peace. To quote from Reverend King's Nobel speech :

this award which I received . . . . is profound recognition that non-violence is the answer to the crucial political and moral question of our time—the need for man to overcome oppression and violence without resorting to violence and oppression. Civilization and violence are antithetical concepts. Negroes of the United States, following the people of India, have demonstrated that non-violence is not sterile passivity, but a powerful moral force which makes for social transformation. Sooner or later, all the people of the world will have to discover a way to live together in peace, and thereby transform this pending cosmic elegy into a creative psalm of brotherhood. If this is to be achieved, man must evolve for all human conflict a method which rejects revenge, aggression and retaliation. The foundation of such a method is love.

The next day, December 11, 1964, Dr. King made the following remarks to students at Oslo University:

Violence as a way of achieving racial justice is both impractical and immoral. It solves no social problem. It merely creates new and more complicated ones. Violence is impractical because it is a descending spiral ending in destruction for all. It is immoral because it seeks to humiliate the opponent rather than win his understanding. It seeks to annihilate rather than convert. Violence is immoral because it thrives on hatred rather than love. In a real sense non-violence seeks to redeem the spiritual and moral lag which is the chief dilemma of modern man. It seeks to secure moral ends through moral means. Non-violence is a powerful and just weapon. Indeed, it is a weapon unique in history, which cuts without wounding and ennobles the man who wields it.

Perhaps non-violence is that philosophy for which mankind has been seeking so desperately as the answer to that resignation toward sudden, devastating, final death which has settled upon the earth. Before it is too late, men will have to discover a way to live together in peace. It may be that the black man's non-violent struggle to be free is offering to Western civilization the "kind of spiritual dynamic so desperately needed for survival." In 1935, Gandhi had prophesied, "Perhaps it will be through the Negro that the unadulterated message of non-violence will be delivered to the world." Do we have here the alternative to war and destruction?

"What then shall we do?" asked Tolstoy, the preacher of love and non-violence of an earlier era. Men weary of war and conflict might look to the counsel of Mohandas K. Gandhi:

Adjudicate, negotiate, arbitrate—otherwise one inter-religious brawl or one race riot will immediately create fuel for another and one war will generate the venoms, fears and military designs which make a second and third more likely.

Have Gandhi and King and Luthuli and the oppressed peoples of India, the United States and South Africa shown the world how to conquer war? Suppose the peoples of the world, oppressed with the greatest threat to life ever, were to withdraw their cooperation from the greatest, most obscene evil ever—war and preparation for war. Suppose they were to refuse to pay taxes for armaments or to serve in the armies or to manufacture weapons of destruction. Suppose the peoples of each nation were to turn to their neighbors and say in the words of Dr. King:

See we will not harm you; our hands are clean and empty. Let us be brothers.

15 The Mystic and the Cold War

It was rumored that the 1960 award had been temporarily passed over because the Nobel committee had decided on Dag Hammarskjold and were reluctant to embarrass him while Premier Khrushchev and the Soviet delegation were seeking to replace the Secretary-General with a troika arrangement. However, the 1961 prize was finally awarded to Hammarskjold (1905–1961) posthumously because, since he was still alive when nominations closed, he was eligible under the rules.

Hammarskjold had been preparing for the job of Secretary-General of the United Nations for generations. As he himself had stated :

From generations of soldiers and government officials on my father's side, I inherited a belief that no life was more satisfactory than one of selfless service to your country—or humanity. This service requires a sacrifice of all personal interest, but likewise the courage to stand up unflinchingly for your convictions.

He wrote in his Diary : "I don't know who—or what—put the question. I don't even know when it was put. I don't even remember answering. But at some moment I did answer yes to Someone—or Something—and from that hour I was certain

209

that existence is meaningful and that, therefore, my life, in self-surrender, had a goal."

His father, Hjalmar Hammarskjold, had been a member of the International Court of Arbitration at the Hague; the head of the Swedish delegation to the 1907 second Hague conference; the president of the Nobel Foundation, and the prime minister of Sweden. The elder Hammarskjold was a member of the select Swedish Academy and at their home in the castle of Uppsala young Dag was to get to know the great minds of Scandinavia. Among these was their neighbor Archbishop Söderblom, whose son Jon Olaf was a fast friend of Dag.

Dag Hammarskjold received his bachelor's degree from the University of Uppsala in 1925 after having specialized in the history of literature, the theory of philosophy, French, and political economics. He went on to receive a law degree from Sigtuna College, to do post-graduate work at Cambridge, and to receive his doctorate in 1933 from the University of Stockholm for a thesis entitled *The Spread of Boom and Depression*. He lectured in economics at Stockholm and was considered a member of the Stockholm School of economics whose theories were grounded in the works of John M. Keynes and Knut Wicksell.

His public career began with service as the secretary to the Commission on Unemployment. From that post he went to the Bank of Sweden where he served as secretary and principal clerk. Ernst Wigforss, the Social-Democratic minister of finance was so impressed with the economic sagacity of the young man that he offered Hammarskjold the top civil service position in his department, that of undersecretary. In this post, which he held for nine years, from 1936–1945, Hammarskjold was responsible for drafting a large percentage of the legislation which was to turn Sweden into a welfare state. For part of this period, from 1941–1948, he served simultaneously as chairman of the board of governors of the Bank of Sweden.

He left the finance ministry in 1945 to become an adviser to the Swedish cabinet on economic and financial problems. In 1946, he renegotiated the Swedish-American trade agreement. The next year, he was appointed undersecretary for foreign affairs. He was detailed to Paris as the top Swedish representative for Marshall Plan matters and for the Organization for European Economic Cooperation (OEEC) where he was vice-chairman of the executive committee. Wigforss was to comment that the respect which Hammarskjold earned at the OEEC "for his acute intelligence, good judgment and ability to find ways out of bothersome situations " was principally what made it possible to launch him as a candidate for Secretary-General.

In 1951 he was promoted to vice-minister of foreign affairs under Osten Unden, and in 1953 he became a member of the cabinet as a non-party minister without portfolio. He was a delegate to the Council of Europe and a member of the Swedish delegation to the General Assembly of the United Nations, serving as vice-chairman and later as acting chairman of the delegation to the sixth and seventh sessions.

It should be noted that during this entire period of public service Hammarskjold acted solely as a technician and never joined a political party. He expressed his philosophy of public service as follows :

You put all the ability you had at the service of the government and of Parliament. If you did not, you would be negating the system under which the country was run.

It was typical of him to state, upon entering the office of the Secretary-General :

In my new official capacity, the private man should disappear and the international public servant take his place.

Therefore, it is understandable why, when the nomination of Hammarskjold was announced, so little was known of the self-effacing bachelor, mountaineer, lover of nature, connoisseur of modern art, devotee of esoteric poetry, mystic and philosopher. But those who were acquainted with the new Secretary-General knew that he brought to the job a "razor sharp mind," and an attitude of complete neutrality and universality. He said :

We are on dangerous ground if we believe that any individual, any nation or any ideology has a monopoly on rightness, liberty and human dignity.

He felt the need :

to reestablish full human contact and communication across geographical and political boundaries.

He explained :

Terrible wars have been fought in the past because people thought they could not live in the world together or because they thought their beliefs were in head-on collision with their neighbors. Then, with time, they found it was not only possible but necessary to make it a working compromise that allowed for the difference. They found that it was not only possible but necessary to accept the principle of diversity in human society.

It would then follow logically that Hammarskjold believed firmly in the processes of negotiation for the settlement of international disputes. As he stated to a university audience in California, he regarded negotiation :

not as something immoral but as a responsible and sensible activity—as a process of working out a mutually satisfactory arrangement—with someone I had to live with. To negotiate with someone never meant to me I had to like him or approve of him, much less that I was willing to sell out my principles.

It is certain that he could take the oath of office without mental or moral reservation :

I solemnly swear to exercise in all loyalty, discretion and con-science the functions entrusted to me as Secretary-General of the United Nations, to discharge these functions and regulate my conduct with the interests of the United Nations only in view and not to seek or accept instructions in regard to the perform-ance of my duties from any government or other authority external to the organization.

The new Secretary-General was greeted at Idlewild Air-port by the outgoing Secretary-General, Trygve Lie, with the statement, "You are taking over the world's most impossible job." A more correct statement would have been that he was taking over a job with the world's most impossible organiza-tion. To fully understand Hammarskjold's tenure as Secretary-General it is necessary to digress briefly in order to consider the basic organizational structure of the United Nations.

This discussion of the organization which embodies the dreams and hopes and aspirations of mankind and which stands as the only forum in the world holding forth the slightest chance for peace — the one tangible symbol of the world com-munity — should be prefaced with the following quotation from Robert M. Hutchins:

We support the United Nations not because it can guarantee peace, but because it is a highly tentative first step toward world government and world law. To say that the discussion of world government is a criticism of the United Nations is like saying that to talk about buying an auto is an attack on the baby car-riage industry. In the meantime we must support the United Nations. It is all we have. Let us not throw out the dirty water.

To repeat Ralph Bunche's statement:

If the United Nations cannot ensure peace, there will be none.

The structure of the United Nations is very similar to that of the United States under the Articles of Confederation from 1781 to 1789. The central government did not have power to regulate trade, levy taxes, draft troops, constitute courts, or issue money. The Articles begin :

Each state retains its sovereignty, freedom and independence, and every power, jurisdiction and right which is not by this federation expressly delegated to the United States in Congress assembled.

The Congress could not impose levies for money or men; these had to be requisitioned from the states. And if the states refused, the United States were helpless. The Charter of the United Nations reads :

The Organization is based on the principle of the sovereign equality of all its members.

The United Nations lacks the attributes of a sovereign state and thus suffers from the same weaknesses which plagued the young United States and the League of Nations. Witness the paralysis of the 19th General Assembly, caused by the impasse over the application of penalties under Article 19 of the Charter. The United Nations cannot impose levies for money or men; it, too, must requisition them. Professor Gilbert Murray, writing about the League, summarized its whole existence in one sentence :

The international anarchy of a world administered by some 60 sovereign independent states with no authority over them, admitting no reciprocal duties and nursing unlimited national ambitions, was a disease carrying the seeds of death.

Little wonder then that Vernon Nash can comment that the "League of Nations was as impotent when it was twenty years old as it was in its first year."

Jawaharlal Nehru's recapitulation of the work of the United Nations to 1956 still holds true today :

Since its foundation, many and varied have been its activities to relieve mankind of many pressures and menaces in the economic and social fields and its efforts even in the field of war prevention and cessation of armed conflicts have had some modest successes. The fact, however, remains that a decade after its foundation the world is more armed, more war-prepared, more sharply divided into camps.

The great powers exhibit their lack of confidence in the world organization by continuing the arms race full blast and by their by-passing of the United Nations in times of crisis on a disquietingly large number of issues.

Here in the West it is customary to blame the veto for the impotency of the world organization on the vital issues affecting peace and security. But even a rudimentary analysis of the constitutional structure of the United Nations will make evident that the veto is inherent to its continued existence. That is why the United States was as insistent at San Francisco as was the Soviet Union on the veto. As Hammarskjold pointed out :

On the day that we can get rid of the veto, there will be no need to get rid of it, because at that time there will be such a measure of unanimity and agreement among the major powers that the veto power will be completely innocuous.

The importance of the veto was over-emphasised by the West while it held the majority vote. Now that the balance of power is shifting to the African and Asian nations, it will be interesting to watch how gracefully the Western powers accept reversals. Britain's Sir Alec Douglas Home, when he was foreign secretary, was already lamenting that :

The balance of responsibility as it was laid down in the Charter has been upset. One country, one vote is an ideal and a very good ideal but if that vote is not used with wisdom, discretion, tolerance and restraint, then the United Nations could become nothing less than a demonstration of power without responsibility.

The United States' Adlai Stevenson echoed :

We are witnessing the first act in a drama which could end with the death [of the United Nations], an ignoble death, as did the League of Nations.

With the Security Council paralyzed by the veto, and resolutions of the General Assembly having only the force of recommendations, the United Nations, instead of being the fulcrum of world authority and a power for peace, becomes, in the words of Winston Churchill :

A mere cockpit in which the representatives of mighty nations hurl reproaches, taunts and recriminations against one another.

The spokesmen for the nations are more interested in scoring debating points than in creating what Hammarskjold would call a "center of reconciliation " through "quiet diplomacy."

In this power void, the position of the Secretary-General is all-important, and the effectiveness of the world organization stands or falls with the effectiveness of the office on the thirty-eighth floor. Or as Conor Cruise O'Brien, the United Nations representative at Katanga, put it :

The Secretariat—rather than the half-paralyzed Security Council or the amorphous General Assembly—was the reality of the United Nations.

Thus, a good deal depends upon the occupant's conception of his office. For instance, the approach of Sir Eric Drummond of the League of Nations was essentially a clerical one of housekeeping with "behind the scenes conciliation and no speaking out in public on behalf of the international point of view." Trygve Lie's approach was that of the politician while Hammarskjold's concept was that of the tough administrator who hews to his own idea of the Charter with what David Ben-Gurion called "legal pedantry." This administrative line is aided diplomatically by the subtlety of Hammarskjold's mind and with what Erik Lundberg described as a :

tremendous power of expressing himself orally in a way that people can't quite follow . . . he never tries to express himself in the easiest sort of way . . . he is not a man of simple statement.

The French delegate once called Hammarskjold the "master of calculated imprecision," and Britain's Selwyn-Lloyd once awarded him the "first prize for ambiguity in these matters." The story is told that Dr. Nahum Goldmann complained to the Secretary-General that he could not get a straight "yes" or "no" answer. Hammarskjold's reply was that "diplomats, no more than women, should never allow themselves to be so cornered."

The world organization had sunk to a low ebb under the administration of Trygve Lie. Playing the role of the politician-statesman he had maneuvered himself completely into the Western camp with the result that the Communist powers refused to have anything to do with his office and with the further result that he had completely abdicated command of the United Nations forces in the Korean War to the American general staff. With the United States paying the bill it encroached further and further upon the preserves of the United Nations until agents of the Federal Bureau of Investigation were conducting McCarthy-type witch hunts among the international staff.

One of the first steps Hammarskjold took to reassert the authority of his organization was to order the FBI off the premises declaring :

You can't be here; whatever permission may have been given in the past is withdrawn.

He called the FBI presence "intolerable, absolutely intolerable."

He then proceeded to fulfill his idea of the position of Secretary-General which was not that of a passive clerk but rather that of one "active as an instrument, a catalyst, an inspirer." Thus began the travels of the "custodian of the brush-fire peace." First he journeyed to Peking in January, 1955, to sup swallow's nest soup and trade rapier wits with Chou En-lai, and to secure the eventual release of the eleven American airmen held as spies. Then followed travels to Egypt, Israel, Lebanon, Jordan, India, Laos, Belgium, the Soviet Union, the Congo, and elsewhere in a pragmatic day-to-day effort to quell the incipient brush fires and prevent the blazing of a conflagration that would engulf the earth.

On returning from a trip to the Middle East, Hammarskjold characterized his work by quoting from Arthur Waley on what an early Chinese historian had had to say about the philosopher Sung Tzu and his followers who lived about 350 B.C.:

Constantly rebuffed but never discouraged, they went round from State to State helping people to settle their differences, arguing against wanton attack and pleading for the suppression of arms that the age in which they lived might be saved from its state of continual war. To this end they interviewed princes and lectured the common people, nowhere meeting with any great success but obstinately persisting in their tasks till kings and commoners alike grew weary of listening to them. Yet, undeterred, they continued to force themselves on people's attention.

Hammarskjold understood, of course, that he was:

working on the brink of the unknown because we have no idea as to what the international society of tomorrow will be. We can only do what we can now to find solutions, in a pragmatic sense, to the problems as they arise, trying to keep a sense of devotion, and then we will see later on what comes out of it.

As he displayed at the very outset in his mission to Peking, Hammarskjold exercised a high degree of "constitutional resourcefulness," within the "competence of his office." In Laos, Lebanon, Jordan, The Cambodia-Thailand dispute, the Near East and elsewhere, he took the initiative while acknowledging, "I did so without precedent and without explicit support from the Charter." Through his constant travels to enable his personal evaluation of trouble situations, and through the device of the United Nations presence, he attempted to contain an explosive world.

He faced his first big test in the Suez crisis of late 1956. Here was a crisis which required, in Hammarskjold's words, "that some one do something which no government itself could do and which none of the national diplomats could do." Because of the nature of the General Assembly, it could only hand the Secretary-General mandates "of a highly general character, expressing the bare minimum of agreement attainable." As Prince Wan Waithayahon, the president of the 1956–57 General Assembly, stated at the closing session :

The General Assembly rapidly passed resolutions couched in general terms and the Secretary-General has implemented them by delicate and arduous negotiations, supported therein by the force of world opinion.

Throughout, the Secretary-General, stuck to the overriding principle that aggression could not be rewarded, and that :

to have peace with justice—adherence to principle and law must be given priority and cannot be conditioned.

To this end, Hammarskjold maintained constant pressure until the British and French troops were withdrawn from Egypt on December 27, 1956, and the Israeli troops on March 8, 1957. Further, the United Nations would not permit the aggressors to have anything to do with salvage work in the Canal and the United Nations assumed full responsibility for the monumental job of clearing the waterway.

To create a buffer zone between the combatants, the Pearson

resolution, as we have seen, authorized a United Nations Emergency Force. By working around the clock with practically no sleep, Hammarskjold had the force organized and on Egyptian soil within one week. Even President Eisenhower felt impelled to pay tribute to the ability and stamina displayed by the Secretary-General :

He has not only shown his ability. The man has displayed a physical endurance that is highly remarkable if not unique; night after night he has made do with one or two hours sleep and worked day and night, and, I can say worked with intelligence and devotion.

Here, too, Hammarskjold scrupulously adhered to Article 217 of the Charter which protects the "domestic jurisdiction of any state," and refused to enter Egypt until he received the consent of its government. He declared that sovereign consent was "axiomatic under the Charter," and that he needed "the consent of the state upon the territory of which it is proposed to station these forces."

Thus, in the words of Joseph P. Lash :

There was no overnight miracle . . . But one more crisis was surmounted, one more brink drawn back from with the help of the United Nations and one more stage passed in the historic withdrawal of Western power from the Middle East with the United Nations rather than a new imperialism filling the vacuum as the peoples of the region took over responsibility for their own destinies.

At the height of his popularity, Hammarskjold was unanimously reelected to his post in September, 1957. Unwilling to be unrecorded in the general chorus of approbation, Israel, who was absent because of the Hebrew high holy day of Yom Kippur, sent in a letter to record its "yea" vote.

By its very nature, the honeymoon could not last. Trygve Lie had written in *In the Cause of Peace* :

Any Secretary-General will find it so if he tries to be the kind of officer that I think the San Francisco charter envisaged. Should his conception be the same as mine, he will find it impossible to avoid the displeasure of one or more greater or smaller states during the years to come. He will be the target of criticism from right, left and center.

Hammarskjold had already incurred the enmity of some of the greater powers in the Laos, Lebanon, Jordan, and Suez crises. Anthony Eden had called him "myopic." The Soviet delegate had questioned his authority. Unfortunately, Hammarskjold was caught in the cross-fire of the Cold War. He had himself commented on the "state of absolute frozenness," that existed between the East and the West and had been disturbed to realize that, "one of the most curious and most upsetting features about the present world situation is that everybody is afraid of everybody." This situation was further aggravated by the intransigent position of each side and by their attempt to convert a political power struggle into a holy crusade.

Hammarskjold had boasted, "Well, as my father used to say, being neutral is not a question of saying 'yes' to both sides, but of saying 'no' to both sides." The Congo crisis was to apply the acid test to the picture that Hammarskjold had delineated at Oxford in May, 1961, of a supranational angel, "politically celibate." In the words of C. C. O'Brien :

So high and unreal a concept, so tame and exigent a conscience, must have made the realities of flesh and blood and history—the making of practical political calculations which could not afford to be always so very lofty—something of a torture.

Day to day, moment to moment, decisions had to be made in the field and each of these affected the political destinies of the various Congo factions. The sympathies of Belgium, Britain and the West rested with the Union Minière du Haut-Katanga, Katanga and Moise Tshombe. As O'Brien stated, "When

Katanga is hurt, money screams and money has powerful lungs." The Soviet bloc felt that the Lumumba faction offered them an opportunity to secure a vital foothold in Africa and they naturally resented the actions of the United Nations which had contributed to Lumumba's downfall. When Hammarskjold refused to place the UNOC (the United Nations force in the Congo) at the disposal of the Lumumba government or to shoot his way into the Congo, the Soviet press accused the Secretary-General of "capitulation before the colonialists."

Hammarskjold's prestige in the Soviet Union was not enhanced by his exchange with delegate Kuznetsov where the Secretary-General declared :

I do not believe that we help the Congolese people by actions in which Africans kill Africans or Congolese kill Congolese and that will remain my guiding principle for the future.

The Soviet press raged over Hammarskjold's "disgraceful role," in dealing with Tshombe, in greeting him and shaking his hand. After the body of Lumumba was found, Hammarskjold was to be denounced as "an accomplice and organizer of the murder of Lumumba."

Premier Khrushchev traveled to the 1960 autumn session of the General Assembly with the avowed purpose of securing the removal of Hammarskjold. While still en route aboard the S.S. Baltika, the Soviet leader wired a statement to the *Daily Express* in London declaring that "colonialists and imperialists are carrying out their policy through the hands of the United Nations' Secretary-General, Mr. Hammarskjold."

In his famous troika address to the General Assembly on September 23, 1960, Khrushchev repeated his charge that Hammarskjold's acts in the Congo had "in effect sided with the colonialists and with the countries that support the colonialists." Declaring that the United Nations structure was out of date, the Soviet premier called for the abolition of the job of Secretary-General and its replacement by a committee of one member each from the Western, Soviet and neutral blocs. In his reply, Hammarskjold declared :

Use whatever words you like : independence, impartiality, objectivity—they all describe essential aspects of what, without exception, must be the attitude of the Secretary-General. Such an attitude may at any stage become an obstacle for those who worked for certain political aims which would be better achieved if the Secretary-General compromised with this attitude. But if he did, how gravely he would then betray the trust of all those for whom the strict maintenance of such an attitude is their best protection in the world-wide fight for power and influence.

He closed with the avowal that he would rather see the office of the Secretary-General :

break on strict adherence to the principles of independence, impartiality and objectivity than drift on the basis of compromise. That is the choice daily facing the Secretary-General.

Khrushchev returned to the fray on October 3rd, charging that Mr. Hammarskjold "has always upheld the interests of the United States and other countries of monopoly capital." The Soviet leader declared that the Congo crisis was only "the last drop" that filled his "cup of patience to overflowing." He continued :

to avoid misinterpretation, I want to reaffirm that we do not trust Mr. Hammarskjold and cannot trust him. If he himself does not muster up enough courage to resign, so to say, in a chivalrous manner, then we shall draw the necessary conclusions from the situation obtaining.

With his "moral magistracy" rejected by the big powers, Hammarskjold had nowhere to turn for support except to the smaller countries. Even Drummond, the first Secretary-General of the League of Nations, had recognized that "the smaller the country the more trust is placed in the Secretary-General."

King Hussein in 1959 had properly called the United Nations the "summit meeting of the small nations."

Thus, in exercising his right to reply to Khrushchev, Hammarskjold keyed his refusal to resign to his responsibility toward the smaller countries. The issue, he began, is not that:

of a man but of an institution. The man does not count, the institution does. A weak or non-existent executive would mean that the United Nations would no longer be able to serve as an effective instrument for active protection of the interests of those many members who need such protection. The man holding the responsibility as chief executive should leave if he weakens the executive; he should stay if this is necessary for its maintenance.

"By resigning," the Secretary-General, who had never shown a lack of courage, continued:

I would, therefore, at the present difficult and dangerous juncture throw the Organization to the winds. I have no right to do so because I have a responsibility to all those states members for which the Organization is of decisive importance, a responsibility which overrides all other considerations. . . . . It is not the Soviet Union, or indeed, any other big powers who need the United Nations for their protection; it is all the others. In this sense the Organization is first of all their Organization and I deeply believe in the wisdom with which they will be able to use it and guide it.

He concluded as the swell of applause almost drowned out the speaker:

I shall remain in my post during the term of my office as a servant of the Organization in the interests of all those other nations, as long as they wish me to do so . . . It is very easy to resign; it is not so easy to stay on. It is very easy to bow to the wish of a big power. It is another matter to resist. As is well known to all members of this Assembly, I have done so before on many occasions and in many directions. If it is the wish of those nations who see in the Organization their best protection in this present world, I shall now do so again.

He had written in his Diary, "Life only demands from you

the strength you possess. Only one feat is possible — not to have run away."

Although the General Assembly expressed its confidence in Hammarskjold by a vote of eighty-three to eleven with five abstentions, the East bloc, for the balance of the 1960 session left no argument untried in :

—a concerted and consistent effort . . . to create conditions for a radical change of the administrative structure of the Organization, with that in view, to corrode whatever confidence there may be among members in the integrity of its Secretariat.

The Soviet delegation announced that "the Soviet government, for its part, will not maintain any relations with Hammarskjold and will not recognize him as an official of the United Nations."

It was Jefferson who stated, "What is practicable must often control what is pure theory." Hammarskjold was to discover that not even the smaller African nations were willing to permit him to adhere to his "principles of independence, impartiality and objectivity." No sovereign African country, practically every one of which was governed along authoritarian lines, could permit the continued existence on African soil of a prosperous secessionist movement bolstered by white mercenaries.

Thus Hammarskjold was steadily propelled toward an assault upon Katanga by force of arms. Conor Cruise O'Brien, the United Nations representative in Katanga, in his book *To Katanga and Back* writes that Hammarskjold deliberately misstated the facts in order to make active intervention by UNOC troops appear to be a defensive action. After saying :

These words will make painful reading for Hammarskjold's admirers; I know this because they are words which are painful also to write.

O'Brien cites United Nations document S/4940 issued on

September 14, 1961, while Hammarskjold was in Leopoldville. This document stated that United Nations troops in Elizabethville were fired upon while proceeding to extinguish a blaze which had been set in a United Nations garage by an arsonist, thus bringing about the assault on that capital city of Katanga. O'Brien, who was on the spot, denies that there had been any arson or a fire in the garage, or an initial attack on the United Nations troops.

This was not the first time that Hammarskjold had been attacked as a "Machiavelli of peace," who pictured himself as "some sort of United Nations field marshal." In his last annual report Hammarskjold had written that the members would have to choose between two different concepts of the United Nations: either a "static conference machinery" or a "dynamic instrument" to shape "an organized world community." He left little doubt which concept he favored. He had stated in his Oxford lecture, "This presents us with the crucial issue : Is it possible for the Secretary-General to resolve controversial questions on a truly international basis without obtaining the formal decision of the organization? The answer is in the affirmative." He had also written :

Only those who do not want to see can deny that we are moving these days in the direction of a new community of nations, however far we may be from its full realization, however often we may seem to have chosen the wrong path, however numerous the setbacks and disappointments have been. Could it be otherwise when no other road appears open out of the dangers a new era has created?

Thus Andrei Gromyko could scoff that Hammarskjold "may assume himself to be the prime minister of a world government and, for all we know, may claim that Les Nations Unies — c'est moi!" Hammarskjold lent fuel to the criticisms, despite his protestations, by too often assuming the role of a "kind of Delphic oracle who alone speaks for the international community," and by his inability to delegate authority to others because of his "too high, too quick, too critical" standards.

In any event, after the outbreak of fighting at Elizabethville, Hammarskjold agreed to confer with Moise Tshombe at Ndola, Northern Rhodesia. One can only speculate whether this meeting was prompted by remorse over the initiation of hostilities or by the pressure of the British ambassador. Whatever the reason, Hammarskjold and a party of thirteen took off on Sunday afternoon September 17, 1961, from Leopoldville airport in a Swedish Transair plane SE–BDI, a DC-6B on charter to the United Nations. The wreckage was discovered the next day seven miles from Ndola. All aboard died.

Thus was fulfilled the messianic prophecy which Hammarskjold had entered in his diary, *Markings,* which he termed "a sort of white paper concerning my negotiations with myself — and with God," that his life would end "on the Cross." Like Alfred Nobel, Hammarskjold was given a state funeral at Uppsala Cathedral. He had written :

> Cry,
> If you can,
> Cry
> But do not complain,
> The path chose you—
> And you shall say thank you.

With the death of Hammarskjold, the United Nations sank back into the paralysis of the cold war. The office of the Secretary-General was muted.

The Nobel prize committee announced on November 5, 1962, that there would be no award for that year. There seemed to be so little use.

16 The War on Babies

Then, on July 26, 1963, President Kennedy addressed the American people in a new "spirit of hope." He reported:

Yesterday, a shaft of light cut into the darkness. Negotiations were concluded in Moscow on a treaty to ban all nuclear tests in the atmosphere, in outer space and under water.

Premier Khrushchev hailed the treaty as "a momentous event."

Despite the presence of their initials on the document, the treaty of Moscow had not been negotiated by Averell Harriman, Viscount Hailsham, or Andrei Gromyko. A cartoon appearing in *The Observer* of London had given a more accurate description of the origins of the treaty. The cartoon depicted Britannia knighting a bearded youth wearing ban-the-bomb buttons and the caption read "Arise, Sir Agitator."

Yes, the test ban treaty had been written by the Aldermaston marchers; by the Women's Strike for Peace pickets at the United Nations; by the Student Peace Union hunger strikers at the White House; by the Committee of 100 sitdowners in Hyde Park; by the Committee for Non-Violent Action paraders in Red Square; by the tormented ghosts of Hiroshima and Nagasaki; by the sailors of the not so fortunate Fortunate

228

Dragon; by demonstrators and marchers and protesters in practically every civilized country on earth.

But above all, the test ban treaty had been written by Dr. Linus Carl Pauling, born in 1901, who was belatedly named as the 1962 laureate on October 10, 1963. Gunnar Jahn, the chairman of the Nobel committee, could well inquire whether the test ban treaty would have been achieved:

if there had been no responsible scientist who tirelessly, unflinchingly, year in, year out, had impressed on the authorities and on the general public the real menace of nuclear tests?

The atomic era was ushered in on July 16, 1945, with the first atomic explosion at Alamogordo, New Mexico. This bomb had an explosion energy of about twenty kilotons or 20,000 pounds of TNT. Similar bombs, a few weeks later on August 6th and 9th, unleashed the full horror of the nuclear age upon Hiroshima and Nagasaki.

Secure in its monopoly, the United States tested two atomic devices at Bikini in 1946 and three at Eniwetok in 1948. The Soviet Union confounded all the experts by exploding its own first atomic bomb well ahead of schedule on September 23, 1949. Competitive testing to perfect more refined and more powerful atomic devices began in earnest in 1951. In that year the United States tested sixteen devices and the Soviets two. In 1952 there were nine more American tests plus the explosion of the first thermonuclear weapon at Eniwetok on November 1. Also, Britain joined the atomic club on October 3, 1952, by detonating her own first device near the Montebello Islands.

The Soviet Union kept pace with the United States by testing its first hydrogen bomb on August 12, 1953. She also tested one other device that year while her American rival detonated eleven and Britain two. In 1954 there were six American atomic tests and one Soviet test. The 1955 score was America fifteen, and Russia four. For 1956 it was America, thirteen; and Russia, seven; with seven for Britain also. That country entered into the even more exclusive thermonuclear club on May 17, 1957. She conducted seven tests that year compared with twenty-four for the United States and thirteen for the Soviets. The first period of unrestricted testing culminated in 1958 with fifty-two United States test shots (including two high altitude tests), twenty-five Soviet and five British.

These explosions swept up into the atmosphere ever increasing quantities of materials made radioactive by neutrons. As the gases in the fire balls cooled, solid dust particles were formed and this fallout dust was carried around the world by winds, to be deposited by rain and snow. This radioactive fallout cannot be seen, felt, tasted, smelled or heard but it accumulates in the human bones and glands.

In the words of Dr. Otto Bastiansen, professor of chemistry at Oslo University, "Pauling's greatest effort was that he calculated the harmful effects of radioactive fallout." Dr. Pauling had projected statistically how many thousand children per megaton would suffer gross physical and mental defects and how many hundreds of thousands or millions in the future would bear these defects plus the number of stillbirth and childhood deaths and embryonic and neonatal deaths. Pauling wrote:

We are the custodians of the human race. We have the duty of protecting the pool of human germ plasm against willful damage.

In association with Albert Einstein and seven other eminent scientists, Dr. Pauling helped organize the Emergency Committee of Atomic Scientists in 1946. He delivered lectures for peace in twenty-six countries and wrote over a hundred articles to educate the peoples of the world on the nature of nuclear weapons and nuclear war.

As the winner of the Nobel prize for chemistry in 1954 for

his theory describing the fundamental nature and behavior of molecular bonds, he brought his great prestige to bear in alerting other scientists to the danger of fallout and in creating an opinion against nuclear tests within the scientific world.

In response to an address delivered by Dr. Pauling on May 15, 1957, before the students of Washington University, St. Louis, Missouri, 9,235 scientists from forty-nine nations spontaneously signed a petition stressing the danger of radioactive fallout to present and future generations and calling for a cessation of tests. Dr. Pauling presented this petition to the Secretary-General of the United Nations on January 13, 1958.

He disputed the attempts of the scientists for death, like Dr. Edward Teller, to minimize the effects of testing and accused Dr. Teller of making misleading statements on the harm caused by radioactive fallout. On the other side of the iron curtain, Soviet scientists agreed with Dr. Pauling. Professor A. M. Kuzin published an article in mid-1958 estimating that if nuclear tests were continued at the current rate :

then the price paid by future generations will roughly be at the rate of seven million lives per generation due to various diseases caused by the appearance in the atmosphere of radioactive products of nuclear explosions.

The authoritative Soviet magazine *Mezhdunarodnaya Zhizn* declared in its October, 1958, issue :

The radioactive products formed after each nuclear explosion contaminate the atmosphere, soil and water. The latter is happening now, in peacetime, after each test. Radioactive fallout is a grave hazard to the health of the people living today and threatens the normal development of future generations.

The peoples of the earth were gripped with a dread fear of the radioactive poison that drifted down from the atmosphere. An almost hysterical concern swept around the world. Prime Minister Sirimavo Bandaranaike of Ceylon expressed that concern most eloquently at a conference of twenty-four uncommitted nations at Belgrade when she cried, "There's not a single mother who can face the possibility of her children being exposed to atomic radiation."

A great outcry arose against the reckless testing that was befouling the planetary environment and threatening to make the planet uninhabitable. Great demonstrations broke out in every corner of the globe denouncing what the French biologist Jean Rostand called "le crime dans l'avenir — the crime against the future."

Questions were raised in the United Nations and among the uncommitted nations concerning the sense of responsibility of the American and Soviet governments. Dr. Pauling and 185 other plaintiffs filed suits on June 21, 1958, against Secretary of Defense Robert S. McNamara, Dr. Glenn T. Seaborg, and the other members of the Atomic Energy Commission, and simultaneously against the Soviet Ministry of Defense, for an injunction to halt all atmospheric tests. They charged that the "defendants' past and future acts did and will cause the plaintiffs to be damaged genetically and somatically."

The first political demand for a halt to atmospheric tests had been made by Prime Minister Jawaharlal Nehru on April 2, 1954. The Soviet Union had suggested a two or three year ban on tests in June, 1957. A conference of experts on detection of nuclear tests during a proposed period of suspension convened in Geneva on July 1, 1958. By August 21, 1958, the scientists from both sides had agreed on the technical fundamentals. Thereupon, representatives of the Soviet Union, the United Kingdom, and the United States met October 31, 1958, at Geneva for the Conference on the Discontinuance of Nuclear Weapons Tests. The next month, each of the three powers announced an unofficial, unpoliced moratorium on testing. Up until that time the United States had conducted nuclear explosions with a total force of 130 megatons, the Soviet Union of fifty megatons.

The calm was not disturbed until France exploded its first atomic bomb in the Sahara on February 13, 1960. Despite widespread protest in North Africa, France conducted two more tests in 1960, and another one in April, 1961. The larger powers had extended the test moratorium unilaterally from year to year conditioned upon the other nations not resuming testing also. Then, after having clandestinely prepared for new tests while pretending to negotiate for their cessation at Geneva, the Soviets resumed atmospheric testing on September 1, 1961, with a series of thirty-one shots, including the largest explosion in history with an energy of fifty-five to sixty megatons.

At first, the United States retaliated with only underground tests in Nevada. But, after assessing the Soviet test program, the Americans decided that they, too, would have to resume atmospheric testing in order to keep abreast in the race towards human annihilation. Thereupon, the United States exploded a medium sized nuclear device near Christmas Island on April 25, 1962, in the first of a series that was to encompass eighty-six shots with an energy force of thirty-seven megatons. The Soviet Union contributed to the atmospheric pollution with forty tests, equivalent to a force of 180 megatons that year, and France detonated one.

The result was a marked increase in the concentration of strontium 90, iodine 131, carbon 14, and cesium 137 absorbed by the plants eaten by food animals, and thus incorporated into the animal's flesh and milk. Britain, Sweden, Canada, Austria, and other countries considered halting the supply of fresh milk to children.

In the United States, dairy farmers from Utah, Minnesota, Iowa, Kansas, Alaska, and Missouri agreed to withhold from the market milk produced by cows grazing in the fields. The levels of contamination approached and exceeded the guide-lines previously established by the Federal Radiation Council, a governmental body chaired by the Secretary of Health, Education, and Welfare. On it sits the chairman of the Atomic Energy Commission, and the Secretaries of Defense, Labor, and Commerce, with the President's science adviser as an official observer.

The Council responded in traditional fashion by changing the name of the unit of contamination measurement from the micromicrocurie to the picocurie and by raising the radiation protection guide level in the same manner that the national debt limit is raised every time it is reached. Congressman John V. Lindsay termed the new guides, "some of the most ingenious administrative double-talk of our time." Dr. Russell H. Morgan, professor of radiological science at Johns Hopkins University School of Hygiene and Public Health, and chair-man of the United States Public Health Service's National Advisory Committee on Radiation, pointed out that these revised guides were above those of the International Com-mission on Radiation Protection and accused the Council of "playing the numbers game."

As a result of the fallout from tests conducted through 1962, the Council predicted that one living person out of 100,000 had a chance of developing leukemia, one out of 300,000 of contracting bone cancer, and that one in 500,000 would bear a defective child. These ratios may be small but the numerical figure becomes significant when these per-centages are applied to a world population of over three billion. The Council further estimated that the over-all toll of those affected by nuclear tests up to that date would be 1.5 million persons, as yet unborn. Herman Kahn had reported in 1961 that it was estimated that every time a megaton of fission energy is released in the Pacific Ocean or the Soviet

Arctic, the resulting strontium 90 may give a thousand living persons leukemia or bone cancer.

The picketing and the demonstrations and the marches and the sitdowns resumed. Linus Pauling picketed the White House and the United Nations. Together with 254 persons from twenty-seven countries, he renewed his suits to enjoin the United States and the Soviet Union from continuing testing. By an overwhelming vote, the General Assembly of the United Nations called on the nuclear powers to end all nuclear weapons testing by January 1, 1963.

That is how the 1962 peace prize award to Dr. Linus Carl Pauling was announced on the same day that the test ban treaty went into effect. The laureate himself commented : "I thought it was a nice day for the committee to make the announcement." The great scientist, Hans Bethe, stated, "without Professor Pauling's awakening of the public conscience on this issue, there would not have been any pressure on governments and there would not have been any test ban."

The only person ever to have won two full Nobel prizes was born in Portland, Oregon. He received his bachelor's degree from Oregon State College in 1922 and his doctorate from the California Institute of Technology in 1925. Study in Europe as a Guggenheim Fellow followed before he returned to Caltech in 1931 as professor of chemistry. Dr. Pauling later became head of the chemistry division and director of the Gates and Crellin Laboratories at the Institute. He held this position until he transferred to the Center for the Study of Democratic Institutions in 1963. During World War II he was a member of the explosives division of the National Defense Research Commission and later worked with the Office of Scientific Research and Development. For outstanding wartime services on rocket propellants and other explosives, on an oxygen deficiency indicator for submarine and aircraft, and on development of a substitute for human serum in medical treatment "among other contributions to the war effort," he was awarded the Presidential Medal for Merit.

The Nobel citation acclaimed Dr. Pauling for his work since 1946 "not only against the testing of nuclear weapons, not only against the spread of these armaments, not only against their very use, but against all warfare as a means of solving international conflicts." But Dr. Pauling, like so many before him, had found that it was not "respectable to work for peace."

Although he had denied under oath that he was a Communist, stating, "I am not even a theoretical Marxist"; although Mr. Jahn in his presentation had noted that:

Anyone familiar with Linus Pauling and his views, anyone who has heard him speak or read his works, should know that he is by no means a Communist;

many publications, such as the *National Review* and the *St. Louis Globe Democrat* had branded the biochemist "a traitor, a collaborator with subversive foreign and alien elements. . . . engaged in subversive Communist activities," and a "moral nihilist."

In 1952 he was refused a passport by the State Department. In 1960 he was subpoenaed by the Senate Internal Security subcommittee and asked to produce all correspondence pertaining to the United Nations peace petition. This he refused to do contending that such disclosure would damage the persons involved and describing the subcommittee as a "discredit to the Congress." In turn, this body accused him in its report of "a consistent pro-Soviet bias. . . . the number one scientific name in virtually every major activity of the Communist peace offensive in this country."

In all too familiar tones, the award was denounced as

"rude," "an extraordinary insult to America," "a weird insult from Norway."

Yet Dr. Pauling had set forth his views clearly. As early as 1950, he had declared, "The problem of an atomic war must not be confused by minor problems, such as Communism versus capitalism." He continued, "It is not necessary that the social and economic systems in Russia be identical with that in the United States in order that these two great nations can be at peace with one another. It is only necessary that the people of the United States and the people of Russia have respect for one another, a deep desire to work for progress, a mutual recognition that war has finally ruled itself out as the arbiter of the destinies of humanity. Once the people of the world express these feelings, the East and West can reach a reasonable and equitable decision about all world affairs and can march together side by side, towards a more and more glorious future."

He had once summed up his philosophy for an interviewer by stating, "I like people. I like animals, too." Thus he wrote in a 1959 paper for the American Journal of Orthopsychiatry entitled *I Like People* :

But I like human beings especially and I am unhappy that the pool of human germ plasm, which determines the nature of the human race, is deteriorating.

Because of his love for humanity, because of his concern that the right of the human race to survive was being squandered, he feared, as he wrote in 1958 in his book *No More War!*, that :

If the world continues along the path of insanity, we are doomed to die—we Americans, all of us, and all the Russian people, and perhaps most of the people of European nations. Our civilization will come to its irrational end.

When the Soviet Union announced in August, 1961, its intention to resume testing, Dr. Pauling condemned that decision as a threat to peace. He also denounced the massive Soviet explosion of October 30, 1961, in a broadcast beamed by Radio Liberty to Eastern Europe, predicting that the blast would cause gross defects in more than 40,000 children born in the next few generations and 400,000 more children in later centuries. He joined with Lord Boyd-Orr and Dr. Albert Schweitzer in protesting the Soviet treatment of the Jews in Russia.

At the same time Dr. Pauling defended his association with the Communist sponsored World Council of Peace by asking how it could be possible to achieve international understanding, disarmament and peace unless the peace organizations of the free and Communist worlds cooperated and met together.

Dr. Pauling filled the need lamented by Norman Cousins :

Belonging to a nation, man has nations that can speak for him. Belonging to a religion, man has religions that can speak for him. Belonging to an economic and social order, man has economic or political orders than can speak for him. But belonging to the human race, man is without a spokesman.

Dr. Pauling was that spokesman. But in preaching that above all nations is humanity he hurled himself for seventeen years at a thousand prejudices, addressing deaf ears, closed eyes and locked minds. The *New York Times* finally acknowledged, "His courage in running against the crowd is now being recognized."

Events again prove the truth of Yevtushenko's lines :

This strange era, these strange times when
Ordinary common honesty was called courage.

The quiet voice of Dr. Pauling grew to an overwhelming world-wide din that had to be heard. The result was the treaty providing for a limited nuclear test ban. The United States insisted on omitting underground nuclear explosions from the ban, claiming such tests could be checked only by detection monitor stations on Soviet soil. However, the United States secretly concealed that it had been monitoring such tests since February 2, 1962, when it had detected seismic signals from the Soviet nuclear weapons proving ground in the Semipalatinsk area of Central Asia.

Nevertheless, Dr. Pauling hailed the treaty as one that "may well go down as the greatest action ever taken by national governments, one that will lead to the abolition of war and development of a system of international law." Dr. Pauling said in his Nobel lecture, entitled *Science and Peace*, "I believe that the historian of the future may well describe the making of this treaty as the most important action ever taken by the governments of nations, in that it is the first of a series of treaties that will lead to the new world, from which war has been abolished forever."

He summarized the importance of the Nobel peace prize :

I consider this a greater honor than the Nobel prize for chemistry because of the significance to humanity and the diminution of human suffering.

We have already discussed the award of the 1963 peace prize to the International Committee of the Red Cross and the League of the Red Cross Societies as a fitting commemoration of the one hundredth anniversary of the founding of that great humanitarian organization by Henri Dunant.

The 1964 award to the Reverend Dr. Martin Luther King, Jr., has also been considered.

With the award for 1965, the Nobel committee of the Storting turned from the war on babies to the healing of children. The United Nations Children's Fund, UNICEF, was the eighth organization to be honored with the coveted prize.

The noble, humanitarian work of this agency, administered without regard to creed, color or ideology, warrants a detailed discussion.

Anne Frank would have approved of the 1965 award. As her fate so cruelly demonstrated, while other eras cherished the child as man's most precious possession, the twentieth century is marked by man's inhumanity to children. The third symbol of our enlightened century, in addition to the mushroom cloud and the huddled refugee, is the forsaken child.

Each of us can call to his mind's eye his own private gallery of horror pictures: the naked, crying, orphaned Manchurian child slumped on the ground while the smoke of war swirls around her; the line of silent, wide-eyed youngsters filing into the death chambers of Buchenwald; the grim rat packs of Italian boys foraging in the ruins; the Chinese boy, with the distended belly, extending an empty rice bowl; the once pretty Javanese girl covered with the sores of yaws; the groping Moroccan boy blind of trachoma; the Utah teen-ager with nodules on the thyroid gland; the ragged beggars everywhere.

The Nobel Peace Prize for 1965 was awarded to an organization which is committed to mitigating the sufferings which society has inflicted upon its children. That organization is the United Nations Children's Fund, universally known as UNICEF.

The world has formulated in words its obligations to its children. The fourteenth session of the United Nations General Assembly adopted the Declaration of the Rights of the Child on November 20, 1959. This resolution declares that, "Mankind owes to the child the best it has to give to the end that he may have a happy childhood." Principle Six of the Declaration goes on to say, "The child needs love and understanding. He shall . . grow up . . . in an atmosphere of affection and . . . security." Principle Ten adds, "He shall be brought up in a spirit of understanding, tolerance, friendship among peoples, peace and universal brotherhood."

Square these noble sentiments with the facts. Three out of four of the world's one billion children are growing up in the developing countries where forty percent of the population is under fifteen. These seven hundred and fifty million children survive under the most abject conditions of privation, hunger, disease, filth, lack of shelter, and ignorance. Four hundred million have no school to go to, no teacher to instruct them. Seventy-five million babies are born each year in these under-developed lands where not more than one mother in four receives prenatal attention or medical or midwife assistance at birth. UNICEF exists to attempt to bridge the gaping span between the realities of every-day life and the objectives set forth in the Declaration.

What is UNICEF? It is something tangible. It is a glass of milk being drunk by a child in Brazil; it is a packet of seeds, fertilizer and garden tools to start a nutrition project in Chad; it is a windmill and sink pump to supply pure water to schools in Uruguay; it is a midwife in Malaya using a UNICEF kit to deliver a baby; it is an Indonesian factory to produce milk-like saridele from soya beans; it is Dr. Ramon Miquel y Suarez-Inclan injecting UNICEF sulfone with a UNICEF hypodermic into a leper child in Ban Phrayun, Thailand; it is Dr. Soomarsono injecting penicillin into a Sidoredje, Indonesia child who is covered with ugly yaw sores; it is a two gallon UNICEF sprayer spreading DDT against malaria in Insein-Ywoma, Burma; it is a nurse applying an antibiotic ointment against trachoma at the Chetla Health Center in Calcutta, India; it is a dairy to produce water buffalo milk in Iraq; it is Miss Johansson setting up a mother and child clinic in Nuevo Mondo, Mexico; it is a hospital reconstructed after an earthquake in Morocco; it is a factory in Quintero, Chile, producing flour from dried fish; it is a line of children in the Uganda jungle waiting for a BCG vaccination against tuberculosis.

UNICEF is a jeep in Nigeria, a wheel chair in Greece, a bicycle in Syria, a blanket in Ecuador, a pair of shoes in Tunisia — fifteen thousand different items used in the fight against childhood's most powerful foes. There are 543 projects, in all, in 118 different countries. In the words of Henry R. Labouisse, executive director, "UNICEF's approach to the needs of children is a practical, down-to-earth approach, as all humanitarian efforts must be if they are to be any good."

UNICEF, the United Nations International Children's Emergency Fund, was created by Resolution 57 of the United Nations General Assembly on December 11, 1946, to bring emergency aid to the millions of sick and starving children victims of World War II. Beginning with the $550,000 left over from the liquidation of the United Nations Relief and Rehabilitation Administration, UNICEF established a lifeline of milk, blankets, shoes, clothing, cod liver oil and medicine to twenty million children in fourteen war torn countries.

In 1948, the field of activity of the agency was extended to aid refugee mothers and children in Palestine. In 1950, the program was further enlarged to encompass children in the underdeveloped regions of the world. The 1953 General Assembly dropped the words International and Emergency from the title and made the Fund permanent. The UNICEF initials, however, had been too well ingrained in the minds of the peoples of the world to be changed.

The guiding spirit of UNICEF, from its inception until his death in January, 1965, was Maurice Pate. In 1960, Mr. Pate was nominated for the peace prize by the Norwegian Committee for UNICEF, but he protested that he could not accept the honor for himself and suggested that UNICEF be named instead.

Mr. Labouisse, a distinguished American career diplomat,

succeeded to the post of executive director in June, 1965. He is appointed by the United Nations Secretary General and is responsible to a thirty nation executive board. The headquarters are in New York City.

UNICEF is more than an international milkman, providing billions of pounds of powdered milk, to give 6,300,000 children—and their mothers—a daily ration of milk. At the time of its award, UNICEF had provided basic equipment for 8,610 health centers and 21,000 sub-centers in 100 countries. It had helped protect forty-five million persons against malaria in twenty-eight countries. It had administered two hundred million BCG vaccinations in forty-five countries. It had examined over 100 million persons for yaws and treated forty-one million in thirty-five countries. It had treated twenty-one million persons afflicted with trachoma in eighteen countries. It had treated two million lepers in forty countries. It had helped equip two thousand five hundred schools and teacher training institutions and four hundred vocational training institutions in fifty-five countries. It had equipped three thousand five hundred day care, youth and community centers, women's clubs and training institutions for welfare workers. It had equipped 198 milk processing plants in thirty-eight countries. It was assisting fifty-five million children and their mothers in health, nutrition, family and child welfare, vocational training, education, and in other essential services.

UNICEF is also an ideal. It holds out a flicker of hope and expectation to the deprived children of the world. It is a concrete demonstration that they have not been abandoned by mankind as lost.

All of this is being accomplished by a staff of under four hundred persons on an annual budget of $33,708,385—less than 3/100 of one percent of the hundred and thirty-five billion dollars spent each year by the civilized countries of the world on armaments; less than ten percent of the monies spent daily for purposes of war. It is the boast of UNICEF that all of its income comes from voluntary contributions from governments and private sources or from fund raising activities, such as the sale of Christmas cards. However, since 77.8 percent of the income comes from contributions of 121 governments, this boast would appear to be a play on words. As we have seen, all contributions made to the United Nations by the member states are, in actuality, voluntary contributions. The receiving governments match UNICEF funds two-and-a-half times in locally available products, buildings and personnel.

In view of the pittance which the UNICEF budget represents, compared to the vast needs, one can understand Mr. Labouisse's complaint : "We never have enough money to do what we want." Twenty-five cents buys enough antibiotics to save two young victims of trachoma from blindness; fifty cents means enough DDT to protect seven children from malaria for one year; seventy-five cents provides the sulfone to treat a young leprosy victim successfully for three years; one penny will provide a hungry child with five glasses of milk; fifteen cents will supply vitamin capsules for a child for three months; one penny vaccinates a child against tuberculosis with BCG; and a nickel buys the penicillin to cure two children of yaws.

Literally, hundreds of million of children, who desperately need these vital food and medicines, must suffer without them because there isn't enough money. What is the current price of a machine gun bullet or a canister of napalm or a missile or an atomic bomb? What is so monstrous is that the world presently possess, as has been demonstrated in an earlier chapter, the capability to eradicate hunger and disease completely from the face of the earth.

These considerations should not detract, in any way, from the holy work being performed each day by the dedicated staff of UNICEF. The highest form of reverence for life is regard for the life of a child. Here, the manifold achievements of UNICEF outrank all others.

But even the act of grace, which is UNICEF, has not been spared its share of abuse. Although the Vatican makes an annual contribution, several Roman Catholic parishes have barred trick-or-treat collections because communist representatives served on the executive board and children in communist countries received assistance. Right wing organizations, such as the John Birch Society, attacked UNICEF as a government charity, tending to create a world welfare state, and promote world government.

The Daughters of the American Revolution characterized UNICEF as a "program designed to promote the world welfare state and to remove the Christ from Christmas." This is the same Christ who said :

Suffer little children to come unto me and forbid them not.

17 Norway and the Cold War

As our quest for peace reaches into the present; it is not invalid to question whether Alfred Nobel chose, in the Norwegian Storting, the most perfect vehicle for the dispensing of his peace prize. Norway has never disarmed or given up its armed forces. As a small nation with a very large merchant marine, it has maintained a sizeable navy. After its traumatic experiences during the Nazi occupation of World War II, Norway completely abandoned any pretense of neutrality. It is a member of the North Atlantic Treaty Organization which is militarily allied against the Warsaw bloc. It has universal military service.

Further, it had to be expected that the members of the Storting would have to be nationalistic, practical politicians, and we have already seen how uncertain is the support given to the cause of peace by this class of statesmen. The reader will remember the furor raised by Prahl's suggestion that the composition of the Nobel committee be international.

Many members of this committee have gone on record as opposed to arbitration, disarmament and an international rule of law. For instance, Hans Jakob Horst, a member of the Nobel committee from 1901 to 1931, was a strong advocate of defense "for the sake of our independence — war crazy, if you will." John Lund favored the strengthening of Norwegian defenses. Halvdon Koht opposed any reduction of arms by Norway and was opposed to arbitration because he thought international law had not advanced far enough to recognize national independence as an inalienable right. Jorgen Lovland held that disarmament endangered peace instead of promoting it. Georg Francis Hagerup openly expressed skepticism of the ability of international law to replace warfare. Carl Bergen helped to found and was the first president of the League of Norsemen, a fraternity of patriotic Norsemen.

Thus, when the announcement was made that the Social-Democratic Storting had awarded the 1951 peace prize to the socialist Jouhaux, it was not certain whether the honor had been given in recognition of a lifetime of work to convert the working class movement into a force for peace, or whether the honor had been conferred because its recipient had saved French and international labor from communism. In other words, was the 1951 award made on the merits or was the Nobel peace prize utilized as another weapon in the cold war against the East?

As we have seen, some laureates, such as Jane Addams, considered works of charity the foundation of world peace; others, such as Boyd-Orr, would base world peace on a drive to abolish hunger; still others maintain that world peace can develop only as an outgrowth of the collaboration of the working classes. Yet, only one other person from the house of labor, outside of Jouhaux, had ever received the Nobel prize (Henderson had held minor posts in the movement). That labor leader was Cremer but that founder of the Amalgamated Society of Carpenters and Joiners had advanced to broader political endeavors before he was named laureate. Jouhaux, on the other hand, had never left the house of labor except for the war years 1941–1945 when he was forcibly removed to a Nazi concentration camp.

The *Communist Manifesto* had proclaimed, "The worker

has no country." During World War I; the Russian revolution under the slogan "Bread and Peace"; the open fraternization of Russian and German soldiers on the Eastern front; the French army mutiny of 1917; the fraternization of French, Belgian and German troops on the Western front; and the mutiny of the Kiel sailors all raised fears that the common soldier, in revulsion against the wanton butchery of modern war, would rear up and put an end to the mass slaughter. Perhaps because of the more intense hatred engendered in World War II or perhaps because of the more impersonal nature of that war, commanding officers in that later conflict were not confronted with any mutinous acts more serious than self-inflicted wounds or shellshock.

Since all predictions of World War III forecast a lightning quick push button holocaust, it does not seem probable that army mutinies will ever again be a factor in halting wars. One must then turn to the working masses who would be required to take up arms and fight and lay down their lives in case of war. Karl Hjalmar Branting, when notified of his designation for the peace prize, had commented :

The only way to peace, however, is through an international organization of the working classes in all countries, both in a political and an economic sense. From that it follows that really effective work for peace can never be performed by a single individual; that being so, the masses ought certainly to have a share in the sum which the Nobel Foundation may be able to disburse for this purpose and then use them to promote a steady and increasingly intensive peace propaganda.

Léon Jouhaux echoed Branting's sentiments when he, in turn, was notified of his selection, claiming that the award was "confirmation of the value accorded to the action of the working class in favor of the organization of peace." Jouhaux's career had well qualified him for the coveted prize. His origins were revolutionary and working class. His grandfather had fought on the barricades in 1848 and his father had been active in the Paris commune.

Jouhaux had had to leave school when he was twelve. He had worked; as a locksmith, a vat boy in a soap factory, and as a wall-paper hanger before he finally became a worker in a match factory in Aubervilliers at the age of sixteen. He became active in the local union of the match factory, and in 1906 was elected as representative to the Confédération Générale du Travail (C.G.T.). He was elected Secretary-General of this federation in 1909, a post he was to hold until December, 1947. During his term of office, the membership of the C.G.T. increased from five hundred thousand to five million.

In those days he was a philosophical anarchist, a revolutionary syndicalist, and he edited *La Bataille syndicaliste* from 1911 to 1921. Together with Jaurès, he had tried to organize an anti-militarist movement with German labor prior to World War I. Shortly before the outbreak of the war, Jouhaux dispatched a telegram to the leader of the German trade unions, Legien, urging a united front. When these attempts failed, Léon Jouhaux supported the French war effort. After the war, he served on the French delegation to Versailles and was a member of the committee on labor which drafted the charter for the International Labor Office. Jouhaux was a perennial labor delegate to this specialized agency; the only one to survive World War II. He was very active in its work which included a long period of service as vice-chairman. From 1925 to 1928 he was a French delegate to the League of Nations. He was active in the Popular Front of the 1930's and was the president of the French Economic Council, a governmental official advisory board on economic matters. During this period he completed his studies on a university level and wrote several books, including a very effective treatise on disarmament.

After the fall of France, Jouhaux, together with other Popular Front leaders, was seized by the Germans. He was removed to the Reich and interred in various concentration camps from 1941 to 1945.

Upon his return to the C.G.T. after his release from the concentration camp by the advancing American Army, Jouhaux discovered that that organization had become infested with communists. When he found that his voice was powerless and that he had to share the post of secretary with the communist Benoit Frachon, Jouhaux led one million of his followers out of the C.G.T. into a new anti-communist federation called, "Force Ouvrière," the French Workers Force. The slogan of this force was "Freedom from all political control." He followed this step by later helping to organize and serving as an executive officer, of the anti-communist International Confederation of Free Trade Unions, an opposition group to the communistic World Federation of Trade Unions. He was a champion of a United States of Europe.

In his eloquent acceptance speech, Jouhaux declared :

Let us be soldiers for peace . . . There can be no peace so long as there is fear, need, distress and injustice, but only where there is confidence and brotherhood. Peace should be the consecration of liberty.

The world press, in commenting on the Jouhaux award, neglected, in the main, the great bulk of his work, concentrating instead upon his efforts to save French and world labor from communism. Whatever doubt might have existed concerning the motivation behind the Jouhaux designation; it was dissipated when the 1953 winner was announced. The Nobel committee of the Norwegian Storting was quite apparently taking sides in the cold war and using the Nobel peace prize as a partisan weapon.

The 1953 peace laureate was General George C. Marshall, the United States Army Chief of Staff in World War II and Secretary of State in the Truman cabinet from 1947 to 1949. While in the latter post, he had delivered an address at the Harvard University commencement in June, 1947, proposing that aid be offered to European nations for economic reconstruction. He said, "United States assistance should not be doled out as crises developed but should provide a cure rather than a mere palliative." A few days later British Foreign Minister Ernest Bevin hailed the address as one that would "rank as one of the greatest speeches made in Western history."

The Congress established the Economic Cooperation Administration in April, 1948, and sixteen Western European nations qualified for aid through the Committee of European Economic Cooperation. Under the Marshall Plan, the United States pumped thirteen billion dollars into Europe in three-and-a-half years to rebuild the economy of the Western nations and to save them from communism. Bevin summarized:

History has decreed that Mr. Marshall's name would be associated with one of the greatest efforts that had ever been made in the establishment of peace and the European recovery program.

Although the plan had originally been open to them, the Soviet bloc, as expected, denounced the Marshall plan as imperialistic, as cold war inspired, and as a counterpart of the military oriented North Atlantic Treaty Organization. It was not unexpected, therefore, to have Pravda greet the award to Marshall with a cartoon showing a sheep's headdress labeled, Nobel Peace Prize, about to be placed on the head of the uniformed General Marshall.

Perhaps the Nobel committee has been mindful of the Chinese proverb that "no good specimen of humanity is ever converted into soldiery as no good iron is made into nails," for

Marshall is the only professional soldier ever rewarded with the Nobel peace prize and his Nobel medallion must have looked incongruously out of place among his many military decorations and combat ribbons. It is questionable whether a professional soldier can be a true advocate of peace. From the beginning of his career, war has provided his only reason for existence; his training has ingrained in him the conviction that war is the ultima ratio for all international problems. Grenville Clark and Louis B. Sohn have observed that the professional soldier is opposed to disarmament "because his training and environment have irrevocably conditioned him to assume that his profession is indispensable."

George C. Marshall was a professional soldier who had spent most of his adult life in the United States Army. Even as a boy, Marshall had set his sights on a military career. Since appointment to West Point was not likely for the son of a Democrat small businessman in Uniontown, Pennsylvania, a heavily Republican state, Marshall enrolled at the Virginia Military Institute at Lexington. In military school, as in his earlier education, the future chief of staff was not an outstanding student. But he did demonstrate leadership in handling and commanding men and became the senior cadet captain.

Upon graduation, he was commissioned. The Army was not a particularly promising career at the turn of the century. The military establishment was meager and promotion was agonizingly slow. At the age of thirty-six in 1915, he was only a lieutenant and he even thought of resigning. Then came World War I and General Pershing's recognition of the abilities of this staff officer, George C. Marshall.

Marshall's postwar career included assignments to the Phillipines and to Tientsin. When a vacancy occurred in the position of chief of staff in the autumn of 1939, he was thirty-fourth in seniority, although he actually ranked fifth because of the rule that the officer selected for the four year term must

be under sixty. Harry Hopkins lent his influence in inducing
Franklin Roosevelt to skip Marshall over the others. The rest
is history.

It should be recorded here that General Marshall, like
General Eisenhower, had misgivings about dropping the atom
bomb on Japan. He is recorded as having stated before
Hiroshima :

We must offset by . . . warning methods the opprobrium which
might follow from an ill-considered employment of such force.

It would appear that Marshall suffered from the same gaps
in his equipment as a statesman that are so common to former
military men. His biographer, Forrest C. Pogue, writes :

Some of his associates deplored his lack of academic accomplishments . . . They also regretted his insufficient knowledge of the
totalitarian ideologies of his time. To these charges Marshall
would have been the first to plead guilty. Like most officers of
his generation, he studied the practice of arms and not the
theory. Like most of them, he had read little in political theory,
international economics or advanced science.

Perhaps this explains the naïveté displayed by Marshall as
the head of the Truman Presidential mission to China. By not
recognizing that the absolute incompatability between the
Nationalists and the Communists foredoomed any coalition
government and by being duped into identifying the Reds as
agrarian reformers, Marshall laid the basis for the disastrous
American policy toward China — a policy that may yet trigger
World War III.

It is doubtful whether Marshall himself ever had any real
hope for world peace. He is on record as having said :

If man does find the solution for world peace, it will be the most
revolutionary reversal of his record we have ever known.

His Nobel acceptance speech evoked echoes of Theodore

Roosevelt with Marshall declaring that "a very strong military posture is vitally necessary today," although he recognized that "it is too narrow a basis on which to build a dependable, long-enduring peace."

These partisan awards renew the persistent query as to whether the Nobel peace prize, as now administered by the admittedly Western oriented Norwegian Storting, retains its prestige and stature as a genuine force for peace. Or has the Nobel peace prize been reduced to a Western intra-mural decoration equivalent in international moral standing to that of the Lenin peace prize? It was precisely for this reason that Jean Paul Sartre declined the 1964 literature prize, declaring that the award only goes to Westerners or rebels of the East.

At this perilous junction of world history, this "most dangerous time in the history of the human race," as the West confronts the East in a balance of terror across a battle line bisecting the globe, there seems to be only two alternatives. Adlai E. Stevenson had eloquently defined these as "co-existence or no existence." In this atomic age, it would appear that peace can be attained in either of only two ways; either we will achieve a peace of the cemetery or we will achieve a peace of accommodation — by patching together a modus vivendi permitting capitalism and communism to co-exist. As long as life continues, Western leaders should be confident that the blessings of liberty will, in time, penetrate even the iron curtain while Eastern dialecticians should be certain that the overwhelming logic of Marxist-Leninist theory will prevail ideologically.

A peace maker must not be thrashing about with his sword in the thick of battle. He must stand apart and aloof from the dust of the fray in order for his voice to command respect and attention. Perhaps, then, it would not be out of order to suggest that the time has come for the Norwegian Storting to re-examine the existing apparatus for the awarding of the

Nobel peace prize. Perhaps this body should consider whether this power should be temporarily delegated to a committee of outstanding world scholars until such a time as Norway is no longer an active member of one of the contending camps.

18 But Few Are Chosen

Nor is it invalid to question whether the Norwegian Storting, in its choice of peace laureates, has carried out the intent of Alfred Nobel's will. Aware that the world is better at supplying tombstones than stepping stones, Nobel had stated to Archbishop Söderblom, "As a rule, I'd rather take care of the stomachs of the living than the glory of the departed." A 1934 editorial in the *Christian Century* best summarized Nobel's purposes:

The founder's intention was to encourage bold dreamers and prophetic spirits whose ideas are too far ahead for their time to win attention without some adventitious aid.

Affidavits by witnesses to the Nobel Will, support this conclusion. One such document states:

He was not in the least interested in giving small sums as a reward without any real use. His desire was, as he always stated, to place those whose work showed promise in a position of such complete independence that they would in the future be able to devote their whole energies to their work.

Nobel was most concerned with smoothing the path for the "dreamers such as possess the gift of poetry but are unknown to the many or are misunderstood by them." He said:

256

I would not leave anything to a man of action since he would be tempted to give up work. On the other hand, I would like to help dreamers for they find it hard to get on in life . . . There are dreamers in this world, seers of things beautiful to be accomplished for the benefit of mankind. But they do not always live under conditions that enable them to convert their visions and dreams into deeds. The world needs just these visionaries.

In this sense, R. W. Strehlenert, a Swedish engineer, co-worker and friend of Nobel and the sole surviving witness to the will in 1933, stated in that year that the founder's intention was to aid younger men. The other witness to the will, Leonard Hwass, in a 1914 article appearing in *Die Woche* of Berlin, had written:

because Nobel knew from his own bitter struggle how particularly difficult it is for the noble-minded, often so sensitively and delicately organized, to make their way, he wished to lighten the life of dreamers . . . . who, impractical and devoid of means, often go to wrack and ruin in the fullness of their mental powers.

Hwass continues by stating Nobel's intention that the

prize should never be bestowed as an honorary prize, but as a promotive prize for the encouragement of new and beneficent work and . . . world renowned personalities with an assured future should be excluded.

The gist of the Hwass article was that Nobel had dedicated his fortune, not as a decoration to those who had already attained the pinnacle of fame and fortune, not as a superfluous distinction for men whose working days were over, but as help and encouragement for those whose life's work lay before them. Free such dreamers from the trammels of economic pressures and they become "the real dispensers of blessings and happiness to mankind."

The founder recognized that if the Nobel peace prize is to have any real influence on the course of history and the quest for peace, it would have to be awarded in recognition of the heroic virtues of creative idealists. If one examines the roster of the peace awards in this light, it becomes apparent that, except for certain isolated and notable exceptions, the prizes have been stripped of any ideality. The prizes have honored the lords of victory instead of those dedicated souls who have labored for that disarmament of the mind which must be a prerequisite to any lasting state of peace. The Stockholm Peace Society complained in 1934 that the prizes had been too often awarded to "presidents, ministers and other high public officials," and too seldom to "working friends of peace or to really radical proponents of peace and disarmament." As George Bernard Shaw expressed it in his inimitable way, the prizes have become "life belts you throw a man after he has reached shore."

Too often, the prizes have added a glow to the sunset instead of a brightness to the dawn. Run down the list of peace laureates. So many were well along in years when the awards were accorded: Dunant, Passy, Ducommun, Cremer, Moneta, Bajer, Beernaert, Asser, Root, Bourgeois, Buisson, Quidde, Kellogg, Butler, Jane Addams, Henderson, Cecil, Hull, Mott, Emily Balch, Boyd-Orr, Jouhaux, Schweitzer, Marshall, Noel-Baker, and Pauling. Four were over eighty: Beernaert, Asser, Buisson, Mott. Only seven were under fifty: Roosevelt, Fried, Stresemann, von Ossietzky, Bunche, Pire, and King. King was the youngest at thirty-five; Bunche the next youngest at forty-six.

Further, the Nobel committee has almost completely ignored the stipulation in the will that the work rewarded should have been accomplished during the preceding year. As early as May 9, 1907, the *New York Times* was complaining in an editorial:

We fear that Nobel's originality will never be allowed much scope by those who have charge of the administration of the fund, for they have from the beginning shown a flagrant disregard of the intention of the founder.

The editorial then goes on to measure the delay between the year of achievement and the year of award for the early winners. The newspaper thus finds a thirty-seven year delay in Dunant's case, twenty-six years for Passy, fifteen for Cremer, and sixteen years for Baroness von Suttner. The editorial concludes that the award came at a time when these workers for peace:

were resting on their laurels. The money, however much needed, will not enable them to do more than they have; the honor, however much deserved, will not add to their fame.

Mme. Rosika Schwimmer summed up in an article published in the January, 1932, issue of *World Tomorrow*:

If the dead really turn in their graves whenever their wills are carried out contrary to their intentions, poor Alfred Nobel, founder of the greatest European endowment for the advancement of humanity, is not having a very restful time for there has seldom been greater inconsistancy between a man's will and its execution.

Perhaps nothing else can be expected when administration is entrusted to a body of practical, successful men. Such a body is not likely to recognize merit in dreamers and is likely to be timid and hesitant at the risk of erroneous judgment in heaping honors upon unproven, controversial idealists. Indeed, from the beginning there has been a lack of sympathy between the professional peace fighters and the Nobel committee, and both the committee and the Norwegian Storting have remained isolated from the organized peace movement. Only one peace professional, in the Passy sense of the term, has been cited in the post World War II period. That was Emily Balch in 1946.

In all fairness, however, it should be stated that while some critics were complaining about the timidity of the Nobel committee, other critics were objecting that the peace prize was being converted into a pacifist prize and that the Nobel committee was showing "a penchant for off-beat, small nation or minority party characters."

Even the relatively narrow range of choice circumscribed by the Nobel committee did not prevent it from being subjected to that criticism which is the lot of any one who seeks to make a selection from among a highly qualified field. The greatest furor was raised by the failure of the prize committee to name either Mohandas K. Gandhi or Count Leo Tolstoi.

With regard to the omission of the Indian non-resistance leader, an editorial in the March 14, 1934, issue of the *Christian Century* expressed the widespread opinion that :

if Gandhi is not the most logical candidate for the Nobel prize, then the popular idea of the function and purpose of that prize needs to be revised.

It was rumored that the peace prize had been offered to Tolstoi but that he had refused it, claiming that it should have been proffered to the Doukhobor sect.

In addition, adherents have advocated the candidacy of peace workers such as Louis Lecoin, Henri Barbusse, Paul von Schoenaich, Eugene V. Debs, Andrew Carnegie, Jean Jaurès, Paul Otlet, Clarence K. Streit of Union Now, Emery Reves, author of the *Anatomy of Peace,* George Duhamel, Salvador de Madariaga, James T. Shotwell of the Carnegie Endowment for International Peace, E. D. Morel, and Bertrand Russell among many others.

Included among the statesmen proposed have been Edward Benes, C. J. Hambro, head of the Norwegian Storting, Paul Harris of Southern Rhodesia, Ramsay MacDonald, Harry S. Truman, Winston Churchill, Jean Monnet, Jawaharlal Nehru, Emperor Haile Selassie (who doesn't seem to hesitate to behead his political opponents), Count Coudenhove-Kalergi, the chief protagonist of Pan-Europa, Thomas G. Masaryk, and Jan Christian Smuts.

Popes Pius XII and John XXIII, Frank Buchman, and Gen. Bramwell Booth of the Salvation Army are numbered among the religious leaders who have been proposed.

Humanitarians suggested include Herbert H. Lehman of the United Nations Relief and Rehabilitation Adminstration (UNRRA), Herbert Hoover, Max Huber, Raoul Wallenberg who was instrumental in the rescue of many Central European Jews during World War II, and Acharya Vinoba Bhave of the Indian land gift program.

Among the jurists whose names have been urged for consideraton we find John Morgan, Robert H. Jackson, Sir Hartley Shawcross, Ewing Cockrell who was one of the first to formulate a United Nations international police force, Giuseppe A. Borgese who drafted a Constitution for a world government, and Raphael Lemkin who coined the word "genocide" and was active in the adoption of a United Nations convention against that evil.

Women proposed to the Nobel Committee include Mrs. Emmeline Pethic-Lawrence, Mme. Rosika Schwimmer, Mrs. Franklin D. Roosevelt; and Mme. Alexandra Kollontay, the Soviet ambassador to Sweden. International civil servants include Sir Eric Drummond and Trygve Lie. Other prominent persons nominated include Baron Pierre de Coubertin, the founder of the modern Olympic games; and Nicholas Roerich who advocated better international understanding through the dissemination of art and culture.

Among the more outlandish nominations, mention should be made of those of Juan D. Peron and Eva Peron, Kaiser Wilhelm II, Nicolai Lenin, Leon Trotzky and Neville Chamberlain who brought "peace for our time" back from Munich.

19 Epitaph

It is customary for a book of this sort to conclude with an epilogue exuding hope and confidence for the future. However, in view of the subject matter of this volume and the utter failure of its quest, it is believed more appropriate to inscribe an epitaph. It would be self delusion of the cruelest form to pretend that the Nobel peace prize has mitigated in the slightest degree the threat of war which its founder called "the horror of horrors, the greatest of all crimes."

Dr. Schweitzer was asked on his 90th birthday, "Can you find any cause for optimism in the world today?" "Optimism," he exclaimed, "how can you speak of optimism when Africa is in the state it is? How can you speak of optimism for the rest of the world?"

Survey the horizons. You will see smoldering fires in every direction: China, India, Kashmir, Taiwan, the Near East, Viet Nam, Malaysia, Korea, Laos, Indonesia, Angola, South Africa, Yemen, Haiti, Cuba, the Congo, Berlin, Rhodesia, and elsewhere. These are not bonfires of peace. No, they are the flames of war which threaten to ignite the world into one devouring conflagration.

What has happened to the "spirit of hope" engendered by the test ban treaty which was signed by over a hundred nations? Admittedly it was a limited treaty; it did not end the threat of nuclear war; it did not reduce nuclear stockpiles; it did not halt production of nuclear weapons; it did not stop research into even deadlier nuclear arms; it did not restrict use of nuclear weapons in time of war. Nor has this small, hesitant step in international cooperation proven to be the "start of a long, fruitful journey" towards true disarmament. The sprout of international confidence has not grown. The first swallow has not heralded the summer. The test ban treaty has been followed by a few meaningless gestures but its impact on great word issues has been termed "completely inconsequential." Dr. Pauling's expectations have not been fulfilled.

What has happened to the Nobel peace prize and to the twentieth century, both of which began as an era of rising expectations tending limitessly upwards and onwards? What has happened to the high hopes of finally beating the swords into plowshares and the spears into pruning hooks? What has happened to the goal of lifting man from savagery under a rule of law under God? Al these expectations, hopes, and goals have evaporated wtth the hissing sound of escaping hope. We have scaled down our horizons to a mere holding action so that, in the words of Hammarskjold :

Where our predecessors dreamt of a new heaven, our greatest hope is that we may be permitted to save the old earth.

The men of strife will never hush their noise long enough so that we may hear the angels sing.

The decision has been taken—taken by default, but a decision nevertheless—by the "millions of over-driven professional men, coal heavers, dentists, tea-shop waitresses, parsons, charwomen, artists, country squires and chorus girls." The final verdict has been given. Man has lost the race between education and catastrophe. Ernest Bevin once truly stated that "the common man is the greatest protection against war." The preamble to the constitution of the United Nations Educational Scientific and Cultural Organization also restates a truism when it declares:

Since wars began in the minds of men, it is in the minds of men that the defenses of peace must be constructed.

We have not utilized the years of the twentieth century towards the development of an enlightened public opinion. We have not succeeded in getting things right at the primary source of policy and action which is the mind of the ordinary man and his way of thinking. Unfortunately, there is not time left to re-educate the common man from the stale phrases and myths that dominate his thinking to the reality of the three R's enumerated by Norman Angell: "reality, relatedness and responsibility." There is no time left to purge our minds of the collection of stereotyped prejudices and sacred cows and wishful misconceptions which misrepresent the nature of things and falsify our judgment of events. There is no time because the hydrogen bomb has wiped out time.

In an age as complex as the twentieth century, the fullest freedom of communication, information and expression is necessary for comprehension. Instead, we find that the nation-states have increasingly shackled the limbs, brainwashed the minds and muzzled the voices of their citizens. Indeed, during the 1962 Cuban crisis, a high-ranking United States official justified lying to the people on the grounds that generation of information is only another weapon in a nation's arsenal.

At the beginning of this century, uninterrupted travel was possible throughout the world without a passport. Now, however, as Emery Reves has observed, "the nation states, like feudal knights, are chaining their subjects to the soil of their homeland, refusing them the most elementary of freedoms, the freedom of movement." Now, no man can budge unless he is supplied with all sorts and shapes of papers. To quote Garry

Davis, "instead of a man there is only a papier-mâché human, a collage of official forms in various hues and sizes."

The closing of the frontiers has been accompanied by a restriction of the free market of ideas. Dr. Schweitzer remarked, "The organized political, economic and religious associations of our time are at work to induce individual man not to arrive at his convictions by his own thinking but to take as his own such convictions as they keep ready-made for him." To read, to listen to radio broadcasts, to think, to express one's self has become treason. The man who searches for truth and reason in this insane world is branded a traitor, a collaborator with subversive, foreign and alien elements, a nihilist, a communist (in Western countries; in Eastern countries the same man would be denounced as an imperialist). As the Russian poet Yevgeny Yevtushenko well knows,

> Sometime posterity will remember
> And will burn with shame
> When they shall have done with shame and lies.
> Those strange times
> When
> Common honesty was called courage.

We may thus begin to understand why the average individual is so desperately helpless to span the ever-widening and unbridgeable gap between the level of his knowledge and the advances of modern science. Science has sped far ahead of mankind's present phase of political, social and emotional development. In the words of Rabbi Julius Mark:

The tragedy of our time is that we have succeeded in splitting the atom before acquiring the wisdom to unite humanity.

Unfortunately, soaring science has pulled loose from its moral and ethical moorings. It has not devoted its wonders to solving the problems of a world which bears an intolerable burden of hunger, disease, poverty, and mutual fear. The first claim on the available resources of genius and money has been assigned, not to the advancement of man's well-being, but to the frenzied accumulation of ever more monstrous weapons of destruction. Even the space race is primarily motivated by military considerations.

Bertrand Russell has described the direction of modern day science :

I see science, which in itself is one of the most splendid of human achievements, permitted to become the minister of death and the education of the young advocated with a view toward increasing their skill as assassins. I see more and more of human effort put into a futile competition in death-dealing engines . . . And in the end, howling hordes of fanatics exterminating each other and all bystanders in a vast orgy of murder.

What is so puzzling is that the average man and his leaders do not seem to realize how successful science has been in perfecting these death-dealing engines. They do not seem to understand that the day of the tournament has long passed into history. They do not see, as Dr. Brock Chisholm does, that:

outbreeding, out-gunning or out-producing other groups can no longer be counted on to provide security, prosperity or peace, or even survival.

It has not penetrated men's minds that the old order of nation-states can no longer provide protection for its citizens; that this old order has, indeed, become a threat to further existence.

They have not read Gordon Dean's "Report on the Atom" :

Whereas, before, the problem was simply one of war or peace, it is now one of oblivion or peace . . . Yet man, even in the atomic age, has not chosen peace. He also has not chosen oblivion and he seems to think he can go on forever without deciding upon one or the other. Maybe he can, but the risks are enormous . . . In flirting with world war in the atomic age, man . . . is playing with the means by which mortal life on earth can be ended.

Imagine what would happen if, by some miracle, man finally chose peace and converted the efforts of science towards works of peace? No less an authority than Professor Harold C. Urey states, "We would have an embarrassment of riches, for we would not know what to do with all the materials that we could produce." Only then would humanity begin to approach an all-embracing peace, an indivisible peace, a peace not achieved in a vacuum but one paced by human progress and translated into bread or rice, shelter, health, education, human dignity and freedom — a steadily better life.

But one must wrench himself away from this dream and face the realities. The economic reality is that the gap between the standard of living of the developed and the underdeveloped is steadily widening instead of narrowing. The political reality was best described by President Eisenhower in an address delivered before the United Nations General Assembly in 1953 :

two atomic colossi . . . doomed malevolently to eye each other indefinitely across a trembling world.

This description brings to mind a painting by Goya at the Prado showing two men, sinking in quicksand, beating each other with clubs.

The brutal reality is expressed by the opinion of qualified scientists like Professor Harold C. Urey, Sir Charles Snow, Herman Kahn, Erich Fromm and others, that the bombs will probably go off within the next ten years.

It is possible, of course, that the premise, namely peace, upon which Alfred Nobel founded his prizes, is a false one. We seem to take for granted, without examination, the preaching of our saints like San Bernardino who said :

So needful a thing it is, this peace. Even its name—pace—leaves a sweetness on the lips.

Pope John XXIII asks:

Is there anyone who does not ardently yearn to see war banished, to see peace preserved and daily more firmly established?

It may be that peace is another one of those icons (like truth, liberty, freedom, democracy, free enterprise, religion, morality, honesty) to which man pays lip service while masking his true feelings, convictions and actions. Certainly, history gives us no justification for concluding by some "romantic fallacy" that man was born of fallen angels instead of risen apes or that he has progressed magnificently beyond his primordial savage state of a "predator whose natural instinct is to kill with a weapon." After all, war is more ancient than history and one military scholar has calculated that in some 3,457 years of recorded history, there have been 3,230 years of war, only 227 years of peace.

Perhaps General Von Moltke understood human nature with a truer insight than Pope John XXIII when the general wrote to Johann Kasper Blantachli, the Swiss scholar:

Eternal peace—that is only a dream and not a beautiful one either. War is an integral part of God's ordering of the Universe.

Otherwise, how can one possibly explain the universal contempt and ridicule accorded by the people to the workers for peace in every country of the world — East or West.

The fact is that there never existed among the peoples a spirit directed toward the realization of peace. It would appear futile to ring the tocsin and alert the artisan at his lathe, the clerk at his counter, the young man at his plow, of the danger that lurks in some obscure corner of the globe, the danger that a spark from some seemingly inconsequential incident may flame into the hell of a nuclear war.

One is reminded of a great passage from Spengler:

Already the danger is so great, for every individual, every class, every people, that to cherish any illusion whatever is deplorable. Time does not suffer itself to be halted; there is no question of prudent retreat or wise renunciation. Only dreamers believe that there is a way out. Optimism is cowardice. We are born into this time and must bravely follow the path to the destined end. There is no other way. Our duty is to hold on to the last position, without hope, without reserve, like the Roman soldier whose bones were found in front of a door in Pompeii, who, during the eruption of Vesuvius, died at his post because they forgot to relieve him. That is greatness.

Could it be that the atomic physicist Ralph E. Lapp does not have Spengler's grasp of the majestic sweep of history when the former bewails that :

The strangest aspect of our perilous time is the ominous quiet. Probably never in history has the human race looked so much like sheep marching silently to slaughter.

But might not the answer be that the human race, in its infinite wisdom, knows that its destiny, like that of the sheep, is the abattoir? The people, with their usual common sense, have realized that it would be futile to flail about against their fate and have resigned themselves without resistance to the inevitable.

It could be that Henry Mencken was right when he said :

All the larger human problems are insoluble. Life is, . . . a spectacle without purpose or moral.

It could be that the only practical thing to do now is to weep. Our revels now are ended. La commeddia è finita.

Appendix

NOBEL PEACE PRIZE LAUREATES

Year	Laureate	Country
1901	Jean Henri Dunant	Switzerland
	Frédéric Passy	France
1902	Elie Ducommun	Switzerland
	Charles Albert Gobat	Switzerland
1903	William Randal Cremer	Britain
1904	Institut de Droit International	
1905	Bertha von Suttner	Austria
1906	Theodore Roosevelt	United States
1907	Ernesto Teodoro Moneta	Italy
	Louis Renault	France
1908	Klas Pontus Arnoldson	Sweden
	Frederik Bajer	Denmark
1909	Auguste Marie Francois Beernaert	Belgium
	Paul Balluet, Baron	

Year	Laureate	Country
	d'Estournelles de Constant de Rebecque	France
1910	Bureau internationale permanente de la paix	
1911	Tobias Michael Carel Asser	Netherlands
	Alfred Hermann Fried	Austria
1912	Elihu Root	United States
1913	Henri Marie Lafontaine	France
1914	Award omitted	
1915	Award omitted	
1916	Award omitted	
1917	International Committee of the Red Cross	Switzerland
1918	Award omitted	
1919	Woodrow Wilson	United States
1920	Léon Victor Auguste Bourgeois	France
1921	Karl Hjalmar Branting	Sweden
	Christian Louis Lange	Norway
1922	Fridtjof Nansen	Norway
1923	Award omitted	
1924	Award omitted	
1925	Charles G. Dawes	United States
	Joseph Austen Chamberlain	Britain
1926	Aristide Briand	France
	Gustav Stresemann	Germany

Year	Laureate	Country
1927	Ferdinand Buisson	France
	Ludwig Quidde	Germany
1928	Award omitted	
1929	Frank B. Kellogg	United States
1930	Nathan Söderblom	Sweden
1931	Nicholas Murray Butler	United States
	Jane Addams	United States
1932	Award omitted	
1933	Norman Angell	Britain
1934	Arthur Henderson	Britain
1935	Carl von Ossietzky	Germany
1936	Carlos Saavedra Lamas	Argentina
1937	Edgar Algernon Robert Cecil, Viscount Cecil of Chelwood	Britain
1938	Bureau internationale Nansen pour les refugés	
1939	Award omitted	
1940	Award omitted	
1941	Award omitted	
1942	Award omitted	
1943	Award omitted	
1944	International Committee of the Red Cross	Switzerland

Year	Laureate	Country
1945	Cordell Hull	United States
1946	John R. Mott	United States
	Emily Greene Balch	United States
1947	American Friends Service Committee	United States
	Friends Service Council	Britain
1948	Award omitted	
1949	Lord Boyd-Orr of Brechin	Britain
1950	Ralph J. Bunche	United States
1951	Léon Jouhaux	France
1952	Albert Schweitzer	France
1953	George C. Marshall	United States
1954	Office of the United Nations Commissioner for Refugees	
1955	Award omitted	
1956	Award omitted	
1957	Lester B. Pearson	Canada
1958	Rev. Dominique Georges Pire	Belgium
1959	Philip J. Noel-Baker	Britain
1960	Albert John Luthuli	South Africa
1961	Dag Hammarskjold	Sweden
1962	Linus Carl Pauling	United States

Year	Laureate	Country
1963	International Committee of the Red Cross	Switzerland
	League of the Red Cross Societies	
1964	Rev. Dr. Martin Luther King, Jr.	United States
1965	The United Nations Childrens Fund	

Index

275